Developments in
Management Information Systems

**DICKENSON SERIES IN
COMPUTER AND INFORMATION SCIENCES**
Fred M. Tonge, Editor

A Clear Introduction to Fortran IV
Richard M. Jaffe

L.I.S.P. 1.5 Primer
Clark Weissman, Systems Development Corp.

PL/1: A Self Instructional Manual
George L. Scott and Joanne Scott, Computer Sciences Corp.

Of Related Interest:

Accounting: An Information Systems Approach
John D. Buckley, University of California, Los Angeles
Kevin M. Lightner, California State University, San Diego

Contemporary Thought in Accounting and Organizational Control
K. Fred Skousen, Brigham Young University
Belverd E. Needles Jr., Chicago State University

Contemporary Accounting and the Computer
Leonard W. Hein, California State University, Los Angeles

Developments in Management Information Systems

Robert H. Trent

Thomas L. Wheelen

McIntire School of Commerce
The University of Virginia

DICKENSON PUBLISHING COMPANY, INC.
Encino, California
Belmont, California

T 58.6
.T67

ISBN-0-8221-0102-5
Library of Congress Catalog Card Number: 72-90752

Printed in the United States of America

Printing (last digit): 9 8 7 6 5 4 3 2 1

To
Joanne   Margy
  John   Kathy, Tommy, Richard

Contents

pg-84

PART FOUR: THE ROLE OF THE COMPUTER

A. Computer Concepts

B. Management and the Computer

C. Computer Applications in Systems

PART FIVE:

STATE OF THE ART IN EMERGING MANAGEMENT SYSTEMS

A. Internal Control

B. Process Control

C. Marketing

Contributors

Russell L. Ackoff

Lee Adler

American Telephone
and Telegraph
Company

Arnold E. Amstutz

James D. Babcock

Kenneth E. Boulding

James B. Bower

W. M. A. Brooker

Ralph J. Brown

Business Week

S. D. Catalano

D. Ronald Daniel

John Dearden

E. R. Dickey

G. W. Dickson

Martin L. Ernst

John P. Fertakis

B. G. Grubbs

Timothy P. Haidinger

Charles W. Hofer

Robert W. Holmes

Richard A. Johnson

Richard A. Kaimann

Fremont E. Kast

R. L. Martino

David B. Montgomery

Bert Nanus

Gerald E. Nichols

John J. Omlor

John Plummer

W. Thomas Porter Jr.

Alfred Rappaport

James E. Rosenzweig

Joel E. Ross

Thomas Rullo

Peter P. Schoderbek

Elliot Schrier

J. Bruce Sefert

N. L. Senensieb

John K. Simmons

Arthur L. Svenson

Glen L. Urban

P. D. Walker

Thomas L. Wheelen

Edgar G. Williams

Stanley Young

Sources

Baylor Business Studies

Bell System's Approach to Business
  Systems

Business Horizons

Business Quarterly

Business Week

California Management Review

Columbia Journal of World Business

Computer Decisions

Data Processing Magazine

Encyclopedia of Management

Financial Executive

Harvard Business Review

Journal of Accountancy

Journal of Marketing Research

Journal of Systems Management

Management Accounting

Management Science

Management Services

Systems and Procedures Journal

Preface

Understanding the concept of systems and the methodology of systems analysis is now generally regarded as necessary for the planning required to achieve the objectives of any organization. Planning, of course, requires information processing, and such processing depends on the current state of information technology. Both the input and the output of information through processing have a value and a cost.

The readings in this volume indicate that there is a definite relationship among systems concepts, the design of systems, and developments in information technology. Implementation of these ideas within an organization can have a significant impact on the structure of an organization as well as seriously affect human relations within the organization. A great deal of material is developing concerning information systems and their analysis, but for the most part, one must have access to a host of current periodicals to stay abreast of new developments. Additionally, some of the early basic writings are most important and should not be discarded. The readings herein bring together some of the important earlier articles and more recent material.

Managers as well as practicing systems analysts will find much useful material included in these readings. A large selection of references has been appended, which will provide additional information on techniques and applications.

The selections have been separated into five catagories:

Theory and Concepts: general systems theory, organizational aspects of systems and the concept of total systems, and the broad scope integrative attitude needed for systems analysis.

Information Technology: the information explosion and its effect on organizations as they attempt to deal with it technologically.

The Design of a System: the problem of designing a system that permits an organizational structure compatible to the human resources encompassed therein, and characteristics of formal and informal organizations and their interrelationships.

The Role of the Computer: the computer's ubiquitous status, who in the organization selects and controls the computer, is the computer paying its way?, new applications such as timesharing, and the concept of multinational computer facilities.

State of the Art in Emerging Management Systems: rapidly developing systems applications and internal control methodology, and system design with a clear view of the objectives of the organization and subject to physical and human limitations.

We are indeed grateful to the many authors and publishers who have allowed us to incorporate their material in this volume. We are also indebted to Dean Frank S. Kaulback Jr. of the McIntire School of Commerce at The University of Virginia; Charles S. Bunker, Babson College; Harry R. Page, The George Washington University; Donald L. Raun, California State University at Northridge; Stanley R. Sitnik, Georgetown University; and Fred M. Tonge, University of California, Irvine. Special thanks are due Mrs. Dorothy Giannini for both her typing skills and her patience. A special note of thanks to Mrs. Sandra Garland for her assistance.

We dedicate this book to our wives, for without their assistance, encouragement and understanding, this book would still be a proposal and not a reality.

> *Robert H. Trent*
> *Thomas L. Wheelen*
> McIntire School of Commerce
> The University of Virginia

1 THEORY AND CONCEPTS

The growing complexity of virtually all of the organizations with which we as individuals must interface has created a tremendous need for systems that can transform data into information for quick, efficient, decision making. In the business organization the emphasis is on effective application rather than theory development; however, it has been said that without theory there can be no practice.

In this section, the idea of a General Systems Theory stemming from interdisciplinary efforts is proposed by Boulding. He concludes that General Systems Theory is the "skelton of science," not only because it can provide a framework or structure of systems, but the reluctance of science to admit the low level of success in systemization makes it a skeleton in the cupboard. Messrs. Johnson, Kast and Rosenzweig describe the general theory as applied management, and illustrate its application to the traditional functional areas of a business organization. A discussion of the dynamics of a business organization as a total system is given next, with a warning by Brooker to beware of confusing general systems with total systems.

A. General Systems Theory

1. General Systems Theory – The Skeleton of Science*

Kenneth E. Boulding

General Systems Theory[1] is a name which has come into use to describe a level of theoretical model-building which lies somewhere between the highly generalized constructions of pure mathematics and the specific theories of the specialized disciplines. Mathematics attempts to organize highly general relationships into a coherent system, a system however which does not have any necessary connections with the "real" world around us. It studies all thinkable relationships abstracted from any concrete situation or body of empirical knowledge. It is not even confined to "quantitative" relationships narrowly defined—indeed, the development of a mathematics of quality and structure is already on the way, even though it is not as far advanced as the "classical' mathematics of quantity and number. Nevertheless because in a sense mathematics contains all theories it contains none; it is the language of theory, but it does not give us the content. At the other extreme we have the separate disciplines and sciences, with their separate bodies of theory. Each discipline corresponds to a certain segment of the empirical world, and each develops theories which have particular applicability to its own empirical segment. Physics, Chemistry, Biology, Psychology, Sociology, Economics and so on all carve out for themselves

*SOURCE: From *Management Science* (April, 1956), pp. 197-208. Reprinted by permission of the publisher.

2

certain elements of the experience of man and develop theories and patterns of activity (research) which yield satisfaction in understanding, and which are appropriate to their special segments.

In recent years increasing need has been felt for a body of systematic theoretical constructs which will discuss the general relationships of the empirical world. This is the quest of General Systems Theory. It does not seek, of course, to establish a single, self-contained "general theory of practically everything" which will replace all the special theories of particular disciplines. Such a theory would be almost without content, for we always pay for generality by sacrificing content, and all we can say about practically everything is almost nothing. Somewhere however between the specific that has no meaning and the general that has no content there must be, for each purpose and at each level of abstraction, an optimum degree of generality. It is the contention of the General Systems Theorists that this optimum degree of generality in theory is not always reached by the particular sciences. The objectives of General Systems Theory then can be set out with varying degrees of ambition and confidence. At a low level of ambition but with a high degree of confidence it aims to point out similarities in the theoretical constructions of different disciplines, where these exist, and to develop theoretical models having applicability to at least two different fields of study. At a higher level of ambition, but with perhaps a lower degree of confidence it hopes to develop something like a "spectrum" of theories—a system of systems which may perform the function of a "gestalt" in theoretical construction. Such "gestalts" in special fields have been of great value in directing research towards the gaps which they reveal. Thus the periodic table of elements in chemistry directed research for many decades towards the discovery of unknown elements to fill gaps in the table until the table was completely filled. Similarly a "system of systems" might be of value in directing the attention of theorists towards gaps in theoretical models, and fight even be of value in pointing towards methods of filling them.

The need for general systems theory is accentuated by the present sociological situation in science. Knowledge is not something which exists and grows in the abstract. It is a function of human organisms and of social organization. Knowledge, that is to say, is always what somebody knows: the most perfect transcript of knowledge in writing is not knowledge if nobody knows it. Knowledge however grows by the receipt of meaningful information—that is, by the intake of messages by a knower which are capable of reorganizing his knowledge. We will quietly duck the question as to what reorganizations constitute "growth" of knowledge by defining "semantic growth" of knowledge as those reorganizations which can profitably be talked about, in writing or speech, by the Right People. Science, that is to say, is what can be talked about profitably by scientists in their role as scientists. The crisis of science today arises because of the increasing difficulty of such profitable talk among scientists as a whole. Specialization has outrun Trade, communication between the disciples becomes increasingly difficult, and the Republic of Learning is breaking up into isolated subcultures with only tenuous lines of communication between them—a situation which threatens intellectual civil war. The reason for this breakup in the body of knowledge is that in the course of specialization the receptors of information themselves become specialized. Hence physicists only talk to physicists, economists to economists—worse still, nuclear physicists only talk to nuclear physicists and econometricians to econometricians. One wonders sometimes if science will not grind to a stop in an assemblage of walled-in hermits, each mumbling to himself words in a private language that only he can understand. In these days the arts may have beaten the sciences to this desert of mutual unintelligibility, but that may be merely because the swift intuitions of art reach the future faster than the plodding leg work of the scientist. The more science breaks into sub-groups, and the less communication is possible among the disciplines, however, the greater chance there is that the total growth of knowledge is being slowed down by the loss of relevant communications. The spread of specialized deafness means that someone who ought to know something that someone else knows isn't able to find it out for lack of generalized ears.

It is one of the main objectives of General Systems Theory to develop these generalized ears, and by developing a framework of general theory to enable one specialist to catch relevant communications from others. Thus the economist who realizes the strong formal similarity between utility theory in economics and field theory in physics[2] is probably in a better position to learn from the physicists than one who does not. Similarly a specialist who works with the growth concept—whether the crystallographer, the virologist, the cytologist, the physiologist, the psychologist, the sociologist or the economist—will be more sensitive to the contributions of other fields if he is aware of the many similarities of the growth process in widely different empirical fields.

There is not much doubt about the demand for general systems theory under one brand name or another. It is a little more embarrassing to inquire into the supply. Does any of it exist, and if so where? What is the chance to getting more of it, and if so, how? The situation might be decribed as promising and in ferment, though it is not wholly clear what is being promised or brewed. Something which might be called an "interdisciplinary movement" has been abroad for some time. The first signs of this are usually the development of hybrid disciplines. Thus physical chemistry emerged in the third quarter of the nineteenth century, social psychology in the second quarter of the twentieth. In the physical and biological sciences the list of hybrid disciplines is now quite long—biophysics, biochemistry, astrophysics are all well established. In the social sciences social anthropology is fairly well established, economic psychology and economic sociology are just beginning. There are signs, even, that Political Economy, which died in infancy some hundred years ago, may have a re-birth.

In recent years there has been an additional development of great interest in the form of "multisexual" interdisciplines. The hybrid disciplines, as their hyphenated names indicate, come from two respectable and honest academic parents. The newer interdisciplines have a much more varied and occasionally even obscure ancestry, and result from the reorganization of material from many different fields of study. Cybernetics, for instance, comes out of electrical engineering, neurophysiology, physics, biology, with even a dash of economics. Information theory, which originated in communications engineering, has important applications in many fields stretching from biology to the social sciences. Organization theory comes out of economics, sociology, engineering, physiology, and Management Science itself is an equally multidisciplinary product.

On the more empirical and practical side the interdisciplinary movement is reflected in the development of interdepartmental institutes of many kinds. Some of these find their basis of unity in the empirical field which they study, such as institutes of industrial relations, of public administration, of international affairs, and so on. Others are organized around the application of a common methodology to many different fields and problems, such as the Survey Research Center and the Group Dynamics Center at the University of Michigan. Even more important than these visible developments, perhaps, though harder to perceive and identify, is a growing dissatisfaction in many departments, especially at the level of graduate study, with the existing traditional theoretical backgrounds for the empirical studes which form the major part of the output of Ph.D. theses. To take but a single example from the field with whom I am most familiar. It is traditional for studies of labor relations, money and banking, and foreign investment to come out of departments of economics. Many of the needed theoretical models and frameworks in these fields, however, do not come out of "economic theory" as this is usually taught, but from sociology, social psychology, and cultural anthropology. Students in the department of economics however rarely get a chance to become acquainted with these theoretical models, which may be relevant to their studies, and they become impatient with economic theory, much of which may not be relevant.

It is clear that there is a good deal of interdisciplinary excitement abroad. If this excitement is to be productive, however, it must operate within a certain framework of coherence. It is all too easy for the interdisciplinary to degenerate into the undisciplined. If the interdisciplinary movement, therefore, is not to lose that sense of form and structure which is the "discipline" involved in the various separate disciplines, it should develop a structure of its own. This I conceive to be the great taks of general systems theory. For the rest of this paper, therefore, I propose to look at some possible ways in which general systems theory might be structured.

Two possible approaches to the organization of general systems theory suggest themselves, which are to be thought of as complementary rather than competitive, or at least as two roads each of which is worth exploring. The first approach is to look over the empirical universe and to pick out certain general *phenomena* which are found in many different disciplines, and to seek to build up general theoretical models relevant to these phenomena. The second approach is to arrange the empirical fields in a hierarchy of complexity of organization of their basic "individual" or unit of behavior, and to try to develop a level of abstraction appropriate to each.

Some examples of the first approach will serve to clarify it, without pretending to be exhaustive. In almost all disciplines, for instance, we find examples of populations—aggregates of individuals conforming to a common definition, to which individuals are added (born) and subtracted (die) and in which the age of the individual is a relevant and identifiable variable. These populations exhibit dynamic movements of their own, which can frequently be described by fairly simple systems of difference equations. The populations of different species also exhibit dynamic interactions among themselves, as in the theory of Volterra. Models of population change and interaction cut across a great many different fields—ecological systems in biology, capital theory in economics which deals with populations of "goods," social ecology, and even certain problems of statistical mechanics. In all these fields population change, both in absolute numbers and in structure, can be discussed in terms of birth and survival functions relating numbers of births and of deaths in specific age groups to various aspects of the system. In all these fields the interaction of population can be discussed in terms of competitive, conplementary, or parasitic relationships among populations of different species, whether the species consist of animals, commodities, social classes or molecules.

Another phenomenon of almost universal significance for all disciplines is that of the interaction of an "individual" of some kind with its environment. Every discipline studies some kind of "individual"—electron, atom, molecule, crystal, virus, cell, plant, animal, man, family, tribe, state, church, firm, corporation, university and so on. Each of these individuals exhibits "behavior," action, or change, and this behavior is considered to be related in some way to the environment of the individual—that is, with other individuals with which it comes into contact or into some relationship. Each individual is thought of as consisting of a structure or complex of individuals of the order immediately below it—atoms are an arrangement of protons and electrons, molecules of atoms, cells of molecules, plants, animals and men of cells, social organizations of men. The "behavior" of each individual is "explained" by the structure and arrangement of the lower individuals of which it is composed, or by certain principles of equilibrium or momeostats according to which certain "state" of the individual are "preferred." Behavior is described in terms of the restoration of these preferred states when they are disturbed by changes in the environment.

Another phenomenon of universal significance is growth. Growth theory is in a sense a subdivision of the theory of individual "behavior," growth being one important aspect of behavior. Nevertheless there are important differences between equilibrium theory and growth theory, which perhaps warrant giving growth theory a special category. There is hardly a science in which the growth phenomenon does not have some importance, and though there is a great difference in complexity between the growth of crystals, embryos, and societies, many of the principles and concepts which are important at the lower levels are also illuminating at higher levels. Some growth phenomena can be dealth with in terms of relatively simple population models, the solution of which yields growth curves of single variables. At the more complex levels structural problems become dominant and the complex interrelationships between growth and form are the focus of interest. All growth phenomena are sufficiently alike however to suggest that a general theory of growth is by no means an impossibility.[3]

Another aspect of the theory of the individual and also of interrelationships among individuals which might be singled out for special treatment is the theory of information and communication. The information concept as developed by Shannon has had interesting applications outside its original field of electrical engineering. It is not adequate, of course, to deal with problems involving the semantic level of communication. At the biological level however the information concept may serve to develop general notions of structuredness and abstract measures or organization which gives us, as it were, a third basic dimension and information processes are found in a wide variety of empirical situations, and are unquestionably essential in the development of organization, both in the biological and the social world.

These various approaches to general systems through various aspects of the empirical world may lead ultimately to something like a general field theory of the dynamics of action and interaction. This, however, is a long way ahead.

A second possible approach to general systems theory is through the arrangement of theoretical systems and constructs in a hierarchy of complexity, roughly corresponding to the complexity of the "individuals" of the various empirical fields. This approach is more systematic than the first, leading towards a "system of systems." It may not replace the first entirely, however, as there may always be important theoretical concepts and constructs lying outside the systematic framework. I suggest below a possible arrangement of "levels" of theoretical discourse.

(i) The first level is that of the static structure. It might be called the level of *frameworks*. This is the geography and anatomy of the universe— the patterns of electrons around a nucleus, the pattern of atoms in a molecular formula, the arrangement of atoms in a crystal, the anatomy of the gene, the cell, the plant, the animal, the mapping of the earth, the solar system, the astronomical universe. The accurate description of these frameworks is the beginning of organized theoretical knowledge in almost any field, for without accuracy in this description of static relationships no acurate functional or dynamic theory is possible. Thus the Copernican revolution was really the discovery of a new static framework for the solar system which permitted a simpler description of its dynamics.

(ii) The next level of systematic analysis is that of the simple dynamic system with predetermined, necessary motions. This might be called the level of *clockworks*. The solar system itself is of course the great clock of the universe from man's point of view, and the deliciously exact predictions of the astronomers are a testimony to the excellence of the clock which they study. Simple machines such as the lever and the pulley, even quite complicated machines like steam engines and dynamos fall mostly under this category. The greater part of the theoretical structure of physics, chemistry, and even of economics falls into this category. Two special cases might be noted. Simple equilibrium systems really fall into the dynamic category, as every equilibrium system must be considered as a limiting case of a dynamic system, and its stability cannot be determined except from the properties of its present dynamic system. Stochastic dynamic systems leading to equilibria, for all their complexity, also fall into this group of system; such is the modern view of the atom and even of the molecule, each position or part of the system being given with a certain degree of probability, the whole nevertheless exhibiting a determinate structure. Two types of analytical method are important here, which we may call, with the usage of the economists, comparative statics and true dynamics. In comparative statics we compare two equilibrium positions of the system under different values for the basic parameters. These equilibrium positions are usually expressed as the solution of a set of simultaneous equations. The method of comparative statics is to compare the solutions when the parameters of the equations are changed. Most simple mechanical problems are solved in this way. In true dynamics on the other hand we exhibit the system as a set of difference or differential equations, which are then solved in the form of an explicit function of each variable with time. Such a system may reach a position of stationary equilibrium, or it may not—there are plenty of examples of explosive dynamic systems, a very simple one being the growth of a sum at compound interest! Most physical and chemical reactions and most social systems do in fact exhibit a tendency to equilibrium—otherwise the world would have exploded or imploded long ago.

(iii) The next level is that of the control mechanism or cybernetic system, which might be nicknamed the level of the *thermostat*. This differs from the simple stable equilibrium system mainly in the fact that the transmission and interpretation of niformation is an essential part of the system. As a result of this the equilibrium position is not merely determined by the equations of the system, but the system will move to the maintenance of any *given* equilibrium, within limits. Thus the thermostat will maintain *any* temperature at which it can be set; the equilibrium temperature of the system is not determined solely by its equations. The trick here of course is that the essential variable of the dynamic system is the *difference* between an "observed" or "recorded" value of the maintained variable and its "ideal" value. If this differnce is not zero the system moves so as to diminish it; thus the furnace sends up heat when the temperature as recorded is "too cold" and is turned off when the recorded temperature is "too hot." The homeostasis model, which is of such importance in physiology, is an example of a cybernetic mechanism, and such mechanisms exist through the whole empirical world of the biologist and the social scientist.

(iv) The fourth level is that of the "open system," or self-maintaining structure. This is the level at which life begins to differentiate itself from not-life: it might be called the level of the *cell*. Something like and open system exists, of course, even in physio-chemical equilibrium systems; atomic structures maintain themselves in the midst of a throughput of electrons, molecular structures maintain themselves in the midst of a throughput of atoms. Flames and rivers likewise are essentially open systems of a very simple kind. As we pass up the scale of complexity of organization towards living systems, however, the property of self-maintenance of structure in the midst of a throughput of material becomes of dominant importance. An atom or a molecule can presumably exist without throughput: the existence of even the simplest living organism is inconceivable without ingestion, excretion and metabolic exchange. Closely connected with the property of self-maintenance is the property of self-reproduction. It may be, indeed, that self-reproduction is a more primitive or "lower level" system than the open system, and that the gene and the virus, for instance, may be able to reproduce themselves without being open systems. It is not perhaps an important question at what point in the scale of increasing complexity "life" begins. What is clear, however, is that by the time we have got to systems which both reproduce themselves and maintain themselves in the midst of a throughput of material and energy, we have something to which it would be hard to deny the title of "life."

(v) The fifth level might be called the genetic-societal level; it is typified by the *plant*, and it dominates the empirical world of the botanist. The outstanding characteristics of these systems are first, a division of labor among cells to form a cell-society with differentiated and mutually dependent parts (roots, leaves, seeds, etc.), and second, a sharp differentiation between the genotype and the phenotype, associated with the phenomenon of equifinal or "blueprinted" growth. At this level there are no highly specialized sense organs and information receptors are diffuse and incapable of much throughput of information—it is doubtful whether a tree can distinguish much more than light from dark, long days from short days, cold from hot.

(vi) As we move upward from the plant world towards the animal kingdom we gradually pass over into a new level, the "animal" level, characterized by increased mobility, teleological behavior, and self-awareness. Here we have the development of specialized information-receptors (eyes, ears, etc.) leading to an enormous increase in the intake of information; we have also a great development of nervous systems, leading ultimately to the brain, as an organizer of the information intake into a knowledge structure or "image." Increasingly as we ascend the scale of animal life, behavior is response not to a specific stimulus but to an "image" or knowledge structure or view of the environment as a whole. This image is of course determined ultimately by information received into the organism; the relation between the receipt of information and the building up of an image however is exceedingly complex. It is not a simple piling up or accumulation of information received, although this frequently happens, but a structuring of information into something essentially different from the information itself. After the image structure is well established most information received produces very little change in the image—it goes through the loose structure, as it were, without hitting it, much as a subatomic particle might go through an atom without hitting anything. Sometimes however the information is "captured" by the image and added to it, and sometimes the information hits some kind of a "nucleus" of the image and a reorganization takes place, with far reaching and radical changes in behavior in apparent response to what seems like a very small stimulus. The difficulties in the prediction of the behavior of these systems arises largely because of this intervention of the image between the stimulus and the response.

(vii) The next level is the "human" level, that is of the individual human being considered as a system. In addition to all, or nearly all, of the characteristics of animal systems man possesses self-consciousness, which is something different from mere awareness. His image, besides being much more complex than that even of the higher animals, has a self-reflexive quality—he not only knows, but knows that he knows. This property is probably bound up with the phenomenon of language and symbolism. It is the capacity for speech—the ability to produce, absorb, and interpret *symbols*, as opposed to mere signs like the warning cry of an animal— which most clearly marks man off from his humbler brethren. Man is distinguished from the animals also by a much more elaborate image of time and relationship; man is probably the only organization that knows that it dies, that contemplates in its behavior a whole life span, and more than a life span. Man exists not only in time and space but in history, and his behavior is profoundly affected by his view of the time process n which he stands.

(viii) Because of the vital importance for the individual man of symbolic images and behavior based on them it is not easy to separate clearly the level of the individual human organism from the next level, that of social organizations. In spite of the occasional stories of feral children raised by animals, man isolated from his fellows is practically unknown. So essential is the symbolic image in human behavior that one suspects that a truly isolated man would not be "human" in the usually accepted sense, though he would be potentially human. Nevertheless it is convenient for some purposes to distinguish the individual human as a system from the social systems which surround him, and in this sense social organizations may be said to constitute another level of organization. The unit of such systems is not perhaps the person—the individual human as such—but the "role" —that part of the person which is concerned with the organization or situation in question, and it is tempting to define social organizations, or almost any social system, as a set of roles tied together with channels of communications. The interrelations of the role and the person however can never be completely neglected—a square person in a round role may become a little rounder, but he also makes the role squarer, and the perception of a role is affected by the personalities of those who have occupied it in the past. At this level we must concern ourselves with the content and meaning of messages, the nature and dimensions of value systems, the transcription of images into a historical record, the subtle symbolizations of art, music, and   poetry, and the complex gamut of human emotion. The empirical universe here is human life and society in all its complexity and richness.

(ix) To complete the structure of systems we should add a final turret for transcendental systems, even if we may be accused at this point of having built Babel to the clouds. There are however the ultimates and absolutes and the inescapable unknowables, and they also exhibit systematic structure and relationship. It wll be a sad day for man when nobody is allowed to ask questions that do not have any answers.

One advantage of exhibiting a hierarchy of systems in this way is that it gives us some idea of the present gaps in both theoretical and empirical knowledge. Adequate theoretical models extend up to about the fourth level, and not much beyond. Empirical knowledge is deficient at practically all levels. Thus at the level of the static structure, fairly adequate descriptive models are available for geography, chemistry, geology, anatomy, and descriptive social science. Even at this simplest level, however, the problem of the adequate description of complex structures is still far from solved. The theory of indexing and cataloguing, for instance, is only in its infancy. Librarians are fairly good at cataloguing books, chemists have begun to catalogue structural formulae, and anthropologists have begun to catalogue culture traits. The cataloguing of events, ideas, theories, statistics, and empirical data has hardly begun. The very multiplication of records however as time goes on will force us into much more adequate cataloguing and reference systems than we now have. This is perhaps the major unsolved theoretical problem at the level of the static structure. In the empirical field there are still great areas where static structures are very imperfectly known, although knowledge is advancing rapidly, thanks to new probing devices such as the electron microscope. The anatomy of that part of the empirical world which lies between the large molecule and the cell however, is still obscure at many points. It is precisely this area however—which includes, for instance, the gene and the virus—that holds the secret of life, and until its anatomy is made clear the nature of the functional systems whch are involved will inevitably be obscure.

The level of the "clockwork" is the level of "classical" natural science, especially physics and astronomy, and is probably the most completely developed level in the present state of knowledge, especially if we extend the concept to include the field theory and stochastic models of modern physics. Even here however there are important gaps, especially at the higher empirical levels. There is much yet to be known about the sheer mechanics of cells and nervous systems, of brains and of societies.

Beyond the second level adequate theoretical models get scarcer. The last few years have seen great developments at the third and fourth levels. The theory of control machanisms ("thermostats") has established itself as the new discipline of cybernetics, and the theory of self-maintaining systems or "open systems" likewise has made rapid strides. We could hardly maintain however that much more than a beginning had been made in these fields. We know very little about the cybernetics of genes and genetic systems, for instance, and still less about the control mechanisms involved in the mental and social world. Similarly the processes of self-maintenance remain essentially mysterious at many points, and although the theoretical possibility of constructing a self-maintaining machine which would be a true open system has been suggested, we seem to be a long way from the actual construction of such a mechanical similitude of life.

Beyond the fourth level it may be doubted whether we have as yet even the rudiments of theoretical systems. The intricate machinery of growth by which the genetic complex organizes the matter around it is almost a complete mystery. Up to now, whatever the future may hold, only God can make a tree. In the face of living systems we are almost helpless; we can occasionally cooperate with systems which we do not understand: we cannot even begin to reproduce them. The ambiguous status of medicine, hovering as it does uneasily between magic and science, is a testimony to the state of systematic knowledge in this area. As we move up the scale the absence of the appropriate theoretical systems becomes ever more noticeable. We can hardly conceive ourselves constructing a system which would be in any recognizable sense "aware," much less self-conscious. Nevertheless as we move towards the human and societal level a curious thing happens: the fact that we have, as it were, an inside track, and that we ourselves *are* the systems which we are studying, enables us to utilize systems which we do not really understand. It is almost inconceivable that we should make a machine that would make a poem: nevertheless, poems *are* made by fools like us by processes which are largely hidden from us. The kind of knowledge and skill that we have at the symbolic level is very different from that which we have at lower levels—it is like, shall we say, the "knowhow" of the gene as compared with the knowhow of the biologist. Nevertheless it is a real kind of knowledge and it is the source of the creative achievements of man as artist, writer, architect, and composer.

Perhaps one of the most valuable uses of the above scheme is to prevent us from accepting as final a level of theoretical analysis which is below the level of the empirical world which we are investigating. Because, in a sense, each level incorporates all those below it, much valuable information and insights can be obtained by applying low-level systems to high-level subject matter. Thus most of the theoretical schemes of the social sciences are still at level (ii), just rising now to (iii), although the subject matter clearly involves level (viii). Economics, for instance, is still largely a "mechanics of utility and self-interest" in Jevons' masterly phrase. Its theoretical and mathematical base is drawn largely from the level of simple equilibrium theory and dynamic mechanisms. It has hardly begun to use concepts such as information which are appropriate at level (iii), and makes no use of higher level systems. Furthermore, with this crude apparatus it has achieved a modicum of success, in the sense that anybody trying to manipulate an economic system is almost certain to be better off if he knows some economics than if he doesn't. Nevertheless at some point progress in economics is going to depend on its ability to break out of these low-level systems, useful as they are as first approximations, and utilize systems which are more directly appropriate to its universe—when, of course, these systems are discovered. Many other examples could be given—the wholly inappropriate use in psychoanalytic theory, for instance, of the concept of energy, and the long inability of psychology to break loose from a sterile stimulus-response model.

Finally, the above scheme might serve as a mild word of warning even to Management Science. This new discipline represents an important break-away from overly simple mechanical models in the theory of organization and control. Its emphasis on communication systems and organizational structure, on principles of homeostasis and growth, on decision processes under uncertainty, is carrying us far beyond the simple models of maximizing behavior of even ten years ago. This advance in the level of theoretical analysis is bound to lead to more powerful and fruitful systems. Nevertheless we must never quite forget that even these advances do not carry us much beyond the third and fourth levels, and that in dealing with human personalities and organizations we are dealing with systems in the empirical world far beyond our ability to formulate. We should not be wholly surprised, therefore, if our simpler systems, for all their importance and validity, occasionally let us down.

I chose the subtitle of my paper with some eye to its possible overtones of meaning. General Systems Theory is the skeleton of science in the sense that it aims to provide a framework or structure of systems on which to hang the flesh and blood of particular disciplines and particular subject matters in an orderly and coherent corpus of knowledge. It is also, however, something of a skeleton in a cupboard—the cupboard in this case being the unwillingness of science to admit the very low level of its successes in systematization, and its tendency to shut the door on problems and subject matters which do not fit easily into simple mechanical schemes. Science, for all its successes, still has a very long way to go. General Systems Theory may at times be an embarrassment in pointing out how very far we still have to go, and in deflating excessive philosophical claims for overly simple systems. It also may be helpful however in pointing out to some extent *where* we have to go. The skeleton must come out of the cupboard before its dry bones can live.

NOTES

1. The name and many of the ideas are to be credited to L. von Bertalanffy, who is not, however, to be held accountable for the ideas of the present author! For a general discussion of Bertalanffy's ideas see "General System Theory: A New Approach to Unity of Science," *Human Biology*, Dec., 1951, Vol. 23, pp. 302-361.
2. See A. G. Pikler, Utility Theories in Field Physics and Mathematical Economics, *British Journal for the Philosophy of Science*, 1955, Vol. 5, pp. 47 and 303.
3. See "Towards a General Theory of Growth" by K. E. Boulding, *Canadian Journal of Economics and Political Science*, 19 Aug., 1953, 326-340.

2. Systems Theory and Management*

Richard A. Johnson, Fremont E. Kast and James E. Rosenzweig

Ludwig von Bertalanfly, in 1951, and Kenneth Boulding, in 1956, wrote articles which have provided a modern foundation for general systems theory. We build on that foundation in applying general systems theory to management.

The general theory is reviewed for the reader. Next, it is applied as a theory for business, and an illustrative model of the systems concept is developed to show the business application. Finally, the systems concept is related to the traditional functions of a business, i.e., planning, organizing, control, and communications.

Introduction

The systems concept can be a useful way of thinking about the job of managing. It provides a framework for visualizing internal and external environmental factors as an integrated whole. It allows recognition of the

*SOURCE: From *Management Science*, Vol. X, No. 2 (January, 1964), pp. 367-384. Reprinted by permission of the publisher.

proper place and function of subsystems. The systems within which businessmen must operate are necessarily complex. However, management via systems concepts fosters a way of thinking which, on the one hand, helps to dissolve some of the complexity and, on the other hand, helps the manager recognize the nature of the complex problems and thereby operate within the perceived environment. It is important to recognize the integrated nature of specific systems, including the fact that each system has both inputs and outputs and can be viewed as a self-contained unit. But it is also important to recognize that business systems are a part of larger systems—possibly industry-wide, or including several, maybe many, companies and/or industries, or even society as a whole. Further, business systems are in a constant state of change—they are created, operated, revised, and often eliminated.

What does the concept of systems offer to students of management and/or to practicing executives? Is it a panacea for business problems which will replace scientific management, human relations, management by objective, operations research, and many other approaches to, or techniques of, management? Perhaps a word of caution is applicable initially. Anyone looking for "cookbook" techniques will be disappointed. In this article we do not evolve "ten easy steps" to success in management. Such approaches, while seemingly applicable and easy to grasp, usually are short-sighted and superficial. Fundamental ideas, such as the systems concept, are more difficult to comprehend, and yet they present a greater opportunity for a large-scale payoff.

Systems defined[1]

A system is "an organized or complex whole; an assemblage or combination of things or parts forming a complex or unitary whole." The term system covers an extremely broad spectrum of concepts. For example, we have mountain systems, river systems, and the solar system as part of our physical surroundings. The body itself is a complex organism including the skeletal system, the circulatory system, and the nervous system. We come into daily contact with such phenomena as transportation systems, communication systems (telephone, telegraph, etc.), and economic systems.

A science often is described as a systematic body of knowledge; a complete array of essential principles or facts, arranged in a rational dependence or connection; a complex of ideas, principles, laws, forming a coherent whole. Scientists endeavor to develop, organize, and classify material into interconnected disciplines. Sir Isaac Newton set forth what he called the "system of the world." Two relatively well known works which represent attempts to integrate a large amount of material are Darwin's *Origin of*

Species and Keynes's *General Theory of Employment, Interest, and Money.*
Darwin, in his theory of evolution, integrated all life into a "system of
nature" and indicated how the myriad of living substances were interrelated. Keynes, in his general theory of employment, interest, and money,
connected many complicated natural and man-made forces which make up
an entire economy. Both men had a major impact on man's thinking
because they were able to conceptualize interrelationships among complex
phenomena and integrate them into a systematic whole. The word system
connotes plan, method, order, and arrangement. Hence it is no wonder
that scientists and researchers have made the term so pervasive.

The antonym of systematic is chaotic. A chaotic situation might be
described as one where "everything depends on everything else." Since
two major goals of science and research in any subject area are explanation
and prediction, such a condition cannot be tolerated. Therefore there
is considerable incentive to develop bodies of knowledge that can be
organized into a complex whole, within which subparts or subsystems
can be interrelated.

While much research has been focused on the analysis of minute
segments of knowledge, there has been increasing interest in developing
larger frames of reference for synthesizing the results of such research. Thus
attention has been focused more and more on over-all systems as frames of
reference for analytical work in various areas. It is our contention that a
similar process can be useful for managers. Whereas managers often have
been focusing attention on particular functions in specialized areas, they
may lose sight of the over-all objectives of the business and the role of
their particular business in even larger systems. These individuals can do
a better job of carrying out their own responsibilities if they are aware of
the "big picture." It is the familiar problem of not being able to see the
forest for the trees. The focus of systems management is on providing a
better picture of the network of subsystems and interrelated parts which go
together to form a complex whole.

Before proceeding to a discussion of systems theory for business, it will
be beneficial to explore recent attempts to establish a general systems
theory covering all disciplines or scientific areas.

General systems theory

General systems theory is concerned with developing a systematic, theoretical framework for describing general relationships of the empirical
world. A broad spectrum of potential achievements for such a framework
is evident. Existing similarities in the theoretical construction of various
disciplines can be pointed out. Models can be developed which have

applicability to many fields of study. An ultimate but distant goal will be a framework (or system of systems) which could tie all disciplines together in a meaningful relationship.

There has been some development of interdisciplinary studies. Areas such as social psychology, biochemistry, astrophysics, social anthropology, economic psychology, and economic sociology have been developed in order to emphasize the interrelationships of previously isolated disciplines. More recently, areas of study and research have been developed which call on numerous subfields. For example, cybernetics, the science of communication and control, calls on electrical engineering, neurophysiology, physics, biology, and other fields. Operations research is often pointed to as a multidisciplinary approach to problem solving. Information theory is another discipline which calls on numerous subfields. Organization theory embraces economics, sociology, engineering, psychology, physiology, and anthropology. Problem solving and decision making are becoming focal points for study and research, drawing on numerous disciplines.

With these examples of interdisciplinary approaches, it is easy to recognize a surge of interest in larger-scale, systematic bodies of knowledge. However, this trend calls for the development of an over-all framework within which the various subparts can be integrated. In order that the *interdisciplinary* movement does not degenerate into *undisciplined* approaches, it is important that some structure be developed to integrate the various separate disciplines while retaining the type of discipline which distinguishes them. One approach to providing an over-all framework (general systems theory) would be to pick out phenomena common to many different disciplines and to develop general models which would include such phenomena. A second approach would include the structuring of a hierarchy of levels of complexity for the basic units of behavior in the various empirical fields. It would also involve development of a level of abstraction to represent each stage.

We shall explore the second approach, a hierarchy of levels, in more detail since it can lead toward a system of systems which has application in most businesses and other organizations. The reader can undoubtedly call to mind examples of familiar systems at each level of Boulding's classification model.

1. The first level is that of static structure. It might be called the level of *frameworks*; for example, the anatomy of the universe.
2. The next level is that of the simple dynamic system with predetermined, necessary motions. This might be called the level of *clockworks*.
3. The control mechanism or cybernetic system, which might be nicknamed the level of the *thermostat*. The system is self-regulating in maintaining equilibrium.

4. The fourth level is that of the "open system," or self-maintaining structure. This is the level at which life begins to differentiate from not-life: it might be called the level of the *cell.*
5. The next level might be called the genetic-societal level; it is typified by the *plant,* and it dominates the empirical world of the botanist.
6. The animal system level is characterized by increased mobility, teleological behavior, and self-awareness.
7. The next level is the "human" level, that is, of the individual human being considered as a system with self-awareness and the ability to utilize language and symbolism.
8. The social system or systems of human organization constitute the next level, with the consideration of the content and meaning of messages, the nature and dimensions of value systems, the transcription of images into historical record, the subtle symbolizations of art, music and poetry, and the complex gamut of human emotion.
9. Transcendental systems complete the classification of levels. These are the ultimates and absolutes and the inescapables and unknowables, and they also exhibit systematic structure and relationship.[2]

Obviously, the first level is most pervasive. Descriptions of static structures are widespread. However, this descriptive cataloguing is helpful in providing a framework for additional analysis and synthesis. Dynamic "clockwork" systems, where prediction is a strong element, are evident in the classical natural sciences such as physics and astronomy; yet even here there are important gaps. Adequate theoretical models are not apparent at higher levels. However, in recent years closed-loop cybernetic, or "thermostat," systems have received increasing attention. At the same time, work is progressing on open-loop systems with self-maintaining structures and reproduction facilities. Beyond the fourth level we hardly have a beginning of theory, and yet even here system description via computer models may foster progress at these levels in the complex of general systems theory.

Regardless of the degree of progress at any particular level in the above scheme, the important point is the concept of a general systems theory. Clearly, the spectrum, or hierarchy, of systems varies over a considerable range. However, since the systems concept is primarily a point of view and a desirable goal, rather than a particular method or content area, progress can be made as research proceeds in various specialized areas but within a total system context.

Within the general theory and its objectives as background, we direct our attention to a more specific theory for business, a systems theory which can serve as a guide for management scientists and ultimately provide the framework for integrated decision making on the part of practicing managers.

Systems theory for business

The biologist Ludwig von Bertalanffy has emphasized the part of general systems theory which he calls open systems [A]. The basis of his concept is that a living organism is not a conglomeration of separate elements but a definite system, possessing organization and wholeness. An organism is an open system which maintains a constant state while matter and energy which enter it keep changing (so-called dynamic equilibrium). The organism is influenced by, and influences, its environment and reaches a state of dynamic equilibrium in this environment. Such a description of a system adequately fits the typical business organization. The business organization is a man-made system which has a dynamic interplay with its environment —customers, competitors, labor organizations, suppliers, government, and many other agencies. Furthermore, the business organization is a system of interrelated parts working in conjunction with each other in order to accomplish a number of goals, both those of the organization and those of individual participants.

A common analogy is the comparison of the organization to the human body, with the skeletal and muscle systems representing the operating line elements and the circulatory system as a necessary staff function. The nervous system is the communication system. The brain symbolizes top-level management, or the executive committee. In this sense an organization is represented as a self-maintaining structure, one which can reproduce. Such an analysis hints at the type of framework which would be useful as a systems theory for business—one which is developed as a system of systems and that can focus attention at the proper points in the organization for rational decision making, both from the standpoint of the individual and the organization.

The scientific-management movement utilized the concept of a man-machine system but concentrated primarily at the shop level. The so-called "efficiency experts" attempted to establish procedures covering the work situation and providing an opportunity for all those involved to benefit— employees, managers, and owners. The human relationists, the movement stemming from the Hawthorne-Western Electric studies, shifted some of the focus away from the man-machine system per se to interrelationships among individuals in the organization. Recognition of the effect of inter-personal relationships, human behavior, and small groups resulted in a rela-tively widespread reevaluation of managerial approaches and techniques.

The concept of the business enterprise as a social system also has received considerable attention in recent years. The social-system school looks upon management as a system of cultural interrelationships. The concept of a social system draws heavily on sociology and involves recognition of such elements as formal and informal organization within a total integrated system. Moreover, the organization or enterprise is recognized as subject to external pressure from the cultural environment. In effect, the enterprise system is recognized as a part of a larger environmental system.

Since World War II, operations research techniques have been applied to large, complex systems of variables. They have been helpful in shop scheduling, in freightyard operations, cargo handling, airline scheduling, and other similar problems. Queuing models have been developed for a wide variety of traffic- and service-type situations where it is necessary to program the optimum number of "servers" for the expected "customer" flow. Management-science techniques have undertaken the solution of many complex problems involving a large number of variables. However, by their very nature, these techniques must structure the system for analysis by quantifying system elements. This process of abstraction often simplifies the problem and takes it out of the real world. Hence the solution of the problem may not be applicable in the actual situation.

Simple models of maximizing behavior no longer suffice in analyzing business organizations. The relatively mechanical models apparent in the "scientific management" era gave way to theories represented by the "human relations" movement. Current emphasis is developing around "decision making" as a primary focus of attention, relating communication systems, organization structure, questions of growth (entropy and/or homeostasis), and questions of uncertainty. This approach recognizes the more complex models of administrative behavior and should lead to more encompassing systems that provide the framework within which to fit the results of specialized investigations of management scientists.

The aim of systems theory for business is to develop an objective, understandable environment for decision making; that is, if the systems within which managers make the decisions can be provided as an explicit framework, then such decision making should be easier to handle. But what are the elements of this systems theory which can be used as a framework for integrated decision making? Will it require wholesale change on the part of organization structure and administrative behavior? Or can it be woven into existing situations? In general, the new concepts can be applied to existing situations. Organizations will remain recognizable. Simon makes this point when he says:

> 1. Organizations will still be constructed in three layers; an underlying *system* of physical production and distribution processes, a layer of programmed (and probably largely automated) decision processes for governing the routine day-to-day operation of the physical *system*, and a layer of nonprogrammed decision processes (carried on in a man-machine system) for monitoring the first-level processes, redesigning them, and changing parameter values.

2. Organizations will still be hierarchical in form. The organization will be divided into major subparts, each of these into parts, and so on, in familiar forms of departmentalization. The exact bases for drawing departmental lines may change somewhat. Product divisions may become even more important than they are today, while the sharp lines of demarcation among purchasing, manufacturing, engineering, and sales are likely to fade.[3]

We agree essentially with this picture of the future. However, we want to emphasize the notion of systems as set forth in several layers. Thus the systems that are likely to be emphasized in the future will develop from projects or programs, and authority will be vested in managers whose influence will cut across traditional department lines. This concept will be developed in more detail throughout this article.

There are certain key subsystems and/or functions essential in every business organization which make up the total information-decision system, and which operate in a dynamic environmental system subject to rapid change. The subsystems include:

1. A *sensor subsystem* designed to measure changes within the system and with the environment.
2. An *information processing subsystem* such as an accounting, or data processing system.
3. A *decision-making subsystem* which receives information inputs and outputs planning messages.
4. A *processing subsystem* which utilizes information, energy, and materials to accomplish certain tasks.
5. A *control component* which ensures that processing is in accordance with planning. Typically this provides feedback control.
6. A *memory or information storage subsystem* which may take the form of records, manuals, procedures, computer programs, etc.

A goal-setting unit will establish long-range objectives of the organization, and the performance will be measured in terms of sales, profits, employment, etc. relative to the total environmental system.

This is a general model of the systems concept in a business firm. In the folowing section a more specific model illustrating the application of the systems concept is established.

An illustrative model of the systems concept

Traditionally, business firms have not been structured to utilize the systems concept. In adjusting the typical business structure to fit within the framework of management by system, certain organizational changes may be required. It is quite obvious that no one organizational structure can meet operational requirements for every company. Each organization must be designed as a unique system. However, the illustrative model set forth would be generally operable for medium- to large-size companies which have a number of major products and a variety of management functions. The primary purpose of this model is to illustrate the application of systems concepts to business organizations and the possible impact upon the various management functions of planning, organizing, communication and control. The relationships which would exist among the top management positions are shown in Figure 1.

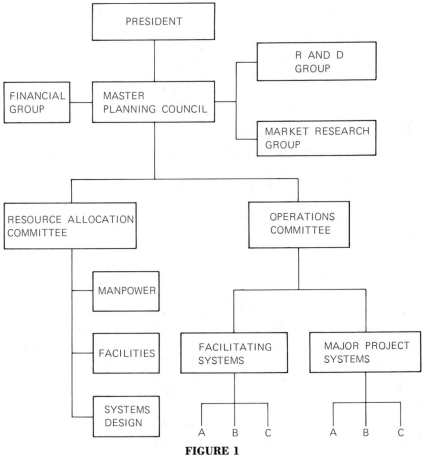

FIGURE 1
The systems model: top management

The master planning council would relate the business to its environmental system, and it would make decisions relative to the products or services the company produced. Further, this council would establish the limits of an operating program, decide on general policy matters relative to the design of operating systems, and select the director for each new project. New project decisions would be made with the assistance and advice of the project research and development, market research, and financial groups. Once the decision was made, the resource allocation committee would provide the facilities and manpower for the new system, and supply technical assistance for systems design. After the system had been designed, its management would report to the operations committee as a major project system, or as a facilitating system.

Facilitating systems would include those organized to produce a service rather than a finished product. Each project system would be designed toward being self-sufficient. However, in many cases this objective may not be feasible or economical. For example, it may not be feasible to include a large automated mill as a component of a major project system, but the organization as a whole, including all of the projects, might support this kind of a facility. A facilitating system would be designed, therefore, to produce this kind of operating service for the major project systems. The output of the facilitating system would be material input for the project system and a fee should be charged for this input, just as if the input had been purchased from an outside source.

A soap manufacturer could have, for example, major project systems in hand soap, laundry soap, kitchen soap, and tooth paste. A facilitating system might be designed to produce and *sell* containers to the four project systems.

Operating systems

All operating systems would have one thing in common—they would use a common language for communicating among themselves, and with higher levels of management. In addition, of course, each system designed would be structured in consideration of company-wide policies. Other than these limits, each operating system would be created to meet the specific requirements of its own product or service. A model of an operating system is shown in Figure 2.

Figure 2 illustrates the relationship of the functions to be performed and the flow of operating information. The operating system is structured to (1) direct its own inputs, (2) control its own operation, and (3) review and revise the design of the system as required. Input is furnished by three different groups: technical information is generated as input into the processing system, and in addition, technical information is the basis for originating processing information. Both technical and processing information are used by the material input system to determine and supply materials for processing. However, corrective action, when necessary, would be activated by input allocation.

This model can be related to most business situations. For example, if this represented a system to produce television sets, the technical information would refer to the design of the product, processing information would include the plan of manufacture and schedule, and the material input would pertain to the raw materials and purchased parts used in the processing. These inputs of information and material would be processed and become output. Process control would measure the output in comparison to the standard (Information Storage) obtained from input allocation, and issue corrective information whenever the system failed to function according to plan. The design of the system would be reviewed continually and the components rearranged or replaced when these changes would improve operating efficiency.

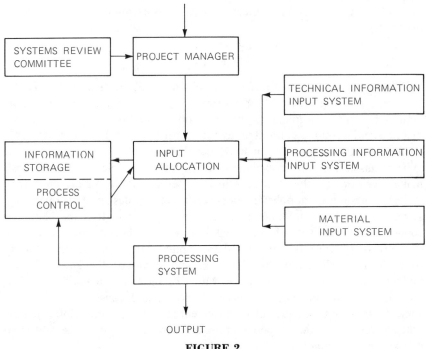

FIGURE 2
An operating system model

Basically, the operating systems would be self-sustaining with a high degree of autonomy. Therefore, they could be integrated into the over-all organizational structure (Figure 1) with a minimum of difficulty.

Systems concepts and management

Managers are needed to convert the disorganized resources of men, machines, and money into a useful and effective enterprise. Essentially, management is the process whereby these unrelated resources are integrated into a total *system for objective accomplishment*. A manager gets things done by working with people and physical resources in order to accomplish the objectives of the system. He coordinates and integrates the activities and work of others rather than performing operations himself.

Structuring a business according to the systems concept does not eliminate the need for the basic functions of planning, organization, control, and communication. However, there is a definite change of emphasis, for the functions are performed in conjunction with operation of the system and not as separate entities. In other words, everything revolves around the system and its objective, and the function is carried out only as a service to this end. This point can be clarified by reviewing each of the functions in terms of their relation to the model of the systems concept illustrated previously.

Planning

Planning occurs at three different levels in the illustrative model. These levels are shown in Figure 1. First, there is top-level planning by the master planning council. Second, the project and facilitating systems must be planned and resources allocated to them. Finally, the operation of each project and facilitating system must be planned.

The master planning council establishes broad policies and goals and makes decisions relative to the products or services the company produces. It decides upon general policy matters concerning the design of the operating systems and selects the director for each new program. It is the planning council which receives informational inputs from the environmental and competitive systems. It combines these inputs with feedback information from the internal organizational system and serves as the key decision-making center within the company. Much of the decision making at this level is non-programmed, unstructured, novel, and consequential. While some of the new techniques of management science may be helpful, major reliance must be placed upon mature assessment of the entire situation by experienced, innovative top executives.

Once these broad decisions have been made, the planning function is transferred to the resource allocation and operating committees. They plan and allocate facilities and manpower for each new system and supply technical assistance for individual systems design. At this planning level it is possible to utilize programmed decision making—operations research and computer techniques.

The third level, planning the operations of each project or facilitation system, is concerned primarily with the optimum allocation of resources to meet the requirements established by the planning council. This planning can most easily be programmed to automatic decision systems. However, the project director would still have to feed important non-quantifiable inputs into the system.

Under the systems concept of planning there is a direct relationship between the planning performed at each of the three levels. The first planning level receives informational inputs from the environment and competitive system and feedback information from within the organization. It translates this into inputs for the next planning level which in turn moves to a more detailed level of planning and provides inputs for the third or project level. One of the major advantages of this systems model is to provide a clear-cut delineation of the responsibility for various types of planning.

Organization

Traditional organization theory emphasizes parts and segments of the structure and is concerned with the separation of activities into tasks or operational units. It does not give sufficient emphasis to the interrelationships and integration of activities. Adapting the business organization to the systems concept places emphasis upon the integration of all activities toward the accomplishment of over-all objectives but also recognizes the importance of efficient subsystem performance.

The systems basis of organization differs significantly from traditional organization structures such as line and staff or line, staff, and functional relationships. As shown in Figure 1, there are three major organizational levels, each with clearly delineated functions. The master planning council has broad planning, control, and integrative functions; the resource allocation committee has the primary function of allocating manpower and facilities, and aids in systems design for the facilitating or project systems. One of the major purposes of this type of organization is to provide an integration of activities at the most important level—that is the individual project or program.

Staff specilization of skills is provided for the master planning council through such groups as financial, research and development, and market research. Their activities, however, are integrated and coordinated by the planning council. There are specialists at the operating level who are completely integrated into each project system. Thus, the activities of these specialists are geared to the effective and efficient performance of the individual project system. This type of organization minimizes a major problem associated with staff and functional personnel—their tendency to associate their activities with specialized areas rather than with the optimum performance of the over-all operation. Yet, under the model the importance of initiative and innovation are recognized. In fact, the major function of the master planning council is planning and innovation. Specific provision for receiving information inputs from product and market research are provided in the model.

There are other advantages of the systems concept. Business activity is dynamic, yet the typical organization is structured to perpetuate itself rather than change as required. There is generally resistance by the various specialized functions to change in order to optimize organization performance. For example, Parkinson's Law states that there is an ever increasing trend toward hierarchies of staff and functional personnel who are self-perpetuating and often do not contribute significantly to organizational effectiveness, or in extreme cases may be dysfunctional. In contrast, a system is designed to do a particular task. When the task is completed, the system is disbanded.

Systems are created from a central pool of resources. Facilities, machines, and manpower are assigned to specific projects or programs. The approach is to create and equip the project system with a complete arrangement of components to accomplish the job at hand. This may result in the duplication of certain activities in more than one operating system; however, this disadvantage is not as serious as it may seem. For example, it may be more efficient to have several typewriters assigned to each system rather than a central pool of typewriters. In the first instance, the typewriters may be utilized less than 100 per cent of the time, but the problems of scheduling the work at the central pool, delays, accountability, measurement of contribution, etc., would soon offset the advantages of centralizing equipment. Too much effort may be spent in creating processing information which accomplishes no objective other than keeping the machines utilized. A reasonable amount of redundancy or extra capacity will provide more flexibility, protect against breakdowns, reduce flow time, require less planning, eliminate many problems associated with interdepartmental communication, and reduce the amount of material handling.

Obviously, there are situations when it is impractical to decentralize a particular facility, because individual systems cannot utilize it sufficiently to warrant its incorporation into each separate operation. In these instances, a facilitating system would be created which would sell its services to any or all of the major project systems. These service systems would have to justify their existence and compete with outside vendors as suppliers to the major project system.

One of the great advantages of the systems concept for organizing pertains to the decentralization of decision making and the more effective utilization of the allocated resources to the individual project system. This has the merit of achieving accountability for performance through the measurability of individual systems of operation.

Control

The systems concept features control as a means of gaining greater flexibility in operation, and, in addition, as a way of avoiding planning operations when variables are unknown. It is designed to serve the operating system as a subsystem of the larger operation. Its efficiency will be measured by how accurately it can identify variations in systems operation from standard or plan, and how quickly it can report the need for correction to the activating group.

We must conclude that error is inevitable in a system which is subject to variations in input. When the lag in time between input and output is great, more instability is introduced. Feedback can reduce the time lag; however, corrective action which is out of phase will magnify rather than overcome the error. Every system should be designed to make its own corrections when necessary. That is, a means should be provided to reallocate resources as conditions change. In our model the Systems Review Committee (see Figure 2) should be aware of any change in operating conditions which might throw the system "out of control." Replanning or redesign may be required.

In controlling a system it is important to measure inputs of information, energy, and materials; and outputs of products and/or services. This will determine operating efficiency. In addition it may be important to establish points of measurement during critical or significant stages of processing. Such measurements would be used principally to help management analyze and evaluate the operation and design of individual components. The best approach is to spotlight exceptions and significant changes. Management can focus their attention on these areas. One important thing to remember is that the control group is not a part of the processing system— it is a subsystem, serving the operating system. Cost control can be used as an example to illustrate this point. The cost accountant must understand that his primary objective is to furnish managers with information to control costs. His task is to inform, appraise, and support; never to limit, censure, or veto. The same principle applies to every control group serving the operating system.

Communication

Communication plays a vital role in the implementation of the systems concept. It is the connecting and integrating link among the systems network. The flow of information, energy, and material—the elements of any processing system—are coordinated via communications systems. As shown in model (Figure 2) the operating system requires information transmission to ensure control. Communication systems should be established to feed back information on the various flows—information, energy, and material. Information on the effectiveness of the planning and scheduling activities (as an example of information flow) would be helpful in adjusting the nature of this activity for the future. Similarly, reports on absenteeism are examples of communication concerning the energy flow (the people in the system) to the processing activity. Information on acceptance inspection is an example of information stemming from the material flow aspect of an operating system. All of these feedback communication systems provide for information flow to a sensor and a control group. Comparison between the information received and the information stored (the master plan for this particular operating system) would result in decisions concerning the transmission of corrective information to the appropriate points.

Relationships within and among various project systems and between the levels of the system as a whole are maintained by means of information flow which also can be visualized as a control device. Moreover, any operating system maintains contact with its environment through some sensory element. Referring to Figure 1, the sensory elements in this case are the groups reporting to the master planning council. The master planning council makes decisions, concerning the product or service the organization will produce, based on information gained from market research, research and development, and financial activities. In a sense, these activities function as the antenna of the organization, maintaining communication with the external environment. The master planning council melds the information received through these activities with other premises covering the internal aspects in order to make decisions about future courses of action. Here again, communication or information flow can be visualized as a necessary element in controlling the course of action for the enterprise as a whole. Based on the feedback of information concerning the environment in general, the nature of competition, and the performance of the enterprise itself, the master planning council can continue its current courses of activity, or adjust in light of developing circumstances. Thus, communication or information flow facilitates the accomplishment of the primary managerial functions of planning, organizing, and controlling.

Communication by definition is a system involving a sender and a receiver, with implications of feedback control. This concept is embodied in the lowest level projects or subsystems, in all larger systems, and in the system as a whole. Information-decision systems, regardless of formal charts or manuals, often flow across departmental boundaries and are often geared to specific projects or programs. The systems concept focuses on this approach and makes explicit the information-decision system which might be implicit in many of today's organizations.

The systems concept does not eliminate the functions of management, i.e., planning, organizing, control, and communication. Instead, it integrates these functions within a framework designed to emphasize their importance in creating more effective systems. Because of the great diversity of operations and environments, particular missions of organizations differ and each system must be unique or at least have some unique elements. Nevertheless, the illustrative model and its application to the management functions of planning, organizing, controlling, and communication can serve as a point of departure in systems design.

Pervasiveness of system concepts

Many of the most recent developments in the environment of business-men and managers have involved systems concepts. For example, the trend toward automation involves implementation of these ideas. Auto-mation suggests a self-contained system with inputs, outputs, and a mechanism of control. Yet the concept also recognizes the need to consider the environment within which the automatic system must perform. Thus the automated system is recognized as a subpart of a larger system.

The kinds of automation prevalent today range in a spectrum from sophisticated mechanization to completely automatic, large-scale production processes. Individual machines can be programmed to operate automati-cally. Large groups of machines also can be programmed to perform a series of operations, with automatic materials-handling devices providing connecting links among components of the system. In such a system, each individual operation could be described as a system and could be related to a larger system covering an entire processing operation. That particular processing operation could also be part of the total enterprise system, which in turn can be visualized as a part of an environmental system

Completely automated processing systems such as oil refineries are also commonplace today. In such cases the entire process from input of raw material to output of finished products is automated with preprogrammed controls used to adjust the process as necessary, according to information feedback from the operation itself.

The systems concept is also apparent in other aspects of automation. The above examples deal with physical processing; another phase which has been automated is information flow. With the introduction of large-scale, electronic-data-processing equipment, data-processing systems have been developed for many applications. Systems concepts are prevalent, with most applications built around the model of input-processor-output and with feedback control established within the instructions developed to guide the processing of data. Here again, there is an entire spectrum of sophistication leading from simple, straightforward data-reduction problems to elaborate, real-time data-processing systems.

Physical distribution systems have received increasing attention on the part of manufacturers and shippers. The concepts of logistics, or materials management, have been used to emphasize the flow of materials through distribution channels. The term *rhochrematics* has been coined to connote the flow process from raw-material sources to final consumer.[4] In essence, these ideas embrace systems concepts because emphasis is placed on the total system of material flow rather than on functions, departments, or institutions which may be involved in the procesing.

In recent years increasing attention has been focused upon massive engineering projects. In particular, military and space programs are becoming increasingly complex, thus indicating the need for integrating various elements of the total system. Manufacturing the product itself (a vehicle or other hardware) is quite complex, often involving problems of producibility with requirements of extremely high reliability. This is difficult to ensure for individual components or subsystems. In addition, each subsystem also must be reliable in its interrelationship with all other subsystems. Successful integration of subcomponents, and hence successful performance of a particular product, must also be integrated with other elements of the total system. For example, the functioning of the Nike-Zeus antimissile missile must be coordinated with the early warning system, ground facilities, and operating personnel. All elements must function as an operating, integrated whole.

The previous discussion has emphasized the mechanistic and structural aspects of the systems concept. Yet, we cannot forget that business organizations are social systems; we are dealing with man-made systems. Obviously, a great deal could be said about the possible consequences of applying systems concepts to human relationships, but such a task is beyond the scope of this article. However, in discussing the impact of the systems concept it should not be assumed that people basically resist systems. Much of man's conscious activities since the dawn of history has been geared to creating system out of chaos. Man does not resist systemization of his behavioral patterns per se. Rather, the normal human being seeks satisfactory systems of interpersonal relationships which guide his activities. Without systematization, behavior would be random, non-goal-oriented, and unpredictable. Certainly, our complex, modern, industrial society demands more systemized human behavior than older, less-structured societies. A common characteristic in a rapidly advancing society is to make systems of interpersonal relationship more formal. While many of these systems have been implicit in the past, they are becoming more explicit. This remains one of the basic precepts of our systems model; systematic interpersonal relationships are necessary for accomplishing group objectives and an effective organizational system should be designed to meet this need.

Summary

General systems theory is concerned with developing a systematic, theoretical framework for describing general relationships of the empirical world. While a spectrum, or hierarchy of systems can be established over a considerable range, the systems concepts is also a point of view and a desirable goal, rather than a particular method or content area. Progress can be made as research proceeds in various specialized areas but within a total system context.

The business organization is a man-made system which has a dynamic interplay with its environment—customers, competitors, labor organizations, suppliers, government, and many other agencies. In addition, the business organization is a system of interrelated parts working in conjunction with each other in order to accomplish a number of goals, both those of the organization and those of individual participants. This description parallels that of open systems in general which maintain a constant state while matter and energy which enter them keep changing; that is, the organisms are influenced by, and influence their environment and reach a state of dynamic equilibrium within it. This concept of the organization can be used by practicing managers in order to integrate the various ongoing activities into a meaningful total system. Regardless of specific adjustments or organizational arrangements, there are certain subsystems or essential functions which make up a total information-decision system. However, the exact form utilized by a particular organization may depend upon the task orientation. We have presented a generalized illustrative model which indicates an approach that may be appropriate for a large segment of modern business organizations.

Managers are needed to convert disorganized resources of men, machines, and money into a useful, effective enterprise. Essentially, management is the process whereby these unrelated resources are integrated into a total *system for objective accomplishment.* The systems concept provides no cookbook technique, guaranteed to provide managerial success. The basic functions are still planning, organization, control, and communication. Each of these activities can be carried out with or without emphasis on systems concepts. Our contention is that the activities themselves can be better accomplished in light of systems concepts. Furthermore, there can be a definite change in emphasis for the entire managerial process if the functions are performed in light of the system as a whole and not as separate entities.

The business organization as a system can be considered as a subsystem of a larger environmental system. Even industry or inter-industry systems can be recognized as sub-elements of the economic system, and the economic system can be regarded as a part of society in general. One of the major changes within business organizations of the future may be the breakdown of traditional functional specialization geared to optimizing performance of particular departments. There may be growing use of organizational structures designed around projects and information-decision systems. The systems concept calls for integration, into a separate organizational system, of activities related to particular projects or programs. This approach currently is being implemented in some of the more advanced-technology industries.

The breakdown of business organizations into separate functional areas has been an artificial organizational device, necessary in light of existing conditions. Management-science techniques, computer simulation approaches, and information-decision systems are just a few of the tools which will make it possible for managament to visualize the firm as a total system. This would not have ben possible two decades ago; it is currently becoming feasible for some companies; and it will become a primary basis for organizing in the future.

NOTES

1. For a more complete discussion see: Johnson, Kast, and Rosenzweig [C], pp, 4-6, 91, 92.
2. Boulding [B], pp. 202-205.
3. Simon [D], pp. 49-50. (Italics by authors.)
4. Rhochrematics comes from two Greek roots; rhoe, which means a flow (as a river or stream), and chrema, which stands for products, materials, or things (including information). The abstract ending -ics has been added, as for any of the sciences.

REFERENCES

A. Bertalanffy, L. von, "General System Theory: A New Approach to Unity of Science," *Human Biology*, December, 1951, pp. 303-361.
B. Boulding, K., "General Systems Theory: The Skeleton of Science," *Management Science*, April, 1956, pp. 197-208.
C. Johnson, R. A., Kast, F. E. and Rosenzweig, J. E., *The Theory and Management of Systems*, McGraw-Hill Book Company, Inc., New York, 1963.
D. Simon, H. A., *The New Science of Management Decision*, Harper & Brothers, New York, 1960.

B. Total Systems

3. Total Systems Concept*

E. R. Dickey and N. L. Senensieb

The total systems concept

The total systems concept is a relatively new aproach to Systems and Procedures (*q.v.*) work in the design of management information systems for timely optimum integration of administrative information. This concept is closely associated with the use of electronic computers and data communications devices as "systems tools" to process large quantities of data, converting them into useful, timely information for managerial decision making in complex modern business organizations. It conceives of a business as an integrated entity composed of interrelated systems and sub-systems.

History

The growth in size and complexity of modern business organizations in recent decades has resulted in ever-increasing volumes of paperwork and the resultant problem of extracting accurate and timely information for meaningful managerial action from masses of scattered data. While the advent of the electronic computer during the 1950's provided a needed capability of processing masses of data rapidly, the simple extension of

*SOURCE: From *The Encyclopedia of Management* by Carl Heyel, Copyright © 1963 by Litton Educational Publishing, Inc., reprinted by permission of Van Nostrand Reinhold Company.

traditional methods to high speed machines fails to produce meaningful information to satisfy the many needs of management.

Concepts of automated and integrated operations are not new. Automation has facilitated the economical integration of factory operations. Integration of systems and sub-systems is traditional in engineering design. Electronic computers have for some years facilitated the integration of machine and human capabilities in many military operations. However, only recntly have serious attempts been started to apply fully such engineered concepts to the administrative process of the business organization *as a whole*.

The over-all approach

Computer capacity to process large volumes of data rapidly can be linked to high-speed data transmission devices which communicate between geographically separated locations, which in turn may be hooked to automated devices to record data where they originate. In order to distill useful information from the masses of data thus available, optimum integration of all the high-speed devices has to be planned as part of effective information systems design. Such system design reflects awareness that a modern organization is comprised of closely interrelated data-flow systems and sub-systems which criss-cross functional and organizational lines and hierarchical levels, and that requirements of managers at different organizational functions require varied information.

These unique information needs must be carefully identified and incorporated into the design of the total system so that it wil collect source data in an economical manner, perform desired manipulations and produce required selective information as a normal function of its processing cycles. The concept of a total business system goes far beyond the more easily recognized cycle of an integrated physical production system which receives raw materials on one end and converts them in phases into a finished product to be shipped out at the other end. Rather, the total system requires full comprehension by its designer of managerial functions and administrative processes, which can best be described as "the dynamic business systems cycle."

Dynamics of the business system cycle

A business system's functions range from the most abstract conceptualization of objectives to the most concrete specifictaion for processing materials. Organization structure also approximates the same abstraction ladder, in that it begins with the board of directors and top management, who concern themselves with more abstract ideas, and extends to the workers at the bottom of the pyramid, who perform tasks as directed by management.

Exhibit I depicts the dynamics of a total business system. It is divided into four quadrants. The top two quadrants picture the abstract part of the business, while the bottom half represents the concrete. The quadrants, from left to right, indicate actions contributing to the input into the business intelligence system or Corporate Memory, while the right quadrants represent the output from the intelligence system.

Data input to the Corporate Memory must be logical and structured in order to be useful and manipulable. No input is expected from a statement of objectives, which are far too abstract for inclusion in such a system. When the objectives are translated into logical statements, as they can be for purposes of prognostication or forecast or statements of policy, the ideas are then in such form as to be capable of logical storage, manipulation, and retrieval. The ultimate in systems design, to be sure, would automate this intelligence system, but these basic concepts remain true of any manual system.

The dynamic process of the system starts at the top of the circle and proceeds counter-clockwise. Since the process is dynamic it is continuous, and iterative. Action is the result of decision, and objectives are altered as a result of action. The cycle starts with the board of directors or chief executive, who arbitrarily establishes some objectives for the enterprise.

The next step in this dynamic process is prognostication. This is the first step to be reduced to logical terms, and constitutes the statement of plans and budgets that can be manipulated by man or machine processes. Prognostications are a matter of judgment and decision, and cannot be derived by rules applied to data, as can a payroll.

The only function left for decision and judgment on the input cycle is the establishment of policy upon which to build the procedural processes. Again policies are arbitrary, but are fashioned to be the basis for accomplishing the objectives and prognostications. (Since the word policy has been badly abused in common parlance, its use here shall be confined to mean authority, responsibility, and criteria.) Once a policy has been reduced to logical statements and stored in a Corporate Memory, the cycle of decision and judgment is virtually accomplished. At this point in the cycle, the system enters the area of performance. Here procedures as to how the information system will operate are designed. These procedures not only must conform to the policy statements previously established, but also to any statutory impingements that are applicable to each enterprise. Procedures must also take into account any contracts with suppliers or customers, since these affect the rules of procedure.

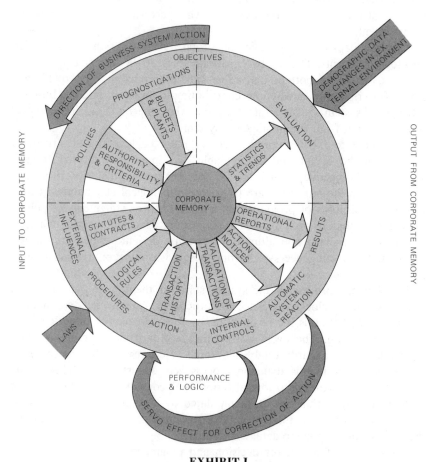

EXHIBIT I
Dynamics of the business system

The last item to enter the intelligence system is the history of transactions. A well designed system can accept into the Corporate Memory explicit and logical statements of all plans, rules, legal situations and records of transactions. With all these statements not only logical but also highly structured, the system is ready to manipulate and retrieve information or data. It may now retrieve data organized in patterns that can be only vaguely helpful to operating personnel, or it can extract the essence of information. Information is confined to data that can be used, and aside from fulfilling legal or curiosity requirements, is the only part of data of value.

The first output from the business system is on a highly concrete level.

The consideration of internal control and validation of prior transactions is paramount. The system can produce action notices, such as low inventory stock notices, employee review periods, etc. by manipulation of rules established via policy statements, in the procedure, transaction history, and time. These outputs also act as correction stimuli to operating personnel much as a thermostat starts corrective temperature action.

The next concrete level output is in the form of selected operating results. These are at a very detailed level, and maximum use is gained by association with the prognostications. This is equally true of formal or informal, manual or automatic systems. It is in this area of operating reports that the greatest amount of money is wasted because of the outpouring of great volumes of unedited paper containing data with low information content.

The last and perhaps most important quadrant of the cycle is the output and evaluation of the essence of information relative to the health of its enterprise and the art of comparing the situation of the enterprise with external conditions. It is extremely important that the information (not data) at this point be valid and complete. It is also essential that great competence be exercised by management to determine that the dynamics of the organization are correct, that the enterprise is healthy, that external conditions are such that success in fulfilling objectives will continue. If any of these factors is askew, correction or new decision and judgment must alter the objectives, prognostications, or policies.

The advantages of a total system approach

Compared with the more traditional individual-problem-oriented, or "fire-fighting approach," the Total Systems Approach is an intellectual discipline under the influence of which:

(1) Objectives are the foundation for formulating a basic policy framework for the enterprise.

(2) Logical operating procedures govern performance toward the effective attainment of objectives within parameters of applicable policies, and related procedures are integrated into logical systems (thus eliminating the inconsistent patch work of policies and procedures found all too frequently).

(3) All mechanization is systems-oriented and utilized where feasible.

The systems orientation of mechanization

The last point is a major one. Mechanization, *per se*, does not make any system a better one. However, the computer, used as a vital systems tool, can make feasible recentralization of all business data in a single Corporate Memory, using a single master file, rapidly accessible, for many kinds of data formerly stored in non-uniform (and often incompatible) terms in various departments, which use different aspects of the basic information for their own ends (sales analysis and sales forecasts in dollars, inventory control in pieces, shipments in finished units, backorders in dollars or units, plant loadings, etc.). The computer Corporate Memory can, in turn, act as the heart of an integrated Management Information System which not only provides a single control point at which all data can be edited, validated, and securely stored, but also in which meaningful relationships of information can be established for rapid provision to all managers.

Other mechanized devices can also measurably assist in optimizing the data flow, as well as integrity of data within the total system. Such devices include equipment for rapid data transmission between distant locations (which, in turn, can facilitate a central computer system), and equipment for accurate collection of transaction data in a machine language at the point of origin. From a systems viewpoint, source data acquisition equipment presents a dual advantage. First, source data acquisition facilitates capturing data at the time of creation as an economical automatic by-product of the initial transaction. Secondly, data captured in a machine language can be immediately transmitted into the computer's Corporate Memory, precluding further clerical efforts to transcribe manually or mechanically any part, thus avoiding attendant costs and possibilities of transcription error. The role of mechanization as a tool in the design of Total Systems can be summarized as: The collection of all transactions data at the point of origin in machine language, validation of the data and assimilation into a single Corporate Memory, for purposes of secure retention and re-arrangement for timely and accurate capsulized dispersal as information to users with an authoritative need to know.

Acceptance and potentials

The Total Systems Approach is gaining acceptance where competent systems and data processing staffs are able to demonstrate its practical applications, and where these analysts have broad enough knowledge of business management and of their own organizations to apply it effectively. The supply of more rigorously trained and oriented systems "generalists" to supplement narrow, specialized technicians will presage more rapid and fuller implementation of the Total Systems concept in American business organizations.

4. Organization as a Total System*

Stanley Young

Increasingly, organizations are being considered from a systems point of view in both descriptive and normative context.[1] Ashby's work would exemplify some of the descriptive work. Systems Development Corporation, Strategic Air Command, and Lockheed are effectively using the systems concept to redesign major phases of organizations in an operational and normative sense.[2] Many companies have expanded similar efforts to certain subsystems, such as steel-rolling mills, oil refineries, and so on.[3]

Our conception of the organization is changing from one of structure to one of process. Rather than visualizing the organization in its traditional structural, bureaucratic, and hierarchical motif, with a fixed set of authority relationships, much like the scaffolding of a building, we are beginning to view organization as a set of flows, information, men, material, and behavior. Time and change are the critical aspects. When we consider the organization from a normative point of view, we find another reason for this trend which is of more immediate concern. This is the working hypothesis of my article. Only when the organization is designed (organization planning) from a systems engineering orientation will it be able to take full advantage of the new and emerging managerial technologies, such as quantitative methods, the computer, information sciences, and the behavioral sciences. The engineering sciences have illustrated unusual success in the rapid creation and application of new technology and will, therefore, represent the guiding model of this analysis.

However, before taking up my thesis, let us note the current problems concerning the effective utilization of managerial technology. One problem relates to the absence of a construct as to how this new technology is to be used in an integrated and systematic manner; or consider it as the absence of a meaningful gestalt, or whole, into which such a technology would logically fit. What does exist might be categorized as a tool chest or "bits and pieces" state.

For example, let us suppose that a personnel manager has a problem of excessive absenteeism. Given the external and internal environment of the firm, the organizational constraints he has as a manager, and a set of behavioral information and managerial tools that he has acquired, how does he reduce the absenteeism rate? He knows something about psychology —perception, cognition, learning, and motivation theory. From social psychology, he should be aware of theories of attitude formation and resistance to change. From sociology, he recalls the implication of group theory. He can calculate the median, mean, and mode, run a correlation, and find a derivative. He is a qualified MBA student. Yet, what specifically should he do to reduce the absenteeism rate? Students and practitioners are given a tool chest filled with some mathematics, some psychology, and so on, and the manager is then admonished to build a better house.

Although one can appreciate the value of these various approaches, one is still confronted with the problem of their integrated application in order to be relatively assured of achieving a desired result. What is missing is the bridge or discipline between tools and organizational results. The engineering sciences represent such a discpline.[4]

Although one can raise many serious questions as to the reality, validity, predictability, and effectiveness of the classical principles approach, nevertheless it can be said that it roughly holds together as a whole or single unit, and its parts are related in logical fashion. Starting with the concept of private property and the delegation of authority, the organizational chart is drawn; authority is allocated; a division of labor is specified; and the functions of management, planning, organizing, and staffing are outlined. A certain internal logic is present, not unlike the economist's model of perfect competition. The parts are related to each other in a particular manner. Viewed as a single construct, the traditional model is understandable and operational to students and practitioners alike.

A systems approach

The same cannot be said for the newer managerial technology. The general management or organization theorist's domain is the whole. One is concerned with the problem of organization space or the distance between subfunctions, subprocesses, tools, and techniques—the interface problems. To those who are concerned with the whole, the partial approach of the new technology is disconcerting. Where and how do all these parts fit together, and what is the relationship between one and another? Sprinkling behavioral and quantitative courses about a business curriculum is of questionable effectiveness. Therefore, as far as the newer technologies are concerned, a gestalt, or general, model has been missing which will integrate all the parts meaningfully. What is being suggested is that the systems approach will provide this model.

Another problem which has emerged, which requires that the organization be designed as a total system, is that all too frequently the organizational context into which the newer technologies are inserted tend to be inappropriate. We are attaching sophisticated techniques to a primitive vehicle—the bureaucratic structure. Organizations should be designed around the techology; technology should not be forced to fit an existing structure. Thus, some corporations, to be fashionable, have created operations research departments which in fact have been given little or nothing to do. One case was reported in which the primary duty of the O.R. official was to solve the school mathematics problems of the corporate president's daughter!

In the history of innovation, one frequently finds that when a new device is invented it is attached to the existing model. For example, when the gasoline motor was first invented, it was connected to a buggy. However, as additional innovations occurred, the vehicle itself eventually had to be modified. If advantage was to be taken of additional improvements, obviously one could not unite a 300-horsepower motor to a light wooden shay. If innovation follows its usual course, we can expect the new managerial techniques to force a modification in the traditional organizational arrangements. This, indeed, has been taking place. The exploitation of the computer has led to a weakening or abolishment of the traditional divisional or departmental lines of authority. Improvements in the control and measurement of operations have the same consequences.

The differences between administrative and engineering analyses that will be taken up are:

• The engineering sciences view of the operation to be analyzed as a system or subsystem.

• The design and implementation of such systems as a sequential analysis of a team effort composed of appropriate specialized personnel.

Research, development, hardware specifications, and pilot and field studies are conducted with at least one purpose: to create and apply an improved technology to the functional operations being considered. Further, historically, the engineering sciences have incorporated the basic sciences of physics, chemistry, and quantitative methods into their analyses.

To demonstrate how the organization may be treated from an engineering point of view, it will first be analyzed as a system, and then the design process will be briefly outlined. In the presentation of the organization as a system, the approach will be analytical—a successive breakdown of the whole into increasingly smaller parts.

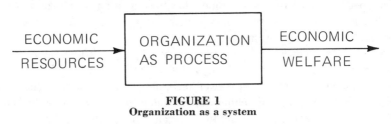

FIGURE 1
Organization as a system

Organization as a total system

In Figure 1, the business organization is presented in its most simplified form. The basic input is economic resources, the organization is the process, and the output is economic welfare. Other organizations can be represented by changing the inputs and outputs. For example, the hospital has a human input (sick patient) and a healthy patient as the output.

In Figure 2, the control or feedback mechanisms is added to the organization, which is represented by management. Or, in terms of control theory, the management segment constitutes the basic control element of the organization. Thus, given a certain welfare objective or expected welfare output (a profit increment), actual welfare is measured against expected welfare. If a difference exists, then a problem is indicated. This information

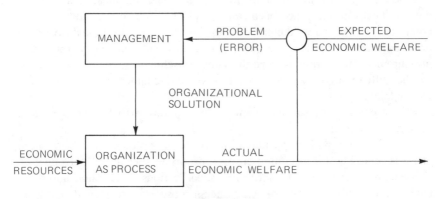

FIGURE 2
Organization with control unit

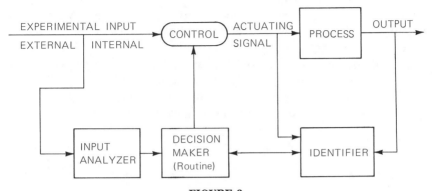

FIGURE 3
Organization as an adaptive system

is sent to the management segment which formulates a solution that is then input into the organization process. This feedback device will operate until the actual and expected welfares are approximately equal.

In Figure 3, the control unit is further broken down into a series of parts, in order to provide an adaptive capability for the organization.[5] Given a change in certain environmental inputs, one initially has an input analyzer, which indicates the nature of such changes. This is an information-gathering or sensory device; somewhat analogously, market research might be so categorized in terms of sensitizing the organization to some of the external variables, as accounting functions for the internal changes. One has also a display device, the identifier, which indicates the state of the organization or any of its subprocesses at any given time.

Hence, if the subprocess were a production plant, the identifier at a given time could indicate the productive capacity, current running capacity, order backlog, inventory conditions, orders in process, production lines in operation, and machine breakdown. Such information is fed to a decision-making unit along with the information from the environment. We assume that a set of rules has been programmed, one of which will be selected for a particular environmental input and a given process point to achieve a certain output.

For example, if the initial input is a large order with a required completion date, the rule may be to go to overtime. This information is called a control signal and is sent to the control unit. The control unit is that element which actually changes the input before it enters the system, or the process itself. The order could have been put into a queue. Such information is simultaneously sent to the identifier. Therefore, at any given time, the identifier tells us what inputs have entered the process, the state of the process, and its outputs.

Because the control signal and the control unit are frequently confused, the difference between the two should be explained. The example that is usually given is the driving of an automobile. If one wants to stop an automobile by depressing the brake pedal, information is relayed to the brakes of the car. It is not the brake pedal that stops the car, but the brakes, which constitute the control unit. Similarly, in a man-to-man system, the control signal and the control unit would appear as shown in Figure 4.

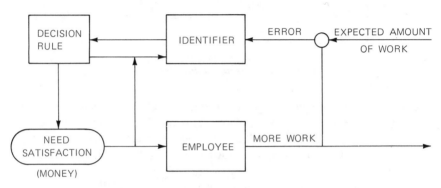

FIGURE 4
The control signal and the control unit

Let us suppose that the total employee population is the basic system, and we want a higher work output. Further, assume that we know exactly what the relationship is between need satisfaction input and expected work output. Given the figure for expected work output, the decision maker will increase or decrease the amount of need satisfaction (for example, money) via a control signal to the financial department, where need satisfaction is stored in the form of money. This department would release funds until the expected work output was achieved. It is not the decision to increase work output or its relay to the employee that constitutes the control element or even the decision to augment wages and salaries, but the reservoir and release of funds that is the control element. In other words, a salary may be to the employee what brakes are to an automobile. For our particular purposes, those subparts of the organizational control mechanism—input analyzer, and so on—give the process an adaptive capability or the ability to adapt to changing inputs so as to maintain a desired or expected output.

In Figure 5, the organization is further broken down into a series of major subprocesses: marketing, production, and so on, with its own adaptor. The adaptor consists of an input analyzer, decision rules, identi-

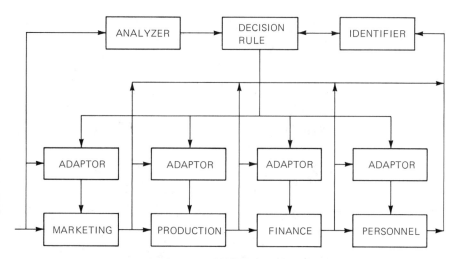

FIGURE 5
Major subprocesses, each with its own adaptor

fier, and control for each subprocess. Moreover, it is assumed that each of these subprocesses can be identified and separated from other subprocesses. A super-adaptor applies a series of decision rules for subdecision makers, to assure appropriate adjustment between processes. It is further assumed that each subsystem's adaptor has this same capability concerning subprocesses. Consequently, the production system may have subsystems of purchasing, inventory control maintenance, and so forth. The inputs and outputs of these subsystems would have to be controlled appropriately with the proper decision rules.

In Figure 6, a learning capability in the form of a designer is added to the adaptive system. A learning capability can be thought of as the ability of the system to redesign itself or learn from past mistakes so as to improve system performance. Given the environmental state of the system and the application of what is thought to be the correct rule, the expected output may still not be produced. This indicates design problems.

The designer would receive information as to system performance. Then, to increase welfare output, he would attempt to improve the adaptive mechanism: by formulating more effective decision rules for the decision-making routine, by improving the identifier in terms of more and better information, by achieving a more rapid response in information from the input analyzer, by improving the sensory devices, and by improving the control mechanisms.

In Figure 7, we now see the total system in some detail. We have our

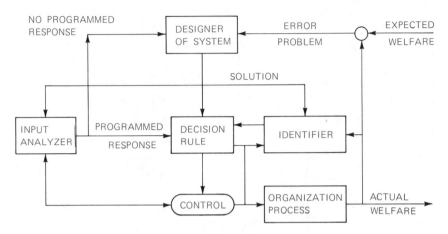

FIGURE 6
Adaptive system with learning capability

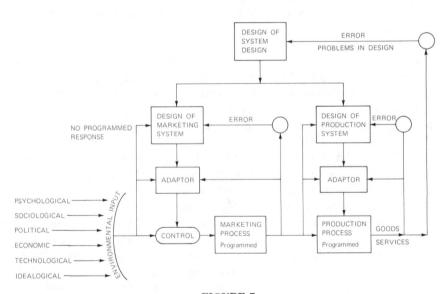

FIGURE 7
Organization as a total adaptive system

environmental inputs on the left, both external and internal (psychological, sociological, etc.). Two basic subsystems are shown: marketing and production, in which the marketing output becomes a production input. Each of these subsystems has its own adaptor, and although not shown, a coordinating adaptor to integrate the two. Further, each subsystem has its own design capability.

The only new feature of the schematic is the box at the top: Design of System Design. This particular function would integrate the work of subdesigners. For example, if the organization is viewed as an aircraft, the design of which is generally broken down into such areas as weight and structures, air frame, power, information system, and so on, design coordination is required. Moreover, this function would also advise as to design technique and strategy, and, ideally, one should be able to reach a stage in which the design itself of subsystems could be programmed.

Thus, in looking at Figure 7, we see in some detail the organization as a total system which is self-regulating and self-learning, at least partially closed, in which the environment can be detailed and in which subsystems are integrated. Further, the adaptor provides for appropriate internal adjustments between subsystems. In other words, the organization without too much difficulty can be considered as a total system. All of its essential elements can be incorporated into a design. Also, with an appropriate index, one can detail the subsystems. Each subsystem can be broken down into its subsystems, and so forth. The indexing of the system's subparts is a complex but not an insurmountable problem. For example, it is estimated that the blueprints for a new aircraft may finally weigh two or three tons— more than the aircraft itself!

System design

In Figure 8, we can briefly go through the design process, which further analyzes the function of the designer. Given a statement of the problem or the type of system with which one is concerned, the next, and key, step is the construction of a model of the system. Such a model would be essentially stochastic in nature and would stipulate the output or mission of the system and the inputs, of which there are three:

• The input upon which the process is to operate or that input which enters the system.

• Environmental inputs which affect the process.

• Instrumental or control inputs which modify the operation of the process or the process itself—and here we are concerned with the technology of processing the load inputs. For example, in a marketing subsystem, if the initial input is a potential customer, he has to be processed through the subsystem so that a sale will result.

The system's logic relates to the set of decision rules or, given certain inputs, the state of the system and a certain control capability, such as

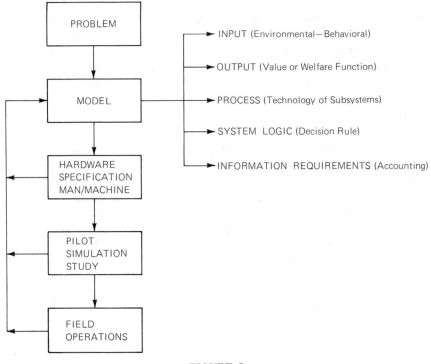

FIGURE 8
System design

more or less advertising—what particular decision rule should be utilized to achieve some expected output? Information requirements relate to the classification, amount, and timing of information, so that the system will operate as expected. Hence, concerning the environmental variables, what information about which variables should be gathered? How often? How much? And how soon would this information have to reach the decision role?

At the outset, it would be a highly worthwhile investment to construct a complete stochastic model of the system with which one is concerned, in which output is the dependent variable, and inputs, environmental and instrumental, are the independent variables. For example, one might be concerned with a personnel selection subsystem in which the output is a certain number of qualified employees. The environmental inputs might be the labor demand for certain occupations, amount of unemployment, the number of graduates, and so on; the instrumental variables might be the recruiting budget, the number of recruiters, the training program, etc.

It is more efficient to construct one model to which various decision rules can be applied than to construct a new model every time a new decision rule is formulated. With the latter approach, one would always be reconstructing the model, given a change in tools. Once the model is constructed, the research and development begins. One can experiment— try different decision rules and different hardware specifications—in terms of devising appropriate controls and measuring devices.

Experimentation requires a certain ingenuity. A grocery chain may have to set aside one of its representative stores for research purposes. It would not only be important to establish the consequences of various pricing strategies, but if possible, the causes for such consequences or, at least, the ability to predict their outcome. Given a new rule on a pilot basis, one can apply it to actual hardware. Naturally, one has to be sure that the data from pilot studies are meaningful in terms of the total system with which one is concerned. Research and development represent the essence of the engineering effort. Experimentation is costly and uncertain, but there is little doubt that the payoff is greater than using an intuitive approach.

If it is successful, the new rule can be applied, and data can be fed back regularly to the designer, so that he can continually improve and refine his initial model. Although one may begin with a relatively unrefined model, with successive experimentation and field experience, hard data will constantly flow back to the designer. This will enable him to improve his model in terms of the nature of the variables, the preciseness of the parameters, and the model's predictability.

Over time, an improvement in the state of the art should occur, if research development is effectively executed. Our grocery chain should have an ever-improving pricing strategy. As for hardware specifications, apart from the consideration of costs, one is concerned with providing components that will execute the operations as specified.

In terms of Figure 8, of particular concern is the problem of how to convert what is essentially a paper model into something that approaches operating reality. We can construct reasonably good stochastic or econometric models which can be used to stimulate different decision rules, but the conversion of these into operating reality with appropriate hardware is a different matter. In an operating context, the stochastic model or identifier becomes an information panel for a decision or rulemaker. In terms of hardware, information collection or sensory devices are needed which survey the environment and send such data to a central location, so that the values of the variables of the model can be displayed. An example is the control room in a public utility, in which the operator watches continually the changing values of significant variables. Only with such a display can appropriate action be taken. However, wiring such a system is a particularly difficult task.

For example, as a member of a team that has been given the responsibility of designing a metropolitan poverty program as a total system, the primary inputs are poverty families, and the outputs are supposed to be self-sufficient economic units. Although there exists some technical assurance that a stochastic model can be constructed, we have not yet been able to reach this design step, because we are at the initial stage of inventing a sensory machine that will give us some running idea of the nature of our changing inputs which, in this instance, is the changing mix of the characteristics of our poverty families. This program appears in Figure 9.

Another area that requires additional work is the control element, which actually modifies the operation of the system. In a man-to-man system, we do not have sufficient information about which variables to vary and by how much, in order to achieve the desired human behavior. The crude reward and punishment system that we have all too often gives us dysfunctional results. Presumably, in the design process, when serious deficiencies arise, research and development should be directed to those areas.

Managerial technology as utilized in system design

Although this view of the organization as a total adaptive system and the design process has been brief, it has been sufficient to indicate how one can take advantage of the newer managerial techniques in the use of system analysis.[6] In terms of the system presented, where and how do these techniques fit? As for the behavorial sciences, our environmental inputs or variables are behavioral in nature. To build a model and eventually a display panel, such knowledge is essential. In the decision box, we would utilize our various decision rules, such as Linear Programming, Game Theory, Dynamic Programming, PERT, and so forth. Because system design requires one to deal eventually with a total subsystem as marketing, in all likelihood we will become increasingly concerned with the problem of combining various decision rules. For example, Gerald Thompson has indicated that we must combine appropriate decision rules to achieve the most satisfactory system output. Under what conditions is it advisable to move from Linear Programming to rule of thumb, and then back to Linear Programming? As Professor Thompson has noted,

> We need to develop heuristics about using heuristics. That is, an executive program that would accept a problem and then decide which of a list of heuristics (decision rules) should be employed to give its solution.[7]

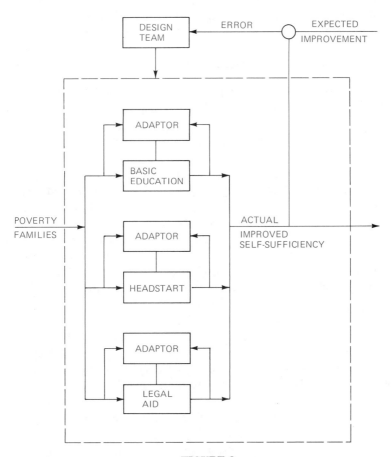

FIGURE 9
Poverty program as a system

The information sciences relate to the input analyzer and the collection, manipulation, and relay of information. Here we have all our data collection and processing problems. The control element relates to the area of control theory, specifically, the direction of human effort. Finally, in designing a specific subsystem, such as personnel or marketing, one should have some knowledge with regard to the technology of these systems; for example, one should be able to use employment tests correctly in the selection process.

In designing the organization as a total system, it would appear rather apparent that one would not only have to be familiar with but also be able to use a wide array of sophisticated managerial techniques and knowledge. The understanding and use of managerial techniques is an integral part of the design process. This is distinctly counter to the bureaucratic structure, which merely attaches such techniques to it with little purpose or place.

Design criteria

Design criteria are rules which are utilized to evaluate designs as to their acceptability. Given a number of designs, which one is the best? Although there are numerous rules, the most widely used are: *measurability, feasibility, optimality, reliability, and stability.* We will consider only the first three.

Measurability is the system's ability to evaluate its performance. If its performance cannot be measured, a system's desirability or undesirability cannot be established. Its particular excellences or deficiencies cannot be known. When models are measurable, the superior system can be inferred from the specific measuring devices used in each. In the model that has been suggested, the identifier as a display panel is the primary measuring mechanism, in that we would know the actual inputs, process, outputs, and decision rules. If the model is not working as expected, the errors would be fed to the designer on a more or less continual basis, so that the system could be redesigned for more effective results.

One of the most serious weaknesses of the bureaucratic design as a management system is that it lacks measurability. When the bureaucratic system is redesigned, for example, from a product to a functional arrangement or when the line of command is lengthened by the introduction of additional levels of managers, no measuring devices exist either in the previous or subsequent design that will indicate what improvements, if any, have occurred.

Feasibility relates to the question of whether or not the model will operate as planned. As the model must be realistic, it must be capable of being installed, of achieving expected payoff, and of performing its task requirements within the environment of the system. If a particular quantitative decision-making tool is suggested, can we be reasonably certain that it can be employed in an operational context? The use of pilot studies or experimental models relates to the question of feasibility.

Given any managerial device, we of course want to know if it will increase organizational payoff when it is utilized; will stockholders, employees, and consumers be better off than before? Organizations are normative systems. All too often, the student and practioner are exposed to quantitative manipulations and behavioral research that are interesting, but either no directions are provided as to how these findings are to be incorporated into the operations of the firm or no measuring devices are suggested that will establish the quantity of welfare that the research results will actually produce.

The end purpose of the manager, as it is viewed in this analysis, is to design subsystems which will actually increase human well-being. The manager is not, per se, a mathematician, statistician, sociologist, or psychologist. However, he must rely on these disciplines in much the same way that the engineer has to rely on physics. This does not mean that continuous research is not required in these disciplines, if designs are to improve. However, such research will not automatically lead to improvements. It is only when the designer is able toincorporate findings into an operating reality that he can achieve the full value of the research.

A corollary to the feasibility criterion relates to the question of balance between the parts of the system. All parts of the system must not only be integrated, but they must also be mutually consistent. One would not put into practice a primitive input analyzer and follow this with a complex regression analysis in the identifier. The final system output will be no more productive than the least productive part of the system. Each part acts as a constraint on all other parts. Consequently, the identifier can never be any better than the input analyzer, and so on. The absence of integration and/or balance is self-defeating.

For example, we frequently find information systems personnel providing voluminous data; that is, the input analyzer is well developed. However, the rest of the system may be missing; there is no identifier or set of decision rules. In other instances, we may have analyses of the use of a single decision rule, linear programming, but nothing else.

As long as we find this type of analysis, managers will always revert, out of necessity, to the most primitive part of the total system, because this part represents the primary constraint. In such a context, increasing sophistication will not meet the criterion of feasibility. Even if it is used, no increment in organizational payoff will result.

For example, in the design of the poverty program system that was mentioned earlier, the staff's initial impulse was to design an econometric model of the program including exogenous variables. We immediately ran into the constraints of the rest of the system and realized that, until we had a relatively effective input analyzer, a set of decision rules, and a control element, we could not move to the sophisticated model we wanted. In other words, when one designs a total system, he is generaly forced to start with a fairly elementary model. Then, when all the parts are developed, he can progress to a more complex system.

The management sciences may be overly concerned with the *optimality* criterion and ignore such other criteria as measurability and feasibility, on the assumption that if one has an optimal solution there is little else that has to be done. But unless all criteria are considered, we will not get the hoped-for results. To have a solution that is optimum but nonfeasible is meaningless. Obviously, a solution has to be measurable, feasible, and reliable, before we can consider its optimality.

For the most part, operating managers stress the feasibility criterion. At the outset, they want something that will work and actually function and are not overly concerned with optimality. In dealing with a complex system, I am sure what constitutes an optimal solution. Russell Ackoff has said:

> One of the things Operations Research has learned about putting results to work is having considerable effect on its methods. This means the team must either translate elegant solutions into approximations that are easy to use or side step the elegance and move directly to a quick and dirty decision rule. Operations Research is learning that an approximation that is used may be a great deal better than an exact solution that is not.[8]

Because design methodology imposes a specific discipline on the designer, we can be assured that new techniques will be effectively utilized.

Conclusions

Some implications

Although this has been a rather broad treatment of the organization as a total system, certain implications can be inferred.

1/On a normative basis, organizations should be viewed as a *total system* if we are to increase organizational output. Different organizations, corporations, universities, poverty programs, and so on can be categorized. Further, although this is by and large an article of faith, nevertheless some empirical evidence does exist (certainly in the area of complex weapons systems) that, if organizations are viewed as a total system, better results will be obtained. We are in the initial stages of this development, and, at this time, we can only block out the basic characteristics of total systems.

2/There has been an attempt to demonstate that the systems approach is a highly conducive vehicle for the *incorporation of current managerial technologies*, unlike the bureaucratic structure. Irrespective of the developing managerial concepts, the bureaucratic structure itself represents such a serious constraint that only minimal advantages would accrue.

3/When viewed in this context, the *essential role of the manager is that of designer of organizational or behavioral systems*, just as the engineer is the designer of machine systems. The design of a large complex system, however, will necessitate a team effort: mathematicians, psychologists, and information specialists. But, as in large machine systems, system specialists will be required to integrate the team effort. There is little reason why efforts cannot be organized to design a marketing system in the same fashion as the F-111 aircraft was designed.

In conclusion, the engineering and management sciences face the same fundamental problem—the creation of improved systems. Both suggest that quantitative modeling be performed, based on their respective underlying sciences, physical and social. However, in the engineering sciences the design and implementation of machine-to-machine systems tends to be organizationally highly systematic, whereas such a development is yet to occur with respect to the management sciences in their designs of man-to-man systems.

NOTES

Portions of this article were presented at the Midwest Academy of Management, Spring Meeting, 1966, Lexington, Kentucky.

1. For example, see Joseph Litterer, *Analysis of Organizations* (New York: John Wiley & Sons, Inc., 1965); Claude MacMillan and Richard Gonzales, *Systems Analysis* (Homewood: Richard D. Irwin, Inc., 1965), Chaps. 11-14; Ross Ashby, *An Introduction to Cybernetics* (New York: John Wiley & Sons, Inc., 1958), Chaps. 10-14.

2. For example, see Donald G. Malcolm, *et al., Management Control Systems* (New York: John Wiley & Sons, Inc., 1960).

3. See Cornelius Leondes, *Computer Control Systems Technology* (New York: McGraw-Hill Book Company, Inc., 1961), Chaps. 15-20.

4. See Arthur D. Hall, *A Methodology for Systems Engineering* (Princeton: D. Van Nostrand Company, Inc., 1962); and Harry E. Goode and Robert E. Machol, *System Engineering* (New York: McGraw-Hill Book Company, Inc., 1957).

5. For a review of adaptive systems, see El. Mishkin and Ludwig Braun, Jr., *Adaptive Control Systems* (New York: McGraw-Hill Book Company, Inc., 1961); and J. H. Westcott, *An Exposition of Adaptive Control* (New York: The Macmillan Company, 1962).

6. For a more complete review, see Goode and Machol, *System Engineering.*

7. Gerald L. Thompson, "Some Approaches to the Solution of Large Scale Combinatorial Problems," Carnegie-Mellon University, Pittsburgh, working paper, p. 25.

8. Russell L. Ackoff, "The Development of Operations Research," *Scientific Decision Making in Business*, Abe Shuchman, ed. (New York: Holt, Rinehart and Winston, Inc., 1963), pp. 59-60.

5. The Total Systems Myth*

W. M. A. Brooker

The purpose of this article is to examine critically the value of the total systems concept and to make predictions on the effects of its application. As is implied in the title, the author does not regard the concept itself as having the practical value claimed by its followers. On the other hand, the belief in this concept is a powerful motivating force among those who have accepted it as a frame of reference.

Why and what is untrue about the total systems concept? The basic error in the total systems concept is the assumption that the total systems approach is the most fruitful; that systems analysis in any situation is the most powerful kind of planning that can precede planned and profitable change for a company.

This article will discuss the foundations of the systems concept, the value of this concept and the limitations of its application. These limitations amount to an inadequacy as to the totality of pervasiveness of the approach, notwithstanding its value in an auxiliary role. We shall then discuss the requirements of an overall approach and outline an alternative in which systems theory ocupies a significant but auxiliary role.

Foundations of the systems concept

The foundation of the systems concept seems to rest on the work of von Bertalanffy, who apparently coined the term "general systems theory."

*SOURCE: *Systems & Procedures Journal* (July-August, 1965) pp. 28-32. Reprinted by permission of the publisher.

Hall, who is referred to by Bertalanffy, defines the system as . . . "a set of objects with relationships among the objects and among their attributes. Objects are simply the parts or components of a system."[1]

More specifically, systems are defined in terms of flows. According to Forrester: The business system is . . . "a system in which the flows of information, materials, manpower, capital equipment and money set up forces that determine the basic tendencies towards growth, fluctuation and decline."[2]

The flows of business system, according to Optner, are in the form of a closed system which . . . "'can be defined as one which is free of variation or disturbance . . . the concept of the black box"[3] of which the basic model is thus:

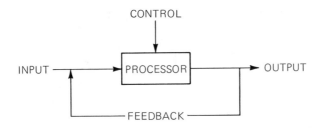

In its business form, this model becomes:

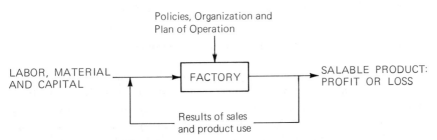

An advantage of the systems approach is that it focuses attention on broader issues than may be contained in a single department. This is because of the emphasis on inputs and outputs. What goes on *inside* the black box is of secondary importance. Naturally this has a healthy effect on any departmental narrowness of viewpoint.

The second advantage of the systems approach is that it aids in the formulation of purposes or objectives for a particular department or operating area. The reason for the existence of any operating area can very neatly be expressed in the formula:

$$P = O - I$$

where P is purpose, O is output and I stands for input.

A third advantage of the systems approach is that it can sometimes be related to decision making. Forrester, for example, in his model for industrial dynamics, shows information flows controlling valves in material and money flows.[4]

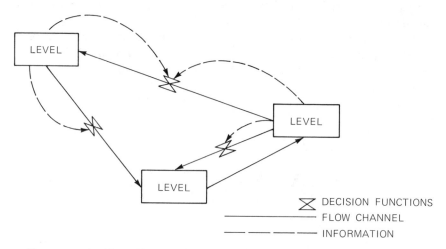

Forrester, incidentally, develops this theme very well in demonstrating the effect of varying sales volume on inventory levels.

Disadvantage of the total systems approach

The author's main quarrel with the approach is that many of the followers of systems theory seem to have translated *general* systems into total systems; they give the impression that if systems are omnipresent they must somehow, like God, be omnipotent. General systems theory is a valid field of interdisciplinary study. Those who profess general systems theory realize its limitations, which are not recognized by those who take the *total* systems approach. As an example of an understanding of the limitations of the approach, let's refer again to Hall. Following his definition of a system quoted previously in this article he continues:

"Systems may consist of atoms, stars, switches, springs, wires, bones, gases, mathematical variables, equations, laws and processes."[5]

Nowhere in this list does he refer to businesses or people; nowhere in his book does he suggest the use of systems engineering models in business.

Bertalanffy remains conservative:

"General systems theory in its present form is one—and still very imperfect—model among others." Even then, this organismic picture would not claim to be a 'nothing but' philosophy: it would remain conscious that it only presents certain aspects of reality . . . but never exhaustive, exclusive or final."[6]

In contrast is the Forrester definition quoted above. Later, in his book, he says:

"Industrial dynamics models in their purpose and origin will be . . . similar to models of engineering systems . . . concentration must be on those factors that determine the characteristics of information feedback systems—structure, amplification and delays."

Even more ambitious is Wiener:

"It is the thesis of this book that society can only be understood through a study of the messages and the communication facilities which belong to it. . . ."[7]

The error in the "total" approach

In a nutshell the objection to the "totality" of systems approach is that there is an assumption that this approach is the most important one.[8] This assumption is translated into practice by writers who define the role of change agents such as systems analysts in terms of the total systems concept.

In terms of this concept, the role of the change agents is to design the business system in terms of *flows* of information, materials, money and people, and to persuade members of the enterprise to adopt the system or subsystem so designed. The author has never come across a situation where this has actually been achieved nor has he read an account of where this has been done. This may be coincidental or it may be because of the following:

1. The total systems opproach in business makes no attempt to explain, predict or understand why the human members of the business system act the way they do. It is concerned with components of a business system in the same way as communication theory is concerned with electronic components in a communications system, but it offers little or no understanding of those components either as individuals or as members of business organizations.

2. If it cannot explain the way things are, the total systems approach cannot be expected to explain the way things are going to be. Insofar as the total systems approach is weak analytically with regard to the most significant aspects of the business system (viz., the people), it must also be weak in predicting future developments with regard to people.

Illustrations of the myth

In order to demonstrate the points we have been making we are going to discuss two articles, both heavily influenced by the total systems concept.

The first is "Analyzing an Overall System" by Charles J. Berg.[9] Early in his article he defines a business system as a:

> "...set of policies, rules, and procedures which defines the actions, responsibilities, and authorities of all elements of a business organization in the day-by-day conduct of its normal activities."

This is all-encompassing, and justifies us as classifying it as being a holistic or total approach. How does Mr. Berg use it? The core of his article is concerned with the stepwise "analytical technique for defining our present position and for use as a systems reference point. Step One is the use of the conventional flow chart of the existing system, with each step analyzed and measured showing the amount of time, money and physical distance required in each processing component. It is not unusual to find at this stage that unnecessary transportation, time and money are incorporated into the system. Step Two relies on the information previously produced, but it is a modified form of the same information. This is the input-output analysis chart. This technique clearly depicts the multitudinous uses of various data. Generally it can be stated that where many inputs are used to devise many outputs, potential systems improvements are of a high order. Step Three is to relate the present system as described in steps one and two above into financial terminology. What lines on the statement are affected and what are the potential improvements available? Step Four is the allocation of people responsibility for the planned systems improvement, along with specific financial obectives to be attained. Step Five is to accomplish the improvements resulting from the analysis of the above information."

Diagramatically Berg expresses his approach as shown in Figure 1.

But the author does not fulfill his promise. In terms of his own definition of a business system his analytical technique is mainly concerned with "procedures and actions." He refers to policies, rules, responsibilities and authorities *of all elements of a business organization* in his definition of a business system quoted above, and says precious little about them in his analytical technique. Under which of his stepwise analytical techniques could one consider the following problems which have to be considered in any business organization?

What business should we be in? For example, should we diversify our operations, or consolidate? Should our business be divisionalized along

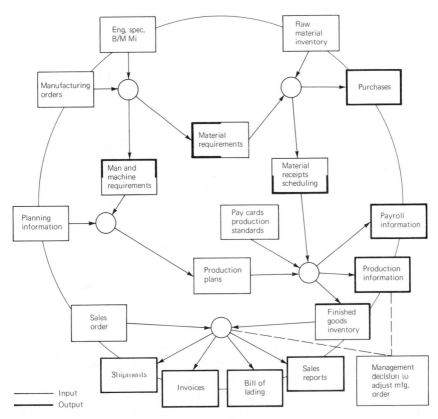

FIGURE 1

The stepwise analytical techniques shown here are too narrow to fulfill the promise evident in the definition of total systems.

ONE: If you have a manufacturing order and this is combined with an engineering specification, bills of material and manufacturing information, manpower and the facilities required can be determined.

TWO: With material requirements being compared to raw material inventories, purchases anr material receipts schedules can be derived.

THREE: Returning now to the manpower and facilities requirements, combining and comparing this with planning infirmation, we can evolve specific production plans.

FOUR: Material receipts schedules and pay cards, along with production standards and the production plans, can be integrated to produce payrolls, production data and finished goods inventory.

FIVE: Coordinating the information of a sales order with that of the finished goods inventory, we can produce shipments, invoices, bills of lading and sales receipts.

SIX: Finally, we can build management decisions into the systems which are necessary to operate it most effectively.

*product lines, customer grouping, or geographic areas? Should our en-
gineering function be centralized or decentralized or along some combination of both?*

In fact these problems cannot be subsumed under the techniques proposed because they are too narrow. The promise of total systems—evident
in the definition—remains unfulfilled in the proposals for its creation.

Similar objections come to mind with a second article by Dr. R. L.
Martino.[10] But in this case the gap between promise and proposal is even
more blatant. The promise lies in the title: "The Development and Installation of a Total Management System."

Most business people are inclined to accept the simple notion that
management is concerned with governing and controlling of the activities
of a company, somewhat analogous to the executive branch of the government of a state. To enlarge "management" to "total management system"
emphasizes the pervasiveness of the phenomena and also its completeness
and orderliness. This promise is not borne out by the following:

> ". . . The primary objective in developing a total management system
> should be the production of detailed up-to-the-minute summaries of the
> past and the use of these summaries to project future activity. In essence
> the functions of a total management system are: (1) To predict; (2) To
> compare the prediction with actual results; and (3) To produce the
> deviations between the predicted and the actual."

In other words, the total system conceptualizers, when they really get
down to it, talk of designing flows of information to enable management
to do its job better. Martino represents this diagramatically in Figure 2.

The figure shows what management does with various kinds of information. In Martino's model, management *itself* is not part of the total
management system, for nowhere is there any phase where management
looks at itself or the organization of which it is a part. It is as though
management were something like the driver of a car, detached; as though,
like a car driver, management made the decisions, the "systems" carried
them out.

Factories, warehouses and saleshouses and other industries, services,
utilities—whatever the business exists for—consist of much more than information handling systems glorified into some state of "totality." Just as a
map of a country may cover the whole of it, it is not a "total" depiction
of it, because in a country there are other dimensions and features that
cannot be shown on a map. Similarly, in a business there are other
dimensions and features which cannot be subsumed under the kinds of
total systems we have been discussing.

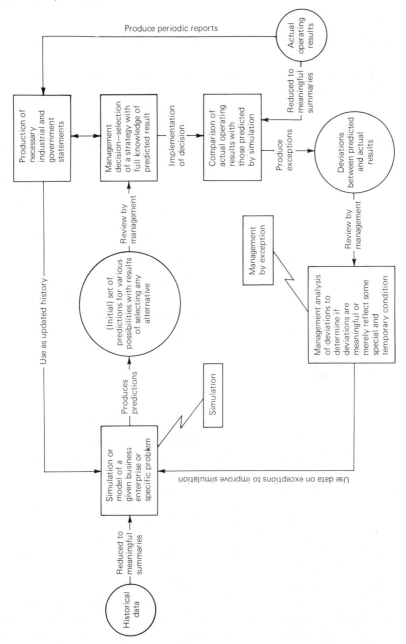

FIGURE 2

This diagram shows what management does with various kinds of information. Management itself, however, is not part of the total management system, for nowhere is there any phase where management looks at itself or the organization of which it is a part.

Requirements of a general business theory

What, then, are the theoretical requirements of change agents in business? The following thoughts are offered as criteria for basic theory:

A. Understanding for action

1. It must be capable of understanding current problems of business. Therefore,

2. It should be capable of realistic predictions on consequences of proposed actions.

3. It should provide a basis for establishing direction for proposed change.

B. Basis for theoretical development

An acceptable basic theory should be broad enough to include other more specific theories. If, for example, we reject total systems theory as a basic tool, the basic tool we do adopt should be capable of covering the valuable aspects of such a theory.

Outline of a basic theory

What follows is a skeletal account of a theory which meets these requirements:

1. A business is primarily a social human group. The machines, however vast, are originated by and operated by human beings. Therefore, the theoretical basis should be human oriented.

2. There are three aspects of human groups which are important to the understanding of a business. They are objectives, or purpose; activities, or the actual work performed; and relationships which include cooperative and functional as well as the ever-present man/boss relationship. In addition, there are three corresponding concepts pertaining to the individual: values, status and activities.

3. The basis of the approach suggested is, first, that there are certain desirable or healthy conditions for these group and individual aspects, particularly in their relationship to one another. Second, it can be assumed that these conditions do not necessarily apply at all times. Third, it is suggested that the lack of desirable conditions applying will lead to the occurrence of certain effects or symptoms. Fourth, the approach envisages the use of various techniques to reveal these symptoms. Fifth, it is suggested that the symptoms can be used to identify the *causes* of malfunction, and

sixth, that planning and executing projects which rectify causes are the proper work of systems analysts, or other change agents, in business.

4. The activities of business are only one of many aspects. Only when this aspect is viewed against its proper background of group purpose (or objectives) and structure, and individuals' values and status, should it be elaborated into a "totality" of system.

5. It is entirely possible to make use of the valuable aspects of systems theory (discussed in the early part of this article) within these other concepts, but then the systems aspect is no longer "total" but ancillary.

A proposed role for systems analysis

How can the role of the systems analyst be met in view of these criticisms? The senior systems man in a company may be analogous to a cabinet minister in charge of communications (embracing, for instance, tele-postal-road-rail and air-communications). A minister of communications is concerned with the development of channels for the transmission of information in whatever form. Similarly, the VP of communications with a firm should be concerned with the development and maintenance of communication networks which best achieve company, and divisional if necessary, purpose(s).

This is far-reaching in that it would be extending throughout the whole but it is not holistic or "total" in the Wiener or Forrester sense. Systems departments, therefore, are not analogous to the management of a *real* whole (e.g., a company, a plant or a division).

Let us again take a geographic analogy. All the cities in North America are connected by a system of roads, but urban development—as in the case of corporate development—means working with the wholes in the situation.

City management and development undoubtedly requires auxiliary and parallel development and modification in the road system, and occasionally cities have to adjust to a road development program under the control of a wider authority which constitutes a natural whole,[11] such as a state government.

Roads in this way are analogous to the communications networks of business. Corporations as natural wholes are composed of other, smaller wholes (divisions, operating departments, staff functions, etc.), and the role of management is the continuous mutual adjustment of these parts to one another in order to achieve company goals. This process of continuous adjustment requires the continuous development of new communications transmittal, reception and storage, and it is the role of the systems analyst to carry out this development.

Sometimes, as in the case of a city having to adjust to the road development by a wider authority, the natural wholes (e.g., divisions, departments) within a company have to adjust to the communications system imposed upon them by the company as a whole.

The total systems concept implies—indeed some of its exponents, as we have seen, are quite explicit—that the communications system is the basis for understanding and changing society, or the micro-society that the corporation forms. This is not true; the systems concept is not that "total."

NOTES

1. Arthur D. Hall, *A Methodology for Systems Engineering*, Van Nostrand, Toronto, 1962, p. 60.
2. J. W. Forrester, "Industrial Dynamics: A Major Breakthrough for Decision-Makers," *Harvard Business Review*, July-August, 1958, p. 52.
3. Stanford L. Optner, *Systems Analysis for Business Management*, Prentice-Hall, Inc., 1960, pp. 3-15.
4. From J. W. Forrester, *Industrial Dynamics*, John Wiley & Sons, New York, 1961, p. 67.
5. *Ibid.*, p. 60.
6. Bertalanffy, *General System Theory—A Critical Review*, Yearbook of the Society for General Systems Research, Vol. VII, 1962, p. 10.
7. Norbert Weiner, *The Human Use of Human Beings—Cybernetics and Society*, Doubleday-Anchor, New York, 1954, p. 16.
8. The reason for the error lies in what the author calls the Magical Fallacy.
9. *Systems & Procedures Journal*, November-December, 1963.
10. "The Development and Installation of a Total Management System," *Data Processing for Management*, April 1963, p. 31.
11. J. C. Smuts, *Holism and Evolution*, Compass Books, New York, 1961.

2 INFORMATION TECHNOLOGY

An effective information system encompasses the use and generation of information. Observed changes in the structure of organizations have created new demands and uses for information. Thus, there is an apparent need for criteria to evaluate the generation and use of information, and for ways to determine the impact of information technology on the structure of an organization. The articles in this section describe elements to be considered in judging information. In addition, assumptions with respect to the quality and quantity of information are treated both pro and con.

The computer, as the agent of information technology, has been praised for its potential, and cursed for its pervasiveness, if not for its perversity. The writings offered deal with both sides of the question. Important evidence relating to changes in organizational structures and processes in manufacturing companies is presented, and the role of the general manager in the development of information systems is discussed.

A. The Nature of Information Technology

6. On the Nature of Management Information*

Gerald E. Nichols

The primary purpose of a management information system is to expose significant relationships that will decrease uncertainty in organizational decision-making with a corresponding increase in the utilization of organization resources. Those concerned with achieving this goal need some criteria for guiding their efforts. The necessary considerations include a knowledge of the types and qualities of information needed throughout the organization, for the fate of the business is determined by the information supplied the decision-maker.

This paper attempts to give the reader some insights into the elements to be considered in judging information. Such knowledge should facilitate both the generation and use of business information.

Classification and information

Man is confronted with a wide and varied environment. To reduce the diversity of his environment to manageable order, man resorts to classification and to the formation of general ideas about groups of things—that is, man simplifies to aid comprehension.

Information generation[1] requires four steps if it is to be useful beyond

---

*SOURCE: *Management Accounting* (April 1969), pp. 9-13, 15. Reprinted by permission of the publisher.

the moment of observation or useful to individuals and groups other than the observer. The steps involve:

1. Classification of data—the basic problem is relating observations to anticipated situations of all classes of economic decision-makers.
2. Establishment of procedures for recording data in a manner facilitating recall, yet sufficiently simplified to enable the operation to be routinized.
3. Summarization of data classified and recorded.
4. Specification of the collection procedure of the system.

Classification reduces the complexity of the material, provides a means of identification by grouping like things together, provides a record of experience, and orders and relates classes of events. Three major characteristics[2] of any classification system are that:

1. Classes must not overlap—they must be mutually exclusive.
2. The classification system must be exhaustive—each item to be classified must be placed in some distinct category.
3. The basis of classification must be significant (related to some specific goal) and in accordance with some predetermined pattern.

The information generating system

The general functions of information systems are to determine user needs, to select pertinent data from the infinite variety available from an organization's environments (internal and external), to create information by applying the appropriate tools to the data selected, and to communicate the generated information to the user. Such a system is depicted in Exhibit I. This presentation uses the three levels of information postulated by Gregory and Van Horn[3] who state that:

"Considered at the *syntactic* level, data consists of collections of symbols or characters arranged in some orderly way to serve as the vehicle for information. Information is the meaning derived from data and represents the *semantic* level—the relationship between a symbol and the actual object or condition that is symbolized. The impact of the objects or conditions on the receiver represents the *pragmatic* level of information."

Thus, "data" is used to refer to perceived and symbolized events (syntactic information); "potential information" refers to meaning derived from data (semantic information); and "information" refers to the impact upon the receiver (pragmatic information). Each of the functions depicted in Exhibit I will be discussed in detail.

Specification of information needs

The specification of needs is necessary since information has meaning only when associated with the decision to be made. This element also

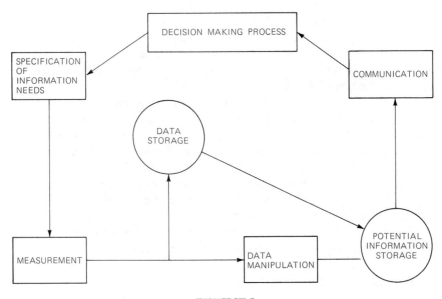

EXHIBIT I
An information system

implicitly includes the specification of the events to be observed and the time and place of observation.

The information that is generated and made available within the organization should be tailored to the task at hand. However, the concept of "tailoring" within the organization is much more comprehensive. "Tailoring" requires that the *decision-maker* and the information required by the decision be matched at each decision point within the organization.

The emphasis is upon supplying each decision point with enough information, of the right quality, when it is needed. This requires that the system be constantly updated. Not only must the information supplied the decision point be current, but the skills, or knowledge level, of the decision-maker, *per se*, must also be kept current. That is, the information to be supplied the decision point must be tailored not only to the specific requirements of the decision to be made but also to the skills, attitudes, and capabilities of the decision-maker. The manager must be supplied with information he can comprehend and use effectively.

Ideally then, the information flowing to any given decision point would be adjusted when changes occurred in the capabilities of the decision-maker, or in the information available or pertinent to the decision; or if the manager responsible for a given decision were changed.

Measurement

As used here, measurement includes the observation and symbolization of the pertinent aspects of the above-specified events in one of the four possible measurement scales: nominal, ordinal, interval and ratio.

The nominal scale refers essentially to classification; whereas the ordinal scale requires that things or classes of things be ranked minimally as either "less than" or "greater than," but may include the assignment of numbers or symbols as a means of ranking multiple objects or classes. The objects ranked must be comparable in terms of some relationship.

The interval scale not only ranks objects or classes but also contains information on how large the interval is numerically. The rules of the real number system are applicable to an interval measure, but not all arithmetic operations can be applied because the interval scale has an arbitrary zero and thus many different scales can be applied to measure the same phenomenon. For example, temperature can be measured in either degrees centigrade or degrees Fahrenheit.

The ratio scale is an interval scale whose origin is absolute zero. All arithmetic operations are applicable to measurements derived using a ratio scale.

Note should be made of the fact that measurement, and thus, data, is concerned only with the *past*, since an event must have occurred before it can be measured.

Data manipulation

Management is concerned with the past, the present and the future. Since data is past oriented, manipulation is necessary to convert data into potential information relevant to the present and the future. In a sense, data may also be potential information, requiring only that it be communicated to management. Johnson, Kast, and Rosenzweig have stated that:

"The information-decision-system must be designed to garner pertinent facts and screen unwanted or unusual data. Screened data may become information for managerial decision-making. However, it is more likely that additional processing is necessary before meaningful information is available."[4]

Time is an essential consideration in developing and presenting information. Therefore, manipulation is also concerned with the timeliness of data determination and presentation, and thus its conversion into potential information. Manipulation is definitely necessary for converting data to potential information concerning decisions affecting the future.

Actually, all decisions concern the future and are based on past experience. In the business organization records of past experience (data) usually

require manipulation such as summarization to expose significant relationships that will reduce uncertainty in decision-making. Other common
manipulations are the determination and extrapolation of trends, correlation
analysis of organization data with economic indicators, simulations, or the
assignment of probabilities to possible situation outcomes.

Data and potential information storage

In this day of absentee ownership and the large organization, the
decision-maker does not usually gather all of the information necessary for
the decisions he makes. Potential information is generated throughout the
organization which requires that some form of intermediary storage be
used. Data covering long periods of time are necessary for some manipulations and decisions. Hence, data must be stored until needed. Data storage
is also necessary where specialization within the information generating
process is used.

It should be observed that data refers to measures of events concerned
with the organization's internal and external environments, while "potential
information" and "information" are internally oriented concepts. Data and
potential information storage may involve such things as written documents,
punched cards, or magnetic tapes, and a concomitant concern with the
method and speed of retrieval.

Communication

Communication problems can be considered from three different levels—
the technical, the semantic and the effectiveness levels. These considerations
are comparable to those previously associated with information. However,
only the effectiveness level will be considered here.

"Effectiveness" implies a relationship to purpose. The effectiveness of a
communication refers to the changes it causes in the pursuit of a purpose.
The effectiveness of a communication is determined by comparing the
purposeful states of the decision-maker before and after receipt of the
communication.

The communication[5] is considered to have been effective if it changes a
purposeful state in one of three possible ways:
1. Informs—changes the probabilities of a choice
2. Instructs—changes the efficiencies of a course of action
3. Motivates—changes the values of the outcomes

Effective communication of information may result from proper sequencing, spacing, coloring, or things of like nature that affect or result in the
reduction of uncertainty in the decision-maker. Thus, potential information
must be effectively communicated and have news content pertinent to a

given decision to be considered information. These considerations tie in with the concept of "tailoring" which stresses the importance of the decision-maker as well as the information supplied a decision point.

The attributes of information

The management information system is, in general, concerned with information pertinent to the achievement of organization goals. Representations of an event require two basic types of information, quantitative and descriptive.

Quantitative information tells how much or how many; but the majority of the information will be descriptive and will serve to identify that which has been quantified. Business information specifically requires information regarding the five basic flows of economic systems—money, orders, materials, personnel, and capital equipment—in a time, or dynamic, context.

A partial list of desirable business information attributes are: relevance, availability, timeliness, objectivity, sensitivity, comparability and quality. The meanings of most of these attributes are self-evident even though there may be some overlap in meanings.

Information *must* possess the first three attributes—relevance, availability, and timeliness—to have value, and thus to qualify as information. Objectivity, sensitivity, comparability, conciseness, and completeness are desirable, but they are present and necessary only in varying degrees. These latter attributes of information are favorably influenced when the information is derived using higher levels of measurement scales, progressing up from the nominal to the ratio. That is to say, quantifiability is desirable.

The last attribute, quality, refers to the presence or absence of ambiguities in information. All information should posses "quality." Measures of quality are validity, accuracy, and precision. These measures of quality are especially important and applicable to quantified information, for quantified information creates the illusion of rightness. However, numbers are of course not sacred and are subject to ambiguities.

Information and the management hierarchy

The amount, or quantity, of information to be provided each decision-maker is a function of the state of arts and the individual decision-maker as determined by the application of the "tailoring" concept. The amount of information supplied management is also a function of the relative position of the manager in the managerial hierarchy and the environment with which the information is concerned—the internal environment of the organization and the environment in which the organization exists, its external environment. It is a well known generalization that internal information should be more and more summarized as the level of management for which the information is prepared increases in the hierarchical structure, with top management receiving the most summarized reports. This contention is based upon the fact that most internal data is control oriented and the lower echelons of management are the most control oriented; while top management is more planning oriented.

This situation is depicted in Exhibit IIA where management activity is bisected into planning and control. Exhibit IIA is to be interpreted broadly and is not intended to portray accurately the actual percentage of the time spent by the various levels of management in either planning or control. However, the representation is roughly correct according to an estimate by Terry.[6]

It seems just as plausible to generalize that information concerning the external environment of the organization should be summarized in a manner exactly opposite to that posited for information concerning the internal environment. This is to say that since the upper levels of management are more planning oriented and since planning necessitates more information concerning the organization's external environment, information concerning the external environment should be increasingly more summarized and selective as the position of the receiver decreases in the managerial hierarchy. This situation is depicted in Exhibit IIB.

Informational constraints

The conceptual nature of information systems makes them difficult to study and understand. There are, however, physical systems whose well developed theories may be beneficially extended or applied to information systems. For example, classification was previously contended to be a necessary device for coping with reality. However, classification creates a paradox, for it at once creates and destroys information. The number of classifications regarding a particular event (that is its information potential) are infinite, while classification systems are finite. Thus, classified data loses all information potential other than the potential possessed by the category into which it is placed.

To achieve its total potential (perfect information) an event would have to be classified into an infinite number of categories, which is to not classify at all. Thus, only a finite amount of information is available in a given system; or conversely, a certain amount of information is not available.

The situation is analogous to that of energy in the physical world. The

A. RELATION OF MANAGERIAL POSITION TIME SPENT IN PLANNING AND CONTROL

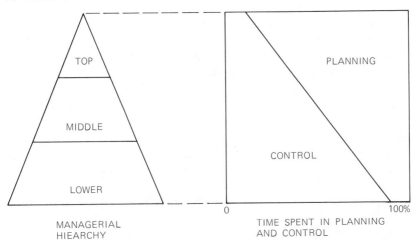

B. RELATION OF MANAGERIAL POSITION TO SUMMARIZATION OF INFORMATION

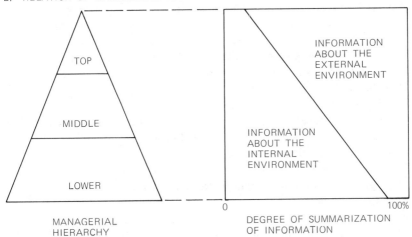

EXHIBIT II
Management levels related to planning control and information

second law of thermodynamics states that in an isolated system the probability that entropy shall decrease is zero (where entropy is the positive measure of disorder). In addition, the conversion of energy from one form to another in a given system is accompanied by an increase in entropy (that is, energy is lost).

The application of these concepts to business information systems makes more obvious some intuitive facts:

1. Information is a function of order.
2. Order, and thus information will not spontaneously increase in an isolated system.
3. The amount of information available in a system is finite; the measure of the unavailable information is a measure of disorder.
4. Conversion of information from one form to another (communication) results in a decrease in available information.

One method of minimizing information loss through communication is to maintain a certain level of redundancy in messages. However, redundancy is related to efficiency of coding or classification by the relationship:

Redundancy $= 1 -$ Efficiency

This relationship reveals that a highly efficient code or message is accompanied by a low redundancy which in turn increases the possibility of loss of information.

To convey understanding, there must be uniformity of meaning of words and numbers used in information systems, and rules or guidelines for the use of resulting abstractions are necessary to assure that the underlying activity is revealed and not obscured or distorted by the reporting process. To this end, the AAA Committee on Basic Accounting Theory proposed five guidelines[7] for the communication of accounting information:

1. Appropriateness to expected use,
2. Disclosure of significant relationships,
3. Inclusion of environmental information,
4. Uniformity of practices within and among entities,
5. Consistency of practices through time.

These guidelines appear to be pertinent to all business information. Other more specific means to improve communication[8] are:

1. Finding out what information is desired,
2. Limiting the quantity of information to the essentials,
3. Highlighting the most important figures on reports,
4. Rounding numbers.

However, communication is much more complicated than has thus far been indicated. Studies have shown that even when executives have all the information they need to make a decision, they do not always make the correct one. These failures are thought to occur either because the executive does not know how to translate information into effective action or because the information has not been adequately communicated to him.

Some feel that the answer is to be found in a better understanding of the manager himself and how he thinks and works. The information purveyor must fit his reports to specific individuals.

Value of information

There are various approaches to the problem concerning the value of information. One approach to the information collection problem centers on the minimization of the sum of two costs: the cost attributable to decision error, and the cost of assembling and analyzing the required information. The information system is restricted by economic limitations to the accumulation of useful information only, and the measurement of usefulness depends upon the ability to relate the cost of gathering information to the benefits received. This approach is ideally correct, but the determination of the requisite costs necessary in applying this approach is in many cases impossible. Many authorities have termed this type of approach impractical and so general as to be useless. More rigorous approaches based upon this philosophy have recently been formulated, but are beyond the scope of this paper.[9]

The following are some non-dollar value guidelines[10] for evaluating information:

1. Information must influence decisions.
2. Increasing the accuracy of information increases the cost.
3. Timeliness influences costs.
4. Shorter delays mean higher costs.
5. The systems capacity affects the cost value of the information.

A pragmatic approach is taken by Kirk who states that a value can be assigned information by simply asking, "How much does the piece of information reduce my uncertainty in this decision situation?"[11]

Adopting a pragmatic approach, information is seen to acquire significance (that its value is increased) only when it is used in conjunction with or judged by comparison with:

1. Other current measures
2. The same measurements in previous periods
3. Standards or targets
4. Forecasts
5. Parallel activities elsewhere[12]

The value of information presented in reports can be increased by maximizing their psychological impact and usefulness to managers. Doris

Cook[13] recently surveyed the attitude of managers towards certain aspects of performance reports. Based upon her findings, she proposed that the usefulness, and thus the value of performance reports can be increased if they:

1. Are provided as frequently as costs and other circumstances permit
2. Are provided as soon after the end of a reporting period as possible
3. Give appropriate credit for favorable performance
4. Include, if possible, the reasons for reported below average performance
5. Provide as much detailed information as specifically needed by each recipient
6. Include only controllable items
7. Are accurate
8. Compare actual results with an accurate, fair and appropriate basis of measurement (where possible the quality of the job should also be measured)
9. Emphasize the *exceptional* items which require the attention of the manager
10. Avoid using performance reports as a pressure device to prod the managers continually to increase output or decrease costs.

The value of information is also increased when the user has confidence in the information. Confidence is increased if the user generates the information himself. When the user and the generator of information are not the same person, confidence, and thus value, is increased by a knowledge of the method of generation and of the generator.

Confidence in the person or group generating the information can be attained by either a personal acquaintance with, or power over, a person; or through some sort of confirmation of or attestation regarding the reliability of the generator. Confidence in the information itself will be increased when the information and the method of generation are standardized, providing the user has knowledge of the standards and their meanings and limitations. Useful standards will involve criteria regarding the previously mentioned attributes of information in addition to the factors outlined above.

Summary and conclusions

The general functions of information systems are to determine user needs, to select pertinent data from the infinite variety available from an organization's environments, to create information by applying the appropriate tools to the data selected and to communicate the generated information to the user. The nature of and criteria for evaluating management information and the information generating system have been presented. Much more research is necessary regarding the interrelationships of information and decision-making. Such a body of theory would be very useful as an aid to individual decision-making but its greater use would be in the designing of information systems for decision-making in the whole business system.

NOTES

1. James W. Giese, *Classification of Economic Data in Accounting*, a dissertation, University of Illinois, 1962, p. 122.
2. *Ibid.*, p. 15.
3. Robert H. Gregory and Richard L. Van Horn, *Automatic Data Processing Systems*, Wadsworth Publishing Company, Inc., Belmont, Calif. 1965, p. 54.
4. Richard A. Johnson, Fremont E. Kast, and James E. Rosenzweig, *The Theory and Management of Systems*, McGraw-Hill Book Company, Inc., New York, 1963, p. 181.
5. Russell L. Ackoff, "Towards a Behavioral Theory of Communications," *Management Services*, April 1958, p. 226.
6. George R. Terry, *Principles of Management*, Richard D. Irwin, Inc., Homewood, Ill., 1964, p. 238.
7. American Accounting Association, *A Statement of Basic Accounting Theory*, American Accounting Association, Evanston, Ill., 1966, p. 13.
8. Harold W. Jasper, "Future Role of the Accountant," *Management Services*, January-February, 1966, p. 53.
9. For example see: Norton M. Bedford and Mohamed Orsi, "Measuring the Value of Information—An Information Theory Approach," *Management Services*, January-February, 1966.
10. Rudolph E. Hirsch, "The Value of Information," *The Journal of Accounting*, June, 1968, pp. 42-43.
11. Andrew Kirk, "Company Organization and Control," *Management Accounting*, England, February, 1966, p. 63.
12. J. A. Scott, "The Management of Performance in Industry," *The Cost Accountant*, England, April, 1963, p. 131.
13. Doris M. Cook, "The Psychological Impact of Certain Aspects of Performance Reports," *Management Accounting*, July 1968, pp. 33-34.

7. Management Information Crisis*

D. Ronald Daniel

In late 1960 a large defense contractor became concerned over a major project that was slipping badly. After 15 months costs were running far above the estimate and the job was behind schedule. A top-level executive, assigned as program manager to salvage the project, found he had no way of pinpointing what parts of the system were causing the trouble, why costs were so high, and which subcontractors were not performing.

Recently an American electronics company revamped its organization structure. To compete more aggressively in international markets, management appointed "area managers" with operating responsibility—e.g., in Latin America, Western Europe, and the Far East. After nine months it was apparent that the new plan was not coming up to expectations. On checking with three newly created area managers, the company president heard each say, in effect:

- "In half of the countries in my area the political situation is in flux, and I can't anticipate what's going to happen next."

- "I'm still trying to find out whether our operating costs in Austria are reasonable."

*SOURCE: *Harvard Business Review* (September-October, 1961), pp. 111-121. Reprinted by permission of the publisher. Copyright © 1961 by the President and Fellows of Harvard College; all rights reserved.

- "I don't know where in South America we're making a profit."

A small but highly successful consumer products company recently followed the lead of its larger competitors by establishing product-manager positions. Although outstanding men were placed in the new jobs, an air of general confusion soon developed, and the product managers began to show signs of frustration. After much study it became apparent that an important cause of the trouble was that no one had determined what kind of information the product managers would need in order to perform their new functions.

In retrospect it is obvious that these three companies were plagued by a common problem: inadequate management information. The data were inadequate, not in the sense of there not being enough, but in terms of relevancy for setting objectives, for shaping alternative strategies, for making decisions, and for measuring results against planned goals.

Assessing the gap

In each company the origin of the problem lay in the gap between a static information system and a changing organization structure. This difficulty is not new or uncommon. There is hardly a major company in the United States whose plan of organization has not been changed and rechanged since World War II. And with revised structures have come new jobs, new responsibilities, new decision-making authorities, and reshaped reporting relationships. All of these factors combine to create new demands for information—information that is usually missing in existing systems. As a result, many leading companies are suffering a major information crisis—often without fully realizing it.

Far-reaching trends

Some idea of the scope of this problem can be gained by reviewing the intensity of the three major causes of recent organization changes in American business:

Growth—Since 1945 the Gross National Product has risen 135%. In specific industries the growth rate has been even greater. Plastic production, for example, tripled between 1948 and 1958; electronics sales nearly quadrupled in the decade from 1950 to 1960. Many individual companies have shown even more startling growth. This growth, in turn, has fostered organizational change:

- Divisions have been created and decentralization has been encouraged.

• Greater precision in defining line-staff relationships has been necessitated.

• Organization structures that were once adequate for $50-million businesses have proved unworkable for $500-million enterprises.

Diversification—Merger and acquisition have accounted for the growth of many large organizations. For these companies, the task of finding, evaluating, and consummating diversification deals—and assimilating newly acquired products and businesses—has required continuous organizational adjustment. Some corporations have diversified by developing new product lines to satisfy shifting market requirements; some have used other means. But always the effect has been the same: different organization structures for parts of or perhaps for the entire enterprise.

International operations—There has been a threefold increase in the value of United States investments abroad since World War II. Major companies that once regarded foreign markets as minor sources of incremental profits, or as markets for surplus production, now look overseas for the bulk of their future profits and growth. They are setting up manufacturing and research as well as marketing organizations in foreign countries. Consequently, we are growing used to seeing a company's "export department" evolve into the "international division," and national companies grow into world-wide enterprises.[1] All this calls for extensive modifications of organization structure.

The impact of any one of the above factors alone would be sufficient to create great change in an enterprise, but consider that in many cases at least two, and sometimes all three, have been at work. It is easy to see why so many company organization structures do become unstable and how this creates a management information problem large enough to hamper some firms and nearly paralyze others.

Linking systems and needs

Organization structure and information requirements are inextricably linked. In order to translate a statement of his duties into action, an executive must receive and use information. Information in this case is not just the accounting system and the forms and reports it produces. It includes *all* the data and intelligence—financial and nonfinancial—that are really needed to plan, operate, and control a particular enterprise. This embraces external information such as economic and political factors and data on competitive activity.

When viewed in this light, the impact of organization structure on needs for management information becomes apparent. The trouble is that in most companies it is virtually taken for granted that the information necessary for performance of a manager's duties flows naturally to the job. To a certain extent this is so. For example, internally generated information—especially accounting information—does tend to flow easily to the job or can be made to do so. Also, in companies doing business in only one industry and having a small, closely knit management group much vital interdepartmental and general information is conveyed by frequent face-to-face contact and coordination among executives. Economic and competitive information from outside is similarly transmitted, the bulk of it coming into the concern informally. Further, through trade contacts, general reading, and occasional special studies, executives toss bits of information into the common pool and draw from it as well.

The point is, however, that while such an informal system can work well for small and medium-sized companies in simple and relatively static industries, it becomes inadequate when companies grow larger and especially when they spread over several industries, areas, and countries. At this point, most large companies have found that information has to be conveyed in a formal manner and less and less through direct observation.

Unfortunately, management often loses sight of the seemingly obvious and simple relationship between organization structure and information needs. Companies very seldom follow up on reorganizations wth penetrating reappraisals of their information systems, and managers given new responsibilities and decision-making authority often do not receive all the information they require.

Causes of confusion

The cornerstone for building a compact, useful management information system is the determination of each executive's information needs. This requires a clear grasp of the individual's role in the organization—his responsibilities, his authorities, and his relationships with other executives. The task is then to—

• Design a network of procedures that will process raw data in such a way as to generate the information required for management use.

• Implement such procedures in actual practice.

Such action steps, while demanding and time-consuming, have proved to be far less difficult than the creative and conceptual first step of defining information requirements. Seldom is the open approach of asking an executive what information he requires successful. For one thing, he may find it difficult to be articulate because the organization structure of his company is not clearly defined.

Further, and more important, there is a widespread tendency among operating executives to think of information exclusively in terms of their companies' accounting systems and the reports thus generated. This way of thinking can be a serious deterrent because:

(1) Many conventional accounting reports cause confusion in the minds of nonfinancially trained executives. Take, for example, the profit-and-loss statement, with its arbitrary treatment of inventories, depreciation, allocated overhead expenses, and the like, or the statistical sales report, which is often a 40-page, untitled, machine-prepared tabulation of sales to individual customers. Such reports have made an indelible impression on managers' thinking, coloring their understanding and expectations of reports in general.

(2) By its very nature traditional accounting fails to highlight many important aspects of business operations. Accounting systems often are designed primarily to meet SEC, Internal Revenue, and other statutory requirements—requirements that, more often than not, fail to correspond to management's information needs. Accounting describes the past in dollars, usually without discriminating between the critical and noncritical elements of a business—the elements that control competitive success in a particular industry and the elements that do not.

(3) Accounting reports generally describe what has happened inside a company. Just consider what this approach omits:

• Information about the future.

• Data expressed in nonfinancial terms—e.g., share of market, productivity, quality levels, adequacy of customer service, and so on.

• Information dealing with external conditions as they might bear on a particular company's operations.

Yet all of these items are essential to the intelligent managing of a business.

Planning needs defined

The key to the development of a dynamic and usable system of management information is to move beyond the limits of classical accounting reports and to conceive of information as it relates to two vital elements of the management process—planning and control. In the pages to follow I shall focus largely on the planning aspect.

We hear more and more these days about new techniques for inventory, cost, and other types of control, but information systems for business planning still represent a relatively unexplored horizon.

Planning, as used in this article, means: setting objectives, formulating strategy, and deciding among alternative investments or courses of action. This definition can be applied to an entire company, an integrated division, or a single operating department.

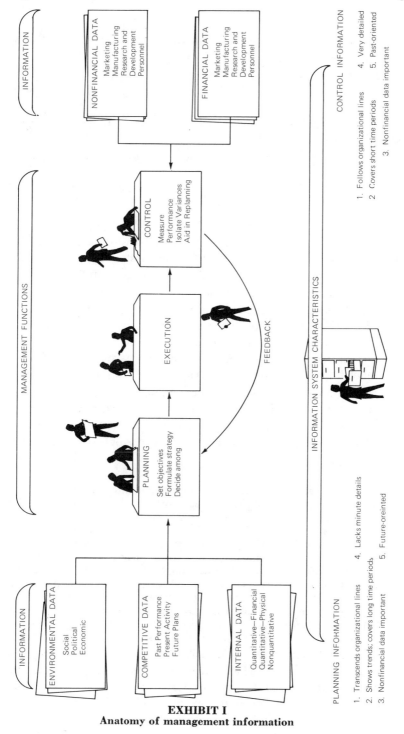

EXHIBIT I
Anatomy of management information

As Exhibit I shows, the information required to do planning of this kind is of three basic types:

1. *Environmental information*—Describes the social, political, and economic aspects of the climate in which a business operates or may operate in the future.

2. *Competitive information*—Explains the past performance, programs, and plans of competing companies.

3. *Internal information*—Indicates a company's own strengths and weaknesses.

Now let us consider each of these categories in some detail.

Environmental information

The environmental data category is one of the least formalized and hence least used parts of a management information system in most companies. Specific examples of the data included in this category are:

- Population—current levels, growth trends, age distribution, geographical distribution, effect on unemployment.
- Price levels—retail, wholesale, commodities, government regulation.
- Transportation—availability, costs, competition, regulation.
- Foreign trade—balance of payments, exchange rates, convertibility.
- Labor force—skills, availability, wages, turnover, unions.

To this list a company operating internationally would add another item —systematic collection and interpretation, on a country-by-country basis, of information on political and economic conditions in the foreign areas where business is being done. Here is an example of what can be accomplished:

> A well-established international corporation with a highly sophisticated management makes a three-pronged effort to get data on local political and economic conditions. (a) There is a small but highly competent and well-paid four-man staff at corporate headquarters which travels extensively and publishes, using its own observations plus a variety of other sources, a weekly commentary on world events as they relate to the company. (b) This corporation has trained all its country managers to be keen observers of their local scene and to report their interpretive comments to headquarters regularly. (c) There is a little-talked-about group of "intelligence agents" who are not on the company's official payroll but are nevertheless paid for the information they pass along.

Certainly, not every organization has to go to these ends to keep itself informed of the situation in which it operates. However, those organizations that ignore environmental data or that leave its collection to the informal devices of individual executives are inviting trouble. Those companies that are knowledgeable concerning their environment are almost always in tune with the times and ahead of their competition. To illustrate:

> (1) Good intelligence on the sociological changes taking place in the United States led several heavy manufacturing companies to enter the "leisure time" field with a great deal of success.
>
> (2) Insight into the possible impact of foreign labor costs on parts of the electronics industry caused some U.S. corporations to acquire their own manufacturing facilities abroad. As a result, the firms were able not only to protect their domestic markets but also to open up profitable operations overseas.
>
> (3) Knowledge of trends in age distribution in the United States added to an awareness of the rate of change of scientific learning provides ample proof for some firms of the desirability of being in the educational publishing field for the next decade.

To be of real use, environmental data must indicate trends; population figures, balance-of-payment data, or political shifts are of little significance when shown for one period because they don't help management make *analytical* interpretations.

The collection and transmission of good environmental data are often problematical. Even in the United States some kinds of information are not readily available and must be pieced together from several sources or acquired *sub rosa* from officially inaccessible sources. Transmitting environmental data, particularly political information, is so awkward that sometimes the data collector must sit down personally with those who need to know the information.

In sum, environmental data are an aspect of planning information that requires more attention and warrants formalization, especially in large geographically dispersed companies. The emergence of the corporate economics department[2] is one development that could lead to better results in this area, but it is my impression that so far the progress of these units has been uneven.

Competitive information

Data on competition comprise the second category of planning information. There are three important types to consider:

1. *Past performance*—This includes information on the profitability, return on investment, share of market, and so forth of competing companies. Such information is primarily useful in identifying one's competitors. It also is one benchmark when setting company objectives.

2. *Present activity*—This category covers new product introductions, management changes, price strategy, and so on—all current developments.

Good intelligence on such matters can materially influence a company's planning; for example, it may lead to accelerating research programs, modifying advertising strategy, or switching distribution channels. The implication here is not that a company's plans should always be defensive and prompted by a competitor's moves but simply that anything important a competitor does should be recognized and factored into the planning process.

3. *Future plans*—This includes information on acquisition intentions, facility plans, and research and development efforts.

Competitive information, like environmental data, is an infrequently formalized part of a company's total information system. And so there seldom is a concerted effort to collect this kind of material, to process it, and to report it to management regularly. But some interesting exceptions to this general lack of concern exist:

Oil companies have long employed "scouts" in their land departments. These men report on acreage purchases, drilling results, and other competitive activity that may be pertinent to the future actions of their own company.

Business machine companies have "competitive equipment evaluation personnel" who continually assess the technical features of competitors' hardware.

Retail organizations employ "comparison shoppers" who appraise the prices and quality of merchandise in competitive stores.

Commercial intelligence departments are appearing more and more on corporate organization charts. An excerpt from the charter of one such group states its basic responsibility thus:

> "To seek out, collect, evaluate, and report information covering the past performance and future plans of competitors in such a manner that the information will have potential utility in strategic and operational planning of the corporation. This means that in addition to reporting factual information, emphasis should be on determining the implications of such information for the corporation."

Internal information

The third and final basic category of planning information is made up of internal data. As it relates to the total planning process, internal data are aimed at identifying a company's strengths and weaknesses—the characteristics that, when viewed in the perspective of the general business environment and in the light of competitive activity, should help management to shape its future plans. It is useful to think of internal data as being of three types:

1. *Quantitative-financial*—e.g., sales, costs, and cost behavior relative to volume changes.

2. *Quantitative-physical*—e.g., share of market, productivity, delivery performance, and manpower resources.

3. *Nonquantitative*—e.g., community standing and labor relations.

In reporting internal data, a company's information system must be discriminating and selective. It should focus on "success factors." In most industries there are usually three to six factors that determine success; these key jobs must be done exceedingly well for a company to be successful. Here are some examples from several major industries:

• In the automobile industry, styling, an efficient dealer organization, and tight control of manufacturing costs are paramount.

• In food processing, new product development, good distribution, and effective advertising are the major success factors.

• In life insurance, the development of agency management personnel, and innovation in creating new types of policies spell the difference.

The companies which have achieved the greatest advances in information analysis have consistently been those which have developed systems that have (a) been selective and (b) focused on the company's strengths and weaknesses with respect to its acknowledged success factors. By doing this, the managements have generated the kind of information that is most useful in capitalizing on strengths and correcting weaknesses. To illustrate:

> An oil company devised a system of regularly reporting its "finding" costs—those costs incurred in exporing for new reserves of oil divided by the number of barrels of oil found. When this ratio trended upward beyond an established point, it was a signal to the company's management to consider the acquisition of other oil companies (together with their proved reserves) as a less expensive alternative to finding oil through its own exploratory efforts.

In the minds of most executives the accounting system exists primarily to meet the company's internal data needs; yet this is often an unreasonable and unfulfilled expectation. Accounting reports rarely focus on success factors that are nonfinancial in nature. Moreover, accounting practices with respect to allocation of expenses, transfer prices, and the like, often tend to obscure rather than clarify the underlying strengths and weaknesses of a company. This inadequacy should not be surprising since the *raison d'être* of many accounting systems is not to facilitate planning but rather to ensure the fulfillment of management's responsibility to the stockholders, the government, and other groups.

Tailoring the requirements

If a company is to have a comprehensive, integrated system of information to support its planning process, it will need a set of management reports that regularly covers the three basic categories of planning data—i.e., environmental, competitive, and internal. The amount of data required in each area will naturally vary from company to company and will depend on such factors as the nature of the industry, the size and operating territory of the company, and the acceptance by management of planning as an essential function. However, it is important in every case for management to *formalize* and *regularize* the collection, transmission, processing, and presentation of planning information; the data are too vital to be ignored or taken care of by occasional "special studies." It is no accident that many of the most successful companies in this country are characterized by well-developed planning information systems.

What is gained if such an approach is taken? What difference does it make in operations? We do not need to conjecture to answer these questions; we can turn to concrete company experience. For instance, Exhibit II illustrates how the information used by the marketing department of an oil company changed as a result of a thorough study of the information needed to formulate effective plans. In this instance, the study indicated an increase in the data required by the vice president and his staff. (However, this result is not inevitable; it holds only for this particular situation. In other circumstances reviews of this kind have led to significant *cutbacks* in information.)

Several points should be noted in examining Exhibit II:

1. The information shown is not all for the *personal* use of the vice president, although much of it is generated and used in his field.

2. For simplicity, most of the information listed in the exhibit was presented to company executives in graphic form.

3. The exhibit highlights only the reports used for retail gasoline marketing; omitted are fuel oil marketing, commercial and industrial marketing, and other topics which the new reporting system also covered.

Many companies have found that the most effective approach to determining requirements for planning information, whether it be for one executive or an entire company, is to relate the three types of planning data described earlier to the steps in the planning process—i.e., setting objectives, developing strategy, and deciding among alternative investments. Thus, one asks himself questions like these:

• What political data are needed to set reasonable objectives for this company?

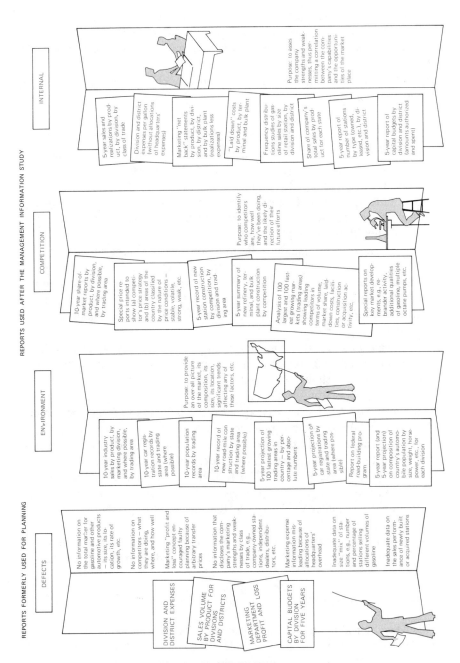

EXHIBIT II
Comparative analysis of marketing planning information

- What sociological and economic data about the areas in which this company operates are needed to formulate new product strategy?
- What competitive intelligence is necessary to develop share-of-market objectives?
- What internal cost information is needed to choose between alternative facility locations?

Contrast with control

In Exhibit I I have listed the five principal characteristics of planning data compared with the characteristics of control data. Note that in all but one case (nonfinancial information) they are different. It is most important to keep these differences in mind, lest the "fuel" for the planning system be confused with the "fuel" for the control system, and vice versa. Hence, I should like to emphasize the contrasts here:

1. *Coverage*—Good planning information is not compartmentalized by functions. Indeed, it seeks to transcend the divisions that exist in a company and to provide the basis on which *integrated* plans can be made. In contrast, control information hews closely to organizational lines so that it can be used to measure performance and help in holding specific managers more accountable.

2. *Length of time*—Planning information covers fairly long periods of time—months and years rather than days and weeks—and deals with trends. Thus, although it should be regularly prepared, it is not developed as frequently as control information.

3. *Degree of detail*—Excessive detail is the quicksand of intelligent planning. Unlike control, where precision and minute care do have a place, planning (and particularly long-range planning) focuses on the major outlines of the situation ahead. In the words of two authorities, L. Eugene Root and George A. Steiner, "The further out in time the planning, the less certain one can be about the precision of numbers. As a basic principle in planning it is understood that, in the longer range, details merge into trends and patterns."[3]

4. *Orientation*—Planning information should provide insights into the future. Control information shows past results and the reasons for them.

Future developments

The heightened interest of management in its information crisis is already unmistakable. Dean Stanley F. Teele of the Harvard Business School, writing on the process of change in the years ahead, states, "I think the capacity to manage knowledge will be still more important to the manager.

. . . The manager will need to increase his skill in deciding what knowledge he needs."[4]

Ralph Cordiner of General Electric Company in his book, *New Frontiers for Professional Managers*, writes:

> "It is an immense problem to organize and communicate the information required to operate a large, decentralized organization. . . .
>
> "What is required . . . is a . . . penetrating and orderly study of the business in its entirety to discover what specific information is needed at each particular position in view of the decisions to be made there. . . ."[5]

Invariably, increasing attention of leaders in education and industry precedes and prepares the way for frontal attacks on business problems. In many organizations the initial reaction to the management information problem is first evidenced by a concern over "the flood of paper work." Eventually, the problem itself is recognized—i.e., the need to define concisely the information required for intelligent planning and control of a business.

Following this awakening interest in business information problems, we are likely to see the acceleration of two developments already in view: (a) improved techniques relating to the creation and operation of total information systems, and (b) new organizational approaches to resolving information problems.

Improved techniques

While the crisis in management information has been growing, tools that may be useful in its solution have been under development. For example, the evolution of electronic data-processing systems, the development of supporting communications networks, and the formulation of rigorous mathematical solutions to business problems have provided potentially valuable tools to help management attack its information problems. Specifically, progress on three fronts is an encouraging indication that this kind of approach will prove increasingly fruitful:

(1) Managements of most companies are far more conversant with both the capabilities and the limitations of computer systems than they were five years ago. This growing understanding has done much to separate fact from fancy. One key result should be the increasing application of electronic data-processing concepts to the more critical, less routine problems of business.

(2) Computer manufacturers and communications companies are learning the worth of their products. They show signs of recognizing that it is not hardware but an information system which is extremely valuable in helping to solve management's problems.

(3) Significant improvements have been made in the techniques of harnessing computers. Advances in automatic programming and developments in creating a common business language are gratifying evidence that the gap is being narrowed between the technical potential of the hardware and management's ability to exploit it.

Organizational moves

The development of new organizational approaches is less obvious. Earlier in this article I noted that: (a) progress in the systematic collection and reporting of information dealing with a company's environment or with its competitive situation has been slow, and (b) traditional accounting reports are often inadequate in providing the data needed for business planning. These conditions may result from a very basic cause; namely, that most organization structures do not pin down the responsibility for management information systems and tie it to specific executive positions. Controllers and other financial officers usually have been assigned responsibility for *accounting* information—but this, of course, does not meet the total need.

Nowhere has the absence of one person having specific and *total* responsibility for management information systems had a more telling effect than in defense contractor companies. In such organizations the usual information problems have been compounded by the rapid rate of technological advance and its attendant effect upon product obsolescence, and also by the requirement for "concurrency," which means that a single product or product complex is developed, tested, produced, and installed simultaneously. Under these conditons, some companies have been nearly paralyzed by too much of the wrong information.

Having recognized this problem, several corporations have attacked it by creating full-time management information departments. These groups are responsible for:

1. Identifying the information needs for all levels of management for both planning and control purposes. As prerequisites to this responsibility it is necessary to (a) define the authority and duties of each manager and (b) determine the factors that really contribute to competitive success in the particular business in question.

2. Developing the necessary systems to fulfill these information needs.

3. Operating the data-processing equipment necessary to generate the information which is required.

To some extent these departments, reporting high in the corporate structure, have impinged on responsibilities traditionally assigned to the accounting organization since they are concerned with financial as well as nonfinancial information. But to me this overlapping is inevitable, particularly in companies where the financial function operates under a narrow perspective and a preoccupation with accountancy. The age of the information specialist is nearing, and its arrival is inextricably tied in with the emergence of some of the newer tools of our management sciences. This notion is not far removed from the concept of Harold J. Leavitt and Thomas L. Whisler, who foresee the evolution of information technology and the creation of a "programing elite."[6]

Conclusion

The day when management information departments are as common as controller's departments is still years away. But this should not rule out concerted eforts to improve a company's information system. In fact, I would expect many broad-gauged controller's organizations to assume the initiative in their companies for such programs.

---

① Does your company regularly collect and analyze information about population, price level, labor, and other important trends affecting the general future of the business?

② If it does, are such analyses reported to operating management in a manner that permits their utilization in the planning process?

③ Does your company regularly collect and analyze significant information about competitors?

④ Is this information effectively "factored into" the planning process?

⑤ How good are your internal data for planning purposes?

⑥ Do you know in what products and in what geographic areas you are making profits?

⑦ Do you know how your costs behave in response to volume changes?

⑧ Are the factors that condition success in your busines explicitly stated and widely communicated in the management group?

⑨ Has your company's organization structure remained unchanged during the past 15 years?

EXHIBIT III
How good is your planning information?

To this end, the nine questions listed in Exhibit III are for the executive to ask himself as a guide to assessing the improvement potential in his organization's planning information. If the answers to these questions tend to be negative, the chances are strong that changes are in order.

The impact of the information crisis on the executive will be significant. To an increasing extent, a manager's effectiveness will hinge on the quality and completeness of the facts that flow to him and on his skill in using them. With technology changing at a rapid rate, with the time dimension becoming increasingly critical, and with organizations becoming larger, more diversified in product lines, and more dispersed geographically, it is inevitable that executives will rely more and more on formally presented information in managing their businesses.

What is more, some organizations are concluding that the easiest and most effective way to influence executive action is to control the flow of information into managerial positions. This notion holds that the discipline of information can be a potent factor in determining just what an executive can and cannot do—what decisions he can make, what plans he can draw up, what corrective steps he can take.

To the extent that this is true, information systems may be increasingly used to mold and shape executive behavior. Better data handling might well become a substitute for much of the laborious shuffling and reshuffling of positions and lines of authority that now goes on. Most reorganizations seek to alter the way certain managers or groups of managers operate. But simply drawing new organization charts and rewriting job descriptions seldom ensure the implementation of new concepts and relationships. The timing, content, and format of the information provided to management, however, *can* be a strong influence in bringing about such purposeful change.

Thus, developments in management information systems will affect the executive in two ways. Not only will the new concepts influence what he is able to do, but they will to a great extent control how well he is able to do it.

NOTES

1. See Gilbert H. Clee and Alfred di Scipio, "Creating a *World* Enterprise," HBR November-December 1959, p. 77.
2. Clark S. Teitsworth, "Growing Role of the Company Economist," HBS January-February 1959, p. 97; and the article by Henry B. Arthur in this issue, p. 80.
3. "The Lockheed Aircraft Corporation Master Plan," in *Long-Range Planning for Management*, edited by David W. Ewing (New York, Harper & Brothers, 1958), p. 151.
4. "Your Job and Mine," *The Harvard Business School Bulletin*, August 1960, p. 8.
5. New York, McGraw-Hill Book Company, Inc., 1956, p. 102.
6. "Management in the 1980's," HBR November-December 1958, p. 41.

8. Management Misinformation Systems*

Russell L. Ackoff

Five assumptions commonly made by designers of management information systems are identified. It is argued that these are not justified in many (if not most) cases and hence lead to major deficiencies in the resulting systems. These assumptions are: (1) the critical deficiency under which most managers operate is the lack of relevant information, (2) the manager needs the information he wants, (3) if a manager has the information he needs his decision making will improve, (4) better communication between managers improves organizational performance, and (5) a manager does not have to understand how his information system works, only how to use it. To overcome these assumptions and the deficiencies which result from them, a management information system should be imbedded in a management control system. A procedure for designing such a system is proposed and an example is given of the type of control system which it produces.

*SOURCE: *Management Science*, Vol. 14, No. 4 (December, 1967), pp. B147-156. Reprinted by permission of the publisher.

The growing preoccupation of operations researchers and management scientists with Management Information Systems (MIS's) is apparent. In fact, for some the design of such systems has almost become synonymous with operations research or management science. Enthusiasm for such systems is understandable: it involves the researcher in a romantic relationship with the most glamorous instrument of our time, the computer. Such enthusiasm is understandable but, nevertheless, some of the excess to which it has led are not excusable.

Contrary to the impression produced by the growing literature, few computerized management information systems have been put into operation. Of those I've seen that have been implemented, most have not matched expectations and some have been outright failures. I believe that these near- and far-misses could have been avoided if certain false (and usually implicit) assumptions on which many such systems have been erected had not been made.

There seem to be five common and erroneous assumptions underlying the design of most MIS's, each of which I will consider. After doing so I will outline an MIS design procedure which avoids these assumptions.

Give them more

Most MIS's are designed on the assumption that the critical deficiency under which most managers operate is the *lack of relevant information.* I do not deny that most managers lack a good deal of information that they should have, but I do deny that this is the most important informational deficiency from which they suffer. It seems to me that they suffer more from an *over abundance of irrelevant information.*

This is not a play on words. The consequences of changing the emphasis of an MIS from supplying relevant information to eliminating irrelevant information is considerable. If one is preoccupied with supplying relevant information, attention is almost exclusively given to the generation, storage, and retrieval of information: hence emphasis is placed on constructing data banks, coding, indexing, updating files, access languages, and so on. The ideal which has emerged from this orientation is an infinite pool of data into which a manager can reach to pull out any information he wants. If, on the other hand, one sees the manager's information problem primarily, but not exclusively, as one that arises out of an overabundance of irrelevant information, most of which was not asked for, then the two most important functions of an information system become *filtration* (or evaluation) and *condensation*. The literature on MIS's seldom refers to these functions let alone considers how to carry them out.

My experience indicates that most managers receive much more data (if not information) than they can possibly absorb even if they spend all of their time trying to do so. Hence they already suffer from an information overload. They must spend a great deal of time separating the relevant from the irrelevant and searching for the kernels in the relevant documents. For example, I have found that I receive an average of forty-three hours of unsolicited reading material each week. The solicited material is usually half again this amount.

I have seen a daily stock status report that consists of approximately six hundred pages of computer print-out. The report is circulated daily across managers' desks. I've also seen requests for major capital expenditures that come in book size, several of which are distributed to managers each week. It is not uncommon for many managers to receive an average of one journal a day or more. One could go on and on.

Unless the information overload to which managers are subjected is reduced, any additional information made available by an MIS cannot be expected to be used effectively.

Even relevant documents have too much redundancy. Most documents can be considerably condensed without loss of content. My point here is best made, perhaps, by describing briefly an experiment that a few of my colleagues and I conducted on the OR literature several years ago. By using a panel of well-known experts we identified four OR articles that all members of the panel considered to be "above average," and four articles that were considered to be "below average." The authors of the eight articles were asked to prepare "objective" examinations (duration thirty minutes) plus answers for graduate students who were to be assigned the articles for reading. (The authors were not informed about the experiment.) Then several experienced writers were asked to reduce each article to ⅔ and ⅓ of its original length only by eliminating words. They also prepared a brief abstract of each article. Those who did the condensing did not see the examinations to be given to the students.

A group of graduate students who had not previously read the articles were then selected. Each one was given four articles randomly selected, each of which was in one of its four versions: 100%, 67%, 33%, or abstract. Each version of each article was read by two students. All were given the same examinations. The average scores on the examinations were then compared.

For the above-average articles there was no significant difference between average test scores for the 100%, 67%, and 33% versions, but there was a significant decrease in average test scores for those who had read only the abstract. For the below-average articles there was no difference in average test scores among those who had read the 100%, 67%, and 33% versions, but there was a significant *increase* in average test scores of those who had read only the abstract.

The sample used was obviously too small for general conclusions but the results strongly indicate the extent to which even good writing can be condensed without loss of information. I refrain from drawing the obvious conclusion about bad writing.

It seems clear that condensation as well as filtration, performed mechanically or otherwise, should be an essential part of an MIS, and that such a system should be capable of handling much, if not all, of the unsolicited as well as solicited information that a manager receives.

The manager needs the information that he wants

Most MIS designers "determine" what information is needed by asking managers what information they would like to have. This is based on the assumption that managers know what information they need and want it.

For a manager to know what information he needs he must be aware of each type of decision he should make (as well as does) and he must have an adequate model of each. These conditions are seldom satisfied. Most managers have some conception of at least some of the types of decisions they must make. Their conceptions, however, are likely to be deficient in a very critical way, a way that follows from an important principle of scientific economy: the less we understand a phenomenon, the more variables we require to expain it. Hence, the manager who does not understand the phenomenon he controls plays it "safe" and, with respect to information, wants "everything." The MIS designer, who has even less understanding of the relevant phenomenon than the manager, tries to provide even more than everything. He thereby increases what is already an overload of irrelevant information.

For example, market researchers in a major oil company once asked their marketing managers what variables they thought were relevant in estimating the sales volume of future service stations. Almost seventy variables were identified. The market researchers then added about half again this many variables and performed a large multiple linear regression analysis of sales of existing stations against these variables and found about thirty-five to be statistically significant. A forecasting equation was based on this analysis. An OR team subsequently constructed a model based on only one of these variables, traffic flow, which predicted sales better than the thirty-five variable regression equation. The team went on to *explain* sales at service stations in terms of the customers' preception of the amount of time lost by stopping for service. The relevance of all but a few of the variables used by the market researchers could be explained by their effect on such perception.

The moral is simple: one cannot specify what information is required for decision making until an explanatory model of the decision process and the system involved has been constructed and tested. Information systems are subsystems of control systems. They cannot be designed adequately without taking control in account. Furthermore, whatever else regression analyses can yield, they cannot yield understanding and explanation of phenomena. They describe and, at best, predict.

Give a manager the information he needs and his decision making will improve

It is frequently assumed that if a manager is provided with the information he needs, he will then have no problem in using it effectively. The history of OR stands to the contrary. For example, give most managers an initial tableau of a typical "real" mathematical programming, sequencing, or network problem and see how close they come to an optimal solution. If their experience and judgment have any value they may not do badly, but they will seldom do very well. In most management problems there are too many possibilities to expect experience, judgment, or intuition to provide good guesses, even with perfect information.

Furthermore, when several probabilities are involved in a problem the unguided mind of even a manager has difficulty in aggregating them in a valid way. We all know many simple problems in probability in which untutored intuition usually does very badly (e.g., What are the correct odds that 2 of 25 people selected at random will have their birthdays on the same day of the year?). For example, very few of the results obtained by queuing theory, when arrivals and service are probabilistic, are obvious to managers; nor are the results of risk analysis where the managers' own subjective estimates of probabilities are used.

The moral: it is necessary to determine how well managers can use needed information. When, because of the complexity of the decision process, they can't use it well, they should be provided with either decision rules or performance feed-back so that they can identify and learn from their mistakes. More on this point later.

More communication means better performance

One characteristic of most MIS's which I have seen is that they provide managers with better current information about what other managers and their departments and divisions are doing. Underlying this provision is the belief that better interdepartmental communication enables managers to coordinate their decisions more effectively and hence improves the organization's overall performance. Not only is this not necessarily so, but it seldom is so. One would hardly expect two competing companies to become more cooperative because the information each acquires about the other is improved. This analogy is not as far fetched as one might suppose. For example, consider the following very much simplified version of a situation I once ran into. The simplification of the case does not affect any of its essential characteristics.

A department store has two "line" operations: buying and selling. Each function is performed by a separate department. The Purchasing Department primarily controls one variable: how much of each item is bought. The Merchandising Department controls the price at which it is sold. Typically, the measure of performance applied to the Purchasing Department was the turnover rate of inventory. The measure applied to the Merchandising Department was gross sales; this department sought to maximize the number of items sold times their price.

Now by examining a single item let us consider what happens in this system. The merchandising manager, using his knowledge of competition and consumption, set a price which he judged would maximize gross sales. In doing so he utilized price-demand curves for each type of item. For each price the curves show the expected sales and values on an upper and lower confidence band as well. (See Figure 1.) When instructing the Purchasing Department how many items to make available, the merchandising manager quite naturally used the value on the upper confidence curve. This minimized the chances of his running short which if it occurred, would hurt his performance. It also maximized the chances of being overstocked but this was not his concern, only the purchasing manager's. Say, therefore, that the merchandising manager initially selected price P_1 and requested that amount Q_1 be made available by the Purchasing Department.

In this company the purchasing manager also had access to the price-demand curves. He know the merchandising manager always ordered optimistically. Therefore, using the same curve he read over from Q_1 to the upper limit and down to the expected value from which he obtained Q_2, the quantity he actually intended to make available. He did not intend to pay for the merchandising manager's optimism. If merchandising ran out of stock, it was not his worry. Now the merchandising manager was informed about what the purchasing manager had done so he adjusted his price to P_2. The purchasing manager in turn was told that the merchandising manager had made this readjustment so he planned to make only Q_3 available. If this process—made possible only by perfect communication between departments—had been allowed to continue, nothing would have been bought and nothing would have been sold. This outcome was avoided by prohibiting communication between the two departments and forcing each to guess what the other was doing.

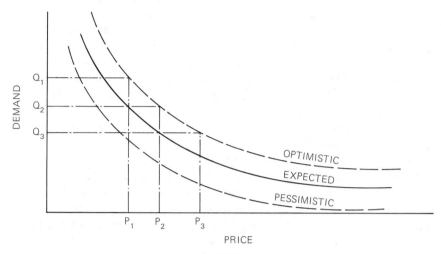

FIGURE 1
Price-demand curve

I have obviously caricatured the situation in order to make the point clear: when organizational units have inappropriate measures of performance which put them in conflict with each other, as is often the case, communication between them may hurt organizational performance, not help it. Organizational structure and performance measurement must be taken into account before opening the flood gates and permitting the free flow of information between parts of the organization. (A more rigorous discussion of organizational structure and the relationship of communication to it can be found in [A].)

A manager does not have to understand how an information system works, only how to use it

Most MIS designers seek to make their systems as innocuous and unobtrusive as possible to managers lest they become frightened. The designers try to provide managers with very easy access to the system and assure them that they need to know nothing more about it. The designers usually succeed in keeping managers ignorant in this regard. This leaves managers unable to evaluate the MIS as a whole. If often makes them afraid to even try to do so lest they display their ignorance publicly. In failing to evaluate their MIS, managers delegate much of the control of the organization to the system's designers and operators who may have many virtues, but managerial competence is seldom among them.

Let me cite a case in point. A Chairman of a Board of a medium-size company asked for help on the following problem. One of his larger (decentralized) divisions had installed a computerized production-inventory control and manufacturing-manager information system about a year earlier. It had acquired about $2,000,000 worth of equipment to do so. The Board Chairman had just received a request from the Division for permission to replace the original equipment with newly announced equipment which would cost several times the original amount. An executive "justification" for so doing was provided with the request. The Chairman wanted to know whether the request was really justified. He admitted to complete incompetence in this connection.

A meeting was arranged at the Division at which I was subjected to an extended and detailed briefing. The system was large but relatively simple. At the heart of it was a reorder point for each item and a maximum allowable stock level. Reorder quantities took lead-time as well as the allowable maximum into account. The computer kept track of stock, ordered items when required and generated numerous reports on both the state of the system it controlled and its own "actions."

When the briefing was over I was asked if I had any questions. I did. First I asked if, when the system had been installed, there had been many parts whose stock level exceeded the maximum amount possible under the new system. I was told there were many. I asked for a list of about thirty and for some graph paper. Both were provided. With the help of the system designer and volumes of old daily reports I began to plot the stock level of the first listed item over time. When this item reached the maximum "allowable" stock level it had been reordered. The system designer was surprised and said that by sheer "luck" I had found one of the few errors made by the system. Continued plotting showed that because of repeated premature reordering the item had never gone much below the maximum stock level. Clearly the program was confusing the maximum allowable stock level and the reorder point. This turned out to be the case in more than half of the items on the list.

Next I asked if they had many paired parts, ones that were only used with each other; for example, matched nuts and bolts. They had many. A list was produced and we began checking the previous day's withdrawals. For more than half of the pairs the differences in the numbers recorded as withdrawn were very large. No explanation was provided.

Before the day was out it was possible to show by some quick and dirty calculations that the new computerized system was costing the company almost $150,000 per month more than the hand system which it had replaced, most of this in excess inventories.

The recommendation was that the system be redesigned as quickly as possible and that the new equipment not be authorized for the time being.

The questions asked of the system had been obvious and simple ones. Managers should have been able to ask them but—and this is the point —they felt themselves incompetent to do so. They would not have allowed a handoperated system to get so far out of their control.

No MIS should ever be installed unless the managers for whom it is intended are trained to evaluate and hence control it rather than be controlled by it.

A suggested procedure for designing an MIS

The erroneous assumptions I have tried to reveal in the preceding discusion can, I believe, be avoided by an appropriate design procedure. One is briefly outlined here.

1. Analysis of the decision system

Each (or at least each important) type of managerial decision required by the organization under study should be identified and the relationships between them should be determined and flow-charted. Note that this is *not* necessarily the same thing as determining what decisions *are* made. For example, in one company I found that make-or-buy decisions concerning parts were made only at the time when a part was introduced into stock and was never subsequently reviewed. For some items this decision had gone unreviewed for as many as twenty years. Obviously, such decisions should be made more often; in some cases, every time an order is placed in order to take account of current shop loading, underused shifts, delivery times from suppliers, and so on.

Decision-flow analyses are usually self-justifying. They often reveal important decisions that are being made by default (e.g., the make-buy decision referred to above), and they disclose interdependent decisions that are being made independently. Decision-flow charts frequently suggest changes in managerial responsibility, organizational structure, and measure of performance which can correct the types of deficiencies cited.

Decision analyses can be conducted with varying degrees of detail, that is, they may be anywhere from coarse to fine grained. How much detail one should become involved with depends on the amount of time and resources that are available for the analysis. Although practical considerations frequently restrict initial analyses to a particular organizational function, it is preferable to perform a coarse analysis of all of an organization's managerial functions rather than a fine analysis of one or a subset of functions. It is easier to introduce finer information into an integrated information system than it is to combine fine subsystems into one integrated system.

2. An analysis of information requirements

Managerial decisions can be classified into three types:

(a) Decisions for which adequate models are available or can be constructed and from which optimal (or near optimal) solutions can be derived. In such cases the decision process itself should be incorporated into the information system hereby converting it (at least partially) to a control system. A decision model identifies what information is required and hence what information is relevant.

(b) Decisions for which adequate models can be constructed but from which optimal solutions cannot be extracted. Here some kind of heuristic or search procedure should be provided even if it consists of no more than computerized trial and error. A simulation of the model will, as a minimum, permit comparison of proposed alternative solutions. Here too the model specifies what information is required.

(c) Decisions for which adequate models cannot be constructed. Research is required here to determine what information is relevant. If decision making cannot be delayed for the completion of such research or the decision's effect is not large enough to justify the cost of research, then judgment must be used to "guess" what information is relevant. It may be possible to make explicit the implicit model used by the decision maker and treat it as a model of type (b).

In each of these three types of situation it is necessary to provide feedback by comparing actual decision outcomes with those predicted by the model or decision maker. Each decision that is made, along with its predicted outcome, should be an essential input to a management control system. I shall return to this point below.

3. Aggregation of decisions

Decisions with the same or largely overlapping informational requirements should be grouped together as a single manager's task. This will reduce the information a manager requires to do his job and is likely to increase his understanding of it. This may require a reorganization of the system. Even if such a reorganization cannot be implemented completely what can be done is likely to improve performance significantly and reduce the information loaded on managers.

4. Design of information processing

Now the procedure for collecting, storing, retrieving, and treating information can be designed. Since there is a voluminous literature on this subject I shall leave it at this except for one point. Such a system must not only be able to answer questions addressed to it; it should also be able to answer questions that have not been asked by reporting any deviations from expectations. An extensive exception-reporting system is required.

5. Design of control of the control system

It must be assumed that the system that is being designed will be deficient in many and significant ways. Therefore it is necessary to identify the ways in which it may be deficient, to design procedures for detecting its deficiencies, and for correcting the system so as to remove or reduce them. Hence the system should be designed to be flexible and adaptive. This is little more than a platitude, but it has a not-so-obvious implication. No completely computerized system can be as flexible and adaptive as can a man-machine system. This is illustrated by a concluding example of a system that is being developed and is partially in operation. (See Figure 2.)

The company involved has its market divided into approximately two hundred marketing areas. A model for each has been constructed as is "in" the computer. On the basis of competitive intelligence supplied to the service marketing manager by marketing researchers and information specialists he and his staff make policy decisions for each area each month.

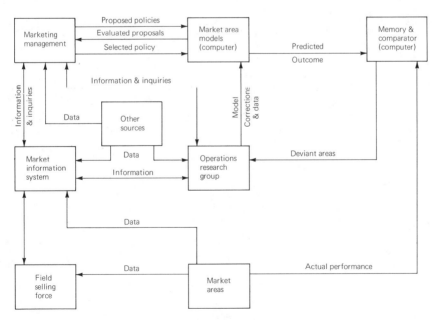

FIGURE 2
Simplified diagram of a market-area control system

Their tentative decisions are fed into the computer which yields a forecast of expected performance. Changes are made until the expectations match what is desired. In this way they arrive at "final" decisions. At the end of the month the computer compares the actual performance of each area with what was predicted. If a deviation exceeds what could be expected by chance, the company's OR Group then seeks the reason for the deviation, performing as much research as is required to find it. If the cause is found to be permanent the computerized model is adjusted appropriately. The result is an adaptive man-machine system whose precision and generality is continuously increasing with use.

Finally it should be noted that in carrying out the design steps enumerated above, three groups should collaborate: information systems specialists, operations researchers, *and managers.* The participation of managers in design of a system that is to serve them, assures their ability to evaluate its performance by comparing its output with what was predicted. Managers who are not willing to invest some of their time in this process are not likely to use a management control system well, and their system, in turn, is likely to abuse them.

REFERENCE

A. Sengupta, S. S., and Ackoff, R. L., "Systems Theory from an Operations Research Point of View," *IEEE Transactions on Systems Science and Cybernetics,* Vol. 1 (November, 1965), pp. 9-13.

9. Management Misinformation Systems — Another Perspective*

Alfred Rappaport

An identification and critical examination of the assumptions made by designers of management information systems is particularly timely. Russell L. Ackoff attempted to do just that in his article, "Management Misinformation Systems" (*Management Science*, December 1967). He identified five common assumptions underlying management information systems design and proposed that these assumptions are unwarranted in many (if not most) cases and lead to major deficiencies in the resulting systems. The purpose of this letter is to examine briefly these assumptions (given in italics) and the supporting illustrations presented in the Ackoff article.

1. The critical deficiency under which most managers operate is the lack of relevant information. Ackoff contends that managers suffer more from an over abundance of irrelevant information than they do from lack of relevant information. This is followed by the suggestion that information be filtered (evaluated) and condensed to reduce the information overload to which managers are subjected. In the face of seemingly endless pages of computer print-outs, book-size requests for equal expenditures, and other forms that consume unnecessary hours of managers' time, suggestions leading to filtered and/or condensed information are likely to be greeted with enthusiasm. This does however raise another important issue: What are the useful limits to filtration and condensation?

*SOURCE: *Management Science*, Vol. 15, No. 2 (December, 1968), pp. B133-136. Reprinted by permission of the publisher.

Just as processing leading to information overload is not in the best interests of the organization, indiscriminate filtration and "over-condensation" can likewise lead to non-salutary results. For example, consider the case of major capital investment proposals originating from various divisions of a company. Assume that book-size capital expenditure proposals are now condensed for headquarters to a single listing of proposed projects (with brief descriptions) and ranked according to some criterion function such as internal rate of return. The headquarters group has two basic options available: (1) accept the divisional estimates; or (2) make a subjective adjustment to compensate for estimated divisional bias. Neither of these alternatives is very comforting since there is no compelling basis for choice except perhaps assessing past behavior which may be neither instructive nor relevant. Here then is clearly a case of "over-condensation" since the report received by headquarters cannot be used to make an intelligent appraisal of the proposals competing for scarce resources since information about the uncertainty underlying key market and cost variables is not available. "Over-condensation" can occur even if risk analysis techniques are actually employed in a company.

In brief, the undesirable state of "over-condensation" is reached when the decision maker no longer has a sound basis for judging the validity of transmittal information.

Filtration has potential as an effective adjustment in the face of information overload. The key question is: where in the system should "filtration decisions" be made? If these decisions were initiated largely at the lower levels of the organization one might question the limited perspective underlying the decisions. Filtration decisions made at the highest level of the organization, however, offer little or no relief from information overload. The relevant strategy then is a function of the confidence that executives have in the filtration decisions made by managers at lower levels.

To illustrate this in context of the capital expenditure analysis example, consider the set of projects enumerated by the divisions for review by the headquarters group. This set consists only of those projects proposed for adoption and excludes projects rejected at the divisional level. Hence, the information presented to headquarters was indeed filtered. If there are no serious conflicts between the way divisions and headquarters perceive organizational objectives and their attitudes toward risk are identical, then the filtered list of projects is in all probability justified. In the overwhelming majority of cases, where the ideal headquarters-divisional relationship does not exist, it would seem to be more appropriate to ask divisions to enumerate their total set of project opportunities with "accept" or "reject" recommendations for each. (Even in this situation divisional managers would undoubtedly filter certain projects, but the potential for filtering is decreased.)

In summary, while managers can often make reasonable adjustments to compensate for information overload, overfiltration and condensation tend to accentuate the biases of lower-level managers and provide the executive decision maker with an inadequate basis for making necessary adjustments. The relevant information for managers is somewhere on the continuum between over-filtration and-condensation, and information overload. I contend that the basic assumption that "the critical deficiency under which most managers operate is the lack of relevant information" remains unchallanged.

2. *The manager needs the information that he wants.* Ackoff argues that the conditions for a manager to know what information he needs are rarely satisfied. The principal problem here is that the decision maker's own conception of an appropriate decision model to fit a specific situation is generally not well developed. I would fully subscribe to Ackoff's subsequent plea for an active collaboration among information systems specialists, operations researchers, and managers in the various stages of system design as the best available strategy for overcoming this deficiency.

The respective roles of the operations researcher-information specialist and manager can be illustrated in the context of the service station problem presented by Ackoff. I would envision the main thrust of the manager's responsibility to be, first, to recognize occasions for making decisions and, then, to frame appropriate questions in light of the decisions to be made. The manager in the major oil company, for example, finds it necessary to make decisions concerning locations of future service stations. An appropriate criterion may be sales or profit maximization subject to certain technological and management-imposed constraints. The manager clearly wants information about future sales potential for alternative service-station locations. *And the manager needs the information that he wants.*

While the task of enumerating relevant variables for forecasting equations should be conducted jointly by the operations researcher and manager, in most situations it would be reasonable to expect that model choice and refinements are largely the domain of the operations researcher. The choice of a statistical forecasting model in this case or any model in the more general case calls for the exercise of careful judgment on the part of the operations researcher. Problem type, relative importance of the problem, time available before decision must be made, and expected degree of utilization of model results by decision makers all qualify as strategic considerations in choosing among alternative models. Finally, the information specialists should present the results to the manager in an easily understood form, without resorting to either information overload or overcondensation.

3. *If a manager has the information he needs his decision making will*

improve. Ackoff points out that because of the complexity of the decision process, managers oftentimes cannot use information well. To support this contention, Ackoff suggests that most managers furnished with an *initial* tableau of a typical mathematical programming, sequencing, or network problem are unlikely to come close to an optimal solution. While one certainly would not want to argue with the validity of this proposition, its relevance to the main argument must be questioned. Specifically, I would submit that to furnish a manager with an initial tableau *is to furnish him with data, not information.* (The decision is explained by Adrian M. McDonough in his book, *Information Economics and Management Systems*: "The term 'data' is used here to represent messages that can be available to the individual but which have not as yet been evaluated for their worth in a specific situation. . . . 'Information' is used here as the label for *evaluated data* in a specifc situation . . . . a given message may remain constant in content and yet, under this approach change from data to information when it is put to use in making a decision") The fact that managers cannot easily convert data to information underlies the very need and justification for developing management decision models. If managers could independently iterate from an initial to a final tableau, the simplex and other related algorithms would become redundant and unnecessary. In the Ackoff case, the manager is not provided information until the results appearing in the final tableau are communicated to him. At that juncture we can only hope that his decision making will improve.

In brief then, Ackoff's illustration fails to invalidate the assumption that if a manager has the information he needs his decision making will improve, because the decision maker was not provided with the *information* he needed. Perhaps, a more interesting and significant question to ask is: to what extent does the information the manager really needs (e.g., final tableaus) improve decision making?

4. Better communication between managers improves organizational performance. It is true that better communication between managers does not necessarily improve organizational performance. Ackoff's example involving a purchasing and a merchandising department in a department store illustrates this point. I believe it is important to emphasize, however, that the origin of the problem described does not lie in the communication, but instead in the conflicting measures of performance used to judge the two departments. Ackoff thus has properly established that interdepartmental communication among departments with conflicting measures of performance may not only be of doubtful value, but may actually work counter to the best interests of the organization as a whole. However, the proposition that well-conceived interdepartmental communication enables managers to coordinate their decisions more effectively when appropriate, nonconflicting measures of performance are present was not invalidated.

5. A manager does not have to understand how an information system works, only how to use it. Ackoff's challenge to the notion that a manager need not understand how an information system works, only how to use it, is particualrly significant. It is difficult to debate the merits of this assumption without a more detailed agreement concerning the degree of understanding Ackoff would require of managers. The best available evidence of intent can be gleaned from the case study presented.

A computerized production and inventory control system was discovered to be costing the company almost $150,000 per month more than the former manual system. Most of this was attributed to excess inventories. Apparently, a major cause of unreasonable inventory accumulation was a program error which confused the maximum allowable stock level and the reorder point. To suggest that the manager understand the information system to a point where he would detect the programming error seems neither reasonable in an organizational plan nor an economical use of the manager's time. Indeed, to argue for understanding and analysis by managers at this level of detail is legitimate cause for cries of "information overload." A more constructive approach would suggest that a manager should have developed techniques and guidelines using exception reporting for discovering a situation where an "improved" system costs $150,000 more than its unglamorous predecessor. Perhaps, event more importantly the manager would be well advised to develop a more reliable system for hiring better systems designers.

While I agree with Ackoff that "no management information system should ever be installed unless the managers for whom it is intended are trained to evaluate and hence control it rather than be controlled by it," my agreement is within the context explained above. To insist upon *detailed* systems design knowledge by managers as a prerequisite for new management information systems is tantamount to calling for an information systems moratorium or at minimum a significant reduction in research and progress in the field.

B. Organizational Implications of Information Technology

10. Emerging EDP Pattern*

Charles W. Hofer

It is commonplace that there has been a great increase in management's understanding of how to apply the computer to a wide variety of tasks, ranging in complexity from simple, routine accounting applications to large simulations of entire industries.

But there has been little knowledge about the overall impact the computer has had on the organizational structures and processes of the companies—both large and small—using EDP.

The purpose of this Special Report is to present the findings of a recent study I conducted in this area, which I feel make some needed additions to our knowledge. But first let me comment that there have been many speculations, opinions, and previous research studies devoted to the effects of the computer on organizations. Each has differed to such a degree, however, that no clear-cut pattern of the total impact of this technology on the organizational structures and processes of businesses has heretofore emerged.

For example, the *predictions* of such observers of the business scene as Harold J. Leavitt, Thomas L. Whisler, Melvin Anshen, John F. Burlingame, and John Dearden differ substantially, as indicated in the ruled insert of page 118.

Likewise, the accompanying *findings* of researchers such as Ida Russa-

*SOURCE: *Harvard Business Review* (March-April 1970), pp. 16-18, 20-22, 26, 28-31, 169-171. Reprinted by permission of the publisher. Copyright © 1970 by the President and Fellows of Harvard College; all rights reserved.

koff Hoos, Donald Shaul, Hak Chong Lee, and Rodney H. Brady differ, although each of their independent studies supports one of the sets of predictions.

Research focus

In search of a clearer understanding of how the use of the computer and related technology has made an impact on industrial companies, I conducted a study of two manufacturing organizations. One was an independent division of a large multiproduct corporation whose total divisional sales exceeded $200 million. The other was a small company with sales of about $8 million. Both organizations were considered to be leaders in their respective industries in the application of computer techniques to management problems.

For example, both utilized nonconventional systems in a batch-processing operation in which the major files were updated daily. Both also had electronic data-collection devices which gathered and transmitted input data from remote locations. In addition, the larger organization utilized a corporate time-shared computer for some engineering and managerial applications.

Unlike previous researchers who had focused their efforts on one or two components of the companies they studied (usually the accounting and/or production scheduling and inventory control activities), I examined the effects of the computer in every type of organizational *component*—such as marketing, finance, engineering, manufacturing, employee relations, general management, and so on—and at every *level* in the hierarchy (from the president's office to the production floor).

Over a period of two years in the two organizations, I interviewed nearly 80 managers, with each set of interviews covering from one to six hours although no single interview took longer than two hours. To supplement and confirm the data obtained from my interviews, I also (a) studied organizational charts, statistics, and job descriptions; (b) analyzed budgeting, operational planning, and measurement and evaluation procedures; (c) constructed detailed decision matrices; and (d) examined computer and noncomputer company reports, all covering a period of 12 years in each organization.

Obviously, however, I could not possibly examine the effects of the computer on all organizational characteristics and processes. Consequently, I focused my attention first on the more important characteristics of formal structure, such as—

. . . the method of task specialization;

Effects of computers on organizational structures and processes

Here are some of the predictions and research findings concerning EDP's impact on manufacturing companies. The references indicated by footnote letters following the authors' names are contained in a list at the end of the article.

A. THE OBSERVERS' PREDICTIONS
Harold J. Leavitt and Thomas L. Whisler[a]
- Jobs at today's middle management levels will become highly structured.
- Top managers will take on an even larger portion of the innovating, planning, and other "creative" functions.
- The programmers and R&D personnel will move upward into the top management group.
- Large industrial organizations will recentralize.

Melvin Anshen[b]
- The new technology will not erode or destroy middle management jobs. Instead it will present opportunities for expanding management capacity and performance in areas that have suffered from scant attention.
- The tasks of middle managers will more clearly resemble those of top management.
- Computer personnel will not assume top management responsibilities or become the fundamental source for top management personnel.
- The trend toward decentralization of decision making will be slowed down.

John F. Burlingame[c]
- If the company's philosophy is one of centralization, then the likely evolution will be along the lines predicted by Leavitt, Whisler, and others.
- If a company's activities are centralized because of difficulties involved in achieving a harmonious unifying of individual creativity and initiative, then the computer will provide a basis for the adoption of a decentralized approach as a more desirable and more effective way.
- If the company's philosophy is one of decentralization, then the technology should strengthen the existing decentralization of operations. Middle management should grow and flourish rather than wither and die.

John Dearden[d]
- The computer will have no impact on the organization of top and divisional management, relatively little impact on the ability of the top manager to control profit centers, and limited impact on management levels below the divisional manager even though there may be some centralization of data processing and logistics systems.
- With the exception of certain routine operating control problems in such areas as logistics, production scheduling, and inventory control, it will not be practicable to operate a real-time information system; and, even if it were, such a system would not solve any of top management's real problems.

. . . the method of coordination;

. . . the span of control;

. . . the size of organizational components.

Then I examined such important organizational procedures as—

. . . the various operational planning processes;

. . . the budgeting process;

. . . the measurement and evaluation process.

Synopsis of findings

With but a few exceptions, my research—which is summarized in Exhibit I and Exhibit II—shows that the effects of the computer were the same in

B. THE RESEARCHERS' FINDINGS
Ida Russakoff Hoos[e]
- Computer applications have led to drastic changes at the middle management level (supervisory to executive junior grade). Many jobs have been either combined or eliminated.
- EDP has systematized and standardized formal information flow and also has seemed to dam up the upward and downward flow of information through both formal and informal channels.
- As more and more operations are programmed, the power and status of new computer personnel have been expanded, while the functions of other departments have been undercut, and the authority of their managers truncated.
- EDP stimulates two distinct kinds of recentralization—one type referring to the integration of specific functions, the other involving regrouping of entire units of the operation and causing sweeping changes of the external structure as well.

Donald Shaul[f]
- While EDP has undoubtedly eliminated a vast amount of monotonous, detailed administrative work, there has been no accompanying reduction in the need for middle managers. Actually, EDP has made the middle manager's job more complex.
- The centralization of *activities* has not been accompanied by an elimination of managerial positions. On the contrary, EDP and the new activities have resulted in the addition of over 50 middle management positions in the companies studied.

Hak Chong Lee[g]
- The nature and magnitude of the EDP impact is basically governed by the computer technology and the management attitude toward the use of the technology.
- Drastic changes (centralization of the decision-making process and reduction in the number of middle management jobs) have not occurred to date in the companies studied during the early period of industrial experience with EDP.

Rodney H. Brady[h]
- Top management does not seem to use the computer directly for decision making.
- The use of the computer by middle management permits top management to:
  — Make some decisions at an earlier date.
  — Gain time in which to consider some decisions.
  — Consider more thorough analysis of some situations.
  — Review several courses of action on many problems
  — Examine analyses of the impact the recommended courses of action will have on the problem or opportunity identified.
  — Obtain additional information from middle managers concerning problems, opportunities, and promising alternatives before making decisions.

both companies even though the one organization was nearly 25 times larger than the other, both in dollar sales and in total employees, and even though the larger one had a rate of growth of less than 2% in dollar sales for the period covered by the study while the other had a compounded growth rate of over 10%. In both companies, the effects of the computer varied according to the organizational characteristics or process examined, the hierarchy level involved, and the nature of the principal tasks of the organizational component involved.

For example, on the one hand, the computer had no effect on the methods of coordination at the general management level or in components whose principal tasks did not involve the processing of large amounts of quantitative data. On the other hand, it did affect both the measurement

EXHIBIT I
Summary of computer impact in a large, multidivision manufacturing corporation

LEVEL IN HIERARCHY	METHODS OF SPECIALIZATION	METHODS OF COORDINATION	SPAN OF CONTROL	SIZE OF COMPONENTS	DECISION MAKING AND DELEGATION OF AUTHORITY	OPERATIONAL PLANNING	BUDGETING	MEASUREMENT AND EVALUATION
General management	No change	No change	No change	No change	No change	No change	No change	Managers able to ask for more detailed back-up statistics on problems
Top functional— Components that do not process large amounts of quantitative data	No change	No change	No change	No change	De facto delegation of some decisions or some decision making process to subordinates	Managers devoted more time to examining ways to improve systems and procedures at the operations level	Managers able to change budgets quickly as projects changed in nature or scope	Quantitative measures of the performance of operations level personnel and components improved in both content and accuracy
Top functional— Components that process large amounts of quantitative data	Creation of position of information systems manager	Some components transferred in hierarchy to improve implementation of computer technology	No change	Some role positions reduced in number because of decrease in size of components at operations level	Additional time allocated to other activities, such as operational planning			
Operations— Components that do not process large amounts of quantitative data	No change	No change	No change	Size of components per dollar sales decreased slightly (about 10%) because of increased efficiency of remaining personnel	Better decisions because of more accurate information	Managers better able to direct attention to areas where efforts would be most productive	Accuracy of manager's budget increased because of more accurate information on indirect costs and greater detail on direct costs	Quantitative measures of the performance of employees, distributors, suppliers, etc. improved in both content and-accuracy
Operations— Components that process large amounts of quantitative data	Creation of roles related to data processing, such as programmers and systems analysts. Elimination of some clerical role positions. Some roles upgraded	Coordination activities increased in frequency, become more formalized. Some components transferred as a result of systems changes	No change	Size of components per dollar sales decreased substantially (30% to 50%) because of elimination of clerical personnel	Some decisions programmed into computer	No change		

EXHIBIT II
Summary of computer impact in a small manufacturing company

LEVEL IN HIERARCHY	METHODS OF SPECIALIZATION	METHODS OF COORDINATION	SPAN OF CONTROL	SIZE OF COMPONENTS	DECISION MAKING AND DELEGATION OF AUTHORITY	OPERATIONAL PLANNING	BUDGETING	MEASUREMENT AND EVALUATION
General management	No change	No change	No change	No change	No change	No change	No change	Managers able to ask for more detailed back-up statistics on problems
Top functional— Components that do not process large amounts of quantitative data	No change	No change	No change	No change	De facto delegation of some decisions or some aspects of the decision making process to subordinates	Managers devoted more time to examining ways to improve systems and procedures at the operations level	No change	Quantitative measures of the performance of operations level personnel and components improved in both content and accuracy
Top functional— Components that process large amounts of quantitative data	Creation of position of data processing manager	Some components transferred in hierarchy to improve implementation of computer technology	No change	No change	Additional time allocated to other activities, such as operational planning		No change	
Operations— Components that do not process large amounts of quantitative data	No change	No change	No change	Size of components per dollar sales decreased moderately (about 20%) because of improved methods	Better decisions because of more accurate information	Managers better able to direct attention to areas where efforts would be most productive	No change	Quantitative measures of the performance of employees, distributors, suppliers, etc. improved in both content and-accuracy
Operations— Components that process large amounts of quantitative data	Creation of roles related to data processing, such as programmers and systems analysts. Some roles upgraded	Coordination activities increased in frequency, become more formalized	No change	Size of components per dollar sales decreased substantially (about 40%) because new activities performed with existing personnel	Some decisions programmed into computer	No change	No change	

and evaluation process at the general management level, and the methods of coordination in components whose principal tasks did involve the processing of large amounts of quantitative data.

In general, the research findings showed that the effects of the computer were:

- Greater on organizational processes and delegation of authority than on the characteristics of formal structure.
- Greater at the operations level than at the top functional level, and greater at both of these levels than at the general management level.
- Greater on the organizational components whose principal tasks involved the processing of large amounts of quantitative data than on components whose tasks did not.

Effects on formal structure

Although I examined all of the changes (over 200) in formal structure which had occurred in both organizations during the 12-year period covered by the study, I found no instances in which the computer had caused changes in structure at either the general management level or at the top functional level in those components whose principal tasks did not involve the processing of substantial amounts of quantitative data.

(In one instance, a computer report served as a catalyst for a change from a functional grouping to a product grouping at the top functional level, but the computer did not influence the nature of the change.)

There were limited changes at the top functional level in components whose principal tasks involved the processing of quantitative data and at the operations level in components whose principal tasks did not. In the former case, the majority of the changes were related to changes in structure which occurred at the operations level. For example:

- In the large company, a 30% reduction in the number of personnel in the general accounting and cost sections permitted the consolidation of these two components, with the consequent elimination of a managerial position.
- In the smaller company, the responsibility for the purchasing component was transferred to the manager of finance, who was also in charge of data processing, when the system and procedures in that area were automated.

The major changes in formal structure brought about by the computer occurred at the operations level in components whose principal tasks involved processing large amounts of quantitative data. Here, new roles were created, while old roles were modified or eliminated. In addition, the coordination mechanisms became more frequent and formal, and organizational components were transferred or combined as a result of new systems and new procedures. Finally, there were substantial decreases in the total number of personnel per total dollar sales at this level, even after taking into consideration the additions of computer-related personnel. For example:

• In the larger company, as the result of the development of a computerized production scheduling system, there was a threefold increase in the number of formal meetings between market forecasting personnel and production scheduling personnel to discuss major changes in production schedules.

• In both companies, after data-manipulation activities had been programmed into the computer, the tasks performed by cost accountants were upgraded.

• In the larger company, because of increased efficiency resulting from the use of computer models in design work, the number of product design engineers decreased about 10%.

• In the smaller company, the automation of accounting records resulted in a 40% decrease in the number of accounting personnel per $1 million of sales.

Why not more changes? Since the effects of the computer on formal structure which I found were far less than many business observers had predicted, I attempted to ascertain why this was the case and also to learn whether further changes in structure were anticipated in the future. In general, the interview responses were to the effect that the computer had not affected formal structure at the general management level or in those components which did not process large amounts of quantitative data because it did not basically alter either the tasks performed by these components or the way in which those tasks were performed. The interviews also predicted that this would continue to be true in the future.

Typical of these kinds of interview responses was this observation by a corporate staff specialist on organizational design and development:

"I do not expect the computer to have much effect on our approach to managing and organizing at the general management level in the near future.

"Most of the information in a business is recorded inside people's heads. All the computer contains is a series of abstractions, and usually financial ones at that, which may serve to alert the general manager to a situation in which he should become involved. When he actually does get involved, it is necessary for the manager to go far beyond these abstractions by talking with the people involved to get at the underlying factors affecting results."

A sales manager offered this explanation as to why there are not more changes in his area:

"There is not much potential for changes in structure in the sales section due to the computer. The way we organize depends on our sales volume, the size and location of our customers, the number and nature of our channels of distribution, the number and diversity of our product lines, and so on, and these factors are not affected by the computer."

An engineering manager viewed the computer's impact in this way:

"I do not expect major changes in the organizational structure of the engineering section in the near future due to the increased use of the computer, although I do feel that the computer will increase the productivity of our present personnel.

"The reason for this is the fact that in the engineering section organizational structure is based on the physical characteristics of the products we produce, the nature of the production process, and the level of new product development and cost reduction activities rather than on the ways we process data."

Finally, this comment was given by a manufacturing manager:

"First, let me say that I could supervise more people than I do now. However, the computer really could not increase the number of men I could supervise. I must evaluate the man as well as the job he does, and the computer could not help there.

"In addition, the real limitation I have is understanding the nature of the tasks performed by each man well enough to evaluate him. The computer does not help too much there, either.

"In the case of my subordinates, the computer has given them better measures, so they could probably supervise a few extra employees. But I prefer them to spend their time improving their supervision of the employees who currently report to them.

"Moreover, the computer has not given them that much more time, because they spend only a small portion of their time in evaluating employees. Most of their time is spent in trying to improve operations by training personnel or by improving methods, and the computer does not help there."

Effects on decision making

My study revealed no direct effects of the computer on decision making or delegation of authority at the general management level. At the top functional level, however, there was considerable de facto delegation to subordinates of the analysis and evaluation phases of certain classes of decisions.

The major reason for this appeared to be the fact that the executives involved felt that the improved systems and procedures enabled their subordinates to handle these tasks on their own. One financial manager put it this way:

"The computer has enabled me to become less involved in day-to-day activities because the system design is such that many tasks that used to occupy my time are now handled routinely by my subordinates. This is possible because the parameters are spelled out in such a way that I know my subordinates can do the job.

"For example, I used to have to worry about our overdue accounts receivable. Now we have a report which indicates accounts receivable for each customer by billing date. We send a copy of this report to each of our customers every month. This eliminates a lot of calls we used to have to make.

"In addition, my subordinates can now follow up on routine cases so that I only have to handle the exceptional ones."

At the operations level, managers in components that did not process large amounts of quantitative data felt they were able to make better decisions as a result of more accurate data. In the components that did process large amounts of quantitative data, a substantial number of decisions were programmed into the computer. These were usually associated with activities such as production scheduling, machine loading, determination of inventory levels, and so on.

Effects on operational planning

The majority of the general managers I interviewed did not become heavily involved with operational planning. Their participation was usually limited to keeping tabs on the activities of their subordinates. The use of the computer did not change this. Thus one general manager commented:

"I do not get deeply involved in the day-to-day operations of the departments reporting to me. In the first place, I do not have the time, and, besides, that is not my job; it's the job of the department general manager. Rather, I just monitor the departments' activities to make sure the managers are doing their jobs.

"In a sense, I'm really not evaluating plans; I'm evaluating people and the way they think, and to do this I must talk with them. A set of statistics cannot tell me how a man thinks."

At the top functional level, however, the computer enabled managers to devote more time to examining ways to improve existing systems and procedures, and it had given them better information to do this. For example, one manufacturing manager described this incident:

"We have three or four peak demands for our punch presses each year. In the past, after each peak period, trained personnel were either laid off or moved to other jobs. Last year, I noted that we were using a lot of overtime and part-time labor to produce these parts during one of the periods of peak demand, so I asked our information systems people to explode our requirements for these parts for the past several years.

"Their figures showed that the total demand was large enough to keep all regular employees busy all year. It did not take me much longer to calculate that it would cost us substantially less to keep those men on full time and build up inventories than to lay them off and then have to work overtime and part-time.

"Without the computer, however, it would not have been possible for me to do this because we would not have had the information stored anywhere. Even if it had been, it would probably have been prohibitively expensive to try to pull it out and process it."

At the operations level, the increased accuracy of computer-prepared reports enabled managers to improve their planning and to direct their attention to areas where their efforts would be most profitable. For example, in the large company, computer reports on tool usage, dollars of expense on tooling, and dollars of maintenance by machine have enabled the engineers to plan replacement, repair, and maintenance work more accurately and profitably than ever before.

Effects on budgeting

Inasmuch as my study only tangentially examined the effects of the computer on the budgeting process, I observed only two types of changes. At the *top functional* level, managers were able to change their budgets far more rapidly when the circumstances on which they were based were also changed.

Thus one engineering manager developed a program for use on a time-shared computer which contained his yearly expense budget broken down by project. Whenever a project had to be changed, he used the program to generate several "alternative" budgets for discussion purposes. When agreement was reached on the changes to be made, he then revised the original program to incorporate the new inputs.

At the *operations* level, utilization of the computer resulted in an increase in the accuracy of the manager's budgets. This occurred because the computer permitted direct costs to be broken down in greater detail than was previously economically feasible. The computer also permitted the development of detailed reports on indirect costs at this level for the first time. The result was better decision making by the managers involved. Typical was the comment of one supervisor who remarked that he was now able to do his job on the basis of facts rather than on intuition or guesswork.

Effects on measurement

One of the few areas in which the computer directly affected the activities of the general manager was that of measurement and evaluation. The major result was that these men were able to request more detailed backup statistics on many problems than previously. In addition, one general manager said that he used the additional information in running his business:

"The availability of almost any sort of information I want makes it possible for me to know where to apply pressure, and/or how I ought to organize activities. For example, before the computer, I had little idea of our costs or profits for our smallest business in the XYZ market on a current basis because these data were buried in other statistics on our major markets. The development of such information has permitted me to examine the problems in a given area more closely and to evaluate the managers involved on the basis of facts."

At both the top functional level and the operations level, the computer changed the measures managers use to evaluate the performance of their subordinates. Here is a typical comment:

"In some cases the computer has affected the way I, and other managers like me, evaluate our subordinates. The ideal measure has not changed, of course, but the actual measure has. For example, we have always felt that the best way to measure the performance of our manufacturers' representatives was by the share of market our distributors got.

"However, since we had no way to estimate total sales for their territories, we used other, less desirable measures. Thus, in the past, if a distributor sent in a large order or if his personal contact with us was good, we felt he was doing well.

"After we got the computer, we started generating reports of quarterly and annual sales by distributor. This revealed that for several distributors the big order did not repeat or that the good contact was a substitute for good sales. These reports have enabled us to upgrade the performance of both our manufacurers' representatives and our distributors, even though we still are not able to measure market share."

A manufacturing manager offered this comment on performance evaluation:

"Previously, I used to have to judge performance on the basis of output. Now I have reports which indicate both machine and labor efficiency for the section as a whole, as well as for each machine and each employee.

They have helped me to identify areas where efficiency could be improved. I suspect, however, that these reports are of even greater value to my subordinates than they are to me.

"For example, the other day one of them told me about a situation in which our labor efficiency report helped him to increase productivity. We had started making parts using a nonstandard material, and he was worried about productivity. But, when he went through the shop, everyone looked busy enough, so he felt pleased.

"The next day, however, the labor efficiency report indicated that one employee's productivity had been extremely low. A quick check revealed that the worker did not know how to machine the new material. A little on-the-spot training solved that problem.

"The point is that without the report the situation would probably have gone unnoticed, since it was a short run. As a consequence, we would have suffered decreased productivity."

Generality of study results

The fact that my research covers only two somewhat similar companies is not as limiting as it might initially seem to be. The results are applicable to many companies in many industries.

I say this because the independent studies described previously (and others like them) tend to support my own research findings. As I mentioned earlier, all of these studies appear to be contradictory when taken individually. However, when one views each as a piece of a larger pattern, rather than as the entire pattern, and then compares each piece with the corresponding portion of my findings, the fit is good indeed.

For example, Hoos's observations of the impact of the computer on the structure and processes of government agencies, banks and insurance companies, and manufacturers of industrial and consumer products dealt primarily with organizational components at the operations level whose principal tasks involved the processing of large amounts of quantitative data.

When her findings (see the ruled insert on page 119) are compared with mine (see Exhibit I and Exhibit II) at the same level for the same types of components, the similarity is unmistakable even though the characteristics of the organizations involved are different.

Similar comparisons of my findings with those of Shaul, Lee, Brady, and others yield the same results. In fact, I found *no* study whose findings are in disagreement with mine when compared in this manner.

Since these studies covered a wide variety of businesses and industries, it would seem that my findings possess substantial generality. Because of limitations in the data available, however, it is not possible to develop a detailed classification system of the types of companies to which the figures would apply.

Future changes

As we have seen, the computer's impact on organizational structure and processes has varied according to the characteristics of the process, the level of the organization, and the nature of the task of the component involved. Will the pattern and magnitude of the effects observed so far remain the same in the future?

It depends. In my opinion, companies which are just starting to use the computer will experience changes such as those described in this Special Report. However, I feel this pattern will change in the future for the two manufacturing companies I studied, as well as for others like them. More specifically, I predict that in such companies this pattern will emerge by 1975:

• The computer will not have any significant effects on any of the major characteristics of formal structure—methods of specialization, coordination, span of control, and so forth—at either the general management or the top functional level.

• The effects on formal structure at the operations level will be similar to those observed here, but the magnitude of these changes will be substantially less than those that have occurred to date.

• For certain important operating decisions, general management will delegate the analysis and evalution phases of the decision-making process to top functional management. As better information becomes available, and as top management becomes convinced that functional managers can do the job, top management may also delegate the responsibility for the final choice.

• Top functional managers will become even less involved in routine, day-to-day decision making. Instead, they will concentrate their time on the important operating decisions delegated to them (for which they will probably begin to use simulation models), and on improvement of system design.

• At the operations level, managers will increasingly be able to focus their attention on those areas with the greatest playback. Fewer decisions will be programmed into the computer than in the past, but the caliber of decision making will increase as information is processed and summarized in more pertinent ways.

• At the general management level, the introduction of financial and other complex simulation models will permit the development of variable budgets. The latter will in turn permit better evaluation of the performance of the general manager involved. Such models should also be useful to general management in the investment planning process.

• There will be continued improvement in the quantitative measures available to evaluate performance at both the functional and operations levels. In a real sense, the computer will make the concepts of both management-by-exception and management-by-objectives operational at these levels.

• In general, the computer is going to affect management decision making and processes—such as operational planning, and measurement and evaluation—substantially more than it will affect the various characteristics of formal structure. This will hold for all levels in the hierarchy and for all types of organizational components.

Conclusion

The computer has brought a number of changes in the structure and processes of businesses. These changes have been less than some would have liked and more than others have wanted. If the same effort and original thinking had been applied to existing operations as was applied to the development of computer systems, some of the changes probably could have been made without the computer. In other cases, the speed and accuracy of the computer were absolutely essential in bringing about the changes.

Further changes will occur in the future. These will primarily involve increases in management efficiency and effectiveness, especially at the top functional level. They will be more subtle and more complex than those changes which have occurred to date and will be more difficult to justify economically, since they will not be accompanied by such substantial decreases in the total number of clerical personnel at the operations level as in the past.

To accomplish these changes will require advances in our knowledge of organizational relationships and business processes, as well as advances in computer hardware and software. Such advances can be aided by management support and training, but they cannot be halted. Kenneth Boulding described the reasons in another context:

"There is probably no way back. The growth of knowledge [computer systems] is one of the most irreversible forces known to mankind. It takes a catastrophe of very large dimensions to diminish the total stock of knowledge in the possession of man. Even in the rise and fall of great civilizations surprisingly little has been permanently lost, and much that was lost for a short time was easily regained. Hence there is no hope for ignorance or for morality [management] based on it. Once we have tasted the fruit of the tree of knowledge, as the Biblical story illustrates so well, Eden is closed to us."[1]

The computer is a tool. Tomorrow's manager will use it in the same manner that today's manager uses a slide rule, or an adding machine, or a telephone.

NOTE

1. *The Meaning of the 20th Century: The Great Transition* (New York, Harper and Row, 1964), p. 23.

REFERENCES

Reference list for the EDP insert, outlining observers' predictions and researchers' findings:

A. "Management in the 1980's," HBR November-December 1958, p. 41.

B. "The Manager and the Black Box," HBR November-December 1960, p. 85.

C. "Information Technology and Decentralization," HBR November-December 1961, p. 121.

D. "Can Management Information Be Automated?" HBR March-April 1964, p. 128; "Myth of Real-Time Management Information," HBR May-June 1966, p. 123; and "Computers: No Impact on Divisional Control," HBR January-February 1967, p. 99.

E. 'When the Computer Takes Over the Office," HBR November-December 1960, p. 102.

F. "What's Really Ahead for Middle Management?" *Personnel*, November-December 1964, p. 8.

G. *The Impact of Electronic Data Processing Upon Patterns of Business Organization and Administration* (Albany, New York, State University of New York at Albany, 1965).

H. "Computer in Top-Management Decision Making," HBR July-August 1967, p. 67.

11. Where Do We Go from Here with MIS?*

P. D. Walker and S. D. Catalano

Organizations, in order to survive, must change as the environment around them changes. Today's organizations are bigger and more complex than any in history: they must be able to cope with technological needs and with the discovery of complex products. Organizational philosophies and practices must keep pace with these changes.

The computer offers a powerful tool for effecting some of the required changes. But just as it would be wrong to place a modern jet engine in a pre-jet age designed aircraft, it is wrong to degrade the potential power of today's management tools by placing them into poorly structured organizations with outdated management conventions.

From 1930 through the 1950s, many organizations, due to rapid growth and dispersed facilities, converted from centralized to decentralized management. Now there is an opportunity for a new form of centralization using modern management techniques based on computers. Organizations now must move toward centralized records and administrative operations that will better serve decentralized day-to-day decision making of operating managements.

The availability of up-to-date data, with capability to use computers to extract meaningful analyses and measures, means that managers of large, diverse business units will be able to perform their jobs in a new way. With

*SOURCE: *Computer Decisions* (September, 1969), pp. 34-37. Reprinted by permission of the publisher.

better information, strategy should be improved and greater efficiency possible on an organization-wide scale. Data, and information extracted from the data, are being recognized as resources as vital as trained personnel or cash to the effectiveness of a business.

Unfortunately there are today few Management Information Systems that allow what we will term general management—managers with total-organization or corporate-wide responsibility—to perform in this manner. The generic term "Management Information System" is being used loosely today and requires more specific definition. Most of today's systems are what should be termed "Management Inquiry Systems."

Rapid changes are now taking place in computer technology. Our concern here will not be with technical aspects, but rather with the ways in which these changes can be harnessed and directed toward running an organization. This shift in emphasis in computer evolution is reflected in the time-diagram.

	56	58	60	62	64	66	68	70	72	74	76	78
COMPUTER GENERATION	FIRST Tubes— Milliseconds		SECOND Transistors— Microseconds			THIRD Integrated circuits— nanoseconds						
BUSINESS NEEDS	OPERATIONAL Management of day-by-day activities					FUNCTIONAL Management of business unit— divisional level				GENERAL Management of entire organization— corporate level		
SYSTEM DESIGN	BATCH PROCESSING Run entire large job through at one time					ON-LINE Direct access to computer for input &/or output				DATA MANAGED Standard data formats & procedures allow organization-wide use of shared data banks		

Management at three levels

Management cannot be viewed as a single entity with a single set of activities. An analysis of a typical three-level management hierarchy is enlightening (diagram on page 134). At the top, we identify general management level; the middle, or functional level, includes such managers as the manufacturing executive or marketing executive. At the base is the operating level concerned with daily productive activities. A product sales manager or manager of a particular production line is at this level. At this level, the time spent by sales managers, for example, to manage the processing of orders, administrative acts, must be minimized to allow more time for their initiative responsibilities, the actual selling.

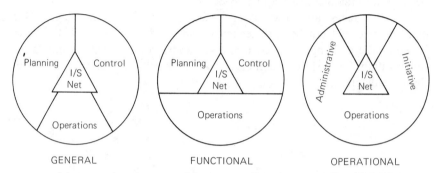

GENERAL   FUNCTIONAL   OPERATIONAL

Management Hierarchy showing the division of activities at different levels.

The information system, designed from the general management point of view, ties the three levels together, and hopefully, allows an increase in the proportion of time spent on initiative-type rather than administrative operations.

In the 1950's and through the early 1960's the computer was primarily a tool for operational problems. It was often applied within a single functional group—finance, manufacturing, personnel. In very large organizations separate computer systems were also used at each particular location even within a single function. Autonomy ruled in the management of computer applications.

Starting in the late 1950's, it was realized that data banks created as a part of these operational systems would be invaluable in providing information for functional management. For example: financial and marketing management now had files of information on customers; purchasing had files on vendors; personnel had files on employees.

During the era of operational systems, development proceeded in an uncoordinated and undisciplined manner. Files were fractionalized because operations were decentralized. It has since become necessary to centralize key files within a functional area to provide management with a consolidated and consistent information base.

Efforts to provide this capability so far have been aimed toward a software system capable of handling a wide range of file formats. Instead more effort should be given to what we call a "data-managed system design," so that the complexity of today's generalized file systems can be replaced with systems built upon standard data bases. Such an approach will permit autonomy in operational and functional systems, but will enable the general management level to extract consistent information from multiple sources throughout the organization.

The next step in the evolving maturity of computer use was the design of functional information systems to consolidate previously uncoordinated operational systems. These systems commenced in the early 1960's and will continue into the early 1970's. But as this system form develops it must be done within the framework of the general management systems which are already recognized as the next step in the progression.

The communications maze that occurred when data flows resulted from poorly planned connections of operational systems is illustrated on the next page. Data streamed from the operation bases of marketing to the operational bases of manufacturing. Top executives in each function were unable to get consolidated information on key actions within their functions because there were no centralized data banks. With so many unique operational systems it proved difficult to make changes demanded by a growing business in a timely fashion. Top executives in manufacturing and marketing could not easily relate the status of marketing demand with production supply. Their data was not timely, nor consistent in formal and data structure. Functional systems with consolidated data are now being installed to solve these problems.

The general manager's role

A broader view of organizational structure is required in preparing to move toward a system design for the general manager. The role of a general manager briefly stated is to maximize the output with minimum resources. Depending on business scope, this is achieved by means of two classes of functional managements. These two classes, illustrated in the diagram, are:

Process management functions, represented by the vertical bars for development, manufacturing, marketing, service and finance.

Resource management functions, represented by horizontal bars for cash, personnel, organization, and product.

These lists of processes and resources are representative and will vary from organization to organization. It is a primary role of the general manager to allocate the use of resources among these various processes.

OPERATIONAL MANAGEMENT SYSTEM DESIGN

SALES
OFFICES   PLANTS

He must be able, for example, to recognize and assess alternative actions when his marketing resources are resulting in the sales of more items than his plant will be able to produce.

Today's large corporations have complex product mixes, subject to shifting markets in fast-paced marketplaces. Faced with many varying decisions, general managers must have the capability to assess the effects of both external conditions and internal plans as they relate to business objectives and operating performance. The general manager's information system of the future must be capable of supporting this responsibility in an extremely timely and accurate fashion.

The conversion of present operational and functional information systems into structures suitable for the general management concept will not be a short-term undertaking. The progression toward such systems must be broken down into a logical sequence of tasks. All tasks do not have to be tackled simultaneously.

The road map

The first task must continue throughout the development cycle. It is concerned with defining precise organizational relationships. It also defines the role of the information systems function and its decision processes, and how these relate to those of other functional areas.

Task 2, *design data specification systems*, includes developing various coding schemes and conventions needed for data management. Code structures must be worked out, for example, to identify resources—people, cash, production equipment, inventory, etc. Objectives of this phase include: a standard accounting scheme for charging and analyzing computer usage throughout the system; a data dictionary and directory identification system; and a standard method for information system documentation retrieval and control.

Task 3, *analyze present and planned information flows*, will provide the "road map" showing how the interdependent information requirements of various business functions relate to each other. In this phase the basic computer applications in support of these business functions, and the information flows involved, must be defined.

Task 4, *define data management principles and standards*, provides the basis for setting up the data files for the organization. For example, in the present system a number of order backlog files might be maintained. In

FUNCTIONAL MANAGEMENT SYSTEM DESIGN

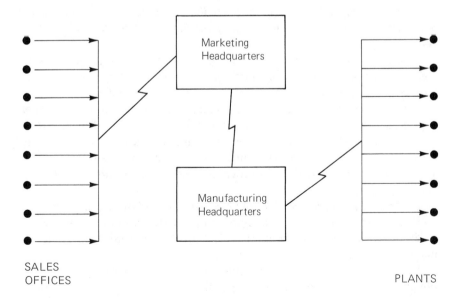

SALES
OFFICES

PLANTS

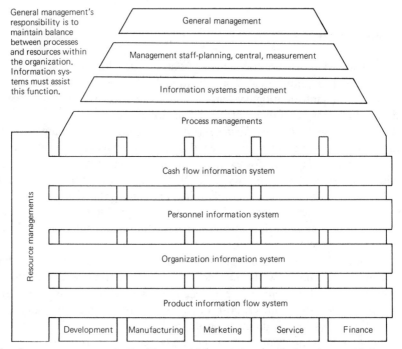

General management's responsibility is to maintain balance between processes and resources within the organization. Information systems must assist this function.

the future system a single file would be maintained, but it would be conveniently shared among multiple dependent functions.

Task 5, *define cost benefit criteria for project selection*, set up priorities so that resources are properly allocated to implement various segments of the system. This assessment should include some measures of user values, management values, and values as they pertain to the overall information system objectives.

Task 6, *define information activities in management terms*, and task 7, *identify management's information requirements*, are closely related and they contribute to task 5. There must be an understanding of how the operational activities throughout the company affect the profits and other key measures important to general management. These are difficult areas. Displaceable costs have not proved an effective measure for justifying application development work. Further work by both management and systems people must be done in order to achieve better definition of these values.

Task 8, *define near-term and long-range business objectives and environment*, is necessary so systems analysts can properly set up the software.

Tasks 9, 10 and 11 are support project involved in setting up the information system.

Task 9, *establish project planning and control system*, provides for obtaining the physical resources and people for implementing the total plan.

Information system architecture can evolve through this sequence of tasks.

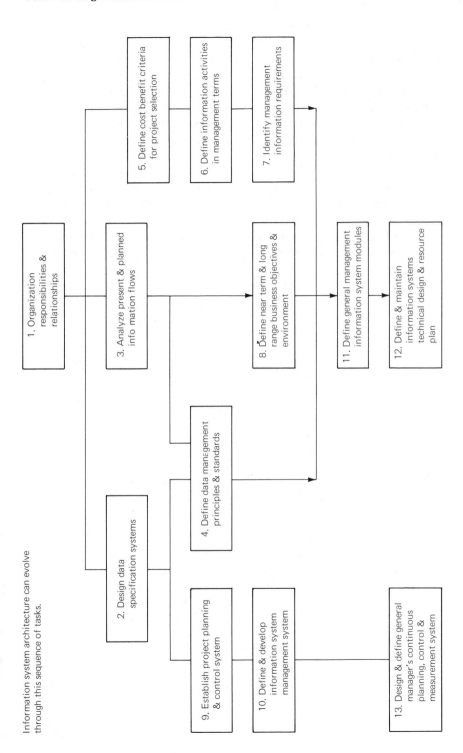

Task 10, *define and develop information system management system*, includes studies of alternate system designs, assigning priorities, planning, controlling and making progress measurements on projects. Task 11, *design general management information system modules*, defines the particular systems modules needed to implement the total design.

Task 12, *define and maintain information system technical design and resource plan*, spells out the technical sequence of events and allocates the necessary resources.

Finally, after all other tasks are well underway: task 13, *design and define general manager's continuous planning, control and measurement system*, begins to bring the use of the total system into the operations of the organization.

These tasks are not defined in a strict time sequence. Many of them must go on continuously even after the system is installed and operating.

12. Next in MIS: 'Data Managed' System Design*

P. D. Walker and S. D. Catalano

Today, we are making a transition from a period in which "data processing" was a pure service function, supporting a single operating unit or location, to a period in which "information systems" are being recognized as an organization-wide function.

In the data processing period, independently-designed operational applications were strung together with little or no concern for the overall perspective required by top management. Today, with the increased emphasis on managing "change" through planning, control and measurement, and with the computer now in use for over 15 years, we can design systems that will yield total "corporate perspective," as illustrated in the diagram to the right. This design aids the "general manager," who is charged with responsibility for choosing among many alternatives, developing organization-wide strategies, allocating resources to meet corporate objectives and competing demands, and directing a highly complex organization. Such managers need consistent and timely data to make decisions. That data must come from widely-scattered sales offices, warehouses, retail stores, and manufacturing plants in a consistent, accurate and timely form. But a full-pledged general manger's information system cannot be built on a weak foundation. We cannot weld previously independent data processing facilities into an integrated system capable of serving general management's

*SOURCE: *Computer Decisions* (November, 1969), pp. 30-33. Reprinted by permission of the publisher.

EXTERNAL ENVIRONMENT: General managers must be concerned with these factors outside the organization:
Customers: Their acceptance of products and reaction to the service received.
Government: Its regulatory actions affecting pricing, advertising, etc.
Investors: Their appraisal of management in terms of growth and stability of the business.
Public: Its influence on corporations growing social conscience; general welfare and the mobility and composition of the work force.
Competition: Their improved technology, new products and merchandising tactics.
CORPORATE: This responsibility includes:
- Continual evaluation and interpretation of how environment will influence corporate policies, practices, plans, performance and products.
- Measurement of operating business units against plans.
GENERAL: These managers infuse corporate policies into the functional and production world by:
- Translating strategic plans into production plans and programs, as well as allocating resources to achieve the goals.
- Establishing a management information system that will ensure balanced corporate perspective.
- Defining control systems to measure functional management's performance.
FUNCTIONAL: Responsibilities include:
- Defining programs that will allow functional groups (finance, developments, etc.) to work within the overall corporate framework. Establishing operating performance quotas and employee motivation programs.
- Installing control systems to ensure that operating, business and functional objectives are consistent with corporate aims.
OPERATIONAL: Activities include:
- Translating performance quotas into resource requirements and specific operating plans.
- Measuring the impact of company policy on employee performance and feeding back worker reactions.
- Executing tasks as a member of a total organization, not in a "production at all cost" vacuum.
- Commenting on how corporate standards can be improved to help day-to-day production.
- Keeping all higher levels of management aware of reactions to the company's products and services.

---

needs in a precise and efficient manner, unless we develop new approaches, new procedures, and new organizations.

The first step in building such systems is to recognize that "data" is a resource, analogous in value to such traditional resources as people and cash. Systems that permit management of the traditional resources already exist. Unfortunately, similar conventions do not exist for data. To carry the comparison a step further:

Resource	Management process
People	Organization
Cash	Budgeting and allocation
Data	Data management

A basic need, then, is to develop systems controlled and managed by a set of organization-wide, "date managed" conventions.

Before discussing the characteristics of such a system, however, it is worthwhile to consider some further needs of general managers in large organizations. An essential function of the general manager is to balance the allocation of resources (people, cash, facilities, data, etc.) among various processes (development, manufacturing, marketing, etc.). In concept, the planning process, coupled with appropriate decision aids ("what if. . ." models), will allow the general manager to perform the function. Unfortunately, in practice, information systems have not been developed to support the planning process in a way that will meet management needs. The planning process generally forces administrative detail onto overworked managers who are required to supply redundant information to budgeting and product planning processes.. In most organizations, plans are usually updated only once or twice a year. This means that top management often makes its decision from outdated, invalid or incomplete data.

There are a number of factors hindering development of general management information systems, even where the basic concepts are intellectually understood. Here are a few of the main obstacles.

• Very few firms have established objectives and strategies for their information systems.

• Lack of top management understanding of, or involvement in, information systems efforts.

• Corporations have not mounted well-defined programs to set priorities for commiting resources. Scarce resources (particularly human resources) continue to be used for low-value activities or insignificant evaluations.

• Today's measurement systems are based on a calendar year, but the general manager's system requires commitment to projects which may evolve over a full decade.

• Many of today's operational managers, the one's handling day-to-day activities, tend to make decisions in the interest of a small portion of the firm, rather than in the best interest of the total organization. This type of manager is usually very aggressive in resisting change.

• Many of today's computer specialists are so involved with technical problems that they often lose sight of overall organizational objectives.

These barriers must be overcome if organizations are to succeed in our increasingly complex world. The environmental factors which affect success and failure are so dynamic that general management must be able to understand and react to them quickly and incisively. Additionally, the cost factor provides another strong incentive for creating integrated systems. The costs for operating separate and independent data processing facilities at every level of management, and for different process or resource groups (with inevitable redundancies), will be much higher than for a highly integrated system.

In order to start toward an information system design, it is necessary to have a road map of the information flows that support related process,

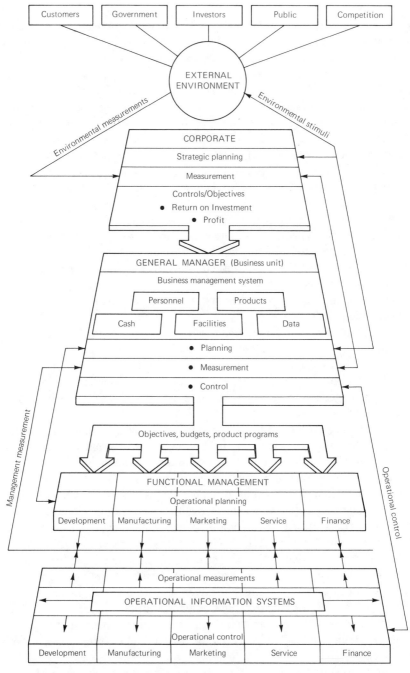

Total corporate information systems based on data-managed design will be highly integrated and interactive.

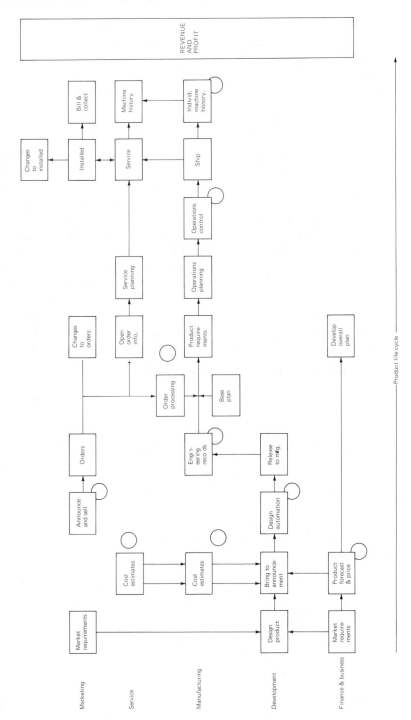

(manufacturing, marketing, etc.) and resource (personnel, cash, etc.) managements. This road map must exist at both the operational and management process levels. The life cycle of a typical product, shown in the diagram, helps to illustrate the business integration that the general manager must accommodate. For operating and functional managers (executives in finance, marketing, etc., are functional managers) to plan and schedule effectively, they must first be aware of the original product plan, and then be kept continuously appraised of actual performance and changes in the plan across the organization.

Today's operational and functional systems designed to process operational data are rarely structured to satisfy organization-wide information requirements. Note in the diagram that individual users—finance, manufacturing, marketing, etc.—each developed different data requirement and data flows to different data banks. The data flowed serially with no regard for consistency between individual systems. For example, in these systems, if the engineering department wants financial information, an engineering manager has to obtain it from an operational system in the accounting department. Chances are the information is not in the proper form to meet the engineer's need. In a data managed system, designed for general management purposes, many users will share centralized data banks.

OPERATIONAL MANAGEMENT SYSTEM DESIGN

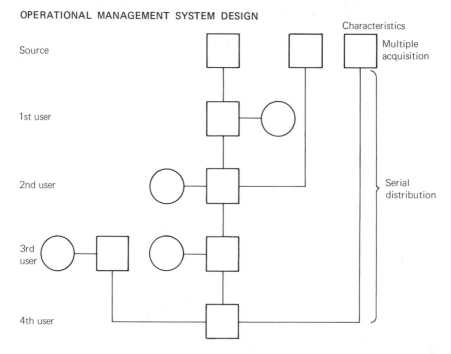

The key to such a data managed system design is the development of an organization-wide data element Dictionary/Directory that includes standard definitions, an index system for defining where used, algorithms for deriving higher levels of data from "basic elements," and security rules for file access.

The final diagram is a conceptual representation of a general business management system of the future. The system will give general management the ability to plan, control and manage the business using current and accurate data. The dynamics of such a system are much more responsive to the changing environment in which general management must work. The system is built upon a "moving file" concept, i.e., as operating data streams in, appropriate adjustments will be made automatically through the system.

GENERAL MANAGEMENT SYSTEM DESIGN

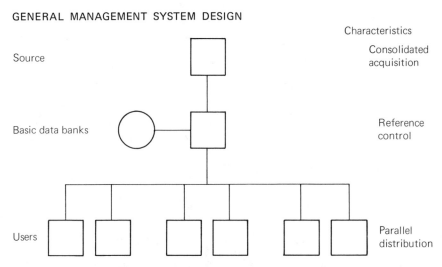

The "moving data bank" reflects both planned and actual performance. Flanking the central, master data bank are data banks containing working plans. One of these is fed by the revenue and product planning groups (to the left), and the other is supplied by the resource planning groups (to the right). At the top of the diagram are resource data banks that are continually reflecting the status of key resources as affected by day-to-day operating events. These operational data banks continuously feed the planning file.

Notice that the master file provides high integrity data to the product strategy model, which is one of general management's decision aid tools. This arrangement allows him to use current information to play "what if . . ." games and see if the firm's performance could be improved, or if the plans should be modified. One use, for example, might be the need to determine whether manufacturing facilities can support increased hiring plans in marketing. At the same time, he can interrogate the central file for other related information as the need arises. Periodic plans can be published in "hard copy" to satisfy areas of management with less dynamic needs.

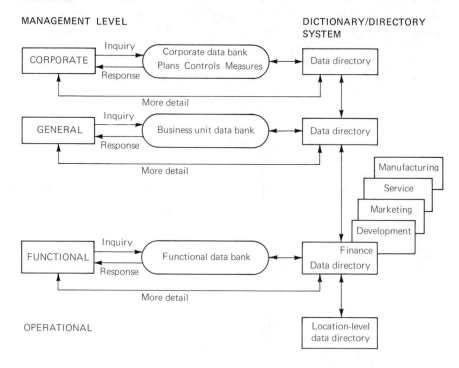

Next in MIS: 'data managed' system design

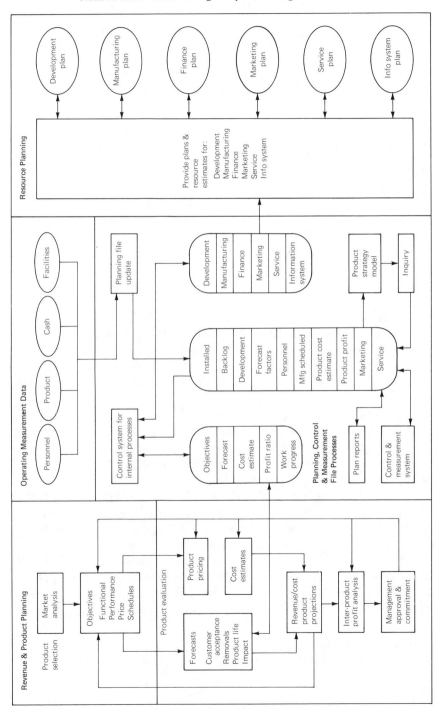

13. What Else Will Computers Do to Us?*

Martin L. Ernst

For more than 20 years growth in the computer business has been fed by technological advances that have made equipment cheaper and better each year, and technological progress is going to continue at a high rate for at least another decade. Costs will continue to go down; performance will improve, and the range of peripheral and input-output devices will expand.

As equipment becomes more diverse, efficient and cheap, more and more applications will become practical. This spread, in turn, will lead to increased anxiety over the social problems associated with the use of computers. Many of the sources of concern arise in a business context and businessmen can alleviate some of them.

We have had early warnings of the social dangers inherent in the growth of computer usage. Until recently, however, these meant little—computers played too small a role in our lives for their negative impacts to be very painful. Our period of grace is now coming to an end.

It is becoming almost fashionable to "blame the computer" even though it is obvious that it is not the computer that is at fault, but our uses of this tool and our development and employment of new institutions and services that the computer is making feasible. Nevertheless, this fact offers no

*SOURCE: This is a revision of an article which appeared in *The Wall Street Journal* (October 21, 1970), p. 18, and is reprinted herein by permission of the author.

excuse for failure to examine the overall social impact, regardless of source, and to seek to find and alleviate areas of social tensions or inequities.

The computer's social impact can be reviewed in terms of three broad areas: Depersonalization, talent bias and vulnerability.

Depersonalization

The origins of depersonalization lie in the high degree of standardization needed to use computers efficiently. As computer activities spread, individuals tend to feel molded to fit the computer's needs rather than the other way around. It probably is no accident that during the first of our major campus riots, at Berkeley, major resentment was directed toward punch cards and computers.

Depersonalization can take place at the corporate level; a concrete example lies in airline reservations systems. A few large airlines have been able to plan and develop computer reservations systems that meet their own needs, but this process is too difficult and expensive for smaller airlines, which must employ existing software. In one case, some 60 significant program changes to the software packages would have been needed for the system to match the operating procedures and philosophy of a small airline. This surgical operation was much too expensive and the airline had to accept the standard programs. It now employs the same basic system as many others and has lost a bit of its special personality.

A far more common encounter with computers involves dealing with a company that has automated its billing operations. The problems here arise from the fact that a system's design is made more complicated by incorporating provisions for dealing with exceptional circumstances. This difficulty is compounded if an organization seeks to get by with minimum training of the clerical staff that examines the customer "inputs" of payments and complaints about mis-billings. The normal result is that the customer writes letter after letter into a non-answering void, his resentment growing at each cycle.

This is a real business failure. Planning to deal with exceptions has been completely inadequate in the design of most computer billing systems and their associated manual procedures. By contrast, very few companies have difficulty picking up changes of address, and most of them make explicit provisions for this when designing their bill formats! None has similarly provided an indicator mechanism for customers to register disagreement with the billing data reported to them.

Another major area of depersonalization concerns privacy—most frequently in regard to credit information, though even more serious invasions may occur in the collection and transmission of health, employment and other data. We have collected and employed credit information for a very long time, but never with the degree of completeness and nationwide access made practical by the computer. How many people deserve a chance to see their own credit information, to make sure that failure to pay a bill because circumstances justified the delay does not appear on their records as a negative mark?

Resentment will probably be slow to rise because of the secrecy surrounding credit information, but this subject may be a time bomb. Only business policies that individuals believe are fair can win social approval. That approval is essential to support collection of information needed for economic and marketing analyses and for solving many of our social problems.[1]

A third area of depersonalization has to do with the opportunities for white collar workers to get started in business. More and more clerks are being displaced by computers. So far, this displacement has been largely made up for by the increasing numbers of people needed to handle input and output information, to design computer programs and to undertake a variety of other new services. However, one very large component of this work force—the personnel responsible for preparing input—is threatened by the development of efficient and economical character-recognition equipment and other input devices. It is likely that in the next decade a significant component of this work force will be eliminated. This means that a certain type of starting job for the white collar worker will disappear in much the sense that the automatic elevator removed a starting opportunity for the least trained blue collar workers. We do not yet have good alternatives available for the starting clerical worker.

Finally, and an extreme case, the use of computers can lead to a form of disenfranchisement. Computers have made practical a rapid increase in the use of credit cards, and we can visualize an almost cashless society. One can ask, what happens then to a man who cannot obtain a credit card? Will he be banned from a form of equal opportunity in our society? Many hotels now require either a credit card or payment in advance. This may be good business, but is it not also a minor indignity of a type that could spread and eventually become a form of real inequity?

Technical training bias

A second broad area of social impact by computers concerns the extension of an existing talent bias in favor of technical training and experience as opposed to the humanities. Until recently, computers have been devoted mainly to clerical areas which, by their nature, already had been routinized within a given company. The management decisions that the computer is now beginning to aid are not standard. We are going to have to develop new techniques, and we will have to acquire large numbers of personnel skilled in developing these techniques and analyzing the output of computer runs. For example, some excellent work has been done in developing the potential of simulations in the decision-making process. But just a few minutes of time on a computer, running a complex simulation, can call for many man-months of analysis to understand the implications of the output. Thus the demand for analytical talent will grow.

This in turn poses problems for our educational institutions; the future demands of business call for certain talents to a greater extent than they probably are naturally present in the human race. These demands tend to cut down the stature and role of the humanities student as he visualizes his position in future society. The new demands place great emphasis on mathematical and analytical skills and tend to split the student body into two components—technically oriented and humanities oriented. This split is resented, and some evidence of rather emotional getting-together of the segments of the student bodies was quite visible during recent riots and protests. A significant number of faculty members are developing an extreme distaste for or even fear of the computer. Some of this will begin to come through to the students that they train.

The use of computers has often led to elimination of some echelons in corporate organizations. They may achieve greater efficiency, but it can also eliminate an important training ground for future management. The result may be an increasing trend for progress in senior managerial positions to come from staff rather than line positions. There are reasons to suspect that, over time, this trend could have disastrous results. As the computer plays more and more of a role, there may be less and less opportunity to develop junior and intermediate management skills.

Vulnerability

While computers can be a source of greater efficiency, they also carry with them many forms of vulnerability. Skills in manipulating computers can unquestionably be employed in ways we have not yet visualized to drain companies and to perpetrate fraud or thefts. This subject has not received adequate and serious study.

We also must face a variety of reliability problems. For example, a lot of attention has been paid to the slowness of moves toward automation on Wall Street. One of the most legitimate barriers to progress has been the reliability of hardware and software. An airline may get into difficulty if its reservations equipment goes down for an hour or more. On a trading floor, a five minute failure of a trading computer could have nearly disastrous results.

In the future we will be faced with the problems as our banking system, our mutual funds, our exchanges and other institutions make increasing use of electronic records. We already have had embarrassing cases in which records were destroyed by mistake or were lost. The size of the largest organization in a given field tends to approach the maximum that is manageable. The use of the computer increases the manageable size of a company but also increases the vulnerability of that company if something happens to the computer.

Sabotage of computers has already occurred, and we must look forward to more instances. In addition, we must anticipate increased industrial espionage. If it is known that a company bases its marketing plans on a simulation or a computer analysis, the simulation itself can become a target for a competitor. It is not difficult in normal situations to arrange for the disappearance of a program—or of input data on sales or customers.

The vulnerability of management

Finally, we face the fact that management itself will become more vulnerable in its decision-making. As we use more complex decision-making tools, and rely more heavily on large data banks, there will be more filtering of information by staff personal before materials for decisions are presented to senior management. Even today, a large fraction of the decisions of senior managers are forced on them by the selectivity of their staffs in providing data and in presenting arguments. As the decision-making apparatus becomes more complex, it will be harder for managers to exercise effective personal control.

This list of problems is obviously not complete. Though the examples range from fairly trivial to moderately serious, all will become far more extensive and more dangerous as our use of computers broadens. Businessmen have an important responsibility for helping solve these problems. If they do not, businessmen will certainly be among the first to suffer from the failure to deal with them.

NOTE

1. This article was written before the signing of the Fair Credit Reporting Act and did not take adequate cognizance of steps taken even earlier by some organizations such as the Associated Credit Bureaus, Inc., to provide for disclosure of file information to consumers. The base for greater equity in this area now exists; the extent to which knowledge of these individual rights is widely available and can be effectively exploited is still, of course, uncertain.

3   THE DESIGN OF A SYSTEM

Whether for the purpose of developing a new system, modifying an existing system, or mechanizing a process, the design of a system requires a conceptualization of system structure. This is true even in the case of the development of human resources within an organization—a matter not frequently considered subject to systemization.

The task of designing systems which may very well consist of an amalgam of human and nonhuman elements requires a spectrum of skills and talents on the part of the analyst. Not only must the systems analyst possess technical and analytical capabilities of a very high order, but he must be cognizant of the human relations problems associated with systems design. Identification and recognition of the impact of informal organizations within formal organizations, coupled with an understanding of the possibility of "dysfunctional" behavior towards a new or modified system, could spell the difference between successful and unsuccessful implementation of a new system.

A. Structural Design

14. The Development and Installation of a Total Management System*

R. L. Martino

Modern business management is faced with a dilemma. At a time when profit margins are shrinking and both foreign and domestic competition are intensifying, heavy expenditures are required for modernization. Such expenditures are considered essential if a business is to remain competitive and if its profit margins are to improve.

In considering modernization, management usually thinks first in terms of facilities and machinery. Too often, however, that is as far as the improvements are carried. The need exists, and has long existed, for modernization of the management function itself. The need is especially accute today because of the great and growing complexity of both products and procedures. Management science has developed many new tools to modernize the management function; it is up to management to take full advantage of these developments.

Management systems in the past have been concerned mainly with the preparation and analysis of historical reports. While this kind of reporting is valuable, rarely is it timely enough to be truly useful. Production figures for January, for example, might not be available until mid-February (or later) when their usefulness will have diminished considerably.

*SOURCE: *Data Processing for Management* (April, 1963), pp. 31-37. Reprinted by permission of Data Processing Magazine, The Publication of Computers and Information Technology.

Objectives

There is an urgent need in business to be able to look ahead as well as behind and to anticipate changes in markets and profit situations. Basically, *a system is required that will forestall the development of an unprofitable business situation.*

Therefore, the primary objective in developing a total management system should be the production of detailed, up-to-the-minute summaries of the past and the use of these summaries to project future activity. In essence, the functions of a total management system, are:

1. To predict
2. To compare the prediction with actual results, and
3. To produce the deviations between the predicted and the actual.

Thereafter, the system should use these deviations to prepare a new, updated set of predictions which can be used as the basis for management decision. This concept is known as *management by exception.* While this term has been bandied about a good deal during the past few years, there are few instances where the concept has been applied in its fullest sense.

The predictive function, it should be understood, includes the determination and consideration of alternatives, and for each alternative, the effects of a decision. The method used in this process is called *simulation,* a technique where in the various factors involved in a given situation are assembled into a model, usually of a mathematical nature. By varying the factors systematically, it is possible to weigh each alternative and its effects. Such information can be of great value to management in making decisions.

A total management system, then, produces basically two kinds of information for all levels of management:

1. Predictions based on historical data and simulation.
2. Suggested changes of present procedures to make the selected predictions possible.

As indicated previously, the predictions are continually compared with actual results to determine deviations. These, in turn, are used to refine or revise the initial set of predictions and strategies. Then, the whole system recycles, producing a new predictions, and so on.

The cycle of a total management system is summarized in the illustration in Figure 1. The upper portion of the cycle diagram, if followed in a counterclockwise manner, represents the regular path. That is, data are used to produce a model which in turn develops predictions are reached by management as to the course of action to be followed, the program is implemented. Then, data obtained from operation of the program are used to produce required statements and reports, and are also used as updated history for the next cycle of the system. The lower half of the diagram

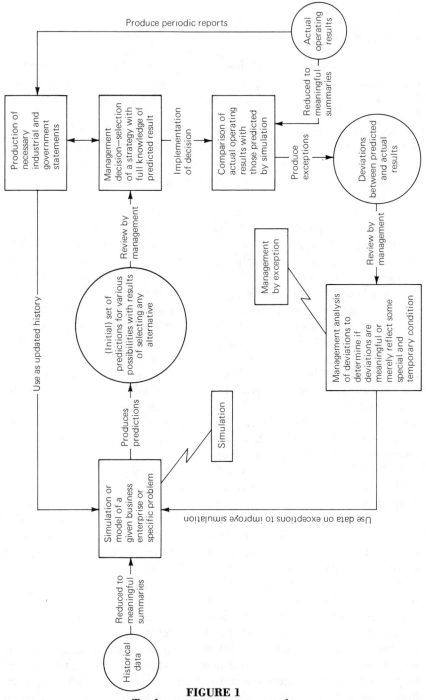

FIGURE 1
Total management system cycle

represents management action required to analyze and correct deviations from the predicted results. The result of such action also becomes a factor in the next cycle of the system.

The value of exception reports drawn from these predictions and historical summaries will vary from function to function in the management system. For example, a daily comparison of predicted and actual sales might be quite useful to an order department, but a daily comparison of predicted with actual profits would not. Decisions as to the type and frequency of reports would be based on the function and on the degree of managed cost control involved.

Scientific methods

In the development and installation of a total management system, scientific methods have played an increasingly important role. Management science involves the application of mathematics to management problems with the aid of the computer to prepare possible alternatives for management decisions. The computer is particularly valuable to management science because it can reduce vast quantities of data to meaningful trends.

When businesses were small and operations were relatively uncomplicated, management decision was often the responsibility of one man—the entrepreneur. Sufficient information was available so that the owner-operator could determine the best course of action by weighing all the alternatives and selecting the best. Whether he knew it or not, the entrepreneur simulated the operation of his business in his mind and, after weighing the various alternatives, made decisions based on the information available to him. And, because the operation was small and uncomplicated, the entrepreneur was in a position to know the consequences of his decisions.

As business volume increased and the organizational structures grew more complex, the lines of communication gradually became less direct and immediate. Without access to the most timely information, management could not know of every alternative course of action, let alone the result of each alternative.

The first attempt to ease the situation was mechanization of the accounting function. Unfortunately, the equipment available could not fully cope with the problem. While it is true that information became more readily available than previously, the voluminous reports in tabulating form were unwieldy and, by the time they reached operating management, they were often too dated to be of real value. To decision making top management, the reports were even less useful.

With the advent of the electronic computer and the introduction of mathematical techniques, management came a step nearer a solution. These new tools make it possible to simulate *all* the operations of an organization and thereby to reduce the overgrown and overly complex problems of business management to a workable form. The electronic computer can be introduced into any present corporate structure with little modification to the line and staff concept so that it is possible to simulate the function of the single entrepreneur without a return to that unrealistic organizational structure.

The emphasis upon computers, mathematics, and the scientific method does not diminish in the least the importance of common sense in distinguishing between what is wanted, what is possible, and what is currently being done. While it is true that methods and machines exist which will produce almost any desired report, economics and common sense must be applied to determine what is realistic. In the development of any management system, too high an emphasis cannot be placed on basic, down-to-earth realism.

Stages of system development

The development and installation of a total management system may be broken down into three major stages. These are:
1. Definition of the problem.
2. Design of the total management system.
3. Programming, cutover to the new system, and system evaluation and modification.

Within each of these areas there are a number of separate operations and activities which must be performed, many of which overlap one another. An arrow diagram[1] has been prepared which illustrates the interrelationship of these activities (see Figure 2). This diagram specifies the various tasks necessary to develop and install a total management system. Whereas the diagram is somewhat abbreviated, the exclusions would be of minor consequences to the overall logic of the plan.

Problem definition

The first stage, problem definition, requires developing a realistic statement indicating the kind of system necessary to produce the reports needed for effective management. This phase must include establishing objectives of a total management system, personnel selection to develop and design such a system, and determining all requisite elements of the system.

Flow charting techniques have generally been used in the problem definition stage, but these charts are cumbersome, difficult to prepare, and difficult to read. Moreover, they often direct management's attention toward simply a mechanization of the old system rather than any bold new approach.

Problem definition for a total management system is based upon data handling procedures. The structure of any operating data system is based upon *data elements* (stock numbers, employee numbers, employee names) which are collected into *data files* (payroll register, stock inventory). Certain rules govern the use of data elements to produce new, or updated, data files. These new files are the *output* reports. The original data elements form the *input* reports to the system.

The rules governing the updating of information fall into three categories. These are:

1. Data movement—the transfer of an element of data from the old document to the new.

2. Arithmetic—the performance of some arithmetic operation upon one or more elements of data during the data transfer.

3. Logical decision—the examination of a data element in the input report to determine a course of action in preparing the output report. For example, the size of gross pay determines the income tax rate.

These three operations form the basis of any electronic computer program since all of the functions that any computer can perform may be reduced to data movement, arithmetic, and logical decision.

In his analysis of a data handling system, the systems engineer will isolate each type of data element and give it a name and number. Then he will determine the interrelationship of the various data elements, such as the format and type of documents in which the data will appear. At the same time, it is necessary to determine the logical selection rules to be used and the arithmetic calculations to be performed on the input data.

The steps in the analysis of a data handling system follow:

1. Determination of data elements.

2. Determination of the interrelationships of data elements and the location of data elements in the file.

3. Determination of rules governing the handling of data elements and data files.

4. Formulation of decision tables where logical choice would govern the selection of one of many possible paths.

5. Formulation of rules governing the production of specific reports required for specific management action.

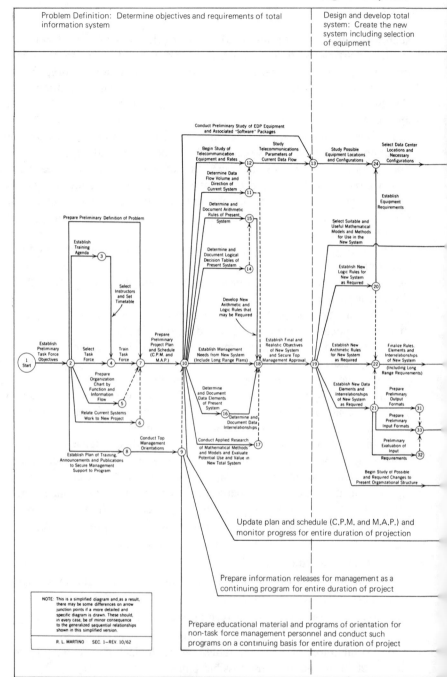

FIGURE 2
A generalized plan for developing and installing a total management system.

The Development and Installation of a Total Management System

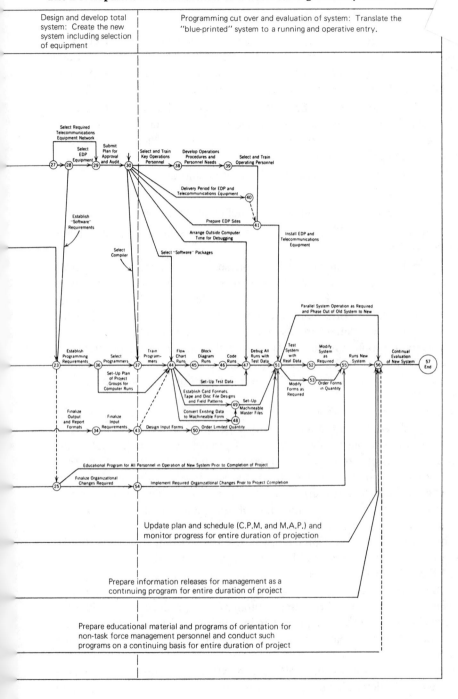

Design and develop total system: Create the new system including selection of equipment

Programming cut over and evaluation of system: Translate the "blue-printed" system to a running and operative entry.

Update plan and schedule (C.P.M. and M.A.P.) and monitor progress for entire duration of projection

Prepare information releases for management as a continuing program for entire duration of project

Prepare educational material and programs of orientation for non-task force management personnel and conduct such programs on a continuing basis for entire duration of project

Various techniques have been devised to assist in the collection of information required for problem definition. The best features of these techniques have been combined in a new system called START (systematic tabulation and analysis of requirements technique).

With this technique, the first step is to define the areas of decision (planning, controlling and operating) necessary to manage the enterprise. These areas of decision are determined from a study of the existing organization, operations and policies.

The problem definition phase, to this point, includes:

1. Establishment of operating objectives.

2. The selection and training of personnel to study the problem.

3. The use of START to analyze the present system and document the required system.

To complete the problem definition phase, management must establish the ultimate objectives of a new system so that parameters and responsive speeds can be determined. This procdure may lead to additions, deletions or revisions in the reports being produced which may, in turn, lead to the introduction of new data elements and the elimination of others.

Throughout problem definition and succeeding stages of the development and installation of a total management system, control should be maintained with the critical path method (CPM) and the multiple allocation procedure (MAP).

The critical path method is a management technique devised for the planning, scheduling and monitoring of large projects. The planning phase consists of drawing an arrow diagram of a project by assembling all of the project activities according to logical sequence and relationships. When time estimates are applied to each of the activities, it is possible to determine the longest (and therefore critical) path of activities. The arrow diagram thus provides easy visual assimilation of the plan and it functions as a working model which can be used to simulate project operations.

The multiple allocation procedure is used to allocate resources to the project and thereby place the plan on a calendar timetable. Resources are levelled to obtain the most economical schedule possible. MAP is applied after the logic of the arrow diagram has been thoroughly analyzed and refined. The allocation of resources automatically produces a schedule for the project. Then, when the project is in operation, data are collected and analyzed on a regular basis to be used in rescheduling or replanning when necessary.

Experience has shown that CPM and MAP used in combination enable management to determine the proper sequencing of activities and to allocate resources needed to perform these tasks in a coordinated fashion.

System design

After the problem has been defined, the next step is to design the new system. This phase should include:

1. The continued examination of various scientific techniques, such as transportation models, simulation, and inventory models, and the final selection of those to be used in the new system.

2. The development of consolidated reports and report formats for historical record keeping to satisfy business and governmental requirements.

3. The testing of selected mathematical techniques which use recent and past experience as the basis for predictions. This would include the generation of management reports that compare the predicted with the actual and offer management various alternatives and the results of each alternative.

4. The selection of a judicious (economic) combination of telecommunications equipment to transmit data over large distances and the establishment of electronic data processing centers to meet present and projected (future) needs.

5. The development of an organization which will program and install the total management system, operate the equipment, and make full and effective use of the results of such a system.

The underlying objective in these considerations should be the most economical combination of equipment and people in an industrial complex in order to provide effective management.

While it is easy to speak of using equipment, especially electronic data processing equipment, one should never become so sophisticated as to overlook the use of pencil and paper. A real distinction between an expert and an amateur in the field of management systems and in the application of electronic data processing equipment and techniques is the ability to distinguish between the proper and improper use of machinery to solve a problem. Quite often the best and most adequate solution involves a simple technique applied with pencil and paper (and sometimes an eraser).

Programming, cutover, evaluation, and modification

Programming, which begins the third phase in formulating a total management system, has been greatly simplified by the great strides made with program compilers, especially COBOL (common business oriented language). With this automatic programming technique a single English language statement can be used to generate many computer instructions— fully checked and integrated in a running program. And looking ahead, it is conceivable that START will lead to the development of a system-type compiler that will eliminate even the block diagramming required with COBOL.

The cutover operation is so interrelated with programming and system design that it is best illustrated by the arrow diagram (Figure 2). Cutover entails such things as the design of forms, conversion of data, installation of new equipment, and the like.

No equipment should be ordered until the system design phase is virtually complete. Delivery should be specified for an appropriate time during the cutover phase. All too often equipment is ordered before the system is designed and then delivered before it is needed. Considering that rentals range between $10,000 and $50,000 per month, a poor decision or an ill-timed delivery can be extremely expensive. In addition, the cost of programming, which often exceeds equipment rental fees, can cause total costs to skyrocket if the programming effort is not phased in properly with the installation of the new system.

Once the new system is in operation, *system evaluation and modification* begin. This phase should be a continuing effort which seeks to take advantage of new developments as they occur. The ultimate evaluation of the system's effectiveness is, of course, the financial statement.

Throughout the period of development and installation of a total management system, a planned program of training must be conducted to ensure the support of middle management for the program. If this is not done, even the best engineered system may never be completely effective.

Summary

This report is an outline of the basic steps, and an introduction to some of the problems, involved in creating a total management system. The task is not an easy one. It requires a great deal of work (particuarly on the part of line personnel), considerable and searching analysis, and some far reaching decisions. The installation of such a system will have tremendous impact. Properly implemented, it will undoubtedly result in increased profits. Moreover, the total management system is designed to put managing back into the hands of management by producing the information needed to "really manage." The opportunity and challenge are here. But if there is any hesitancy—to do the work, to make the decisions, to commit the necessary funds—then there is no point in even starting.

NOTE

1. *How to read an arrow diagram.* Each job or activity in a project is represented by an arrow. Work flows from the tail of an arrow to the head, but the length of the arrow and the direction in which it points are immaterial. Dotted arrows do not represent real activities but are used to maintain logical relationships. The junction points of arrows are called events; they are numbered so that the tail of an arrow has a number smaller than the head. Events represent points in time as opposed to arrows which represent activities that consume time. The event also indicates the point in time when all preceding activities have been completed and succeeding activities can start.

15. Designing Management Systems*

Richard A. Johnson, Fremont E. Kast and James E. Rosenzweig

The vast growth in size, complexity, and diversity of operations of the modern business organization has made the managerial function exceedingly difficult, but even more essential to the success of the enterprise.

During the past few years there have been many new concepts advanced for improving management; e.g., organization theory, decision theory, planning theory, and the behavioral theory of the firm. Each of these philosophies has helped to sharpen management skills; however, there is still a need for an operative theory of management—a theory which provides a conceptual framework of better business design and operation. It is our contention that today's large-scale business enterprise could apply the systems concepts to meet the growing complexities and proliferation of operations, for systems theory provides a conceptual framework within which the manager can integrate his operations effectively.

We are concerned here with design—the key activity in implementing the systems concept. This function is the means for establishing subsystems and larger systems into a composite, integrated whole. However, for completeness of presentation we will review general systems concepts briefly. Specifically, we will:

- Show the relationship between the systems concept and managing,
- Set forth a practical model using the systems concept,

*SOURCE: *The Business Quarterly* (Summer, 1964), pp. 59-65. Reprinted by permission of *The Business Quarterly*.

- Discuss the scope of the design function,
- Introduce flow concepts in systems design,
- Discuss systems design as the implementation of the systems concept and
- Appraise some of the constraints on the design function.

Systems concepts and management

A system is "an organized or complex whole; an assemblage or combination of things or parts forming a complex or unitary whole." The term system covers an extremely broad spectrum of concepts. For example, we have mountain systems, river systems, and the solor system as part of our physical surroundings. The body itself is a complex organism including the skeletal system, the circulatory system, and the nervous system. We come into daily contact with such phenomena as transportation systems, communication systems (telephone, telegraph, etc.), and economic systems.

The systems concept is a useful way of thinking about the job of managing. It provides a framework for visualizing internal and external environmental factors as an integrated whole. It allows recognition of the proper place within which businessmen must operate are necessarily complex. However, management via systems concepts fosters a way of thinking which, on the one hand, helps to dissolve some of the complexity and, on the other hand, helps the manager recognize the nature of the complex problems and thereby operate within the perceived environment. It is important to recognize the integrated nature of specific systems, including the fact that each system has both inputs and outputs and can be viewed as a self-contained unit. But it is also important to recognize that business systems are a part of larger systems—possibly industry-wide, or including several, perhaps many, companies and/or industries, or even society as a whole.[1]

The theory of systems is not new, for much of it has been developed and used in the natural sciences for many years. Further, it is being used to some degree in business. For example, systems theory is used in administering certain military programs where specification and time requirements are critical, and in some single-venture programs, e.g., construction projects. There is no reason, however, why this concept is not equally applicable to appliance manufacturing, retailing, or banking.

A model of the systems concept

Traditionally, business firms have not been structured to utilize the systems concept. In adjusting the typical business structure to fit within the

framework of management by systems, certain organizational changes will
be required. The following Model illustrates *one* arrangement which would
implement the systems concept. We do not imply that this Model is the
most effective arrangement only that it illustrates the use of "systems thinking" in managing a business.

Referring to Exhibit I, a master planning council engages in high-level
design activity and establishes guidelines for the entire organization. This
council would make decisions relative to the products or services the company supplied. Further, it would establish the limits of an operating
program, decide on general policy matters relative to the design of operating
systems and select the director for each new product. New-project decisions

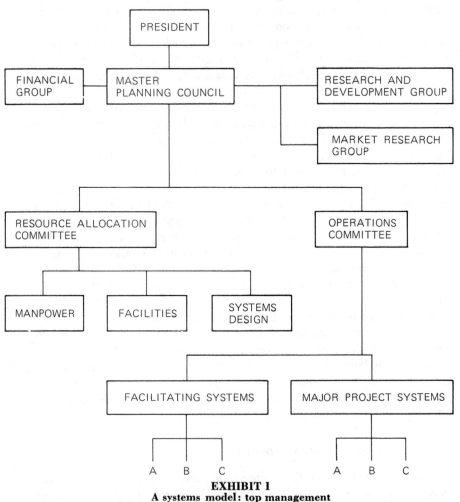

EXHIBIT I
A systems model: top management

would be made with the assistance and advice of the product research and deveolpment, market research, and financial groups.

Within that framework, design activity is carried on by the resource-allocation planning group—a group which combines manpower and facilities to form working systems designed to accomplish given objectives. In both facilitating systems[2] and major project systems, additional design activity—systems review—is necessary to maintain working systems on a current basis.

The master planning council must have a definite approach to developing premises which serve as the basis for systems design. Meaningful information must be translated from environmental data on such questions as economic activity, political developments, and social trends. It is important that top management develop clear-cut systems of such information flow which will provide inputs for planning and decision making. In most companies such systems are left to chance, or at best, periodic review.

Scope of the design function

Design means to "mark-out, designate, or indicate." It includes combining features or details and often calls for preparation of preliminary sketches or plans. The design function is important in establishing a relationship between the various stages or phases of a system, linking them together, and outlining the composite whole. For business systems the design function includes the arrangement of physical facilities for production and auxiliary activities. It also covers the arrangement of people and communication networks established to provide information concerning the process.

When establishing a new business operation, the design function seems fairly straightforward. However, the scope of systems design also covers the function of "redesign," assessing existing systems with an eye toward change. This activity has received considerable attention over the years under headings such as systems and procedures, work simplification, systems analysis, or systems engineering. Of these terms, *work simplification* seems to have the narrowest connotation in that it applies primarily to simple man-machine operations or clerical activity. However, as with most tools and techniques, its practitioners have proclaimed its applicability to a wide range of problems. In any case, it applies to existing systems rather than to the establishment of new systems.

Systems and procedures work has been pointed up as an all-encompassing activity, covering many facets of the business operation. However, implicitly it seems limited to the office, the flow of paper work, and the design of forms. Since the advent of electromechanical equipment, systems and procedures activity has included the designing and programming of data-processing systems. Unfortunately, EDP has been overemphasized in recent years to the exclusion of broader concepts of systems design. The specific aspects of programming, form design, and routing of paper work—as a part of the information-decision system—should be fitted into the overall systems design.

Another term used in describing this general sphere of activity is systems analysis. It also is focused on existing systems rather than on the design of new systems. Systems analysis often has a connotation of application primarily to information flow in the office and does not seem as applicable to a production or processing environment. This is not to say that it is not feasible; rather, most of the literature on the subject deals with information-processing problems.

Systems engineering implies the creation of systems as well as the analysis of existing systems. Systems engineering sometimes is assumed to deal only with physical components; that is, it deals with the integration of components and subcomponents into a total product such as a computer or missile. Using the definition of enginering as "the art and science by which the properties of matter and the sources of power in nature are made useful to man in structures, machines, and manufactured products," there is systems implication. Moreover, systems engineering can be defined as "making useful an array of components designed to accomplish a particular objective according to plan." This approach implies the interaction of more than equipment. It suggests the development of a man-machine system which could function as a task-oriented assemblage. Systems engineering comes closest to implying design activity. In many cases the systems-engineering function involves "starting from scratch" to develop subsystems, larger systems, and a composite whole.

Flow concepts in design

One general approach to systems design involves identification of material, energy, and information flow. These three elements are part of every system and subsystem. Consideration of them plus the use of flow concepts facilitates thinking about systems of systems.

Material

The material aspects of any system include both the facilities involved and the raw material, if any, which flows through the process. A system must be designed to ensure the *acquisition* of raw materials and/or components necessary for processing into finished products. The systems design would include identification or transportation means required to move the raw material to the processing location.

The processing operation needs to be designed in terms of constructing new facilities or realigning existing facilities. Questions of plant layout and materials-handling equipment would be a vital part of the systems-design function for in-plant processing and in-plant material flows. Industrial engineers have considered problems of this nature for many years and have developed detailed methods and techniques for optimizing layout and material handling. The trend toward automation has been evident in many material-processing operations.

Much attention also has been focused on distribution of finished goods. Where items become raw material or components in additional processing operations, the distribution problem is often straightforward. In such cases the material flow would be considered part of the flow of raw materials for a subsequent processing operation. Physical-distribution management, for items moving from producer to ultimate consumer, can be a much more difficult problem. In this case, channels of distribution vary from direct producer to consumer to a myriad of combinations of middlemen. Inventory management, at various points along the distribution channel, must be considered, as well as modes of transportation. In many cases transportation costs have been isolated for analysis without reference to the impact of such decisions on stocks of material in the pipeline. Systems design, in this sphere, would concern itself with identifying the flow of materials and with the development of an explicit network of distribution, recognizing *all* the costs involved—handling, inventory, and transportation costs. Increased effort is being devoted to the design of explicit material-flow systems from a raw-material stage through the production process and to the final consumer.[3]

Whenever the operation in question involves the flow and processing of material, appropriate systems can be designed. For business operations such as insurance companies or other commercial institutions, there may be no flow of material *per se*. Rather, the material in these systems is represented by the facilities and equipment involved. Regardless of whether there is any material flow, all business operations, whether processing a product or service, contain elements of energy and information.

Energy

Some source of energy is present in any operating system. It may be electricity obtained from available sources or generated by a firm's own power plant. The process may require natural gas, petroleum, coal or other fuel for production. A business usually requires electrical energy for operating facilitating systems, if not for the main processing operation itself.

Another obvious source of energy is people. Both physical and mental energy are required to operate business systems. People represent a renewable source of energy, at least for the short run. As an energy source, people are quite variable as individuals. However, *in toto*, the group represents a reasonably stable source of energy for the system.

Electricity, natural gas, or petroleum can be described in terms of flow concepts. Energy flows are under continual inspection by systems designers. However, they are concerned primarily with the energy or power system itself, not the integration of the energy system with other subsystems and the whole. It is somewhat more difficult to visualize people, or the work force, in terms of flow concepts. However, in a very real sense, this is entirely appropriate. There may be a continual flow of workers in terms of shifts where 24-hour, 7-day weeks are scheduled. Even for 5-day, 40-hour weeks there is a systematic flow of worker energy into the operation. In a larger sense, a business operation maintains a flow of worker energy throughout its life—from the recruiting, hiring, and orientation stages, all the way to retirement. Thus all energy can be considered as a flow process both in and of itself and as a part of other systems.

Information

Another basic element in any system is information. It facilitates interrelationships among subsystems and provides the linkage necessary to develop systems of systems. Information flow may be developed to flow along with the routing of material. Requisitions, orders, bills of lading, packing slips, receiving information, inspection reports, accounts payable, and cheques might represent the information flow connected with the acquisition of raw material. The information flow appropriate to production control is another example. In this case production instructions, material requirements, processing information, inspection requirements, routing, and scheduling would be developed from engineering drawings and/or other specifications. The information would flow through the system along with the material necessary to accomplish the planned objectives.

The accounting system requires a flow of information toward the development of income statements and balance sheets for tax purposes or stockholder reports or both. While many data-processing systems have developed on the basis of periodic batch processing, more and more systems are being developed which call for flow concepts approximating real-time activity; that is, the action or activity to be considered is recorded at the time it happens and action is taken at that time.

Information flow is the primary focus of attention for systems designers in many cases. If manufacturing facilities are fixed and if layout requirements are rigid, then the only variables remaining are raw materials (which may be uniform), energy (in the form of power and/or people), and information (in the form of plans and instructions). Systems design in such cases must concentrate on the arrangement of people and the use of information flow to optimize decision making within the system under observation. For many other systems where manufacturing and material flow are not present—service, commercial, and many governmental organizations—the flow of information is the critical element. Information must flow to key decision points where action is taken with regard to a service to be performed by the organization in question. In such cases the system can be defined primarily on the basis of the flow of information to appropriate decision points. Subsystems can be identified on the basis, and they in turn can be interrelated to define the total system.

Unfortunately, most present-day systems of this nature have been established on the basis of people relationships and organization charts without regard for project systems or task-oriented groups. In many cases these organizations function primarily on the basis of informal relationships and informal communications systems. One of the main points in systems design is the necessity of recognizing the natural relationships of informal subsystems in developing a total system. It is by means of these flow concepts that the total system can be conceptualized as a system of systems. Particular emphasis will be placed on the design of information-decision systems. Such systems are integral parts of any operating system, whether it is designed to yield a product or service.

Integrating flow concepts

Basic to the theory of systems is the premise that given certain inputs, the processor will give certain outputs or operate within established limits. However, the business firm, as a whole, is not a structured or predictable system. Its equilibrium cannot be determined by equation, and it will change, within limits, as the components of the system are rearranged or as the inputs are reallocated.

In more advanced form, a system will include some means of control, i.e., a sensor for measuring output or related characteristics, a means of comparing the measurement with a standard, and an activating group to adjust inputs to correct the indicated deficiencies. The objective is to control variables so the system will tend to stabilize near the ideal equilibrium point. The objective is possible only if the ideal standard can be determined and if the operating values can be measured. A complete system, including control, is illustrated in Exhibit II.

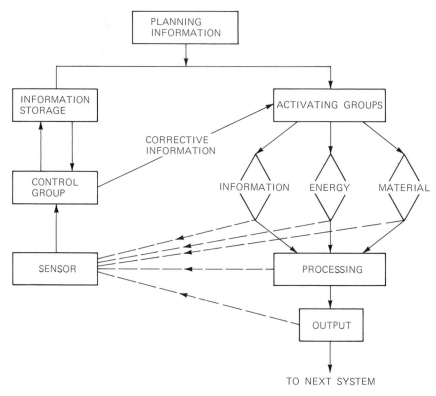

EXHIBIT II
An operating system

It shows the flow of planning information as it releases resources of materials, energy, and processing information. A record of the plan is stored where it can be used as a standard for control purposes. The resources are released by an activating group. For example, detailed schedules are planned (processing information), workers are assigned to specific tasks (energy), and the necessary raw materials or purchased parts are provided (materials). The combination of these inputs into the system results in the performance of a task (processing), and output is produced.

Sensory devices are placed at strategic points in the system flow to measure performance or output. These measurements are fed back to a control group, and this information is compared with the standard. As significant deviations from plan are recognized, information to correct the situation is released to the activating group, which in turn will change the release of resources or information, energy, or materials.

Designing operating systems

Operating systems have one thing in common: they should all use a common language for communicating among themselves and with higher levels. In addition, of course, each system designed should be structured in consideration of company-wide policies. Other than these limts, each operating system can be created to meet the specific requirements of its own product or service.

The operating system is structured to (1) direct its own inputs, (2) control its own operation, and (3) review and revise its own system design as required. Input is furnished by three different groups: technical information is generated as input into the processing system, and in addition, technical information is the basis for originating processing information. Both technical and processing information are used by the material input system to determine and supply materials for processing. The operating system has its own control unit, which measures the inputs and outputs of system. However, corrective action, when necessary, would be activated by input allocation.

This model of an operating system can be related to any business situation. For example, if it represents a system to produce television sets, the technical information would refer to the design of the product, processing information would include the plan of manufacture and schedule, and the material input would pertain to the raw materials and purchased parts used in the processing. These inputs of information and material would be processed and become output. Process control would measure the output in comparison with the standard (information storage) obtained from input allocation and issue corrective information whenever the system failed to function according to plan. The design of the system would be reviewed continually, and the components rearranged or replaced when these changes would improve operating efficiency.

A systems-review function is an integral part of each project system. The system as a whole should be reviewed periodically by means of a thoroughgoing analysis and synthesis of the system and its components. The system should be broken down into its individual subsystems, and each of these should be evaluated in terms of the likelihood of continuing efficiency. Adjustments can be made on the basis of the results of such analysis. Then a process of synthesis must take place in order to restructure an integrated whole.

Why is it that subsystems and/or project systems must be reviewed and adjusted continually? One obvious reason was mentioned above; system requirements change over a period of time, and hence the system must be redesigned in the light of evolutionary trends. Static systems design goes out of date almost immediately. In fact, the battle cry of some systems analysts and designers is, "If it works, it must be obsolete!" As a particular project progresses through its life cycle, the product mission may change, as may other environmental or competitive conditions. Organizational adjustments may be required, or technological advancements may allow improvements in handling of either material or information flow.

Some systems are built around individuals within an organization. If identification of decision points is based on strong or dominant personalities, the information-decision system may be disrupted completely whenever key-personnel changes are made. Hence systems must be redesigned in order to accommodate the changes in managerial personnel.

The original allocation of resources may have been temporary in the sense of availability of necessary elements either internally or externally. Make-shift systems have a way of perpetuating themselves regardless of inefficiencies. It is important to reappraise the situation otfen enough to make sure that such temporary arrangements are revised when conditions allow.

Another typical problem is the tendency toward empire building, the accumulation of more than enough material, manpower, and facilities to accomplish given objectives. The project manager must resist the tendency towards bigness for the sake of prestige or status. A semi-detached, hopefully objective systems-review group can help nurture such a point of view.

Continuing attention must be devoted to systems review and the implementation of proposed changes. Follow-up is necessary because of the seemingly inherent resistance to change on the part of people involved in the system. Unless such resistance can be overcome, poor systems may be prolonged. Once the atmosphere is established for continual analysis and review, implementation of change becomes progressively easier.

Constraints on the design function

In order to place the systems-design function in proper perspective it is important to consider the various constraints on this activity. Policy decisions on the part of the master planning council not only provide guidelines for systems design at lower levels, they also provide boundaries. If top management does not embrace the systems concept as a managerial philosophy, systems design cannot be implemented. The proper atmosphere must be created at all levels in order for this approach to be utilized.

Other limiting factors include the amounts and kinds of facilities available as well as the work force and its skill mix. Elaborate and sophisticated systems designs might be forthcoming which could not be implemented because of lack of facilities and/or manpower. However, we suggest that the systems-design group start with designs for systems that are needed rather than those which obviously can be implemented. The organization will progress if it is forced to strain toward goals and objectives. If the design proves too much of a "cloud nine" approach, the system can always be scaled back to meet existing resources.

The resource-allocation council places constraints on the system-review function in terms of policy decisions with regard to allocation of the resources between major projects systems and facilitating systems. It may be that systems analysts within major project systems have designed optimal arrangements for their own operation without regard to other project systems. The resource-allocation planning group may decide that certain facilitating systems common to several or all project systems should be set up to serve the entire group. Thus policy decisions throughout the total system provide constraints within which systems designers must operate.

Along with policy decisions and equipment and facility limitations, another constraint which must be taken into consideration by systems designers is people. The remark "It would be a great system if it weren't for the people involved" is appropriate here. Problems of resistance to change or of out-and-out antagonism are evident throughout the literature describing impacts of automation and electronic data processing. Similar reaction is often evident when designing information decision systems which call for realignment of people and equipment according to the systems concept. These human factors are important variables in systems design and must be given consideration.

Conclusion

Systems design is the key activity in implementing the systems concept. This function provides an overall framework by establishing subsystems, larger systems, and a composite, integrated whole.

We cannot overemphasize the fact that, first and foremost, the systems concept is a frame of mind. Management must be receptive to this approach and develop a philosophy in which planning, organizing, controlling, and communication are accomplished in terms of subsystems integrated into a composite whole. Once there is acceptance of the systems concept and the feasibility of organizing on the basis of a master planning council, a resource-allocation planning group, and an operations planning group (with facilitating and project systems reporting to it), the systems-design function can be carried out in a progressive atmosphere. The atmosphere created is all-important; it fosters creativity and innovation on the part of systems designers.

NOTES

1. For a more comprehensive discussion of these concepts see R. A. Johnson, F. E. Kast, and J. E. Rosenzweig, *The Theory and Management of Systems,* McGraw-Hill Book Company, Inc., New York, 1963.
2. Facilitating systems are those designed to serve major projects systems, e.g., a computer center.
3. See Stanley H. Brewer and J. Rosenzweig, "Rhochrematics and Organization Adjustments," *California Management Review,* Spring, 1961, pp. 52-71.

16. A Systems Approach to Management Development*

Ralph J. Brown

Progressive managers are deeply involved in long-range strategic planning. They establish marketing forecasts for five to ten years in the future, and they determine financial and logistic requirements for their long-range plan. But sooner or later arises the question: who will implement and manage the plan?

When managerial requirements are matched against the company program, a gap often appears: a gap between the requirements and the company's capability of meeting them internally.

Statistically, this gap was caused by the drop in birth rate during the depression years; there are not enough potential managers born in the early 1930s to meet current demand. There are enough capable internal managers in their early and mid-fifties, but they will be retiring within the span of the ten-year plan. There are plenty of young college graduates with keen technical abilities, but they have limited managerial competence. And managers with 25 to 30 years of experience may not be able to keep pace with the tremendous growth of technology, particularly the technology of the computer and sophisticated management information systems.

In an attempt to solve the problem, development activities have been accelerated. Senior managers are finding themselves back on campus or in numerous lengthy seminars. The college graduates are carefully screened

*SOURCE: *Financial Executive* (April, 1970), pp. 21-25. Reprinted by permission of the publisher.

during their first few years of employment, and the better performers are being placed on the "fast track." Training and development specialists are diligently developing new techniques and appropriate methods to fill the gaps of future managerial needs.

In spite of the abounding activity in the field of management development, the subject is both confusing and frustrating to the majority of line or operating managers. They accept their own responsibility to provide suitable replacements, yet they usually profess a lack of understanding of staff activities in training replacements. In fact, they find it difficult to define a suitable plan of action of their own. They admittedly search for clear, definitive policy statements and programs, but are all too often faced with piece-meal activities of good intent but minimal results.

The interrelation of staff and operations departments in planning and implementing management development activities is a universal problem. The line manager is too busy to give required attention to training problems. He is usually satisfied with allowing a staff specialist to take over the job. An integrated systems approach, as well as sound management development principles, is needed to give impetus to change and to provide the needed direction in devloping the managers of tomorrow.

To illustrate how an integrated management development system operates, I would like to describe the experience of a large manufacturing division of a medium size diversified corporation located in the Midwest.

Training steadily improved

Before describing the development of the system in the division, it might be helpful to give some background information.

The division has a total volume of approximately $150 million with a total employment of 2,000 people.

Following the end of World War II, the division gave prime attention to training managers required for an expansion of manufacturing facilities. The division management's support of the training resulted in an acceleration of activity during the early and mid-fifties. The training was very professional, but was inclined toward a shot-gun approach rather than toward an identification of individual needs. For example, every manager in the division attended a four-week managemnt program.

Although there was undoubtedly wasted motion in such an approach, the principle that "management is the art of getting things done through people" become well established throughout the division. Management responsibility for development of subordinates was crystal clear. Unfortunately, however, the responsibility for identifying and providing training needs remained a staff activity. As a result of this dependency on staff, line management did little to evaluate the result of the training efforts.

During the late fifties and early sixties, loss of key people through corporate expansion and normal turnover had depleted the number of managers who had been trained earlier. However, the value and importance of training and development was still well recognized within the division.

The recession of 1960-61 created a unique problem for the division. A drastic drop in profits forced a reduction of salaried personnel, accompanied by an emphasis on the part of all management for increased earnings. During this period, it became increasingly evident that some change in the management development policy was required. There was, by necessity, a conversion to a more rifle-like approach than had been prevalent during the earlier years.

The first evidence of actual change in approach was a planned policy shift to result-oriented appraisals (ROA) from the group appraisals which had been procedural for six to seven years. Acceptance of a management-by-objectives program quickly followed this shift to provide a more objective evaluation of performance. The objectives were, of course, purposefully dovetailed with result-oriented appraisals. Although the means for improved assessment of managerial performance were then present, managers were still willing to relinquish to staff departments the responsibility for developing subordinates.

As the results of result-oriented appraisals were documented and analyzed over the next few years, tremendous gaps in managerial talent and potential for long-range plans became all too apparent. Results of lack of follow-up on training and development activity became obvious.

A program for identifying people suitable for promotion was adopted, along with accelerated development activities for those people so identified. But still the lack of managerial potential or reserve remained insurmountable. Segmented department managers recognized the problem, but they were without any integrated method to deal with the complexities of either identifying or developing candidates.

At this point a recommendation was made to consider a systems approach to management development. The environment for accepting this proposal had been developing for several years. In 1964, an organization change had coupled management information systems with the personnel function into an administration division. The MIS group for several years had been actively involved in the design and implementation of what at that time was called a total management information system centered around order processing and scheduling. This program, by necessity, involved operational management, and managers' participation was evident at every level in the division. Because the managers were so involved in the MIS program, they readily accepted a systems approach to management development. They understood the feasibility and proposed efficiencies of a systems approach, and that a management development system would require the necessary inputs, a transformation element, and outputs. The chief agent of the transformation element was, of course, to be the operational manager. Since such a system gets its inputs from other operational systems, it could not exist in isolation. All interrelated systems had the same goal—the profitability and growth of the division.

Feedback is essential to optimize efficiency in an integrated system. The purpose of feedback is to return some of the output as input. Without this

EXHIBIT 1

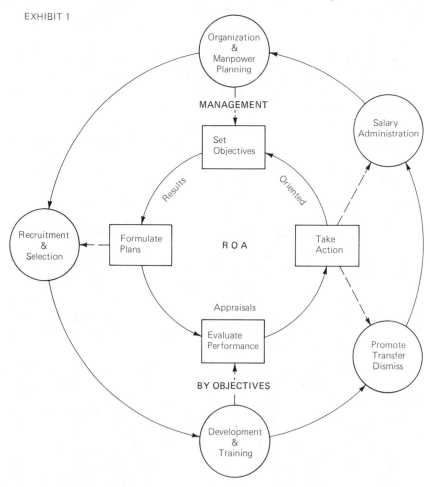

relationship, progress toward an identified goal cannot be identified. With it, however, the manager has the opportunity to increase the efficiency of his system. Since part of the output is returned as input, there has to be some way of measuring output. Thus, in the integrated management development system, if the operating manager does not make an effective transformation of his inputs, the output—the supply of needed managers for the future—can never become a reality.

The systems approach to management development was pursued in the typical manner with the design of related subsystems with appropriate inputs—outputs. The subsystems initially involved management by objectives and result-oriented appraisals activities. As outlined in Exhibit I, management by objectives and result-oriented appraisals relate setting objectives, formulating plans, evaluating performance, and taking action. In addition to the four main inputs/outputs, there was a related peripheral system for organization and manpower planning, recruitment and selection, promotion, transfer and dismissal, salary administration, and training and development. The inputs and outputs of the secondary field were further refined as an integral part of the management development system. Individual activities in salary administration, organization planning, development and training, etc. were defined, and the information flow, inputs—outputs, and feedback circuitry were designed as in Exhibit II.

Existing control reports for each segment of the subsystems were then documented to make management aware that feedback data was available for analyzing variances and auditing results. Some additional operating control reports were devised where information had not before been readily available. Some of the information was on an annual basis, such as revised position descriptions, job evaluations, salary ranges, and retirement projections. Some was available in the normal personnel reports on a monthly basis. Where there was no regular reporting, the method of requesting special reports through administration was clarified. The recent redesign of the personnel subsystem and allocation of the information to a basic computer data file were tremendously helpful in providing control data.

An administration team

Development of several improved approaches in some segments of the system helped to increase interest in the systems approach and to provide better input resources. In the organization planning area where organization changes occurred, an administration team was assigned, when possible, to assist the operating manager in defining the job for maximum efficiency and increased worker satisfaction and performance. The administration

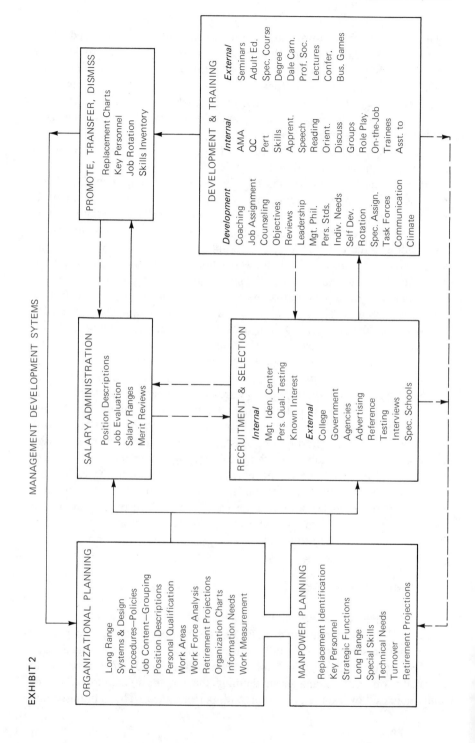

EXHIBIT 2

MANAGEMENT DEVELOPMENT SYTEMS

PROMOTE, TRANSFER, DISMISS
Replacement Charts
Key Personnel
Job Rotation
Skills Inventory

DEVELOPMENT & TRAINING

Development	Internal	External
Coaching	AMA	Seminars
Job Assignment	QC	Adult Ed.
Counseling	Pert	Spec. Course
Objectives	Skills	Degree
Reviews	Apprent.	Dale Carn.
Leadership	Speech	Prof. Soc.
Mgt. Phil.	Reading	Lectures
Pers. Stds.	Orient.	Confer.
Indiv. Needs	Discuss	Bus. Games
Self Dev.	Groups	
Rotation	Role Play	
Spec. Assign.	On-the-Job	
Task Forces	Trainees	
Communication	Asst. to	
Climate		

SALARY ADMINISTRATION
Position Descriptions
Job Evaluation
Salary Ranges
Merit Reviews

RECRUITMENT & SELECTION

Internal
Mgt. Iden. Center
Pers. Qual. Testing
Known Interest

External
College
Government
Agencies
Advertising
Reference
Testing
Interviews
Spec. Schools

ORGANIZATIONAL PLANNING
Long Range
Systems & Design
Procedures—Policies
Job Content—Grouping
Position Descriptions
Personal Qualification
Work Areas
Work Force Analysis
Retirement Projections
Organization Charts
Information Needs
Work Measurement

MANPOWER PLANNING
Replacement Identification
Key Personnel
Strategic Functions
Long Range
Special Skills
Technical Needs
Turnover
Retirement Projections

team consisted of a personal analyst and a systems analyst. The personnel analyst was responsible for job content, job interest, training needs, motivation, salary ranges, safety, personal qualifications, selection criteria, union coordination, and work area. The systems analyst was responsible for systems design, information flow, input-output requirements, computer application, business logic instructional sheets, procedure requirements, numerical statements, and work measurement. The administration team was able to combine technical disciplines and to provide the department manager with information and tools which had not been integrated before. It also had the effect of reminding the manager to consider all the inter-related inputs and outputs in the management development system.

In the area of recruitment and selection, a management identification and development center was established. The purpose of the center was to establish an assessment system for the early identification and evaluation of characteristics required for managerial success. The assessment system concept had been used for some time by several larger companies, such as American Telephone and Telegraph. Their assessment centers, which were quite sophisticated, were scheduled for approximately a week's duration. Not being able to afford the expense of this amount of time, the division designed and implemented a more condensed version. A list of 16 managerial characteristics was carefully compiled to gauge supervisory potential of any hourly and salaried employees who requested an evaluation. There was a real need in the overall management development system for early identification of supervisory capability as well as a means of having all employees feel that their individual skills and abilities could be recognized.

The center was made up of a six-man team consisting of a division management development manager, who was responsible for coordination of the program, one assessor from the personnel department, and four other assessors from production or engineering. Each assessor was thoroughly trained in tools utilized in the center. The tools consisted of ten psychometric devices and observable behavior techniques. The six assessors spent ten hours in a single day observing and evaluating a group of ten candidates as they completed the carefully planned activities of the center. The following morning, the assessors went over the performance observed the previous day and rated the participants on each of the 16 managerial characteristics and their overall potential as supervisors. A follow-up interview was then held with each participant by qualified counselors to discuss the results of the assessment center. A final report containing specific recommendations for the development of the employee was communicated to his direct supervisor and the pesronal department.

Employees and management alike received the management identification and development center enthusiastically. The center revealed a number of overlooked employees with real potential and also identified significant individual remedial training needs in the supervisory ranks. Of equal importance, it illustrates the importance of the manager as the transformation agent in the overall system and the value of feedback information in effective management development.

As a final step in the design of the new system, policy and procedures related to the individual segments were revised, and new procedures were written where required.

Guidelines developed

With the full support of the general manager, a communication program was then activated through all levels of management to describe the system. It stated clearly that management development was a basic ingredient in managing the business. It clarified the management-by-objective cycle and established the importance of participative development of managerial objectives.

During this communication period, it became clear to division executives that, although individual procedures were well understood, there was a real need for some basic or overall management development guidelines to assist operational managers in their implementation of the system. To satisfy this need, the following basic guidelines were developed by the administration division and integrated with the system:

- All development is self-development.
- Development activities should be designated for the individual.
- Development is a line responsibility.
- Determination of development demands the supervisor's perception and understanding the needs of the individual.
- Development requires appropriate action and controls through feedback of results obtained.
- Development is a long and continuous process.
- Company atmosphere is a vital factor in development. This atmosphere includes the organization structure, the people both present and planned, and the boss and his attitudes. All of these are in an interdependent system and are in a constant state of change.
- Developing managerial competence occurs on the job.
- Internal group instruction and external training supplement and motivate growth on the job.
- A manager cannot develop others without developing himself.

As in any case history, there remains the question of how successfully the program achieved desired results. Although time alone can test the success of the program, there was considerable immediate evidence which indicated that some momentum had been generated in the desired direction. Result-oriented appraisals were completed on schedule, and development activities planned for the ensuing year were improved. Managerial objective-setting became sharper. The five-year strategic plan gave considerable attention to realistic manpower planning for the first time. The most significant factor, however, was that managers and supervisors at all levels were planning and carrying through training and development activities on their own and using staff only on an advisory basis.

17. Systems Analyst Training: Objectives and Comment*

Joel E. Ross

"After growing wildly for years, the field of computing now appears to be approaching its infancy."[1] This conclusion by the president's Science Advisory Committee fairly represents what can be expected regarding the growth of the computer industry and the need for skilled people to utilize the computer to something approaching its potential. It is generally recognized that the bottleneck to greater utilization is not improved hardware but properly trained persons who can design better applications: qualified systems analysts.

The need for properly trained systems analysts can only be described as enormous. Despite the difficulties of forecasting this need to any degree of precision, some estimate can be made. The American Federation of Information Processing Societies (AFIPS) estimates that there were about 60,000 systems analysts in 1965 and that 200,000 will be needed in 1970. One report of the federal government estimates that by 1970, more than 500,000 persons will need initial or updated training in systems analysis and related subject matter.[2] This latter estimate includes subject matter specialists and related occupations (e.g., methods analysts) needing some training in systems analysis.

In 1967 the federal government undertook to determine the need for

*SOURCE: *Journal of Systems Management* (February, 1969), pp. 7-9. Reprinted by permission of the publisher.

and the content of training for systems analysts in both industry and government. More than 40 national leaders from industry, education and government assembled in Washington for week-long workshops on the topic. The author was principal consultant to this effort and editor of the proceedings.[3] The results are summarized in this article.

What is the analyst's job?

The tasks of a systems analyst differ from industry to industry. Generally speaking, however, there is sufficient agreement on a broad set of duties. For this purpose we can adopt the recently defined position description published by the United States Civil Service Commission, a description representing the duties of about 18,000 government analysts.

> Computer Systems Analysts develop basic plans or "computer applications" by which subject-matter processes can be organized and accomplished by computer methods. They require a comprehensive understanding and analysis of subject-matter work processes, actions, criteria, as well as supporting controls, reports, documentation, etc., involved in the function to be automated. Also essential is the ability to devise procedures, to develop methods for generating and processing data, and to integrate these data into processing systems and plans. Typically, specific assignments may include: Feasibility or "profitability" studies; the development of detailed systems logic charts and diagrams; the development of data reduction and coding instructions, dictionaries, data banks, and the like. In addition, these positions require a substantial knowledge of computer capabilities and processes, and a basic understanding of programming principles and methods. They analyze and organize subject-matter work processes and functions so that they can be converted into workable computer programs and routines. Furthermore, systems analysts must be able to foresee some of the specific problems posed in the subsequent programming processes required, as well as some of the possible solutions to such problems.

Educators, industry and government ADP executives, and systems analysts generally agree that the above description fairly represents the job of a systems analyst. Yet, some executives feel that the depth of skills inferred by the position is greater than the supply of personnel who can be hired or retained in this category. Typical of this feeling was the comment that "this description is for a much heavier person . . . consequently, persons doing systems work are frequently occupying other positions and higher paying jobs."

ADP executives from both government and industry appeared to lean away from the technical description and more to the "logical problem solver and designer" approach as expressed in these typical comments regarding what was expected of an analyst:

- Understand the intellectual tools capable of being used to look at the relationships between complex activities.
- Probe and evaluate objectives. Determine best methods for achievement. Design systems to accomplish and follow up to assure conformance.
- Find the simplest ways of taking each objective in implementing a program and devising the methods and procedures that would attain the end result forecast.
- Plan, fact-find, analyze, determine findings, develop general systems design and documentation and oversee implementation.
- Design workable problem solutions for users.
- Plan and design information systems in cooperation with various user groups in an organization. Become deeply involved in implementation.
- Take a logical approach to improvement of the system of the organization.

Whatever the job of the systems analyst, it is clear that he is required to be a broad-gauged individual who must bring considerable technical and personal talent to the organization.

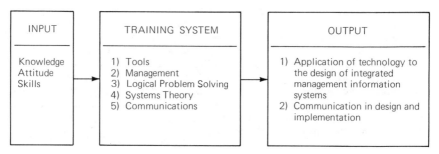

Objectives of training

It is axiomatic that the teaching or learning process be related to an objective—some predetermined body of knowledge that should be transmitted or some behavioral change that should be undergone by the learner. It is of little use to teach, for example, systems theory to an analyst unless it results in application or improvement of some kind.

If the foregoing job description is taken as the objective of training, it becomes clear that something is missing. This "something" can be related to the need for the analyst to: (a) communicate, and (b) think like a manager in designing systems for management uses. Summarizing this widely held view by top ADP executives are typical comments such as these:

- Should be trained to use ADP as a management tool.
- Bridge gap between problem desk (input) and machine configuration (output).
  - Must know how to solve problems on the computer.
  - The analyst must know salesmanship and communication.
  - He must be a diplomat—know when *not* to use a computer.
  - Must understand input/output use of information—not throughput.

The objectives could be summarized in terms of input, output, and the system may be depicted as shown above.

Content of the training program

A remarkable degree of agreement existed among educators and ADP executives regarding the structure and content of the total training program curriculum for the systems analyst. The program is listed here:

Analysis and design concepts

I. Problem solving

The theory and practice of logic, decision making and creative thinking. The use of these and other problem-solving principles in the analysis and design of systems.

II. Organization principles

Classical and contemporary principles of organization design and analysis. An understanding of the structure, decision centers, information flow and other organizational considerations in systems design.

III. Management

The basic functions of management, with special emphasis on planning and controlling through information systems. Consideration and understanding of facilitating the management process with systems.

IV. Systems planning

Determining systems objectives and planning time, cost and resource allocations. Design proposals. PERT/CPM input/output considerations.

V. Systems theory

Theory of information systems operation and design. Control theory. Integrated and total systems concepts. Planning and control through information feedback systems.

VI. Systems evaluation

Measuring efficiency against goals. Input/output review and review of objectives.

VII. Human interaction in systems

Gaining acceptance and "selling" ADP. The impact of automation on personnel. Getting cooperation. Interpersonal relationships. Applied psychology.

VIII. Quantitative techniques in systems design

Application of operations research and other management science techniques. Formulation of decision rules. Simulation and modeling.

Analysis and design techniques

Systems planning

Network analysis technique for logical structuring of planning.
Preliminary systems survey.
The feasibility study.
The cost evaluation and analysis.
Analysis of time requirements.
Planning quality elements of the system.

Systems analysis and design

Analytical techniques and documentation (work measurement, flow charting, forms design, source data automation, etc.) Input/output alternatives.
Communications, interviewing, and selling.
Principles of systems design.[4]

Implementation and follow-up

Planning site preparation, personnel, organization, other considerations.
Training the user.
Evaluation and audit.

Computer concepts and capabilities

I. Hardware characteristics

Mainframe capability, peripheral equipment remotes and linkage, input/output devices, time-sharing, on-line systems, etc.

II. Software

Language options (COBOL, ALGOL, FORTRAN, etc.)
Other software options (compilers, subroutines, etc.)

Additional skill requirements

I. Programming

Ability to program in one language.

II. Quantitative techniques

Management science techniques in systems design.

III. Communications

Graphics and visual presentations.
The oral and written staff report.

Conclusion

The foregoing curriculum, with its accompanying objectives, represents the most comprehensive effort thus far to identify and document the majority of the important elements of a managerial development or training program for systems analysis. This effort should not only provide a basic foundation for the many thousands of seminars, university courses and related training efforts, but should also provide the practicing systems analyst a guide to which he can compare his background and experience with a view toward improvement.

NOTES

1. The White House, *Computers in Higher Education*, U.S. Government Printing Office, Washington, February 1967, p. 1.
2. U.S. Office of Education, *The Relationship of ADP Training Curriculum and Methodology in Federal Government*, Association for Educational Data Systems, Washington, July 1967, pp. 12-13.
3. *Ibid.*
4. A new body of systems principles analagous to principles of management. See Ross, Joel E., and Sullivan, J. W., *Development of Systems Theory*, Foundation for Administrative Research, Colorado Springs, 1967.

B. Human Relations and Systems Design

18. Human Factors in Systems Design*

James B. Bower and J. Bruce Sefert

The growing mechanization of data processing operations, particularly the automation brought about by the application of electronic computers, has intensified the human relations problems inherent in the design of business systems. As a result, business managers and system analysts are devoting increased attention to the impact of the financial information system on the people within their organizations—and to that of the people on the financial information system.

Many trade unions, with some public support, have attacked automation as a leading cause of unemployment. There have even been proposals that automation and data processing revisions be banned altogether.[1] The relation of automation to unemployment remains unclear. Congressional hearings have provided a sounding board for automation's opponents and proponents but no satisfactory answer.

Management opinion is divided as to the actual effect on employee wage levels, job security, advancement, and morale of the many changes that are taking place in both factory and office as a result of changes in procedures, work simplification, elimination of manual data handling, and the advent of high-speed communication. These changes are not confined to companies installing computers but are magnified and highlighted there.

*SOURCE: *Management Services* (November-December, 1965), pp. 39-50. Reprinted by permission of *Management Services*, Copyright © 1965 by The American Institute of CPAs.

Since systems changes involve people, they do not always have the same effects. Sometimes they are or seem to be beneficial to one or a group of the people involved; sometimes, harmful. Some studies of the effects of wholesale revampings of data processing methods have indicated that the employees were on the whole happy with their new jobs, that they generally benefited through higher wages, and that no hardship of any significant duration was visited upon anyone.[2] Other studies have reported employee disillusionment with the new jobs, the elimination of many promotion opportunities formerly available, complaints of being "chained to the machine," empire building by a new elite of EDP specialists, stagnation of middle management, and other adverse effects.[3]

In any case it is clear that there is need for extensive planning of every major procedural or data processing change. Provision should be made in advance to combat any possible harmful effects of systems change on the employees concerned and to take account in the systems design of the effect of human factors upon the operation of an economical and efficient system.

Human factors

The human factors principle of systems design, namely, that the design of a system should be consistent with applicable human factors since people are responsible for the effectiveness of the system, has been proved by experience to be a vital guide to the systems analyst in his work. The term human factors includes all those personality traits that consciously or unconsciously shape the actions and reactions of the people who must use the system as finally designed as well as those same traits reflected in the systems analyst himself as they may affect his ability to achieve an objectively efficient and successful design.

Only the more significant human traits can be explored here and those only as they affect systems design. Some factors, such as resistance to the new and strange, desire for job security, tendency to be influenced by the opinions of others, and preference for familiar work habits are basic in all employees at all levels but may apply with particular force or in particular ways with certain types of employees. Other factors become a problem only with certain groups.

For convenience in examining the effect of human factors on systems design, two levels of management are distinguished in this article. Top management consists of those executives who participate in companywide policy formulation, including the chief executive and those who report directly to him. The term middle management is used to encompass not only the usual group of middle and junior executives, such as division managers, department heads, and their staff functional advisers, but also operating supervisors and foremen since the human factors that affect this group as a whole are similar. Nonsupervisory employees are treated separately since their reactions to systems changes are usually different from those of people on the managerial levels. For purposes of this article the systems analyst is assumed to be either a member of a company's internal systems and procedures staff or an outside specialist in this field, who might represent an accounting or management consulting firm.

Some of the more important human factors that should be considered by the systems analyst in applying the human factors principle are illustrated in Exhibit I. Unforeseen problems, including problems caused by human factors, often arise during the actual implementation of a new or revised financial information system, requiring adaptations. By taking as many human factors as possible into account during the planning of the system, however, the analyst improves his chances of producing an efficient, well accepted system with few subsequent revisions.

In the discussion that follows the components of the human factors principle are applied in detail to each of the three levels of personnel previously identified.

Top management

It is axiomatic that the wholehearted support of top management is required for systems acceptance and success. Middle management and nonsupervisory employees are quick to take their cue from the attitudes that flow downward. In the past, top management often viewed work procedures and systems study as a specialized function worthy of its attention only when a crisis arose. With the advent of computers, which are often so costly as to require justification to boards of directors or stockholders and which have been so heavily publicized as to become status symbols, top management has become much more involved in the problems of data processing.

This is fortunate, for continued top management attention is vital to the eventual success of any system. At several points during the systems project top management must review interim findings and approve or disapprove recommendations for further action. Careful consideration and prompt decisions are essential.

Mere interest and support from top management is not the whole answer, however. The analyst must take account of many human factors at this level in determining management's information needs, in alerting top executives to the full implications of any large-scale revision in the data processing system, and in making sure that executives are aware of and capable of obtaining the full range of benefits available.

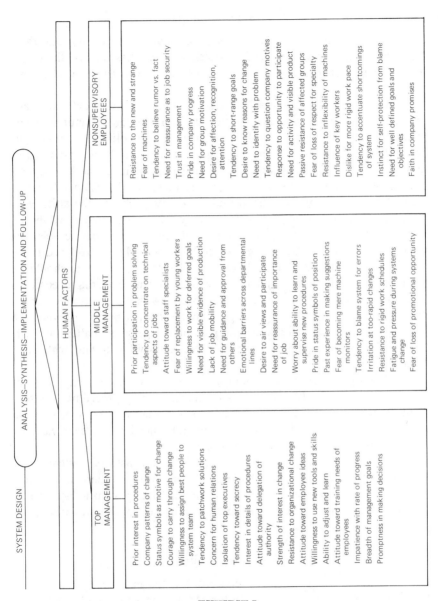

EXHIBIT I
Focusing on human factors

SYSTEM DESIGN

ANALYSIS—SYNTHESIS—IMPLEMENTATION AND FOLLOW-UP

HUMAN FACTORS

TOP MANAGEMENT

Prior interest in procedures
Company patterns of change
Status symbols as motive for change
Courage to carry through change
Willingness to assign best people to system team
Tendency to patchwork solutions
Concern for human relations
Isolation of top executives
Tendency toward secrecy
Interest in details of procedures
Attitude toward delegation of authority
Strength of interest in change
Resistance to organizational change
Attitude toward employee ideas
Willingness to use new tools and skills
Ability to adjust and learn
Attitude toward training needs of employees
Impatience with rate of progress
Breadth of management goals
Promptness in making decisions

MIDDLE MANAGEMENT

Prior participation in problem solving
Tendency to concentrate on technical aspects of jobs
Attitude toward staff specialists
Fear of replacement by young workers
Willingness to work for deferred goals
Need for visible evidence of production
Lack of job mobility
Need for guidance and approval from others
Emotional barriers across departmental lines
Desire to air views and participate
Need for reassurance of importance of job
Worry about ability to learn and supervise new procedures
Pride in status symbols of position
Past experience in making suggestions
Fear of becoming mere machine monitors
Tendency to blame system for errors
Irritation at too-rapid changes
Resistance to rigid work schedules
Fatigue and pressure during systems change
Fear of loss of promotional opportunity

NONSUPERVISORY EMPLOYEES

Resistance to the new and strange
Fear of machines
Tendency to believe rumor vs. fact
Need for reassurance as to job security
Trust in management
Pride in company progress
Need for group motivation
Desire for affection, recognition, attention
Tendency to short-range goals
Desire to know reasons for change
Need to identify with problem
Tendency to question company motives
Response to opportunity to participate
Need for activity and visible product
Passive resistance of affected groups
Fear of loss of respect for specialty
Resistance to inflexibility of machines
Influence of key workers
Dislike for more rigid work pace
Tendency to accentuate shortcomings of system
Instinct for self-protection from blame
Need for well defined goals and objectives
Faith in company promises

Company patterns

Most established companies have certain patterns of activity that affect their approach to innovations. One systems analyst has likened these patterns to the rituals of a South Seas tribe, complete with dances to drive out evil spirits.[4]

In some organizations duties and responsibilities are well defined; many small, closely knit companies prefer a freer, looser structure.[5] Some managers are direct and forceful in ordering changes; others prefer devious and indirect methods. Some top managements are simply not prepared to make any substantial changes in the organization or in methods of operation. In such situations the systems analyst must decide whether to adapt the system to accommodate the attitude or to try to change the attitude.

The pattern of change in a company may have been molded by special factors that operated in the past. A top executive may feel that he holds his present position because of some procedure or method he introduced many years ago; he is not likely to welcome any change.[6] Special care should be taken to see that the new system, instead of endangering this executive's sense of value to the company, can be identified with his contribution as an outgrowth of it. Another top manager may have a pet project to which he gives special attention and which is part of his personal pattern of self-esteem. The analyst must always be alert to avoid colliding with such "sacred cows."[7]

Individual personalities are important, too. One executive may be a so-called detail man who likes to have a hand in designing procedures himself. Another may be an idea man interested only in the broader aspects of the system or a results man interested only in end objectives. In each case the analyst must adapt his approach accordingly.

If the company has a history of orderly and considered attention to continued improvement rather than one of patchwork solutions to immediate crises, the analyst can conclude that the top management is likely to be systems-oriented and ready to support him in designing and installing a new system.

Management climate

Companies that show sincere concern for the employee as a human being build up an employee trust in top management that is of great value in gaining acceptance of change. If management has been willing in the past to use employees' ideas, imagination, and suggestions and to pay attention to workers' feelings in visible ways, the systems analyst's task will be eased considerably.

He should, therefore, appraise the management climate of the organization as early as possible so that he can take into account in systems planning. If he finds a climate of teamwork and understanding among departments, delegation of authority by management, and stimulation of the challenge of problem solving, he can devote his primary attention to technical problems. If he finds a climate of top management isolation, rigid departmental barriers, little or no downward communication, and a reluctance to keep employees informed of company plans and policies, he may need to educate top management about the importance of attention to people in assuring the success of any proposed new system.

An aspect of management climate that has particular significance for the systems analyst is the extent to which authority has been delegated to lower levels. If all decisions have traditionally been made from above, the analyst is likely to find managers and employees alike hesitant to make suggestions and express opinions; their ideas have dried up from lack of encouragement.[8] In such a situation top management needs to give visible evidence of its support of the systems porject. It should, for example, select capable representatives from the departments that will be affected by the systems study to help the analyst with it, and it should give them the time and authority needed to do a proper job.

A detailed study of fundamental systems changes made over a five-year period in a large electric utility[9] provides a striking example of the way in which differences in prior participation in planning and problem solving can affect departments' contribution to and acceptance of change. In the accounting department much effort had been spent over the years in developing participation in management by intermediate and first-time supervisors. The result was a high degree of employee satisfaction, trust, and good will, which proved very valuable during the transition from one system to another. In the sales department, for a variety of reasons, the employees had never participated in management to this degree. Furthermore, this pattern continued during the systems changeover. Communication of information about the change was much less complete at all levels than in the accounting department. No attempt was made to present the new system to the sales employees in relation to their special interests and objectives. As a result, the sales employees never understood the system as well as the accounting employees, had less confidence in it, and presented more difficult problems during the transition.

As recent experience with large-scale computer installations has demonstrated, employee acceptance of change depends heavily on top management's willingness to make assurances about job security, salary retention, opportunity for training, and rules to be followed in reassignment.[10] As the plans for a major systems change unfold, top management will have to chart its course of action in the field of human relations.

What attitude should it adopt toward displaced labor? Is it willing to assure to all affected employees the opportunity for continued employment regardless of the changes in data processing methods and departmental and individual functions? Is it willing to bear the expense of retraining employees? Will it show concern for the employees' self-respect and personal improvement during periods of change and at other times?[11]

Although these decisions are not the systems analyst's to make, he cannot—and should not—avoid some involvement in them. He has a responsibility to take account in his planning of any position for utilization of present employees, their training and retraining, and their job mobility. He should, therefore, press for early top management decisions on these points.

In fact, the analyst's ability to obtain prompt policy decisions from top management on all questions that arise throughout the study will be an important factor in the success of his work. Procrastination in making difficult decisions is a basic human trait. The systems analyst must press firmly for such decisions while using every means available to demonstrate the logical basis of his proposals. In one manufacturing company the systems and procedures staff personnel were forced to spend 60 percent of their time on attempts to obtain final decisions. In the words of one staff member, attempting to get a decision was "like trying to tie a rope around a pile of sand."[12]

Decisions will be particularly difficult to get if a basic change in organizational structure is required or if the proposed change will create an embarrassing personnel problem. If the organizational pattern of the company has tended to develop around personalities rather than being based upon logical division of functions, the difficulties of change will be magnified. If top management is adamant in refusing to make an indicated organizational or personnel change, the systems analyst may have to build around the existing structure or person, recognizing that a good system that has the support of management is to be preferred to the best system if the latter will not be supported or used.[13]

Desire for improvement

If the systems analyst finds that top management has a genuine desire to solve any systems problem discovered to exist, it is likely that he will also find the desire and courage to make the changes necessary to implement the solution.

Top management's willingness to assign good people to work with the analyst and to give them the necessary time and responsibility is one test of its real interest and concern. Too often the tendency has been to make such assignments on the basis of availability rather than suitability. If management shows such a tendency, the analyst needs to point out the importance of having outstanding people on the planning group and the benefits to be expected.

The use of a project team made up of representatives of the various departments affected, operating with or under the analyst, may be a new problem solving procedure in the company. It has, however, many advantages. Not only does it usually produce a sounder systems design but it also greatly facilitates acceptance of the system, both by the members of the team and by others. The representatives of the personnel and industrial relations departments can help in determining the human relations climate of the organization and in helping to plan the final proposals regarding employee utilization. The representatives of the operating departments can be useful in alerting the analyst to any special human factors problems that may arise in their areas.

The strength of top management's desire for improvement will be further tested as it is informed of the training time and costs of installation that will probably be involved in any large-scale systems revision. A realistic appraisal of such factors during the planning phase of the systems project will give management an opportunity to determine its step-by-step involvement.

If cost cutting has been the principal factor in top management's motive for change, it may be desirable for the analyst to reorient management toward the goal of labor saving in the broadest sense, that is, the use of saved labor to make possible improved and faster information for decision making. A system that provides better tools for management is more valuable over the long run than one that simply reduces costs. This shift in emphasis toward a broader goal also will help to ease the fears of operating personnel about labor displacement.[14]

The systems analyst bears much of the responsibility for educating top management about systems in general and about his system in particular. He should do what he can to help management understand what the system can provide and how it can be of value in planning and decision making. At the same time he should be laying the groundwork for further systems advances. The managers of tomorrow must have a broad knowledge of the interdependence of all parts of the business and the potential for improving decision making offered by the increased variety of information made possible by a modern data system. The system analyst can play a vital role in top management's data processing education.

Middle management

An understanding of the human factors at work in the middle management group of managers and supervisors is especially important to the
systems analyst. The personnel at this level hold the key to success or
failure of a new system. Top management relies on them for the organization's everyday efficiency and smooth operation; the nonsupervisory
employees take their direction and set their course from them. The systems
analyst has traditionally found it necessary to work closely with middle
management. In systems analysis he must depend heavily on the information they furnish; in systems implementation and follow-up he needs their
acceptance and cooperation.

Problems

Middle management presents a number of special problems for the
systems analyst. Typically, managers below the top management group
and supervisors have a narrow perspective on company operations. They
are so immersed in their own jobs and their own departments that they
cannot see the significance of what is going on elsewhere in the company.
The systems analyst will have to devote considerable educational effort to
the task of building up in the middle managers a feeling for the total job
that is being attempted.

Typically, too, middle managers concentrate their attention on the
technical rather than on the administrative and human relations aspects of
their work. Thus, the analyst will need to keep emphasizing to them the
importance of teaching the new system to the employees under them and
the need for selling the system to the workers.

Another human factor that is important at the middle management level
is the increased resistance to change that accompanies increased age. This
resistance is likely to be especially intense in large and stable organizations.
Age increases resistance to change partly because of growing reluctance to
alter familiar and comfortable established work patterns and partly from
the ever-present fear of inability to compete with younger people in the
organization. This resistance is partly unconscious. There is an instinctive
tendency to organize experience in a manner that will be minimally
threatening and to believe what one wants to believe.[15]

Furthermore, middle managers are consciously fearful of automation.
Any substantial reduction in the number of employees is likely to reduce
the number of supervisors needed as well. Forecasts that the computer, by
taking over routine decision making, will wipe out middle management have
been highly publicized. Certainly the inflexibility of program necessary to
ensure uniform input, processing, and output in a large-scale computer

system changes the scope of middle management decision making. This may, as some claim, leave the manager free for higher activities, but some middle managers are understandably skeptical.

As with any other employee group, middle management's past experience with systems change is a powerful determinant of its current attitude. A manager whose last experience with a staff specialist was unfortunate may be convinced that all staff men are arrogant, impractical, and opinionated and that it is a waste of time to deal with them. Perhaps he once suggested an improvement that was not acknowledged or that was adopted without credit. If so, he is probably still nurturing his hurt feelings. The systems analyst will have to dig out such attitudes and convince the supervisor that suggestions will be welcomed and used.[16]

Past experience also, although unfortunately less frequently, can be a help. If earlier systems analysts have dealt with middle managers, successfully—and particularly if top management has made a practice of encouraging middle management participation in problem solving and decision making—the systems analyst will find his path easier.

One advantageous characteristic of middle managers is that they are usually acustomed to working toward long-range goals, such a promotion, retirement, and education of their children. Thus, they do not need evidence that a change will bring them immediate benefits to the extent that lower-level employees do.

Preliminary study

Even before the study has actually begun, the systems analyst will need to be at work allaying the fears of middle management and employees alike. In any organization it is difficult to get ahead of the rumor network. As early as possible top management should make a definitive announcement of the scope of the study. If this announcement can also contain assurances of job security and other measures for employment stabilization, so much the better. In case top management does not recognize the importance of informing employees early, the systems analyst should consider it his responsibility to point out the need for such announcements and recommend their timing and content. Reasons for the change should be stated, with emphasis upon the broader goals and the benefits to be derived by everyone. If possible, better use of labor rather than cost reduction should be stressed. Some companies planning computer installations have given employees as much as three years' notice of impending changes in order to accustom them to the idea.

Subsequent interim reports are also desirable. These should be as specific and factual as possible and should continue to stress positive benefits. Middle management in particular needs to be kept continuously informed so that it can answer questions from employees and interpret to them the aims and policies of top management.

Analysis phase

The analysis phase of the study, when the systems analyst is gathering information on current procedures and work flows by interviewing middle managers and employees, gives the analyst one of his best opportunities to obtain supervisory cooperation and reduce supervisory fears.

The middle manager's fear of loss of self-esteem and status can be countered by stressing the increased importance of each manager or supervisor through his part in supplying better information for decision making. The increased need for the manager as a trainer of personnel can be emphasized as an offset to any diminution of his personal responsibility for decision making.

Middle managers will be anxious about possible decreases in employment and the effect on them. The systems analyst can reiterate any assurances previously given by top management as to job security, displacement policies, and retraining and can explain probable new positions and their duties. More generally, he can point out that studies of current employment trends indicate that the number of professional and technical workers will increase more than 40 percent over the next decade and that the number in clerical and sales occupations will increase by 30 percent.[17] He must be careful, however, not to promise upgrading to any specific manager.

Managers and supervisors may be worried about their ability to learn new techniques and keep ahead of their subordinates. Many will doubt their ability to supervise under the new methods. The systems analyst can cite the experience of other companies installing automated data processing systems to show that many persons over 45 have been trained to fill technical positions in the computer field, often more rapidly than younger persons could be trained. These companies have found that older employees' greater sense of responsibility, their reliability, their care for details, and their mature judgment have made such a policy advantageous.[18]

More generally, the systems analyst can build up the middle manager's confidence by treating him as an intelligent equal, competent to understand the system and its problems. The analyst should avoid all signs of condescension or any implication that there is the slightest question about the supervisor's ability to handle any situation that may arise.

In addition to allaying middle management's fears, the analyst should attempt to build positive support for the new system. If the supervisor is given an opportunity to air his views on the present system and take part in the planning for improvement, he will become interested in the ultimate success of the new procedures. The analyst should recognize the super-visor's experience and remember to be a good listener. Whenever appro-priate, he should visibly record suggestions so that credit can be given for them if they are adopted.[19] And he should stress middle and top manage-ment's common interest in building the best possible system. Often it may be wise to interview the supervisor away from the office atmosphere to keep work pressures from interfering with his objective consideration of new ideas and to ensure that he will be free to discuss controversial aspects of the present and proposed systems.

The systems analyst's approach has been likened to that of a doctor whose objective is essentially preservative. He should adopt the view that the organization is basically sound and healthy and that he is not there to tinker for the sake of tinkering. In this way he will impress the supervisor with his concern for people and their problems and his willingness to conserve ideas that have survival value.

Implementation

Other problems arise during implementation of the system. When possible, the analyst should anticipate these problems and do what he can in the planning stage to minimize or offset them.

One source of job dissatisfaction for workers and supervisors alike after the installation of automated systems is the lack of visible evidence of the product of their labor. Workers have a basic need to see that their jobs are significant. A series of entries, a list prepared, a report are all visible evidence of accomplishment. Closely related is the feeling that to be producing one must be doing. In many new systems supervisors and workers see no end product of their work, nor is the work itself visible. This trend is likely to continue.

The only solution for the systems analyst is to begin educating middle management to other job satisfactions as early in the systems project as possible. This will not be easy since these other satisfactions tend to be more abstract than the old. The analyst also should remind supervisors that they will have to plan to give more attention to worker morale and develop new methods of praise and reward. Most middle managers will need training in human relations, and the analyst should make certain that such training is provided.

The relatively greater inflexibility of highly integrated data processing systems will create problems for middle management. Because of the interdependence of parts of the system, the supervisor will be blamed for delays further down the line. He will be subject to greater pressure for adherence to higher work standards, and he will find that improved feed-back will pinpoint responsibility more surely than before.[20] If he is caught off guard by these changes, he may become resentful and resistant—and transmit this feeling to his subordinates. The systems analyst can forestall these reactions by holding briefing sessions with both supervisors and employees and by meeting regularly with individual supervisors during and after the system implementation to check on their reactions and on the morale of their employees.

Unreasonable deadlines can provoke resentment in both supervisors and employees. The analyst should work with top management to keep deadlines realistic. If it becomes evident that the deadlines set cannot be met through no fault of the supervisors or employees, he should relieve their anxiety by assuring them that no blame attaches to them.

During the entire systems design period middle management's work load will be increased. Learning new procedures, training employees, being interviewed, attending meetings, and supervising two parallel work processing systems during testing periods can combine to create tremendous pressure on middle management, pressures that are not conducive to a kindly feeling toward any new system. By careful preplanning the analyst should attempt to minimize these pressures so far as is possible.

It is just as important for the systems analyst to enlist the understanding and support of the rank-and-file employees as of the managers. A group of nonsupervisory workers can sabotage a system they do not accept just as effectively as a supervisor can. In fact, their sabotage may be even more difficult to combat since it may be more subtly applied through group action.

Although the basic human factors that affect the nonsupervisory employee are the same as those that operate at the top and middle management levels, his different position in the organization and normal lack of contact with top management plans and policies lends added weight to some of them. For example, because nonsupervisory workers, particularly younger ones, tend to have shorter-range goals than management, it is difficult to sell them change based upon some abstract general benefit. They demand an immediate personal advantage.

The nonsupervisory employee is generally more group-oriented and less of an individualist than the manager. He is more susceptible to rumors and to the influence of his fellow-workers' opinions. Other human factors that are particularly important at the nonsupervisory level include the desire to produce a visible product as evidence of work accomplished; a need for recognition, affection, and attention; the importance of status in the eyes of co-workers, friends, and family; a need for activity in work as contrasted with the relative inactivity of merely monitoring a machine; the need to lean on others for support and encouragement; and the social need for working in groups. Automation is making the worker more isolated at his work place at the same time that there seems to be a growing number of other-directed persons in our culture who look to others for guidelines and approval.

The basic instinct of resistance to the new, strange, and unkown is intensified in employees by the common human fear of machinery as a displacer of labor. Recurrent periods of unemployment help to keep this fear alive. Automation seems to have replaced the loom and steam engine of the early Industrial Revolution as the public and trade unions symbol of danger from impersonal forces outside the worker's control.

The systems analyst cannot completely prevent the operation of these basic human factors. It will take a long time to substitute new values and new job satisfactions. If, however, he is aware of these forces at work, he may be able to offset them or at least minimize their effects by proper training and by introducing contrary forces.

Even the employee who would admit the desirability of proposed systems changes if he were capable of being objective is likely to develop a core of passive resistance under the influence of his fears and his fellow-workers. The systems analyst must exert continuous positive pressure to overcome this tendency.[21]

The importance of keeping the employees informed has already been stressed. The inevitability of rumors negates the theory that information which might upset the employees should be withheld. They will be upset anyway, and they need reassurance as to their job security, opportunities under the new system, and steps to be followed during the changeover. In addition to the usual meetings, bulletins, and newsletters, the union may sometimes be used as an effective channel of communication.

Many of the employees the analyst interviews will question the real motives of the company in making the changes. The analyst can break down this skepticism by relating the company's general systems problems to each individual's own work experience, thus demonstrating the need for improvement. Often it is wise to devote extra effort to convincing the opinion leaders within employee groups so that they in turn can become salesmen to their fellow-employees. Such employees should be given opportunities to air their views, and the analyst should return to them for further suggestions as the project develops. The analyst must be careful to sell the ideas on their own merit rather than by mere personality; there should, of course, be no misrepresentation.

To counteract employee fear of loss of status, the analyst can emphasize the new job values, which will place a premium on responsibility. He can encourage employees to apply for new positions as they open up. By showing genuine interest in the individuals he is interviewing, the analyst can do much to boost employee morale and build confidence

As with middle managers, nonsupervisory employees should be prepared for the greater rigidity of mechanical equipment and the importance of interdepartmental teamwork in keeping the work flowing. The analyst should emphasize the importance of adherence to work standards, both to keep the employee on his toes and to keep him from blaming breakdowns on "the system" rather than on human errors. Any tendency to blame the system for errors can create serious operating problems by undermining confidence in the system and thus encouraging the human tendency to create additional records as protection against possible blame for error. The plan for system implementation should include provision for continuous checking by the analyst to uncover possible sources of breakdown and eliminate trouble spots promptly.

Another systems design technique that is helpful in preventing breakdowns is to build some flexibility for limited self-adjustment into the system. Allowing affected departments to adjust for unforseen contingencies without having to wait for a formal systems change prevents irritants from growing and gives both employees and supervisors a sense of identification with the system.

The analyst himself

As a human being, the systems analyst is, of course, subject to some of the same human factors that operate in managers and employees—and to some of his own. When given an opportunity to comment, employees have variously accused systems men of demonstrating a narrow perspective, of having a tendency toward isolation, of talking in language incomprehensible to the ordinary person, of cutting across lines of authority, of empire building, and of stirring up jurisdictional disputes. Some analysts have given the impression of automatically opposing any methods in use before they arrived on the scene, seting themselves almost by instinct against the old to favor the new.

The advent of electronic data processing and the necessity of combining on management and operating teams persons of technical training and scientific background with those having only operating experience have compounded the problems of human relations in the systems field. Often the specialized personnel are accused by the others of setting themselves apart from the regular organization, of adopting a tough attitude, and of seeming to feel that human frailties are a nuisance best avoided by adding equipment.

The natural suspicion that an expert arouses when he comes into a department to begin an analysis of work flows and procedures makes it all the more important for him to establish cooperative relationships as quickly as possible. Among the more desirable qualities in a systems analyst are humility, a realization that his mission is one of service, not an end in itself, and a genuine interest in people. He should be a good listener, willing to accept suggestions, analyze them objectively, and give due credit for any ideas adopted. Giving credit for an idea to the person whose acceptance of it is sought can have a strong influence on the employee's interpretation of a situation.[22]

The systems analyst's awareness of the problems that human factors can cause for him in his work makes it all the more important for him to analyze his own methods critically to see whether any of the difficulties he may be encountering in obtaining cooperation and acceptance from employees may stem from his own failure to practice good human relations. Like Caesar's wife, he should be above reproach.

NOTES

1. *Automation and Unemployment*, Economic Research Department, Chamber of Commerce of the U.S., Washington, D.C., 1961, and William G. Caples, "Automation in Theory and Practice," *Business Topics*, Autumn, 1960, p. 7.
2. Einar Hardin, "The Reaction of Employees to Office Automation," *Monthly Labor Review*, September, 1960, p. 925.
3. Albert A. Blum, 'Electronic Data Processing and the Office Worker," *Data Processing*, June, 1961, p. 11; and Ida R. Hoos, "When the Computer Takes Over the Office," *The Harvard Business Review*, July, 1960, p. 102.
4. Allen Y. Davis, "Gaining Acceptance of New Ideas," *Ideas for Management—1959*, Systems and Procedures Association, Detroit, 1959, p. 219.
5. Keith Davis, *Human Relations in Business*, McGraw-Hill Company, Inc., New York, 1957.
6. "Computers," *Business Week*, June 21, 1958, p. 68.
7. Abner W. Boyd, "Human Relations in System Changes," *N.A.A. Bulletin*, Vol. 40, July, 1959, p. 69.
8. Dr. Thomas J. Mallinson, "Human Relations," *Ideas for Management—1960*, Systems and Procedures Association, Detroit, 1960, p. 234.
9. Floyd C. Mann and Lawrence K. Williams, "Observations on the Dynamics of Change to Electronic Data-Processing Equipment," *Administrative Science Quarterly*, September, 1960, p. 217.
10. Ben Conway and Duane E. Watts, "Putting Electronic Data Processing to Work," *The Price Waterhouse Review*, Vol. 3, September, 1958, p. 19.
11. "Human Side of Enterprise," *Factory*, Vol. 118, August, 1960, p. 84.
12. Richard F. Neuschel, *Management by System*, McGraw-Hill Book Company, Inc., New York, 1960.
13. N. C. Pollock, "The Systems Function," *Ideas for Management—1959*, Systems and Procedures Association, Detroit, 1959, p. 185.
14. Virgil F. Blank, "The Management Concept in Electronic Systems," *The Journal of Accountancy*, January, 1961, p. 59; and Harold Koontz, "Top Management Takes a Second Look at Electronic Data Processing," *Business Horizons*, Spring, 1959, p. 74.

15. Donald N. Michael, "The Social Environment," *Operations Research*, Vol. 7, July, 1959, p. 506.

16. Philip E. Wheatley, "The Human Element in Systems Surveys," *Systems and Procedures*, May, 1960, p. 33; and "Change Requires Employee Support," *Nation's Business*, August, 1959, p. 33.

17. Louis F. Buckley, "1960 Manpower Trends and Automation's Impact," *Commercial and Financial Chronicle*, August 18, 1960, p. 660.

18. *Adjustments to the Introduction of Office Automation*, U.S. Dept. of Labor Bulletin No. 1276, Washington, D.C., 1960.

19. John M. Emery, "Systems and Procedures Development," *Journal of Machine Accounting*, December, 1959, p. 12.

20. G. H. Cowperthwaite, "The Challenge of Mechanization," *Systems and Procedures*, May, 1960, p. 20.

21. Edwin S. Raub, "Applied Psychology for the Systems Man," *Systems and Procedures*, April, 1961, p. 23.

22. Robert E. Schlosser, "Psychology for the Systems Analyst," *Management Services*, November-December, 1964, p. 34.

19. Lessons from the Informal Organization*

Arthur L. Svenson

The informal organization is nature's response to management's artificial structuring of an orderly business event. Driven by assumptions about functional division of work, the formal organization splits the natural unity of a business event into segments according to title authority. Informal organization attempts to heal the managerial rupturing by weaving an authority of knowledge about the fracture.

Frequently a system analyst is called upon to repair a faulty management system. Likely as not, this condition of systems disrepair is of a chronic nature. Equally as probable is that past systems repair has been made on a spot or bursh-fire basis. That is, the cause of conflagration has not been studied; attention has been directed only to certain obvious symptoms.

Before the systems analyst makes the required adjustments to the faulty management system, he should analyze the nature, structure and operations of the informal organization existing within the network of the system. The lessons he learns from his informal organization may provide clues to

*SOURCE: Systems and Procedures Journal (May-June 1968), pp. 14-17. Reprinted by permission of the publisher.

remedial action. For it is this informal organization that has permitted the ailing system to function at all. It is this organization that has bolstered the formal one, assisting it to overcome the explicit, damaging shortcomings of the original flow specifications.

Lessons gained from the informal organization will, in all probability, reveal why, how and where the formal organization of people, resources and methods have failed to produce the planned output of the system.

In a word, the systems analyst can gain valuable insight into the realities of the actual system. Only from the informal organization may these realities be seen. The systems analyst has to move behind the facade of formal structure in his attempt to ascertain the cause and points of faulty flow.

The first point about informal organization that the systems analyst must absolutely respect is that the structure is nonlegal. In terms of management planning, approval, and decision making, no legal status attaches itself to this form of human association. Since legality is never a factor, the issue of legitimacy may not be used as a defense, right, claim, or privilege. The relationships, contacts, and information that the system analyst may develop from informal organization carry neither recognition nor approval.

It is important that the systems analyst respect this nonlegal dictum, for whatever lessons he may learn from the membership of that association can never be verified or confirmed by official record. Information gained from such a group cannot be considered proof-positive.

Thus, informal organization is a personal relationship developed outside official bounds and official sanction. Its authority is nonmanagerial, but uniquely its authority rests strictly on the management purpose to be accomplished. Because of this, informal organization contains the paradox of an illegitimate method toward a legitimate goal.

The characteristics of informal organization, aside from this landmark circumstance of nonlegality, are much the same as those characteristics found in other human associations. A communications network, information and communications centers, language, signals, standards and measurements are all present. The informal counterpart—can engage in the distribution of power and in the adjustment of policy and, further, in the adjudication of conflict. But with all this similarity, the informal system is a private delegation of power and a private handling of information by private authorities.

While attempting to understand a total business event (it may be total system, major system or subsystem), informal organization also attempts to integrate the man within the system totally with that event. That man's attitude, dedication, loyalty, physical and mental strength, and knowledge are involved.

Something approaching a unity of outlook, state of mind, vision and behavior result to the end that one man within the system can talk meaningfully to another man within the system. And this occurs despite the splintering effect induced by formal organization structure.

The reader has many times seen the instance of informal organization pushing through the formal. He has witnessed a work process being completed by a display of willingness to work beyond the brutish limitations of a job classification or a work jurisdiction clause. Or he may have experienced the reverse.

As the systems analyst draws aside to study the informal organization at work, it is immaterial what system or subsystem he observes. It may be the system for inventory control, for customer billing, for new product development, or for the organization of the executive office.

The analyst will find constants of informal organizational behavior regardless of the area of corporate task. He becomes a clinician viewing a non-natural process that is attempting to draw as near to working reality as possible. As the analyst dissects the why, what, when, where of informal organization, he gains greater understanding of the manner in which they interact with things and information. He perceives those ingredients essential to systems life and the manner in which they combine to reach an output.

These are some of the lessons he may learn.

Lesson one: Forbidden information

Forbidden information coupled with forbidden knowledge and know-how call the informal organization into being. These give shape and form to common endeavor. The configuration of demands made by the system causes legal information to be used illegally. Where there are information gaps, the needs of the system induce the fabrication of forbidden information.

Usually, forbidden information is that data that have been restricted; it is that information that has not been supplied to the system; it is information that has been prohibited by constitutional fiat from circulating within the system. Yet the participants, on finding that forbidden information is required, develop their own set in order that they may perform work.

In this respect, informal organization seeks Garden of Eden information rather than that data presented by the formal organization of the system.

In part, the search for and the gathering of forbidden information is prompted by curiosity, by the desire to know more about one's operation or about the company than one has been told. But in greater part, this information is sought to make performance possible. One wants to know what goes on before and what follows one's work so that contributions can be more effectively made.

However, much curiosity is a factor in the formation of forbidden information; the rationale lies in gathering information to get a job done. This invariably means that personnel within the system reach out for noncodified, nonlegal, nonrational data. For working information transcends the arbitrary, antiseptic categories of "what one should know" and "what one should not know."

In order for resources to be made productive through human intelligence and combined human effort, the informal organization considers all and any information fair game if it contributes to the system's output. Barriers of rank, job title and organizational level are meaningless in the face of this pressure for information.

The systems analyst should train himself to hear and to listen to the nature of this extralegal information. If he is capable of this, he will be able to identify information that is vital to the system's accomplishment but is not an indigenous part of the system's information flow. Furthermore, he will quickly train himself to detect and separate the nonlegal but relevant data from those that are merely interesting.

The analyst can do nothing about this latter category of forbidden information. Undoubtedly, this data will be sought and accumulated, come what may.

But the analyst can do something about data falling into the first category. When redesigning or repairing the faulty system, he can make certain that this vital but forbidden information becomes an integral part of the system's flow; he can impart recognition and circulation to it.

Lesson two: Forbidden knowledge

In Lesson One, forbidden information employed in informal organization was linked with forbidden knowledge. These represent a duality not readily separable since information of any description requires the vehicle of human knowledge to be made effective.

As he studies the informal organization of the system, the analyst will observe that knowledge and human expertise exceed the authority of the formal organization as defined by formal job descriptions. These codified restrictions are exceeded in several important aspects:

1. Human capability moves beyond the limit of talent demanded by the formal job description;

2. Locations of decisions shift from their formally designated positions to those locations where substance founded on relevant data and knowledge are logically joined;

3. Personnel who are truly capable and responsible for producing an output exercise spontaneous judgment and decision; and

4. Leadership follows the path specified by the authority of knowledge and expertise rather than the path specified by constitutional authority.

These four patterns of informal organization, generated by the linkage of forbidden information with forbidden knowledge, describe the actual chain of the system's authority, command and decision making. Together they spark the manufacture of the system's short-cuts; they provide a climate for the release of talent beyond the straitjacket of personnel classification; they are responsible for the wealth of tools and techniques that have for decades eroded the work of time and motion, and methods and procedures specialists.

But mainly, the analyst will find that clinical study of informal organization will reveal the basic structure and nature of knowledge and expertise required by the system. Inevitably over a passage of time, outlawed knowledge erupts through the strata of codified formal organizational authority. This knowledge pushes through the locations where decisions are bottlenecked; it moves those decisions to the natural locations where expertise lies. It represents the response of interested, committed people to the real demands of the system's output.

Lesson three: Nature, sources of information

Living as it does on forbidden information and nonlegal knowledge, informal organization has to create its own operational data. It does this by combining formally released data with information begged, borrowed or stolen from other sources. Information from these sources is then batched and mixed with the regularly supplied information.

In a strict sense, what results is an informational potpourri, but it is workable. This workability is its justification and its rationale.

The mixture directs people; it permits them to organize themselves about physical inputs, processes and decisions; the informational potpourri makes the nonhuman resources amenable to human manipulation. Thus, whatever information comes to hand and services is admissable.

Sources of information for the informal organization are intensively and extensively cultivated on the justification that a production has to be accomplished within the system. The search for sources cuts across functional lines; it employs information derived from other plans, systems and decisions; it draws upon information that flashes from the starburst of memory or insight.

For example, if a subsystem for production requires cost data, budgeting data or marketing data, members of the system will seek to secure the missing but vital information. While the design of the original system may have specified that this is a production system (i.e., not a costing, not a budgeting, not a marketing system), the need for additional information will be acted upon by the personnel of the system. And thus a private search for information sources begins.

As the system analyst observes and studies informal organization, he should concern himself only with the fact that *sub rosa* information is present and in the system. How this information arrived there and the manner in which it was culled and cribbed from its mother sources are no concern of his for he is not a truant officer. The wonder is that the sources actually were identified and exploited for their informational benefit to the system. Later, when the analyst repairs the system, he will have opportunity for building channels of information flow that tap the required sources.

One further detail of Lesson Three should be noted: The substance of illegal information involves both technical and nontechnical sources. Systems analysts are encouraged not to become so enamored of hardware as to overlook the presence of nontechnical information. For this information constitutes the lubricant that makes technical operations possible; this is what makes "unnatural systems" human.

Lesson four: Flow of information

Spread before the analyst as he studies an informal systems organization will be two road maps documenting the information flow of the system. The formal map will indicate the officially accredited highways of information travel, setting forth distances, junctions, road conditions, entrances and exits. This map represents the regulated, approved content and direction of information flow.

The other map will not be as clearly defined since it reflects the path of information travel not approved. It will concentrate on the byways, the short-cuts, the areas that represent wilderness and the frontiers of official thought.

This second map will show when and how information travel has been rerouted in content and direction. It will reveal those places in formal organization where information flow has come to an abrupt halt, where it has no place to go, where arterial communications cannot support the decision to be made. This map of informal organization reveals the unexplored wastelands and the gaps of official systems planning.

Within the context of this lesson, the systems analyst has opportunity of learning the manner and the direction in which information actually flows from person to person, from decision location to decision location, to make output attainable.

As we have already noted, this second may will be unclear at first reading. It is necessarily fogged over to escape official detection and censure; this plan of information flow leads a subterranean life, moving from mind to mind and not from officially plotted point to point.

But with the exercise of patience and analytical skill, the systems analyst will be able to reconstruct the flow of informal information. He will find that the teeming variety of information circulating through the informal organization makes the official chart look like a primary grade reader. If what he finds appears to be illogical and random, it means that the analyst has somewhere missed the essence of information flow in informal organization. The hard logic of practice still outwits him.

Lessons from the informal organization are not difficult to derive. The systems analyst has but to listen and record. But usually he is so pressed with the demand to take action that he can not afford to be objective about the system he is analyzing.

Thus, he moves into a systems situation where amber caution signals flash, but he does not heed them. Instead, he pastes and patches and improvises. He places further burden upon personnel already overburdened in their desire to make the faulty formal system operative.

People working within the flow of a system can only be effective and efficient through information. This is what joins them with work assignments, with schedules of production, with machines, physical plant, materials and supplies.

When that information is not a function of the approved flow, when it is absent totally or in part, a search begins to unearth it and to weave it into the hidden data and into the data flow of the informal organization. When totally absent, source and substance are comparatively easy to find. The fact that vital information is missing stands out in glaring relief.

But when the information is partly supplied within the formal flow, the search is much more difficult. For in this instance, official comprehension of system needs is to be questioned absolutely. In this instance also, greater official security may have been exercised against the prying and the leverage exerted by personnel of the informal organization.

Studying the informal organization of a faulty system, the analyst will undoubtedly discover an underworld of information and information flow. This underworld is premised on the assumption that work is to be accomplished.

Members of this twilight organization must then make bids for illegal information which they insert into the system's flow. Through subterfuge, a dual system of information flow develops. This duality heightens illegal knowledge and expertise. It alters decision content and decision location. It seeks to make the formal system viable.

The systems analyst will also perceive that a scandal route or a rumor route parallels the flow of illegal information through the informal organization. To obtain his primary objective of repairing the system, it is perhaps best for the systems analyst to close his eyes and ears to the content and path of this highly personal, highly colored information. He is advised not to violate personal confidence. It may be that at some later time his management will permit him to speak objectively and impartially about this phase of the life of informal organization and about what it means to management.

But in order to repair a faulty management system, lessons from the informal organization provide invaluable source reference for the systems analyst. If he will study the anatomical structure and information content of this organization, and if he will refrain from exercising hasty spot action (which would undoubtedly muddy the situation still further), the systems analyst should gain perspective and understanding of the remedial action to be undertaken.

20. The Behavioral Side of MIS*

G. W. Dickson and John K. Simmons

To enjoy the technical benefits of management information systems, it is often necessary to solve the dysfunctional side effects stemming from behavioral problems—in short, people problems. Reactions to the installation of MIS may range from failure to use the output to outright sabotage. The authors identify three types of dysfunctional behavior—aggression, projection, and avoidance—that may appear in four groups—operating personnel, operating management, technical staff, and top management. Only the technical staff—being designers and agents of change—shows no dysfunctional behavior. Operating management, the group that should enjoy most of the system benefits, goes farther than any other group in its resistance, and exhibits all three forms. The authors suggest ways of minimizing the behavioral problems that may follow introduction of MIS.

Time and time again it has been said that the "people problem" is the major difficulty firms encounter when they attempt to design, develop, and

*SOURCE: *Business Horizons* (August 1970), pp. 59-71. Copyright © 1970 by the Foundation for the School of Business at Indiana University. Reprinted by permission.

implement management information systems. Recently, McKinsey and Company conducted a survey of thirty-six large computer users to investigate their computer practices and achievements. The analysis of the survey results strongly suggests that computer expenditures are not being matched by rising economic returns, and that the underlying reason is essentially behavioral in nature.[1]

The same point was dramatically brought home when we interviewed seventeen firms associated with the University of Minnesota's Management Information Systems Research Center concerning their research interests relative to the "management of management information systems." Such topics as project identification and selection, project time and cost estimation, project control and documentation, and the entire area of operations management were felt by the firms to be far less crucial than topics involving people problems in some way. The conclusion is inescapable that, in order to achieve the technical benefits of management information systems, the dysfunctional side effects stemming from behavioral problems must be minimized, and that any systems designer who "gives a complete hardware description to his charge without suggesting or forecasting problems in the social system does a disservice to himself and to his organization."[2]

This article will examine the effect of information systems on various levels of the organization consequences of introducing management information systems. The organizational groups considered to be relevant are: operating personnel (both nonclerical and clerical); operating management (first-level supervision through middle management); technical staff; and top management. One of our major propositions is that each group plays a different role in the development and use of management information systems, is affected differently by their introduction, and, therefore, must be discussed separately. Another of our basic points concerns the management information system (MIS) itself, which we will consider first.

Conceptual framework for MIS

Whenever managers or technical persons connected with organizational electronic data processing (EDP) systems get together and are confronted by the term "management information systems," the first question they usually ask is how the term should be defined. The typical response is to avoid the question or to combine several "buzz words" in order to so obfuscate the issue that the questioner becomes frustrated and passes on to other topics. In fact, it is quite safe to say that to our knowledge no satisfactory definition of MIS exists.

There is no doubt that the lack of an adequate definition makes discussion of the area as difficult as describing the daily activities of a resident of Shangri-la. In fact, it is highly probable that much of the trouble has been caused by speakers and authors, who, when referring to management information system, are actually speaking of EDP systems that do not provide (nor were they designed to provide) management with any information whatsover. In order to clarify the discussion, we shall subdivide the term into four subareas differentiated by the objective that the system is intended to satisfy:

> Clerical system—To substitute computer processing for manual record keeping.
> Information system—To supply information (not data) that is oriented toward management decision making.
> Information-decision system—To go beyond the simple provision of information to the decision maker and actually to assist the way in which the decision is reached.
> Programmed systems—To have the system rather than human decision makers make the decision.[3]

Later in this article we shall discuss how each of the organizational groups is affected by the different types of systems and what their behavioral reactions to each may be. Before getting to this level of detail, however, it is necessary to consider the general consequences of an organizational change.

Consequences of change

People tend to resist the new in favor of the old. Greenberger highlights this phenomenon in commenting that "explanation of human inertia would cite man's tendency to resist the new and espouse the old, his need for security, and his fondness for familiar objects even while exploring the unfamiliar."[4] Since unfavorable behavioral consequences often accompany any significant organizational change, it should not be surprising when a new management information system encounters resistance. In order to minimize or, better, to prevent these unfavorable consequences, management must not only recognize that introduction of an information system is likely to trigger trouble among personnel, but must also have some knowledge of the particular factors that underlie this type of behavior.

Factors influencing behavior

Many factors, including the magnitude of the change itself, may cause persons to resist change. Five factors, we believe, are especially related to dysfunctional behavior upon the introduction of MIS.

First, most complex organizations have definite departmental boundaries and divisions of formal responsibility, and changes in these boundaries and divisions often occur in connection with the introduction of a new information system. These changes may be planned in advance or occur as part of unforeseen adaptations necessary to the successful use of the system. Reif points out that "resistance will be inevitable as departmental boundaries are violated and entire functions are deleted or several combined in the name of greater operating efficiency."[5]

Second, the effect on the informal structure of an organization is also important. An organization tends to develop a system of values, ethical codes, taboos, special working relations, and sometimes even a special language among members. This structure often tends to be a strong force in the day-to-day functions of an organization. The impact of a new system on the informal structure can be as serious in terms of creating behavioral disturbances as the impact on the formal structure.

Third, personal characteristics and background of the particular members of the organization will affect behavior toward the new system. These factors include age, length of service, personality, cultural background, attitude toward the computer, organizational level, and experiences with previous organizational change.

Younger people with fewer years of service with an organization tend to be less opposed to change than older people with many years of service. Over-all personality and cultural background are also important in determining reaction. Schlosser refers to these factors when he reminds system designers that the personal characteristics of those affected may cause difficulties and create a situation where the individuals may not be ready to accept change.[6]

Some people simply view the computer in a negative light. Greenberger emphasizes that to many people the computer represents the most recent intrusion of the machine into man's private domain.[7] In addition, publicity in recent years has tended to justify the cost of computers through replacement of people. When these two factors are combined with a possible feeling of awe and a lack of understanding, the likely result is an unfavorable predisposition toward any system that incorporates the computer.

Reactions are also likely to vary with the organizational level affected. Most writers tend to agree that the middle-level manager can and often does offer the most resistance to change. Beckett articulates this point with the comment that "there is no disrupting the resistance that precedes major system changes—particularly from members of the middle management group."[8] The effect of organizational level and the role of the middle manager are, we believe, especially important regarding information systems.

Fourth, the members of an organization are more likely to respond favorably to a proposed change if the managerial climate maintains open communication and permits all grievances to be heard. The members of an organization can also sense the overall attitude of top management toward the system and the extent to which it has top level backing or support. Past experiences with organizational change may have a great deal to do with how new changes are accepted; if previous changes have not established a feeling of trust, confidence, and cooperative spirit, then the members of an organization may come to feel that management or special staff groups are likely to try to "put something over on them." Under such conditions, changes (or new systems) face trouble.

Fifth, at least one writer, the late Douglas McGregor, implies that the method employed to introduce a change may be the most important variable affecting its likelihood of success: "A fair amount of research has pointed up the fact that resistance to change is a reaction primarily to certain methods of instituting change rather than an inherent human characteristic."[9]

Not everyone would agree that the method used to implement the change is the primary variable influencing acceptance of change (remember the earlier quotation from Greenberger). However, research studies in this area suggest that the method by which a system is introduced is highly pertinent to the reaction to be expected from the organization members.

Outputs of behavior

Mention has been made of dysfunctional behavior associated with a new system. What specific forms do these outputs of behavior take? We have identified three general types.

Aggressive behavior represents an attack (either physical or nonphysical) intended to injure the object causing the problem. The most dramatic aggression toward the system occurs as sabotage—when persons attempt to destroy systems components. A less dramatic but more common aggression occurs when persons attempt to "beat the system." People are always smarter than systems and will be motivated to prove it if a system is operating in a way that offers a pay-off from beating the system (tangible or mere self-satisfaction). The authors saw this type of situation in a recent research investigation.

> The setting was an information system in a complex organization designed to collect man-hours in different work stations on a daily basis. Workers were frequently rotating from one work station to another during the day, and were supposed to clock in and out each time they moved from one station to another. During the course of an interview,

one worker indicated that there had been some "ganging up" on an unpopular foreman. Workers would not punch out of a particular area when leaving for another station or would punch in at the unpopular foreman's area and then work in a different area.

In a systems setting, *projection* exists when people blame the system for causing difficulties that are in fact caused entirely by something else. In many instances, the system may be blamed for failings actually caused by such factors as excessively rapid implementation, unrelated factors such as the general incompetence of the indivdual or individuals involved, or a wrong decision properly made in light of the best information available at the time.

When people defend themselves by avoiding or withdrawing from frustrating situations, they are exhibiting behavior known as *avoidance*. In the area of MIS, this behavior often takes the form of ignoring the system output, particularly when it does not fulfill information needs. The authors recently investigated the use of computrized accounting information in managerial decision making. Managers had developed other sources for the same information and were, to a large extent, ignoring the computer output.

Thus far, the reactions to organizational change (especially in an MIS context) have been discussed in a general fashion. We shall now turn to explore in more depth the behavioral consequences of introducing or modifying computerized information systems.

Organizational impact of MIS

There is good reason to believe that each of the organizational groups listed at the beginning of the article interacts uniquely with management information systems. Because of these differences, generalizations about how all members of an organization may react to information systems is bound to be inaccurate and, in many instances, inappropriate. Recognizing the difficulties associated with all generalizations, we believe that we can be somewhat more accurate by discussing the likely behavioral reactions of the various organizational subgroups to the introduction or modification of an organizational information system. Figure 1 summarizes the relation of each subgroup to information systems and the dysfunctional behaviors that are most likely to occur in each subgroup.

Operating personnel

This group includes all nonmanagerial persons in the organization exclusive of those who may be classified as technical staff. The operating

ORGANIZATIONAL SUBGROUP	RELATION TO MIS	PROBABLE DYSFUNCTIONAL BEHAVIOR
Operating personnel		
Nonclerical	Provide system inputs	Aggression
Clerical	Particularly affected by clerical systems; job eliminated, job patterns changed	Projection
Operating management	Controlled from above by information systems; job content modified by information-decision systems and programmed systems	Aggression, avoidance, and projection
Technical staff	Systems designer and agents of systems change	None
Top management	Generally unaffected and unconcerned with systems	Avoidance

FIGURE 1

Work groups, MIS interaction, and probable types of dysfunctional behavior.

personnel can be segmented into two classes, nonclerical and clerical. The nonclerical operating personnel, essentially the same group often called the blue-collar workers, have a quite different relation with the information system than do the clerical workers, whose tasks are directly associated with the system.

Nonclerical workers provide inputs to the system—punching time clocks, filling out forms giving processing times, entering pre-punched cards in a source recorder, or serving as subjects for time studies. About the only system output this group receives comes from a clerical system and takes the form of the payroll check.

As an organization computerizes and expands its clerical systems and develops information and information-decision systems, more and more responsibility is placed upon the workers to provide accurate and timely input. In many cases, confronted with a new or modified system, they exhibit behavior that prevents the system from being as effective as was intended. All too often systems personnel discover that the input data being transmitted are either in error or are missing altogether. Problems of this sort help account for why new systems often fall behind schedule or, in other cases, why dual systems (both the old and the new) must be maintained so long. A more dramatic case was encountered in another situation:

> An organization that had poor labor-management relations introduced an on-line management information system in one of its branches. Soon after, the discovery was made that source recorders were inoperable because honey had been poured down them. Others were mysteriously run over by work-lift trucks. In still others, paper clips had been inserted rather than badge cards. In addition, the system was being plagued continuously by errors in the input.

Fortunately, outright sabotage of this sort is rare, but it represents the extremes to which the dysfunctional aggressive behavior of the work force can go. Making purposeful errors or "forgetting" to use the system are more subtle forms of aggression often encountered in this subgroup.

Projection is a more frequent type of behavior observed in workers. Statements such as, "How can I get my work done when I have to spend all my time punching my jobs in and out on this transactor," are symptomatic of projection. In many cases, a new or modified system will assume the role of a scapegoat and will be blamed for many shortcomings for which it is not responsible. In most cases, workers' dysfunctional behavior toward information systems takes the form of projection and never reaches the stage of overt aggression. The manager and systems designer should, however, be wary when the system is blamed, for projection often is evident before aggressive behavior takes place.

The part played by clerical workers in information systems is principally one of processing inputs and converting them into outputs. One major function of this group is that of converting data into a form acceptable as system input. The relation of clerical workers to information systems, thus, is one of being a part of the system itself. The relationship with systems is shared by the technical staff, but the clerical workers have far less control over the destiny of an organization's system than does the staff. The three other groups—nonclerical workers, operating managers, and top management—are usually outside the systems development and operations effort, and their behavior is influenced accordingly.

The word best describing the relationship between clerical operatives and information systems is "change." They may be faced with the change from a manual system to an EDP system; they often must adapt to changes in EDP systems because of reprogramming for modified applications; and they may have work patterns changed as an organization develops information or information-decision systems. Because the higher level systems (information and information-decision systems) make so much use of the computer in the processing function (conversion of inputs to outputs), the major interface between clerical systems of this type is data preparation. With regard to clerical systems, these workers often perform some processing functions in addtion to supplying input data in the correct form and format.

As a result of the increased use of the computer to perform clerical tasks, many people predicted that job opportunities for clerical workers would decline in the age of information technology, and that those remaining would be routine and boring. Recent experience, however, shows that these predictions were in error. Currently, clerical workers are more in demand than ever before, and, as higher level information systems are developed, even more clerical workers will be needed. We believe that this state of affairs can easily be explained. Originally, the reason for introducing computer systems was to achieve a saving in clerical labor costs; had this trend continued, perhaps the above predictions would have been correct. Instead, two changes in direction have dramatically affected the role of clerical workers:

> *First,* the types of clerical systems now being computerized are so complex and of such magnitude that they could not even have been considered had manual processing been involved. In other words, these are now applications, not conversions of old manual clerical systems. On-line airline reservation systems and on-line bank teller systems are examples.
> *Second,* the emphasis on developing systems is to provide information that supports management decision making.

Thus, although some clerical jobs have been eliminated, the development of systems never before contemplated has opened up more clerical jobs than before to provide these systems with input data. Moreover, many of these jobs are more challenging and require more education and formal training. Partly because of these new conditions, we argue that a great many clerical workers are involved in system development and expect new, modified, and more complex systems. Consequently, clerical employees generally have little fear of displacement. Thus, the dysfunctional behavior that may be expected on the part of clerical workers is, in most cases, not due to fear of job loss, is much less pronounced than is usually anticipated, and is frequently associated with systems change.

Like most people, clerical workers get used to certain ways of doing their work. They may react negatively when told to modify their work patterns and work group relationships, a common request since change and EDP systems are virtually synonymous. One type of behavior is acceptance of the change, accompanied by a bit of projection toward the "new" system. Statements such as, "There never were as many errors when we did things the old way," or, "I sure could get a lot more work done before they changed the system," are frequently heard. Other dysfunctional behavior is not likely to occur unless the managerial climate is poor or the clerical workers have had bad experiences with previous systems changes.

Operating management

The second organizational group directly affected by management information systems is operating management. This group consists of first-line supervisors up to and including what is usually identified as middle management. Unlike operating personnel, operating management is only slightly affected by clerical systems, but this group is (and will be) greatly influenced by information systems, information-decision systems, and programmed systems.

The reason for this relationship is that the group forms much of the organization's operating decision structure. Since all MIS levels above the clerical level are directly associated with making management decisions, it follows that operating managers are the target of most of the outputs of such systems. Information systems are designed to provide the input to the management decision process; decision systems go one step further and are directed toward assisting the manager's decision-making process itself; and programmed systems actually replace the manager by "making" the decision.

Observers do not agree as to how operating managers will be affected by computerized systems. Predictions run all the way from the elimination of many jobs on the operating management level to freeing the operating manager from many of the time-consuming routine decision that prevent him from activities such as long-range planning, systems development, and working with people. There is general agreement and some empirical evidence that computerized information systems tend to centralize decision making and increase the ability of higher level managers to control their subordinates.

Whereas the operating personnel constitute the group primarily responsible for inputs to management information systems, it is the operating management that, ideally, should be the group which enjoys most of the system benefits in terms of outputs that enable them to make more effective decisions. Unfortunately, the real world often falls far short of this ideal. A principal reason for the difficulty is the behavioral reaction of operating managers to MIS—no other organizational group goes so far in their resistance. Operating managers exhibit all the types of dysfunctional behavior (see Figure 1).

Perhaps the most frequent reaction of the typical operating manager to computerized systems and/or decision aids is one of avoidance. He wants no truck with systems specialists, operations researchers, and the like. Seldom do operating managers seek out relationships with these persons. Most often systems are developed after they are dictated by top management. Parenthetically, it should be added that top management is usually reacting in such cases to a proposal originated by the systems' staff.

When operating managers do become involved with systems (usually after a great deal of coercion), their behavior often takes the form of aggression or projection. They fight the system through inadequate support, or they fail to use the information or decision suggestions provided by the system. They blame the system for operational failures having other causes, especially during the shakedown period of new systems.

Many persons have expressed the opinion that operating management has, in general, abdicated the responsibility for the development of management information systems to the technical staff specialists. No wonder, then, that the reaction of the operating, management group to the product provided by the technical staff is less than ideal. Although much of the blame for this state of affairs can be attached to the operating managers, the technical staff is also at fault.

Technical staff

The organizational group most involved in an operational sense with MIS and least affected behaviorally is the technical staff, such as programmers, systems designers, and operations researcher. These persons, being "systems people," are the agents of organizational change in the MIS area. Being intimately involved with systems development and committed to change, the technical staff is the one group in the organization that exhibits no dysfunctional behavior in the usual sense regarding change and introduction. We are suggesting that the involvement of the technical staff is such that it is unlikely that a member of this group would ever fight a new system or avoid using its output. Thus, while they do not exhibit dysfunctional behavior, they may be guilty of inducing it, especially in operating management.

Conflict between line-and-staff personnel is well documented. In the case of the operating manager vis-a-vis the systems man, the conflict may reach proportions of open warfare; the technical staff is not usually dedicated to smoothing the relationship. In many cases, the line manager is considered to be an old fuddy-duddy, undereducated, flying by the seat of his pants, and standing in the way of progress. Systems staff members tend to be younger, more highly educated, and less experienced than the line managers with whom they must deal. Also, in many cases, they have recently emerged from some prestigious graduate school with the attitude that they are ready to step in as the chief operating officer of a firm standing no lower than number 189 of *Fortune's* 500 industrials. As a result, one can observe these "whiz kids" in conflict with the operating managers, many of whom wish to rely only on their experience and judgment in making management decisions.

We have observed several interesting situations that, although atypical and perhaps overdramatic, serve to demonstrate how bad the conflict between technical staff and line managers can get.

> In one large organization a line manager and a systems analyst had to be physically restrained by others to prevent them from having a fist fight over a systems policy matter.

In several cases we have known operating managers and systems personnel who were not on speaking terms with one another. This was a carryover from working "together" on various systems studies.

Most persons who have ever worked in a large organization having a significant systems development effort can probably add many war stories of their own regarding the conflicts between the systems staff and the operating management. As more and more organizations move toward increased development of information, information-decision, and programmed systems, we expect the conflict between these systems designers and the systems users (operating managers) to get worse, not better.

Top management

The top management of our contemporary organizations have a special relationship with the computer and management information systems—one of avoidance and noninvolvement. Despite the fact that they pay lip service to the importance of the computer as an assistant to the top manager and the fact that many top managers attend short computer courses run by hardware manufacturers, it is a well-documented fact that the average top manager is little affected by the computer. Two recent publications, as a matter of fact, attach much of the blame for shortcomings in the MIS field on top management's lack of involvement in the design of corporate systems.[10]

Top managers, by the nature of their job, are little affected by clerical systems or programmed systems. On the information or information-decision system level, however, these managers have much to gain. Yet their typical reaction is to avoid any involvement with MIS. An example of one of the few exceptions to this type of behavior is the role taken by Terrence Hanold, president of the Pillsbury Company, in the development of that firm's MIS.[11] Partly because of Hanold's involvement, the company is often used as one of the best examples of how the computer should be employed as an aid to management. Unfortunately, the Pillsbury case is one of the few bright spots in an otherwise gloomy picture.

The behavior we have described in the various organizational groups does not occur without good reason. In all cases, the type of work being performed and the type of system with which interaction takes place influence the behavioral reaction. In addition, other factors help to predict behavior that must be considered. Figure 2 summarizes the specific factors that may be most important in causing dysfunctional behavior in each organizational group.

	OPERATING (NONCLERICAL)	OPERATING (CLERICAL)	OPERATING MANAGEMENT	TOP MANAGEMENT
Threats to economic security		X	X	
Threats to status or power		X	X*	
Increased job complexity	X		X	X
Uncertainty or unfamiliarity	X	X	X	X
Changed interpersonal relations or work patterns		X*	X	
Changed superior-subordinate relationships		X*	X	
Increased rigidity or time pressure	X	X	X	
Role ambiguity		X	X*	X
Feelings of insecurity		X	X*	X*

FIGURE 2
Reasons for resistance to MIS (by working group)

X = The reason is possibly the cause of resistance to MIS development.
X* = The reason has a strong possibility of being the cause of resistance.

Minimizing dysfunctional behavior

Recognition of potential dysfunctional behavioral consequences of installing or modifying a management information system does not, by itself, solve any problems. Special attention must also be given to specific steps or procedures designed to prevent or minimize such consequences. The point must be emphasized that there is no single solution—rather, each situation must be diagnosed carefully to determine which procedures apply.

Proper atmosphere

It is important to investigate the nature of the overall organizational climate for its potential effect on the information system. Critical aspects are the attitudes of both management and any affected employee, organizational cohesiveness, and organization culture. The attitude of top management should be one of full support for the system. There should also be open lines of communication between different levels of management, between management and employees, and between line and staff. An overall feeling of trust and cooperative spirit should exist, free of excessive concern over job stability, security, and so forth. If significant problems exist in any of these areas, the systems analyst may have to attempt to create the proper atmosphere; in other words, preconditioning may be necessary.

Participation

Participation in decisions pertaining to the basic structure of the system —which items will be included, what information will be given to whom, and possible job modifications—should be on a widespread basis. Participation by those who will be affected by the system is essential. This is especially true for operating managers. Huse states that specialists have had too much responsibility for information systems and operating managers too little.[12] The specialist must not dominate the installation, and more responsibility should be given to the operating manager than has often been the case.

A system should not be forced upon members of an organization in a "bulldozer" approach. Along with participation in decisions pertaining to the structure of the system, an attempt should be made to achieve harmony between individual and organizational goals. Schlosser makes a strong point concerning the need for the systems analyst to create attainable goals for employees involved in the system if the employee is to accept and learn to use the system. He cites a case in which foremen who were convinced that their ultimate goal of self-advancement would be helped by the system became staunch allies of the system analyst.[13] Of course, relating the goals of the information system and those of the individual may be somewhat difficult in some cases; a substantial amount of probing may be necessary to find the key to obtaining the needed acceptance and support from those members of the organization affected by the system.

Clarity of the system

The purpose and characteristics of the system should be as clear as possible to those who have any direct contact with it; effective use or support cannot be obtained if there is confusion or a lack of understanding. This means that the nature and detail of a system must be fully explored and discussed with those affected before, during, and after installation. Generally, much more explanation is necessary than is usually thought to be required; those of us who have many years' experience in the classroom know that this basic problem applies to many situations. In order to minimize the dysfunctional consequences of a general lack of understanding of the system, a substantial percentage of the systems analyst's time— perhaps 25 to 30 percent—should be reserved for communication with users of the information. Full communication is essential.

Another factor of importance is minimizing initial system errors. The authors have often encountered situations where confusion, misunderstanding, and failure to use output have been caused by numerous errors during the first few months of operation. Frequent mistakes can delay or even completely undermine a potentially good system. User reaction to errors must be recognized, and every effort made to have an error-free operation before implementation. Finally, with regard to system implementation, realistic goals and deadlines must be set. Implementation at too fast a pace creates confusion and numerous errors in addition to short tempers and tired minds.

Plan scope

The fact that a computer has the ability to do something that a man can do—even more efficiently—does not necessarily mean that the computer should do it. In the overall interests of the organization and for the most effective system, certain tasks may need to remain in the hands of individuals. Whisler points out that "managers with whom we have talked are reluctant to admit that computer systems, in any way, tell them what to do. The idea of 'sharing control' is somewhat more palatable." Hofstede calls attention to the possible need to deliberately plan a certain amount of scope for the individual within a computer-controlled system, resulting in a "calculated inefficiency" that can save the humanity within the systems.[14]

The individual must retain his sense of dignity and importance as a human being along with the feeling of worthy contribution to the needs of the organization. Acceptance of the system is not likely if the individual has the feeling, rightly or wrongly, that the computer has usurped his position.

New challenges

Calculated inefficiency may not be necessary in most cases. New challenges may be opened up by the installation of a computerized system. Although certain tasks may be taken over by the computer, there are often less routine and important jobs that, because of lack of time or pertinent information, have not been receiving adequate attention. Such situations are to occur most often at the lower and middle management levels.

Beckett comments that the loss of decision-making power by middle managers under advanced systems turns out to be in part an illusory loss. The decision-making prerogative that is given up may be of such low quality (routine) that it is questionable whether a manager should have devoted time to it in the first place. Whisler comments, similarly, that the real problem is that we have not discovered the new decision problems that are the real challenge for the people whose old decision problems are being removed by information technology. We have not taken a look at what decision makers ought to be doing that is more important and satisfying than what they did before.[15] The systems analyst should attempt to discover and emphasize these new challenges in his discussions with management at all levels if he is to obtain the most effective implementation of the system.

Reexamine performance evaluation

Neither tasks nor their relative emphasis should be modified in a new system without reexamining the performance evaluation criteria. Huse notes that "one of the things that struck me in some of my research is the fact that managers resisted the new computer programs because they could no longer maintain control of their own subunit and yet they were still being rewarded on this basis."[16] Huse also comments that there will have to be a shift from rewards based on individual accomplishments to rewards based upon group achievement if integrated programs are to be successful.

The most effective reward system, especially in complex situations, is a topic upon which there is substantial disagreement; there are few guidelines to offer the systems analyst. Yet it is an area with which he must be concerned, where tasks or the emphases on tasks change extensively in conjunction with the new system. Management must work out the reward system to the satisfaction of those affected if the system is to be accepted.

User orientation

In order to design the appropriate management information system, the analyst must attempt to determine how user behavior will be affected by the manner and form in which the outputs are communicated. The design of the system must fulfill the needs of the user if he is to be satisfied with the output; otherwise, he is compelled to maintain his own system, which, of course, defeats the basic purpose of the installation. The longer the user runs his old system in parallel, the more difficult it is to get him to supply accurate data to a new one that is not serving his needs. The system designer should be careful not to overwhelm the user with a large volume of output which the user either cannot understand or cannot use effectively. Walker makes the pertinent point that the integration of a computer system with a manager does not mean that the manager's thought processes will suddenly accelerate and allow him to keep up with unrestrained outpourings of the computer.[17]

Attempting to maintain a user orientation is perhaps the key factor for the systems analyst; this factor relates not only to the form, content, and volume of the information, but also to the other suggestions for minimizing dysfunctional behavior. User orientation encompasses other factors we have not discussed—guaranteed employment, retraining, recognition of seniority, and so forth—that may be key factors to consider in a given situation.

There is no single factor that represents the panacea for behavioral ills. Each situation must be analyzed carefully to determine the optimal procedures for preventing or curing dysfunctional behavioral consequences surrounding the modification or installation of a system.

The most probable dysfunctional behavioral consequences occurring as a result of a system installation or modification varies with the type of system and the organiaztional level affected. The backgrounds of both the organization and the individuals interacting with the system are also important. There is no single answer for preventing dysfunctional behavior, but the general recommendations may be helpful. The systems analyst must give careful consideration to these factors in solving the people problems and achieving a successful installation.

NOTES

1. See, for example, J. Diebold, "Bad Decisions on Computer Use," *Harvard Business Review*, XLVII (January-February, 1969), p. 15, and *Unlocking the Computer's Profit Potential* (New York: McKinsey and Company, 1968), pp. 14-15.
2. L. K. Williams, "The Human Side of a Systems Change," *Systems and Procedures Journal* (July-August, 1964), p. 199.
3. See G. W. Dickson, "Management Information-Decision Systems," *Business Horizons* (December, 1968) for additional discussion of these subareas.
4. M. Greenberger, "The Computer in Organization," in C. A. Walker, ed., *Technology, Industry, and Man* (New York: McGraw-Hill Book Company, 1968), p. 304.
5. W. E. Reif, *Computer Technology and Management Organization* (Iowa City: Bureau of Business and Economic Research, University of Iowa, 1968), pp. 37-38.
6. R. E. Schlosser, "Psychology for the Systems Analyst," *Management Services* (November-December, 1964).
7. "The Computer in Organization," in *Technology, Industry, and Man*, p. 309.
8. J. A. Beckett, "The Total Systems Concept: Its Implications for Management," in C. A. Myers, ed., *The Impact of Computers on Management* (Cambridge, Mass.: M.I.T. Press, 1967) pp 221-222.
9. Douglas McGregor, "The Scanlan Plan Through a Psychologist's Eyes' in *Technology, Industry, and Man*, p. 124.
10. "Bad Decisions on Computer Use" and *Unlocking the Computer's Profit Potential*.
11. "Beyond Flour Power," *Time* (December 13, 1968), p. 96.
12. E. F. Huse, "The Impact of Computerized Programs on Managers and Organizations," in *The Impact of Computers on Management*, p. 290.
13. "Psychology for the Systems Analyst," p. 206.
14. T. L. Whisler, "The Impact of Information Technology on Organizational Control", in *The Impact of Computers on Management*, p. 40; G. H. Hofstede, *The Game of Budget Control* (Ansen, The Netherlands: Royal Van Gorcam, 1967), p. 304.
15. "The Total Systems Concept: Its Implications for Management" and "The Impact of Information Technology on Organizational Control."
16. "The Impact of Computerized Programs on Managers and Organizations."
17. *Technology, Industry, and Man*, p. 318.

21. Changing Systems and Behavior*

Edgar G. Williams

The popularity of the systems approach has accelerated change in organizations. Change is not easy, primarily because of the people who were deeply involved in the old system. This article explores the variables: emotional, cultural, and perceptual; pointing out that the key to successful, orderly, and planned change lies in the manager's understanding of human behavior and properly applying this knowledge.

Creating and innovating, the hand-maidens of change and progress, do not always contribute to stable modifications of existing systems or to the smooth introduction of newly designed ones.

The early stages of implementation often prove difficult, appear to be less economical in the short run, and on the surface, less effective. How often have you heard the comment, "Why don't they leave well enough alone?" Chances are good that we have all heard that statement at one time or another, and chances are equally as good that the person saying it has found a new system or a new method less to his liking than a previous

*SOURCE: *Business Horizons* (August 1969), pp. 53-58. Copyright © 1969 by the Foundation for the School of Business at Indiana University. Reprinted by permission.

one. It may well be that the new system is a bit more difficult; it may well be that all of the "bugs" have not been anticipated or obviated—thus causing it to be more cumbersome and requiring closer attention. Either of these results will make it appear to the individuals involved that the change is a step backward rather than forward.

On the other hand, the new system or modification may be properly planned and designed, yet great difficulties may be experienced in getting it installed and operating smoothly because of the people involved. The real cause for the problem may be an individual who views the new system as a threat to his personal security; it may not match his skills as well as that which it replaced; or he may even have some emotional hang-up in that the degree of participation that he enjoyed in creating, planning, or implementing the new system may be viewed by him as being totally inadequate.

Two types of problems are commonly associated with the introduction of a new management system or the modification of an existing one: those that relate to the system itself and have to do with its nature and design, and those that have to do with people who either are, or think they are, going to be affected by the innovations and changes inherent in making the newly designed system work. The purpose of this article is to discuss some of the ways and means by which "people problems" may be avoided.

As a creator of change, the manager must understand that planned change, orderly change, is his immediate goal. There are four general reasons for designing orderly change:

1. To improve the means for satisfying somebody's economic wants
2. To increase profitability
3. To promote human work for human beings
4. To contribute to individual satisfaction and social well-being.

What is change in this sense? Simply put, change is a modification of existing relationships; it is an alteration of the status quo. The most difficult relationships to adjust or accommodate to, when one views change in this respect, are organization or behavioral in nature.

If we are going to manage for change successfully, the values that result must contribute directly to the ultimate objectives of the business firm. Technological and/or managerial innovations make change essential. It is essential to competitive well-being and growth. Planned growth usually has a direct relationship to profitability. Profitability, in turn, has much to do with the personal satisfactions that individuals and groups get out of their interactions and individual contributions of energy and ideas. These satisfactions are the means toward social improvement, which, whether one likes it or not, are one of the most compelling long-run reasons for the introduction of change into a business environment.

Important variables in change

Change involves a number of variables. The most common types of change have to do with machinery and equipment, methods and procedures, work standards, personnel and organizational adjustments, interrelationships with those who hold authority and power, responsibility and status, and changes in objectives (in direction, plans, and policies). The systems manager may be involved with one, or even all, of these at one time or another. To be a real change agent, he must be able to influence others in a positive fashion. This skill is tested as he anticipates and designs ways and means of overcoming what in many cases is a natural reluctance or resistance to anticipated change.

Not all change is resisted by all people. Some welcome change. It provides them with hope for adjustment in existing work situations; alterations in relationships that exist among their associates; and opportunities to become more successful in line with their personal aspirations.

Resistance to change

Probably there are more people who resist change for one reason or another than there are those who accept it when first it is introduced. Resistance tends to focus on human relationships rather than on the structural and procedural changes in the systems themselves or the accompanying changes outside the systems. People resist change because it upsets their established patterns of behavior. They often see it as a threat to their security.

Economic reasons

Some resistance is based on economic fear—the fear of becoming temporarily displaced or unemployed. Individuals may see a reduction in their work hours, which they relate to reduction in income; they relate this, in turn, to an attack on their economic security. They may look upon the new system as a work accelerator of some kind which speeds up the normal leisurely pace which they have been enjoying and puts them, as they would say, on a treadmill. They may come to the conclusion that the new system will not improve their material well-being in any way, and they say, "Well, why should I go along with it? It doesn't mean anything to me." *There may be some truth to that, too.*

Economic reasons for resisting change cannot be separated completely from the more personal reasons. Barriers to change, from the viewpoint of an individual, are perceptual, emotional or cultural in nature. Perceptual barriers have to do with the mental limitations of the individual and his ability to vizualize what the proposed changes may mean to him; he may be unable to visualize the total picture and never really understand how he fits into it.

Emotional barriers

Emotional barriers include fear and biases. If people do not understand new equipment and new methods and have heard from others how they have worked, or not worked, apprehensiveness may develop. It is normal also to bring prejudices that have built up during one's lifetime to the job as a result of personal experience and exposure to others. Moreover, he may perceive the change as one involving greater effort or a higher degree of difficulty—thus adding to his resistance.

Cultural barriers

Cultural barriers are the limitations and hang-ups that individuals have as a product of their culture. It is often unhandy, but we must learn to accept people in the same sense that we accept the system. We have to accept the whole man; we cannot employ part of him. We cannot hire a portion of a man to work for us during the day any more than we can take a portion of a system and equate it to a total system. Therefore, when we pay a man's salary we are buying not only his work effort but his fears, biases and social inhibitions as well. Ways must be found to make the system work with and for him.

Perceptual barriers

Individuals resent implied criticism. When somebody comes in and says, "Look, we're going to change the way this is being done; we're going to go to a different type of machine; we're going to alter the procedures or we're going to change the policies," there is the possibility that the individual will feel that the new development implies personal criticism. Therefore, the reasons for the change must be carefully explained in advance, in order that he will have a chance to think about it and to ask questions.

The individual may also fear that the need for either mental or physical skills involved in the job will be diminished by the substitution of systems and hardware. It may be too, that an individual will resist because he anticipates greater monotony and boredom after the systems analyst has completed his task. Sometimes this is true. Yet, sometimes, we can go in the other direction and enlarge the dimensions of the job and make it more meaningful and satisfying.

The individual may not be happy about the time and effort that will be required of him to retrain or to relearn. An excellent example of this situation exists now in colleges and universities—particularly in business schools. We have brought in, over a period of time, a large number of mathematicians and behavioral scientists. We have introduced their disciplines and related information into all of our courses, and now suddenly we have a group of top professors who, if they are not obsolete, run a tremendous risk of becoming obsolete unless they are willing to relearn and to be "retooled" in the behavioral sciences and in mathematical analysis. According to a colleague, many of us are engaged in a footrace between obsolescence and early retirement, and the only way that we are going to win that race is to change our attitudes toward relearning.

Probably the greatest single personal barrier is that individuals do not understand or refuse to accept the reasons for the change or the need for it. Unfortunately, it is not always easy to equate the reasons and the needs and to communicate them in meaningful and compelling language.

The social system

Several social reasons support resistance in the development or modification of management systems. New social relationships will develop on the job as well as off the job, because existent relationships cannot very well be shut off in most communities when work ends at night. Individuals do not want present social relationships altered. They may resent what seems to them to be undue outside influence on their little informal organizational groups. They may feel that there is nothing to be gained as individuals by cooperating, or it may be that they resist because others are resisting, (a form of "me-tooism").

Overcoming resistance

Usually, when initiating a new system, some resistance to change can be anticipated. The planner can overcome this condition to the extent that he can minimize disrupting well-established interpersonal relationships by bringing people together with common or similar frames of reference well before the new system is introduced. He can alleviate resistance to the extent that he presents himself to the people who are going to be affected as an assistant in helping to overcome some of the problems that they perceive in meeting their objectives and to the extent that he minimizes threats and assists calming anxiety.

It is normal for an individual to be concerned when there is a change in the offing; but it is not normal for that individual to let anxiety keep on developing to the point it serves as real fear. This is a difference between the two conditions: fear is introduced from an element that is external to an individual. He becomes afraid of something outside himself. Anxiety grows from within—a sort of self-induced dread. Those of us interested in the development of new systems and their proper implementation can anticipate the fear. We can also anticipate the development of some anxiety and we must do whatever we can to aid the individual in controlling his own dread of what is liable to happen to him under the new set-up.

In general, we can overcome resistance to the extent that we can generate feelings of personal acceptance in the people who are going to be involved and to the extent that we use appropriate timing and strategies in planning and implementing the changes.

Influencing behavior

Let us examine the problem of influencing behavior, the real problem when systems men ask individuals to change their behavior. When we introduce a new system or modify the present one, we are asking people to do two things: unlearn the old and to accept and to learn the new. Too often we forget and do not give enough attention to the first requirement. We are quite willing to ask them to accept and learn the new, but fail to spend enough time trying to get them to unlearn the old. This problem is highlighted by the "persistency of set." Having learned to do something one way often makes it dfficult to learn the new method, approach or technique. This "set" or behavior pattern persists and complicates new learning.

Factors in learning

New learning is based on a number of factors. One must first get the individual's attention, and the individual must have the desire to learn. Learning cues, which automatically trigger certain responses in people, are another factor. If we are going to change a system, we are going to have people learning something new; this means that we have to change the cues as well, because people tend to do what they have done before. As a change agent, the systems man must find out what it is that triggers desired behavior. He should try to anticipate the responses he would like to have, then work backward and figure out what will cue that response. Then he must ascertain what is going to appeal to the specific individual in terms of personally satisfying values. Somehow, wants and needs must be related to the rewards that are available. Individual expectations can be matched with available opportunities and the system can be fully implemented.

To help individuals change their behavior patterns, the reasons for the proposed change must be made clear to them; the new behavior must appear necessary and real incentives must be provided. This does not necessarily mean financial incentives; it may be that nonfinancial incentives will prove most valuable. If we are going to get people to accept a new order of things, we must remember to remove the rewards for their old behavior patterns. If we continue to reward people for doing what they have in the past, they will continue to behave that way. We must remove the old rewards at the same time that we are trying to induce changes in behavior. To stimulate individuals to change their behavior adequate time and improved methods for retraining must be allowed plus adequate time to make the transition from the old to the new.

Finally, the systems manager must demonstrate sympathetic understanding of the problems that the individual is experiencing or likely to experience as a result of the change. He can't just say, "Oh, hell, Joe, that's no problem", or "That's your problem, you worry about it." If he wants to get his new system introduced smoothly, he had better offer a certain amount of sympathetic understanding to the individuals involved.

The role of the group

Groups in themselves are often effective change agents. When a group and its various subgroups have harmonious relationships and well-understood objectives and goals, the group itself may become the prime mover in getting a change effected. When a shared feeling for the need for change has been generated from within the group, the group itself will often cause the change to be implemented and implemented smoothly. This should provide a tip-off to the systems man who is picking an appropriate timing strategy. Whether he chooses a cautious action strategy, a mass offensive strategy or some other other form of strategy, he may be able to utilize what some people have called the "boring from within" concept—plant the idea and get strength from inside the group, and then have the group ask for the change. Impetus for change that comes from within the group it self is probably the strongest and most effective way of producing it.

Recent research shows that when a decision involves some risk to all members of a group, the group as a whole is more willing to venture into a change than is the individual leader of that group. The leader's sense of responsibility seems to make him cautious, and the group itself proves more ready to take the risk. There must be a lesson here, too, for those of us who are planning the introduction of a new way of doing things that is likely to affect a sizable group of people. The reluctance to assume risks represents one of the major obstacles that we must contend with in dealing with individual managers.

In planning for change we should make clear the need for the change and try to provide a climate in which others feel free to identify with such needs. Relevant group participation in clarifying and expanding the concept of these various needs must be encouraged. We are obligated to state the objectives to be achieved in clear, concise, and, if possible, quantitative terms. We must establish broad guidelines for achieving the objectives, guidelines in terms of administrative polices that can be communicated and procedures that can be readily understood.

A word of caution seems advisable at this point. It is possible to overplan for change. We can plan to the point where no room is left for the exercise of any intelligent initiative on the part of those who are going to have to work with the change and make it operate. Therefore, in planning we will do well to determine the actions that are necessary—who-when-where—and then leave the how to last and as much as possible to those persons directly concerned with implementation and operation.

Rewards or benefits to indivduals and to the group must be carefully communicated. To materialize these benefits or rewards, the opportunities that are inherent in the change must be related to the expectations of the people involved. In order to match expectations and opportunites, the systems manager may have to go all the way back to a consideration of the basic human wants and needs of individuals and give consideration to the different kinds of growth with which he is to deal.

People can make any change work if they want it to work. The key to successful, orderly, planned change lies in the systems manager's understanding of human behavior—individually or collectively.

4 THE ROLE OF THE COMPUTER

*The importance of the computer in facilitating the implementation of infor-
mation-decision systems is an acknowledged fact. The matters now requiring
attention include: (1) the proper placement of the computer (and its control)
in the organization so as to obtain its most effective use; (2) the degree to
which operating management is active in the development of information-
decision systems; (3) the manner in which computers are evaluated in terms
of profitability; (4) the establishment of computer project priorities; (5) keeping
abreast of new developments in computer technology, e.g., timesharing; and
(6) appraising new applications elsewhere to determine potential usefulness to
the organization. The readings offered in this section, in addition to discussing
basic computer concepts, should provide insight into these questions.*

A. Computer Concepts

22. Computers: Basic Concepts*

American Telephone and Telegraph Company

Probably the first thing to remember about computers is that they are not "thinking machines." About all they can do is add, subtract, multiply, divide and compare figures in order to choose from a number of alternatives. And to do these things, they have to be told, step by step, exactly what to do. But computers perform so rapidly—some computers can execute a quarter of a million additions per second—it appears that they can do much more complex operations. When a computer solves the differential equation governing the trajectory of a ballistic missile, for example, it reduces that equation to a series of thousands of additions, subtractions, and alternate decisions according to the instructions of its human programmer.

Just as previous machines, such as the hammer and the microscope, extended the capabilities of man's muscles and eyes, the computers can be said to have extended the capacity of man's central nervous system. They "remember" information—some large computers can store billions of numbers—and can perform rudimentary calculations and logical operations. From this point of view, men have used some form of computers for a long time.

Nature gave man his first *digital* computer—his fingers. Digit comes from the Latin word *digitus*, meaning finger. Since man has ten fingers, it was natural for him to use a decimal base (10) when he began to count. Thus, our counting is based on a system of ten digits. It could easily be based on two, five, or any number. As we shall see, digital computers—the kind of

*SOURCE: Extracted from *The Bell System's Approach to Business Information Systems,* brochure published by the American Telephone and Telegraph Company, 1965. Copyright © 1965 by American Telephone and Telegraph Company. Reprinted by permission of publisher.

computers used by businesses—use a binary system based on two digits for their arithmetic.

Representing information

Modern digital computers use a number of different methods to record and represent information. The oldest method and the one still most commonly used for gathering information is the *punched card*. Punched cards contain eighty vertical columns and each column has ten rows, numbered from zero to nine, as in the diagram. Each column represents a character; the five row punched in a column, for example, represents the number five.

There are also two unmarked positions above the top of the 0 row, which are called *zones*. The combination of a zone punch with a number punch produces an alphabetic character. "B," for example, is formed by a punch in the top zone combined with a two punch.

A particular item of information, such as a seven-digit telephone number, is represented on a card by punches in a consecutive group of columns called a field. Data may also be printed at the top of the card to allow people to read the card more easily.

Punched cards are usually "read" by electromechanical readers. The cards pass from a hopper between an electrically charged roller and a metallic brush. The card acts as an insulator between the roller and the brush, and current passes only when there is a punch. An electrical impulse, caused by a punch, along with corresponding timing signals, represents information to the machines. Different types of punched card equipment use this information to sort, collate, print, or perform arithmetic operations.

With the advent of high-speed computers, punched cards alone became too slow and cumbersome. Paper tape, such as used in Teletype equipment systems, came into wide use for recording information. But *magnetic tape*, the fastest of all, is used for storing information for today's high-speed computer operations.

Information is stored on magnetic tape in *binary* language. In the binary counting system, there are only two digits, zero and one. In computer jargon, one and zero are called bit and no-bit. "Bits" is a contraction of binary digits. The binary system is used by digital computers since the two possible states of an electrical component—on or off, magnetized or unmagnetized, positive or negative—can be used to represent the two digits.

Binary numbers sound incredibly complex to the layman, but they are really quite simple. In our ordinary system of counting—the decimal system —we have ten digits. When we use them all up, counting from zero to nine, we "carry" a place and start all over, counting from ten to nineteen.

Binary numbers work the same way. When all the digits are used up—

when we count from zero to two—we "carry" a place and start over again. Thus, we would count: 0, 1, 10, 11, 100, etc. Figure 1 shows the binary equivalents of decimal numbers from zero through nine. Notice that all powers of two (2, 4, and 8) in the decimal system are equivalent to powers of ten (10, 100, 1000) in the binary system.

DECIMAL CHARACTERS	BINARY CHARACTERS
0	0000
1	0001
2	0010
3	0011
4	0100
5	0101
6	0110
7	0111
8	1000
9	1001

FIGURE 1
Decimal values 0-9 and their binary equivalents

Although there are simple formulas for converting binary numbers to decimal and vice versa, people find them inconvenient to read. Thus, for almost all business applications, digital computers use the simpler *binary coded decimal* system. This system uses a four-bit binary number to represent each digit in a decimal number. Thus, the programmers who have to communicate with the machines need only learn the digits zero to nine in binary to be able to read the computer's output. Figure 2 gives an example of a binary coded decimal number.

As on punched cards, nonnumeric characters, such as letters and punctuation marks can also be represented in binary by the addtion of two zone bit positions. A total of six bit positions is used to represent a single number, letter, or other charcter. However, most computers also use a seventh bit—a *check* or *parity bit*—to watch for errors. If there is an error the computer informs the operator that something is wrong.

Information on magnetic tape is sometimes represented by these seven-bit characters written on the tape much as sound is recorded on a tape recorder. Different pieces of information, on records, are separated by an empty space on the tape called an *interrecord gap*. A read-write and an erase head on the tape machines associated with the computer perform their functions much as do their counterparts on a tape recorder. The tape is moved over the heads, and long loops of tape in vacuum columns and other devices permit repid acceleration of the tape without tearing.

In large-scale accounting operations, source data is usually put onto tape

DECIMAL	BINARY
5	0101
1	0001
2	0010
7	0111
4	0100
3	0011

FIGURE 2

Binary coded decimal uses a four-bit binary number to represent each digit in a decimal number. For example, the number 512,743 can be read as shown.

from punched cards and paper tape. Magnetic tape may be used to store data, such as billing and collecting records, and may also be used to store the instructions, or programs, for particular operations. The actual arithmetic and logic of an operation, however, is carried out inside the computer, in its *memory* and in other circuitry.

There are several types of computer memories, but the most common is magnetic cores. Magnetic cores are used for action in a computer. They are tiny ferrite cores, wired in matrices, which can be magnetized in two different directions, each direction representing a one or a zero bit (Figure 3).

There are many other types of computer memories. One of the Electronic Switching System memories uses stacks of ferrite sheets containing tiny magnetic dots. Other devices such as photographic plates and thin magnetic films are also being studied as memory units. Several kinds of *bulk storage* devices, such as magnetic drums and disks, are also used as auxiliary storage in computer systems.

Besides memory, the inside of a computer also contains circuitry called *machine logic*, which carries out arithmetic and logic operations. All operations, no matter how complex, are based on four basic logical functions: *and, or, not,* and *memory*. These functions are performed by fundamental circuits called gates, triggers, and inverters. More complex combinations of thes circuits, called delay circuits, clock circuits, counters, and adders, perform the actual operations of addition, subtraction, multiplication, division, and comparisons. Other circuits control the flow of information in the computer and route information to and from storage. Computer circuit design, however, is an extremely complex subject, far beyond the scope of this book.

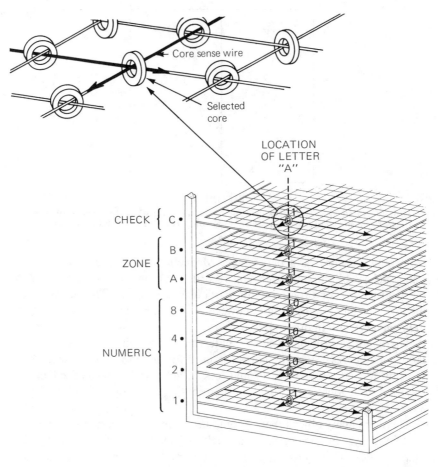

FIGURE 3
This vertical array of 6 bits and 1 check bit make up the letter "A"
(1110001) in core storage.

Programming

The real control and direction of the computer is in the hands of the human beings who use it. To carry out a particular operation, the computer must be told what to do by a set of instructions called a *program*. A program for a typical telephone company billing and collecting job would contain tens of thousands of individual instructions, with thousands of alternate paths through the program for the computer to choose from, depending on the circumstances of each operation. Some fundamental understanding of programming will assist the manager in communcating his needs to the programmers working on his operations.

As an approach to programming, we can look at how a simple telephone billing entry on a tally sheet might be made by a human bookkeeper. Let us say that we have a stack of punched cards for long distance toll calls, and that we want to tell a new clerk how to compute the cost of the call and enter it on the tally sheet. Our instructions (greatly simplified) might start like this: 1) Take the first card. 2) Copy down the originating telephone number, the called area code and telephone number, and the time of the call. 3) Look on the rate table for the proper rate to the area code at the given time. 4) Is the time three minutes or under? 5) If it is three minutes or under, enter the three-minute rate on the tally sheet and go to step 10. 6) If it is over three minutes, write down on scratch paper the number of minutes over. 7) Multiply this by the per minute rate. 8) Add this product to the three-minute rate. 9) Write the sum on the tally sheet. 10) Is there another card? 11) If there is, go back to 1. 12) If there is not, stop.

In this sequence of instructions, there are a number of different types of operations. The clerk must look up information on cards and in tables; he must write information down on scratch paper and on the tally sheet; he must subtract, multiply, and add, and he must make certain decisions which determine what steps to go to next. The computer operates in much the same way, and the diagram of this operation, which is called a *flow chart*, is the way the programmer outlines his problem before he puts it into language that the computer can understand.

In this flow diagram (Figure 4), there are a number of operations requiring special attention. We have already seen how computers read and write information from tape and cards, and how they perform arithmetic operations. In addition to these operations, this flow chart requires the computer to make a number of decisions. The first decision—the diamond shape—is based on whether the telephone call was less than, equal to, or greater than three minutes. If it is more than three minutes, we want the computer to do one thing; if it is less than or equal to, we want it to do something else. In computer jargon such an instruction is called a *branch*, and in this case, a *branch on high* since the exception occurs if the number of minutes is higher than three.

At the second branch, the computer must look to see if there is another card (or if there is another entry on tape). If there is a card, the computer will perform a loop. That is, it will go back to a previous instruction, as directed, and continue through the diagram once again. This ability of a computer to loop is based upon its ability to store and operate on instructions, as well as data.

Unlike the human bookkeeper, the computer has no eyes to see where the data and instructions it needs are stored. Therefore, each piece of information in the computer is given a memory location. Each location is numbered and the number is called the information's *address*. For example,

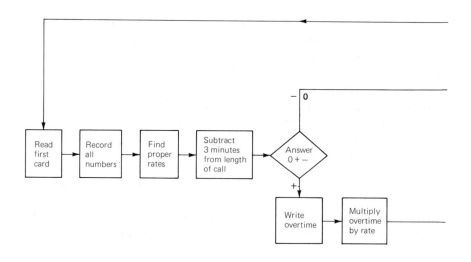

FIGURE 4

A simplified diagram of the way a programmer "outlines" his problem. Each box represents an action to be taken or a decision to be made in the program.

a computer with 10,000 locations would have addresses numbered from 0000 to 9999.

For many computers, information to be added or multiplied must first be placed in a special register called an *accumulator*. To perform our first instruction then, the computer must be told in language it can understand, what to read and where to place the information. If we let the symbol R stand for read, and 0500 for the address of where we wish to place the information, our first instruction in machine language could read: R 0500. This would mean: "Place the information on the card in location 0500." We then compare this information to a constant—three minutes. Thus, we would write S 0019, which would tell the computer to see if the time in location 0500 is greater than the constant we stored in location 0019. A subsequent instruction would tell the computer where to look for its next instruction depending on its findings.

The rest of the sample simplified program for this problem is worked out in Figure 5 with explanations. Note that the instructions themselves also have locations. These instructions—the entire program—are loaded into the computer's memory at the start of an operation. The instructions are read

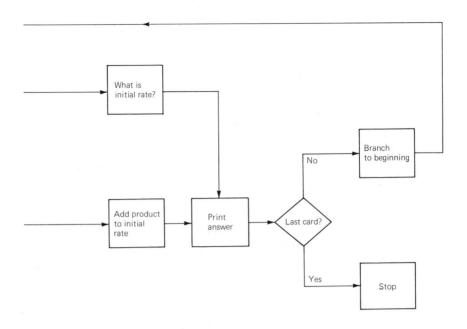

from punched cards or magnetic tape, in the same way data is read. Often there will be too many instructions in a program to fit in the computer's memory. In cases like this, a skilled programmer will take advantage of the fact that many instructions are not needed after they are used. Hence they may be erased and subsequent commands put in their place as the program is running. Similarly, large tables of data, constants, and other intermediate results can be erased and replaced at will to make the most efficient use of the computer's storage capacity. A typical program will contain hundreds of different types of instructions beyond what we have shown here. Certain computational techniques, such as rounding numbers and simplifying equations and other operations, such as moving information from one address to another or planning print out formats, must also be used. But they are beyond the scope of this book.

Because of the complexity and size of most programs, certain subtle errors such as wrong storage addresses or endless loops almost always arise in the first runs of a new program. When an error occurs, the computer will inform the operator at the control console by printing out instructions, by halting or by other means.

One way in which computer users cut costs and programming time is through the use of subroutines. These are portions of programs, ranging from a few to hundreds of instructions, which are present in many different

INSTRUCTION LOCATION	INSTRUCTION	EXPLANATION
0000	R 0500	Read card into locations 500-507
0001	RAD 0501 (3-9)	Put in accumulator card field for called no.
0002	LE 0600	Look up number in accumulator in rate table
0003	B (Error)	Check for error (error routine not shown)
0004	ST 0018	Store rate found in work space
0005	RAD 0502 (8, 9)	Put in accumulator length of call in min.
0006	S 0019	Subtract constant in 0019 from time
0007	BM 0015	Go to Instruction 15
0008	BZ 0015	If minus or zero answer
0009	M 0018 [5, 9]	Multiple overtime by rate
00010	A 0018 [0, 4]	Add initial rate
00011	ST 0550	Store answer in print space
00012	P 0550	Print answer
00013	BLC 0017	Branch if last card to 0017
00014	B 0000	Branch to start
00015	RAD 0018 (0, 4)	Put initial period in accumulator
00016	B 0011	Go in Instruction 11
00017	H 0000	Halt
00018	DA	Use for work space
00019	DC 3	Store constant 3 in memory work space

FIGURE 5
A simplified program for rating toll

kinds of programs. Standard subroutines may be kept on cards or tape in libraries and used as necessary. In addition, companies in the Bell System have found it practical to share some basic programs, thus eliminating duplication of effort.

Finally, programming is both an art and a science which goes far beyond what we have said here. One problem has been to make the language that the computers understand more similar to human language. This has resulted in a number of programming languages that allow machine commands to be written in a form very close to English. COBOL (COmmon Business Oriented Language), widely used for business applications, and FORTRAN (FORmula TRANslation), used in scientific and engineering applications, are two of the most well known. In addition, compilers and supervisory and executive programs, which make the preparation of programs easier and less expensive, have been devloped by computer manufacturers on a competitive basis to lure new customers. The amount of this *software* that a computer manufacturer will supply with his machines is one of the most important factors in choosing a computer today.

23. Seven General Guiding Principles of Data Processing*

Richard A. Kaimann

Volumes have been written on how to design information systems. All of it, however, can be boiled down to a few simple principles.

The following guiding rules sum up the basic concepts that every data processing system should follow. A full-length article could be written about each of them. Here they are distilled as a basic reference tool.

Anyone beginning the design of an information system would do well to keep them in mind. Practicing systems analysts and data processing administrators might also review them from time to time to make sure that the system still conforms to these ground rules.

1. It is financially inappropriate to collect and process all the data that an organization might generate.

2. On inadequate supply of essential data is likely to lead to the failure of the organization.

3. Data should be collected at each stage of the operation to enable the organization to optimize its ability to attain its goals and objectives.[1]

*SOURCE: *Management Services* (May-June 1967), p. 20. Reprinted by permission of *Management Services*, Copyright 1967 by the American Institute of Certified Public Accountants, Inc.

4. Data, once recorded, should not be re-recorded at other stages in the information stream.

5. An item of information is meaningless until it is related to another item or fact.

6. Data should be recorded in a manner that is appropriate to their eventual use.

7. Information should be collected, arranged, stored, retrieved, and manipulated in such a way as to satisfy the goals and objectives of the institution economically and efficiently.

NOTE

1. R. N. Schmidt and W. E. Meyers, *Electronic Business Data Processing*, Holt, Rinehart, and Winston, New York, 1963, p. 30.

B. Management and the Computer

24. The Proper Placement of Computers*

Peter P. Schoderbek and James D. Babcock

The business computer has not yet reached its full profit-making potential. The most significant determinant of success is the organizational climate. The research studies of the authors have indicated that EDP departments are moving away from the accounting department, becoming independent, and progressing upward in the managerial hierarchy. At present, independent computer systems positioned at higher corporate levels are among the more successful departments.

Although many business-operated computers are not utilized to their full capabilities, their profit-making potential remains great. Having a computer does not automatically guarantee success it is only one of the many requisites for the operation of a successful electronic data processing installation. One of the significant, if not the main, determinants is the organizational climate within which it must function. Some writers feel strongly about this:

*SOURCE: *Business Horizons* (October 1969), pp. 35-42. Copyright, 1969 by the Foundation for the School of Business, at Indiana University. Reprinted by permission.

> Nothing is more significant to the success of EDP operations than a strong, well-defined organization . . . . The organizational strength of the EDP group will be the single most important limitation on the extent to which EDP is effectively applied to the information processing needs of a company. The strong organization will successfully produce the sound application definitions, computer system design, effective operating procedures, and control-oriented programs which are essential to well-managed operations.[1]
>
> Perhaps top management's prime interest in the EDP installation program is getting it properly organized so that it has a reasonable chance for success.[2]

Failure to recognize the important organizational condsiderations can directly impair the efficiency and effectiveness of the computer's function. "Somewhere, somehow management must carve out a place in its organization chart for a major responsibility which has to do with the entire process of information gathering."[3] Where the responsibility for guiding and directing this function should lie is a matter of controversy. The two major arrangements mentioned most frequently are:

1. Locate the activity within the accounting or financial department.
2. Establish an independent electronic data processing section.

EDP in the accounting department

When the computer was first introduced, the plausible course of action was to give the responsibility for computer systems to the controller or accounting department. This was done for a number of reasons:

1. The first interest in using computers arose among people in this area.
2. This is the traditional location of the punched card data processing equipment.
3. Many of the most easily mechanized data processing applications occur in the accounting areas.
4. The functions of the controller cut across all areas of the organization.[4]
5. The data flow is well-established and information needs are well known.[5]

One of the advantages of this location is that typically the controller is already experienced in the operation of management information systems and is also well qualified to become the manager of an electronic data processing system. Joplin notes some of these qualifications:

> The accountant, because of his experience with the only existing information system, has certain qualifications which should be considered when choosing the manager of information systems. Because of the length and nature of his association with top management, he is presumed to

have their confidence, an important attribute in systems development. He
has the knowledge of management's needs for information and the extent
to which management relies upon such information for decision making.
He is aware of the problems and limitations involved in supplying information for decision making.[6]

Another advantage of the acounting position would be a smoother transition to fully integrated computer systems. Since many accounting functions
have already been mechanized by punched card applications, these can be
easily converted without drastic changes in system and procedures.[7]

Locating the EDP system in the accounting department also has a
number of disadvantages associated with it. The tendency of the accountant
to place higher priority on his own work than on that of other user
departments or of the company as a whole is scored big. Withington
states that:

> The financial and accounting applications will always receive favored
> treatment, and there may be a reluctance to start employing the computer
> in an operational or decision-making role which is foreign to personnel
> familiar only with accounting work . . . . It is difficult for the computer
> activity to provide important services for departments other than the one
> in which it is located, for however well intentioned they may be, the
> personnel dealing with the computer system's operation and the develop-
> ment of its future applications are naturally going to be most responsive
> to those who control their promotions and salary reviews. As a result,
> most or all of the organization's available resources for computer ap-
> plications development will be channeled into the "parent" accounting
> department.[8]

Another drawback to this organizational set-up is the accountant's
limited knowledge of new methods and techniques for handling information.[9] Often he will tend to slight these new approaches and concentrate
more upon his functional area. Since he is usually judged on his performance in the accounting area rather than on his knowledge of computer
techniques, any deficiencies in EDP may be rationalized by claiming insufficient time to accomplish both objectives.

EDP as an independent function

An alternative to the above and one which finds acceptance in many
companies is the operation of EDP as a separate activity reporting to one
of the members of top management. The main advantage of this alignment
is its neutrality and independence from pressures of particular groups in the
organization.[10] Decisions will be made in the interest of the entire company

rather than that of the department controlling the computer. The needs of the various departments will presumably be objectively evaluated, and service will be extended on the basis of priorities set by top management. Some departments will no doubt receive higher priorities for their applications, but this decision will be based on organizational requirements.

A second advantage is that the staff already has detailed knowledge of EDP equipment and techniques. They know how to utilize available information, how to derive information from new data, how best to secure data not in the system, and how to do all this at the lowest possible cost.[11]

A third benefit is that the computer department tends to take a broader view of systems problems. Operating managers too often take a narrower point of view and regard systems problems as separated by departmental lines. The staff does not confine its planning to existing organizational structures but looks at the firm in terms of overall flow of information.

This arrangement is, however, not without its shortcomings. One likely disadvantage is that operating managers may view the actions of this department as an intrusion into their area, especially if the computer personnel try to by-pass management. Thurston notes this condition:

> Operating people resist planning in which they have no part; they resist the efforts if specialists to seek information or to install systems changes; and they delay accepting responsibility for new operating systems installed by specialists.[12]

Another possible disadvantage is the EDP staff's limited knowledge of the functional areas of departments of the company. The data processing personnel may have some difficulty in assembling the information necessary for systems decisions and in recognizing the changes needed to improve the operation. However, much of this can be alleviated by placing people knowledgeable in specific areas (accounting, production, and inventory control) into the EDP activity.

Analysis of location

Although the EDP function has traditionally been within the controller's domain, the decline of the accountant's control of the computer function has been such that his department no longer enjoys the dominant position it once held.

Were the computer to process only accounting work, there would be little reason to challenge the placement of this function within the accounting department.[13] However, increasing experience and greater confidence in the use of computers has provided a growing recognition of the computer's full potential. More and more companies are shifting to new and more sophisticated applications, and the percentage of computer time spent on routine accounting is steadily decreasing.

Booz, Allen and Hamilton, in a 1966 study, determined that in many companies the finance and accounting applications comprised slightly less than half the computer effort. The 1968 study by the same firm indicated a continuance in the trend away from these applications. In three to five years, finance and accounting applications are estimated to decrease to only 29 percent of the total computer effort as against the 44 percent of the present time. Some of the results of these studies are presented in Table 1.

TABLE 1
Major computer installations

APPLICATION	PERCENT 1966	PERCENT 1968	PERCENT 1972*
Finance and accounting	47	44	29
Production	16	19	24
Marketing	12	13	15
Distribution	11	10	12
Research, development, and engineering	8	11	13
Planning and control	6	3	7

*Estimated.
*SOURCES: James W. Taylor and Neal J. Dean, "Managing to Manage the Computer," *Harvard Business Review* (September-October, 1966), p. 102; and Neal J. Dean, "The Computer Comes of Age," *Harvard Business Review* (January-February, 1968), p. 89.

At least four facts play a major role in determining success in computer systems and which have significant bearing on the location of responsibility. These factors are:[14]

1. Understanding of the objectives of an operation and knowledge of the existing operating patterns, coupled with ability to relate the information system to operating needs.

2. Ability and organizational position to work with operating people to effect change.

3. Competence in the designing of information systems.

4. Motivation to make systems change.

Because of the varying nature of the above factors, each company must decide for itself which organizational form can best fulfill these conditions for success. Placement of the EDP function will depend to a large extent upon the basic company philosophy and the capabilities of certain key personnel.[15] The obvious or presently convenient location may be inadequate for full utilization of computer facilities since conditions within the firm are continually changing and what is appropriate under present circumstances may be totally inadequate for future applications.

Organizational level

Regardless of the locational preference of the EDP function, it is imperative that the individual in charge be afforded sufficient postion in the
organizational hierarchy to operate effectively. Many experts feel the
responsibility for the EDP function should be at a high level in the organization,[16] in fact, some recommend that the level be no more than one step
below the president or operating head of the company.[17]

Locating this function at lower organizational levels can create difficulties
for the person in charge. Since it is necessary for the EDP function to cut
across company lines, it could easily fail if buried under several layers of
uninformed management.[18]

> Locating data processing at the lower organizational levels can cause
> its share of problems. The manager of data processing cannot easily
> discuss proposed systems changes with other functional vice-presidents;
> he must do his talking through his superior. Proposals tend to be "watered
> down" in the course of such a process. Also, the other executives, busy
> with the problems of their own functions and perhaps not confident about
> their knowledge of data processing, tend to proscrastinate on data process-
> ing problems.[19]

Results of the study

The sample used for this investigation comprised 200 firms selected at
random from *Fortune* magazine's listing of the top 500 industrial firms in
the United States during 1967. A questionnaire was mailed to the EDP
managers in these companies. A total of 109 usable responses (58 percent)
were received and utilized in this study.

Organization unit responsible

The results of this study corroborate many of those reported in the
literature. One of these findings is that the location of the computer activity
in the organization is shifting away from the accounting department.
Although 69.7 percent of the companies responding indicated that the
original position of EDP was within the accounting department, at the
present time only 45.0 percent have continued with this arrangement. A
separate and independent electronic data processing function has been
established in 49.5 percent of the firms, and miscellaneous departments
comprise the remaining 5.5 percent. This information is summarized in
Table 2.

TABLE 2
Department responsible for EDP function ($n=109$)

DEPARTMENT	DEPARTMENT ORIGINALLY RESPONSIBLE		DEPARTMENT PRESENTLY RESPONSIBLE	
	NUMBER	PERCENT	NUMBER	PERCENT
Accounting	76	69.7	49	45.0
Data processing or systems	26	23.9	54	49.5
Administrative or management services	4	3.7	4	3.7
Information services	—	—	—	—
Functional department	2	1.8	1	0.9
Other	1	0.9	1	0.9
	109	100.0	109	100.0

A total of 45 companies (41.3 percent) have altered the organizational placement of the computer system from the original setup. EDP was deemed important enough by 37 firms to give it a separate identity and organizational status, while in only five instances did the accounting department retain control; however, in these cases EDP was moved to a higher level within the department.

The reasons given for changing the location of the computer facility are listed in Table 3. As indicated, the main inducement for change was the increased importance of the EDP function as a company-wide service for all departments, and not only one or two as was past practice.

TABLE 3
Reasons for changing original location of EDP function ($n=45$)

REASON	NUMBER	PERCENT
Increased importance of EDP as an independent function	24	53.3
Need for better control	2	4.4
Organizational change	4	8.9
Increase efficiency	1	2.3
Need for more timely information	2	4.4
Other	12	26.7
	45	100.0

One of the more significant findings of this study is that 95.4 percent of the respondents believed that the EDP function should be independent of all operating departments. This weighty figure indicates that an independent activity is judged to be most advantageous and efficient for realizing the computer's potential. What makes this even more meaningful is that only 49.5 percent of the businesses are presently organized in this manner. Even the companies with the computer located within the accounting department overwhelmingly favored functional independence.

The arguments advanced for this type of organizational design parallel those found in the literature. Most respondents (58.7 percent) felt that the computer activity should serve all departments equally and that the best way to accomplish this was to remove it from the jurisditcion of all functional areas, particularly that of the accounting department. Such action would tend to eliminate biases occurring when data processing personnel report to an operating manager. Over 12 percent concluded that independent status is also more conducive to management involvement while another 10.6 percent believed this arrangement gives more economical and efficient service to all users.

Two of the respondents who were accounting managers considered the accounting department the most appropriate location for EDP. No reasons were given for their viewpoint. Three respondents were of the opinion that the organizational location was of little consequence. According to them an effective computer system depends more on the individual in charge than on the organization. A competent and agressive executive is the key ingredient without which even a well-organized system would fail.

Further support for the independent position can be found in an examination of the problems associated with EDP organizational location (see Table 4) Most problematic situations are encountered in companies where the accounting department has responsibility for the computer; of the 49 firms (45.0 percent) with this design, only ten encountred no significant problems. Accounting and financial bias was indicated by 17 companies as the main shortcoming. On the other hand, an independent EDP service created fewer problems. Of the 54 respondents granting autonomy to their computer departments, 35 (64.8 percent) experienced no significant drawbacks related to the organizational design. The two main shortcomings that did occur were accounting bias and lack of management involvement. Although the weaknesses listed may not necessarily be a result of the structure of the data processing activity, there may be a relationship between computer location and the presence or lack of problems.

Organizational level

The results of this study indicate that the level of the EDP function in the managerial hierarchy has been moving upward. The survey conducted by Ernest Dale in 1960 showed that most of the EDP managers queried were members of middle management.[20] However, in the companies sampled, only 51.8 percent were originally in the middle management level or below, and the number presently at these levels has decreased even more (see Table 5). Now middle management comprises 28.7 percent of the total, lower managemnt 1.9 percent, while the majority (53.7 percent) are located at the *upper* management level.

TABLE 4
Problems occurring at various organizational locations of EDP function* (n=109)

DEPARTMENT RESPONSIBLE FOR EDP FUNCTION	NO SIGNIFICANT PROBLEMS		ACCOUNTING BIAS		NO MANAGEMENT INVOLVEMENT		CONFLICT OVER PRIORITIES		POOR UTILIZATION		POOR COORDINATION		OTHER		TOTAL	
	NO.	%	NO.	%	NO.	%	NO.	%	NO.	%	NO.	%	NO.	%	NO.	%
Accounting	10	9.2	17	15.6	8	7.3	4	3.7	4	3.7	4	3.7	2	1.8	49	45.0
Data processing	35	32.1	6	5.5	7	6.4	2	1.8	1	0.9	3	2.7	—		54	49.5
Administrative services	1	0.9	—		1	0.9	1	0.9	—		—		1	0.9	4	3.7
Information services	1	0.9	—		—		—		—		—		—		1	0.9
Other	1	0.9	—		—		—		—		—		—		1	0.9
	48	44.0	23	21.1	16	14.7	7	6.4	5	4.6	7	6.4	3	2.8	109	100.0

*Totals do not add up to the amount indicated because of rounding.

TABLE 5
Level of EDP function in the managerial hierarchy ($n=108$)

LEVEL OF MANAGEMENT	PREVIOUS LEVEL OF MANAGEMENT		PRESENT LEVEL OF MANAGEMENT	
	NUMBER	PERCENT	NUMBER	PERCENT
President/vice-president	9	8.3	17	15.7
Upper management	43	39.8	58	53.7
Middle management	51	57.2	31	28.7
Lower management	5	4.6	2	1.9
	108	100.0	108	100.0

Another indicator of the significance of EDP activity in the organization is the position of the executive in charge of the computer system (see Table 6). This study also bears witness to the loss by the financial officer of his control of computer operations. While he still directs half of the installations, at one time he was responsible for over three-fourths of them. More responsibility has accrued at the vice-presidential level (an increase from 7.9 percent to 28.4 percent). It is interesting to note that the president or chief executive still has not taken direct responsibility as was suggested might happen.

TABLE 6
Executive responsible for EDP activity ($n=109$)

EXECUTIVE	EXECUTIVE PREVIOUSLY RESPONSIBLE		EXECUTIVE PRESENTLY RESPONSIBLE	
	NUMBER	PERCENT	NUMBER	PERCENT
President	3	2.8	2	1.8
Vice-President	8	7.3	31	28.4
Secretary/treasurer	3	2.8	4	3.7
Financial officer, controller	86	78.9	55	50.5
Director, management services	2	1.8	3	2.8
Director, data processing	4	3.7	10	9.2
Director, information	—	—	2	1.8
Functional department manager	2	1.8	—	—
No answer	1	0.9	2	1.8
	109	100.0	109	100.0

From Table 7 it can be seen that the higher the level of the computer location the more successful EDP appears to be. Of the 31 installations reporting to vice-presidents, 25 have experienced no significant problems. On the other hand, 45 of the 55 departments reporting to the financial executive encountered organizational problems. In general, EDP activity appears to be most efficient when placed at a high level in the organization.

The findings of this study indicate that the location of computer activity in the organization is shifting away from the accounting department. An independent EDP department was found in half of the firms participating

TABLE 7
Problem occurrence and organizational location of EDP function ($n=109$)

EXECUTIVE TO WHOM COMPUTER ACTIVITY REPORTS	NO SIGNIFICANT PROBLEMS		ACCOUNTING BIAS		NO MANAGEMENT INVOLVEMENT		CONFLICT OVER PRIORITIES		POOR UTILIZATION		POOR COORDINATION		OTHER		TOTAL	
	NO.	%	NO.	%	NO.	%	NO.	%	NO.	%	NO.	%	NO.	%	NO.	%
President	1	0.9	1	0.9	—	—	—	—	—	—	—	—	—	—	2	1.8
Vice-President	25	22.9	1	0.9	3	2.8	1	0.9	—	—	1	0.9	—	—	31	28.4
Secretary/treasurer	2	1.8	1	0.9	—	—	—	—	—	—	—	—	—	—	4	3.7
Financial officer, controller	10	9.2	19	17.4	11	10.1	6	5.5	4	3.7	3	2.8	2	1.8	55	50.5
Director of management services	—	—	—	—	1	0.9	—	—	—	—	—	—	1	0.9	3	2.8
Director of data processing	4	3.7	1	0.9	1	0.9	—	—	1	0.9	3	2.8	2	1.8	10	9.2
Director of information	2	1.8	—	—	—	—	—	—	—	—	—	—	1	1.8	2	1.8
No answer	1	0.9	—	—	—	—	—	—	—	—	—	—	—	—	2	1.8
	45	41.3	23	21.1	16	14.7	7	6.4	5	4.6	7	6.4	6	5.5	109	100.0

in the survey, and nearly all the respondents stated that this function ought to be independent. The main reason given was that EDP serves many different departments in the firm and should not be subservient to any one function. Fewer problems were found to occur in organizations with functional independence for the computer activity.

The level of the EDP activity has been moving up in the managerial hierarchy. At the present time almost three-fourths of the EDP departments are located at the upper management level, indicating that companies are recognizing the importance of this function. Computer systems positioned at the higher levels were found to experience fewer problems than those located at the lower levels.

NOTES

1. Michael R. Moore, "A Management Audit of the EDP Center," *Management Accounting* (March, 1968), p. 25.
2. Richard G. Canning, *Installing Electronic Data Processing Systems* (New York: John Wiley & Sons, Inc., 1957), p. 11.
3. Robert Beyer, "Management Services—Time for Decision," *Journal of Accountancy* (March, 1965), p. 48.
4. E. Wainright Martin, *Electronic Data Processing* (rev. ed.; Homewood, Ill.; Richard D. Irwin, Inc., 1965), p. 484.
5. Bruce Joplin, "Can the Accountant Manage EDP?" *Management Accounting* (November, 1967), p. 3.
6. "Can the Accountant Manage EDP?" p. 7.
7. William E. Reif, *Computer Technology and Management Organization* (Iowa City, Ia.: Bureau of Business and Economic Research, 1968), p. 33.
8. Frederic G. Withington, *The Use of Computers in Business Organizations* (Reading, Mass.: Addison-Wesley Publishing Co., 1966), pp. 159-161.
9. Phillip H. Thurston, "Who Should Control Information Systems?" *Harvard Business Review* (November-December, 1962), pp. 137-138.
10. Rudolph Borchardt, "Computer Systems: How Now Their Effects on the Organization?" *Systems and Procedures Journal* (May-June, 1967), p. 29.
11. C. I. Keelan, "Your Data Processing Organization 15 Years From Now," *Office* (June, 1969), p. 140.
12. "Who Should Control Information Systems?" p. 137.
13. Winford H. Guin, "EDP Systems in Organizational Structure," *Management Accounting* (October, 1966), p. 45.
14. "Who Should Control Information Systems?" p. 138.
15. James E. Ewell, "The Total Systems Concept and How to Organize for It," *Computers and Automation* (September, 1961), p. 10.
16. Lowell H. Nattery, "Organizing for Data Processing Systems," *Advanced Management* (March, 1961), p. 25.
17. Marshall K. Evans, "Master Plan for Information Systems," *Harvard Business Review* (January-February, 1962), p. 101.
18. I. C. Hume, "He Can Make the Difference Between Profit and Loss," *Iron Age* (Jan. 2, 1964), p. 178.
19. Roger L. Sisson and Richard G. Canning, *A Manager's Guide to Computer Processing* (New York: John Wiley & Sons, Inc., 1967), p. 15.
20. Ernest Dale, *The Decision-Making Powers in the Commercial Use of High Speed Computers* (Ithaca, N.Y.: Cornell Studies in Policy and Administration, Graduate School of Business and Public Administration, Cornell University, 1964), p. 20.

25. At last—Management More Active in EDP*

Peter P. Schoderbek and James D. Babcock

This is the second article dealing with a study of the organizational design of computer activity in the firm. The location and organizational level of the data processing function was described in the first report; this article measures management involvement and examines current trends. The early and continuous participation of top management is essential to the success of an EDP system, and the study indicates that managers are indeed taking a more active role. Operating managers now originate over half of the new applications in half of the companies surveyed. The study also indicates that the trend in computerization is away from financial and accounting applications. The greatest increases were noted in the areas of marketing operations and research, development, and engineering.

For better or for worse, the computer has altered the traditional organizational structures of industry. Most firms with computer installations have

SOURCE: Business Horizons (December 1969), pp. 53-58. Copyright, 1969 by the Foundation for the School of Business, at Indiana University. Reprinted by permission.

found them to be profitable, but some have made the painful discovery that increased efficiency is not achieved by computer alone. Many endogenous factors involving computer use, such as organizational location, reporting authority, and the degree of involvement by line personnel, largely determine the effectiveness of its deployment. It is with these organizational considerations that this article is concerned.

An examination was made of the organizational design of computer activity in various firms. Two hundred were selected at random from *Fortune's* list of the top 500 industrial firms. These companies were surveyed by mail questionnaires, and 109 (54.5 percent) provided usable data. The objectives of the study were:

> To investigate the location of the electronic data processing function in the organization and to determine if this position is most advantageous.
> To determine the organizational level of the EDP function in the management hierarchy.
> To ascertain the actual and desired degree of management involvement in the purchase of new electronic equipment and in the implementation of computer applications.
> To examine the current trends in computer applications.

A report concerning the first two objectives of the study has already appeared in *Business Horizons*.[1] Those results will be summarized briefly before proceeding to the report on the last two objectives.

Summary of earlier results

Although approximately 70 percent of the respondents indicated that the accounting department was originally responsible for the computer activity, only 45 percent have continued with this arrangement. In about 50 percent of the firms participating in the study, an independent data processing department has been established, in contrast to 24 percent when initially organized. The reason given for this change is that the computer has become a company-wide service, no longer catering to only one or two departments.

One of the more significant findings of the study was that 95.4 percent of the EDP managers believed that the EDP function should be independent of all operating departments, including accounting. What makes this opinion startling is that only 49.5 percent of the firms are now organized in this manner. Even those EDP managers in companies were the computer is located within the accounting department overwhelmingly indicated the operational independence was clearly desirable.

Companies with an independent EDP department faced fewer problems than did those with the function located within the accounting or financial department. Of the fifty-four respondents granting autonomy to the computer department, thirty-five suffered no significant drawbacks. On the other hand, thirty-nine of the forty-nine firms with the accounting department responsible for the computer system encountered problems related to organizational design; accounting and financial bias was the main short-coming.

At the present time, 70 percent of the EDP departments are at the upper level of management compared to 48 as previously reported. Those reporting to middle management have decreased from 47 to 29 percent, and to lower management from 5 to 2 percent. Most respondents felt that computer activity at a high level cut across operational boundaries and produced a more effective computer organiaztion. Another indication of the lofty position of the EDP in the managerial hierarchy is the location of the executives in charge of this function. The number of companies assigning executive vice-presidential status to this position has grown four-fold—from 7.3 to 28.4 percent.

The computer systems located at higher levels of management seem to enjoy more success than those at lower levels. At twenty-five of the thirty-one installations reporting to vice-presidents, no significant weaknesses emanating from the organization were reported, but organizational problems were cited at forty-five of the fifty-five departments reporting to the financial executive.

Management involvement

The matter of management involvement in the computer function is the first of the last two objectives to be dealt with in this article. The early and continuous participation of top management is one of the key factors in the development and successful operation of a sound EDP system.

The case for involvement

In view of the capital outlay and the organizational implications involved, top management cannot afford to stay aloof.

> If EDP is to be responsive to the total needs of top management, it demands total involvement on the part of that management. The executive look at EDP has got to be more than a glance through the plate glass window. They have to grasp the significance of a dynamic EDP operation, to see that EDP can give their organization a mighty weapon in the wars with competition, to understand that EDP is much more a profit maker than a cost cutter.[2]

> EDP policies must be geared to the overall policies and objectives of the company. . . . Chief among the executive decisions to be made are those pertinent to setting the objectives for the computer installation, objectives which, as with other basic operations within the company, may be changed from time to time, and establishment of priorities of objectives which are sought through effective use of the computer. Many times the priority value assigned to particular applications by the computer technicians are not at all similar to the values assigned by management in its broader understanding of the company's needs and requirements.[3]

A McKinsey & Company study in 1963 corroborated this concept of top management involvement, finding that firms with the most successful computer operations were precisely those in which top management participated actively in the function.[4] If top management has committed itself to the support of an effective computer system, it will expect equal support from its operating managers, each directly responsible for his own function. He must accept responsibility for adopting new improved information techniques and utilize these techniques on his own initiative. If he does not, top management may demand it of him, and if he fails to comply with these demands, he may be replaced by someone who will.[5] When operating management takes major responsibility for end results and participates in project selection and project manning, the computer systems have usually proved successful.[6]

It is also well known that people tend to resist changes that they have not helped to make; consequently, decisions made by computer personnel that affect the operating personnel, but which reduces their role to that of mere spectators, will not win general acceptance. The criticism frequently leveled at the computer staff—that they lack an awareness of operating realities—may carry considerable weight, thus further reducing their effectiveness for implementing changes.

In many instances, the lack of management involvement can be directly traced to apprehension about the computer. If the computer is viewed as an all-powerful device understandable only to computer specialists (and there is some evidence that this is indeed the case), then predictably the operating line personnel will avoid it at any cost. There are far too many known instances where operating personnel did not utilize the information presented to them simply because they lacked knowledge of how the information was derived or for what is was to be used.

However, the evidence mounts that line managers today are not nearly as mesmerized by the computer as they were five years ago, and in many instances the operating personnel are actually taking the initiative. The reason for this can be attributed to the increasing number of training programs offered by computer manufacturers, to the commercial training programs, and to the in-house training programs. Line personnel have come to realize that if they are to be held accountable for the results of their operations, they ought to have control of their information system, which in turn requires knowledge of the system. Also, it is almost impossible to evaluate an information system unless one has direct knowledge of the intricacies of the system itself.

Analysis of results

The findings of this study indicate that managers are taking a more active role. At one time almost all new computer applications were initiated by the EDP department; now, however, this department is responsible for less than 45 percent of these new jobs in 72.4 percent of the firms responding. Table 1 shows how computer applications are generated in all of the companies. Operating managers now originate over half of the new applications in 50.5 percent of the companies surveyed. The increase in participation can in part be attributed to the education of these managers in computer concepts, and in part to the practical demands of the system itself.

TABLE 1
Initiation of new computer applications $(N=109)$

PERCENTAGE OF NEW COMPUTER APPLICATIONS	REQUESTED BY LINE MANAGERS		PROPOSED BY EDP DEPARTMENT		DIRECTIVE OF TOP MANAGEMENT		OTHER	
	NO.	%*	NO.	%*	NO.	%*	NO.	%*
Not ascertained	4	3.7	4	3.7	4	3.7	4	3.7
None	4	3.7	14	12.8	19	17.4	85	78.0
1-15	8	7.3	20	18.4	40	36.8	15	13.8
16-30	29	26.5	30	27.5	22	20.2	1	0.9
31-45	9	8.3	15	13.8	7	6.4	1	0.9
46-60	27	24.8	12	11.0	13	11.9	—	—
61-75	13	11.9	10	9.2	2	1.8	—	—
76-90	12	11.0	2	1.8	1	0.9	1	0.9
91-100	3	2.8	2	1.8	1	0.9	2	1.8
	109	100.0	109	100.0	109	100.0	109	100.0

*Rounded off.

Formal EDP training is given to functional managers in 74.3 percent of the companies examied. The type of education naturally varies, but it usually takes the form of in-house training programs, computer manufacturers' schools, or some combination of the two. In-house instruction was offered in 75.3 percent of those firms offering schooling and was the only instruction in 16.0 percent of the cases. Computer manufacturers' facilities alone were utilized by 81.5 percent or in combination with some other program. University or college courses were used only in conjunction with other training and in those instances were used only 27.2 percent of the time.

Although the top management level proposes fewer projects than other levels, a considerable number are introduced by this group (see Table 1). The applications initiated by these executives are usually company-wide projects with high priority, or concern areas where functional departments are not making the necessary innovations. In the latter case, once top management makes the initial move, the departmental manager usually steps in to accept responsibility for its successful operation. Increased management involvement in the selection of new applications is favorably regarded by the computer personnel. They feel that the operating managers are the individuals best suited to decide the needs of the functional areas and that the computer staffs' role is to provide guidance for implementation.

Once new applications have been considered, they must be evaluated. The EDP staff, which usually investigates their feasibility, presents its findings to top management for approval or disapproval. That top management makes this decision is true in 44 percent of the cases; the manager of the user department in 23.8 percent of the cases; and the financial officer in 16.5 percent of the cases. Under present arrangements, the EDP staff makes the final decision only 13.8 percent of the time. Correlation analysis shows a positive association of .55 between present procedures and what is considered the desirable method. This high value indicates that many firms are satisfied with their degree of management involvement in implementing new computer applications.

Top management takes an even more active role in the purchase of new electronic equipment, an action to be expected since a large capital outlay is usually involved. The final decision concerning purchase of new equipment is made by top management in eighty-two of the companies (75.2 percent), although in a few cases this is just formal approval of the recommendations made by the data processing staff. The financial officer makes this decision 15.6 percent of the time and the EDP department 7.3 percent. A positive correlation of .64 exists between the present strategy and the ideal procedure.

It is important to note, however, that this decision is by no means arbitrary. Comprehensive feasibility studies are required, and several criteria must be met before approval is given. Economic consideration, the main factor, is involved in 88.1 percent of the decisions and is the only factor 33.9 percent of the time. More information is desired in 50.5 percent of the firms and more timely information 51.5 percent. All three are required 35.8 percent of the time.

Trends in applications

For the purpose of this study, computer applications can be broken down into six categories:

> Financial and accounting—Financial reporting and analysis, accounting, payroll, invoicing, billing
> Management planning and control—Capital investment analysis, resource allocations, mathematical model simulation
> Marketing operations—Sales forecasting, sales analysis and control, market research, sales order processing
> Distribution operations—Warehouse operations, shipment order processing, traffic, in-the-field inventory control
> Factory operations—Materials control, production scheduling, quality control, in-the-plant inventory control
> Research, development, and engineering—Product test, engineering, research, product design and evaluation.[7]

This study indicates that the trend of computerization is away from financial and accounting applications (see Table 2). The percentage of applications in each of the above areas (44 percent in accounting) corresponds very closely with the results of Neal J. Dean's study presented in the earlier article.[8] The greatest differences occurred in the areas of marketing operations (20 in contrast to 13 percent in the Dean survey) and research, development, and engineering (7 in contrast to 11 percent in the Dean study), but none of these differences are significant.

TABLE 2
Percentage comparison of major computer applications* in two studies

COMPUTER APPLICATIONS	DEAN'S STUDY 1968	AUTHORS' STUDY 1969
Finance and accounting	44	44
Production	19	18
Marketing	13	20
Distribution	10	9
Research, development, and engineering	11	7
Planning and control	3	2
	100	*100..*

*Multiple responses.

An inverse correlation of -.35 was noted between the percentage of accounting applications and the number of persons employed by the firm, and a correlation of -.48 between the number of EDP personnel and the percentage of accounting applications. This implies that, as the company and data processing activity grow, less emphasis is given to the accounting aspect of computer operations.

The figures in Table 2 reflect the average percentage of each application in the companies surveyed; the range of each of these applications is described in Table 3. While the accounting projects average 44 percent, they account for 45 percent or more of computer time in 40.9 percent of the companies providing this information. Although 68 percent of the respondents stated that all departments had equal access to the computer, special priorities are given to several departments or to special applications. The accounting department is given priority most of the time, as Table 4 indicates.

TABLE 3
Types of computer application (N=109)

PERCENTAGE OF TOTAL COMPUTER APPLICATIONS	ACCOUNTING OR FINANCIAL		MANAGEMENT PLANNING AND CONTROL		MARKETING		DISTRIBUTION		FACTORY OPERATIONS		R&D OR ENGINEERING	
	NO.	%	NO.	%	NO.	%	NO.	%	NO.	%	NO.	%
Not ascertained	21	19.3	21	19.3	21	19.3	21	19.3	21	19.3	21	19.3
None	—	—	68	62.4	23	21.1	37	34.0	21	19.3	47	43.1
1-15	6	5.5	18	16.5	21	19.3	37	34.0	25	22.9	31	28.4
16-30	21	19.3	2	1.8	23	21.1	11	10.0	23	21.1	4	3.7
31-45	25	22.9	—	—	11	10.0	1	0.9	13	11.9	5	4.6
46-60	18	16.5	—	—	9	8.3	1	0.9	5	4.6	1	0.9
61-75	9	8.3	—	—	1	0.9	1	0.9	1	0.9	—	—
76-90	7	6.4	—	—	—	—	—	—	—	—	—	—
91-100	2	1.8	—	—	—	—	—	—	—	—	—	—
	109	100.0	109	100.0	109	100.0	109	100.0	109	100.0	109	100.0

TABLE 4
Computer applications receiving special priorities (N=109)

APPLICATION	NUMBER	PERCENT
Finance and accounting	22	20.2
Marketing	6	5.5
Factory operations	4	3.6
Research, development, and engineering	2	1.8
Other	1	0.9
None	74	68.0
	109	100.0

It was not too surprising to discover that twenty of the companies giving the financial area special priority have located their computer system within the accounting department. Although there may be other factors involved, this finding tends to support the suspicion that such a location gives preferential treatment to the department. There were some indications that, as the organizational level of the computed activity increase, special priorities decreased. A correlation of .44 exists between the level of EDP in the organization and the presence of accounting priorities.

The success of a computer installation is due in no small part to the degree of leadership and the continuous involvement of top management in the computer function. The findings of this study indicate that managers are indeed taking a more active part in the many areas affecting and affected by the computer. And as computer usage decreases in the area of finance and accounting and increases in the other functional areas of production, marketing, and so on, it can be expected that even more personnel will be involved with the computer, either by choice or by decree. In any event, it will be essential that all areas of the organization, both functional and staff, be considered in order to achieve a truly integrated information system.

NOTES

1. Peter P. Schoderbek and James D. Babcock, "The Proper Placement of Computers," *Business Horizons* (October, 1969), pp. 35.42.
2. Arnold E. Keller, "EDP—Power in Search of Management," *Business Automation* (June, 1966), p. 51.
3. Raymond J. W. O'Toole and Edward F. O'Toole, "Top Executive Involvement in the EDP Function," *Management Controls* (June, 1966), pp. 125, 127.
4. John T. Garrity, "Top Management and Computer Profits," *Harvard Business Review* (July-August, 1963), p. 10.
5. John Dearden, "IIow to Organize Information Systems," *Harvard Business Review* (March-April, 1965), p. 69.
6. "Management's Role Spells Computer Success," *Steel* (April 22, 1963), p. 31.
7. "Computer Usage in the Manufacturing Industry," *Business Automation* (October, 1966), p. 54.
8. Neal J. Dean, "The Computer Comes of Age," *Harvard Business Review* (January-February, 1968), p. 89.

26. The Manager's and The Systems Analyst's Roles in MIS Development*

Thomas L. Wheelen

The past decade has seen two management trains passing in the night on parallel tracks. The first train is participation management which has been adopted in varying degrees by most firms. The second train is management information systems. This era has been characterized by billions of dollars being expended on computers, systems development and utilization of these systems and computers. It would only seem logical from a management point of view that these two developments should have been fully integrated with each other. This doesn't seem to be the case.

Participation management vs. completed staff work

Participation management involves both mental and emotional involvement on the part of the manager.[1] Instead of this active mental and emotional involvement, the managers employ the concept of completed staff work. One interviewed analyst substantiated this point when he said:

"You are called in by the manager and given a tentative problem(s), usually in very broad terms, for which he feels the solution is to put it on the computer. You are told to freely call on him or his staff for assistance, then you are asked how long it will take to develop a system to handle this

*SOURCE: Prepared for this book.

problem. My chief problem arises when I go back to have a meeting of the minds on the key issues involved with this manager. I am told to do what I think is best or work it out with my staff since they are closer to the problem."

Another analyst said:

"Once you complete the system and turn it over to the operating unit, then either of two things will happen. If all goes well, you will hear nothing, *but* if any bugs appear or it's not exactly what they visualized, even though you fully discussed the subject with them before going operational with the system, then you will receive the classical call from the manager—Your system doesn't work. Please get it squared away as soon as possible."

In essence, both analysts are talking about completed staff work. Several other analysts interviewed described the typical participation by the manager in a similar manner. One said:

"I am called in and given a recurring problem or a need for some information that they feel only the computer can provide. I am then left on my own, not by choice, (1) to isolate the problem, (2) analyze the alternative ways of handling it, (3) choose the best one, usually without much assistance on the part of the unit involved, and (4) then implement it. The basic concept is all right, but I do need their active assistance and that includes the manager. Most times this is missing."

This is not to say that all managers don't actively participate in systems development, but a significant number don't and this could be one of the primary reasons why management informations systems doesn't, in many instances, live up to managers' expectations.

One analyst suggested a reason for this lack of participation on the part of the managers—"Most managers aren't sure of their responsibilities in systems development or what to expect from the systems man except a completed system. So, they approach it from the point-of-view of delegating the job to the staff man (the analyst)." A basic management tenet is that you cannot delegate your responsibility. So, the manager should be held responsible for the effectiveness or ineffectiveness of his information system.[2] This author feels the manager can and should have to delegate the design and development of new systems, but the manager must actively participate in the process, since, in the final analysis, this will be his system. Once a system goes operational, then, in essence, the manager has approved of it, and its success or failure should be adjudged to him. This is like completed staff work where the manager affixes his signature to the report—it is now his report. It is time that managers come to recognize they are *responsible* for the effectiveness of their informations systems, and top management should closely appraise them in this area. One way to accomplish this is for managers to fully understand their responsibilities at various stages of systems development and what to expect from the analyst and when.

The manager and the systems analyst

One operating manager said:

"I have attended several in-house type seminars on MIS and its utilization. None of these seminars ever addressed these basic questions, First, what was expected of me, except in broad terms (e.g. request new systems or improvements in existing ones when necessary or we should provide the systems people with full cooperation and assistance) or second, what I could expect from the systems people and when? I don't ever remember anyone asking these types of questions."

Exhibit I was designed to provide a vehicle for communication between the manager and the systems analyst, in order that they might clarify their roles and responsibilities to each other. This is accomplished by listing the duties and responsibilities of both parties for the various stages of management information systems development.

EXHIBIT I

SYSTEMS ANALYSIS is concerned with reviewing the existing system with emphasis on the constraints under which the present system operates. It also is concerned with defining the project and scope of the project to be analyzed.

DUTIES

MANAGER	*SYSTEMS ANALYST*
1. Primary responsibility is to provide analyst with complete and accurate picture of the present system	1. Thorough review of the existing system —(1) how it should work (documentation), (2) how the users perceive it works, and (3) how it actually works with emphasis on what it consists of
2. Assist analyst in learning proper definitions for all jargon	
3. Reviews present documentation with analyst	2. Concerned with:
4. Discusses data information requirements and reasons for them with his staff. Analyst should be present, if at all possible	a. Input and output of present system
	b. Processing required to convert input into output
	c. Quality of present output
	d. Problem areas in existing system
	e. Policies under which existing system operates
	f. Interfacing of present system with other existing systems
	3. Complete list of documents and annotated Reports, forms and records Data source, volume, purpose, frequency, accuracy, time lag of input into output
	4. List of controls against errors
	5. Systems flow chart (if necessary)

Overall: An agreement between the system analyst and the manager on existing system.

SYSTEMS DESIGN is concerned with specifying with exactness a new system, that will improve upon or supplant the existing system.

DUTIES

MANAGER

1. Develops an understanding of the systems analyst's job, philosophy and attitudes
2. Should exert concurrent review over the output of the analyst
   a. Primary duty is to review proposed system for adequacy
      Can be performed on a sub-system approach, but entire system should also be reviewed
   b. This type of review should prevent major problems from occurring in the implementation stages of the system
3. Discuss proposed system with his staff with analyst present

SYSTEMS ANALYST

Prepares the following documents:
1. Systems flow chart
2. Program flow chart
3. List of controls
4. Procedures manuals
5. Document design and layout
   a. Input
   b. Output
6. File design and layout
   Timing estimates
   a. Conversion to new system
   b. Run times
8. Costs
   a. Conversion to new system
   b. Maintenance and up dating
9. List of organizational charges
   a. Job descriptions
   b. Notify Personnel department, if union issues involved

Overall: An agreement on what exactly the proposed system will do, costs involved, and its affect on personnel.

PROGRAMMING, TESTING AND EVALUATION includes the conversion of the program flow chart into the desired computer language; the development of the files; debugging; and evaluating the new system as meeting its original goals.

DUTIES

MANAGER

1. Assists the analyst in gathering data inputs for file making and testing
2. Reviews design
3. Provides extra help as required
4. Issues new manuals and withdraws old ones
5. Holds meeting with personnel involved and *fully* discusses new system
6. Issues new job descriptions
   Discusses these with personnel involved
7. Provides necessary training for personnel
8. Reviews entire system
   Does it meet original specification, both in output and cost?

SYSTEMS ANALYST

1. Conversion of program flow chart into desired language by programmer
2. Establish the necessary files
3. Provides test data
4. Fully tests new system
5. Documents system for internal controls and run procedures
6. Writes up training materials
7. Prepares new procedural and uses manuals
8. Assists personnel department
   a. Job descriptions modify existing ones or prepare new ones
   b. Meet union officials if necessary

Overall: A new system designed, debugged and evaluated by the manager and the systems analyst.

IMPLEMENTATION conversion from old system to new one.

DUTIES

MANAGER	*SYSTEMS ANALYST*
1. Utilize system	1. Provides assistance as required
2. Reviews it for problems	
Staff noting problems	
3. *NOW IT'S YOUR SYSTEM*	

Overall: System made operational. Responsibility for its effectiveness now rests with the manager.

FOLLOW UP is the forgotten step in successful system utilization. A system can be viewed as a moving target which requires monitoring. In order that it meets the needs of the changing environment in which it functions.

DUTIES

MANAGER	*SYSTEMS ANALYST*
1. Notes changes in environment that	1. Audits system
affect system	
Have modifications made or new	
system design, if required	

Overall: Continuous monitoring of the system and its environment by the manager and his staff, and the systems analyst.

Briefly listed below are the salient responsibilities and duties of the manager and the systems analyst in the development of management information system.

1. Systems analysis

Manager provides the systems analyst with a complete and accurate picture of the existing system. He reviews and discusses existing system and information with the systems analyst. In the process, the manager should obtain an undertanding of how the systems analyst approaches his job and his jargon. *Systems Analyst* is concerned with a thorough and accurate review of the existing system. How should the system work? How is the system thought to work? And how does the system actually work? He is concerned with existing systems—(1) strengths and weaknesses, (2) problems, (3) constraints under which they operate, (4) their interfacing characteristics with other systems, and (5) all documents used in the existing system.

2. System design

Manager should exert concurrent review over the proposed system. His staff should be fully involved in this review. *Systems Analyst* designs a system to meet the necessary information needs of the operational unit. Deals with (1) cost for conversion and usage, (2) affects of changes on personnel—job description, training, eliminating, and (3) flow chart new system. Review thoroughly the system with manager and get his approval.

3. Programming, testing and debugging

Manager provides assistance and actual help as required, holds meeting to discuss system with staff, deals with personnel problems and thoroughly reviews and evaluates system as to it original goals. Once reviewed and made operational, he alone is responsible for its effectiveness.

Systems Analyst is concerned mainly with (1) conversion of the new system into the desired computer language, (2) establishing required files, (3) testing and debugging the system, and (4) documenting the system and assisting in the personnel department.

4. Implementation

Manager and his staff fully utilizes the system and note any problems. It is now their responsibility. *Systems Analyst* converts the operating unit from the existing system to a new one. He provides assistance where and when needed.

5. Follow-up

Manager and staff note changes in environment and request modifications when necessary. *Systems Analyst* audits system. This should provide both parties with an empathic point of view as to the others job and responsibility in developing efficient and economical management information systems.

Conclusions

It is time that we fully integrate the concepts of participation management and management information systems. Only with the active participation of the manager will we effectively harness and utilize the great potential of systems management. This lack of participative management on the part of the manager may be the reason why so many systems have not lived up to expectations.

One suggested way to obtain this fusion of these two concepts is for the manager to more fully understand what is expected of him and his staff. Also, what can and should we expect from the systems analysts? In turn, the above holds true for the analyst. This empathic point of view is vital, if we are to have effective management information systems. This fusion should already exist since a manager is responsible for information systems and not the systems analyst once the system is made operational. A stimulant would be for top management to include an appraisal of the effectiveness of the manager's information system in his yearly performance evaluation.

A new tenet of systems management should be that participation management and management information systems be synonymous.

NOTES

1. Keith Davis, *Human Relations at Work* (New York: McGraw-Hill Book Company, 1967), p. 128.
2. John Deardon, "How to Organize Information Systems," *Harvard Business Review*, March-April, 1965, p. 67.

27. Will Your Computer Pay its Way? *

John Plummer

The application possibilities of the computer are unlimited. The software is ready and a third generation of hardware is in place. The profit potential is imposing, but the dollar returns still are found principally in promise and the imagination. Too often, managers have failed to realize that the computer will contribute significantly to profits only if they learn to manage in new ways with their new information. The project approach to the planning and control of computer activities is no different in principles from management's traditional approach to any capital investment. It takes the mystique out of computer planning and focuses attention where it belongs—on the profitability of the computer as a business investment. Mr. Plummer directs the manager to three basic questions: where in the business might the computer be profitably used? which projects should be done first? how can objectives be achieved?

One of the most significant facts of U.S. business life in the past decade has been the phenomenal growth of computer power. Forty thousand

*SOURCE: *Business Horizons* (April 1969), pp. 31-36. Copyright © 1969 by the Foundation for the School of Business, at Indiana University. Reprinted by permission.

computers, or 65 percent of the world's total electronic brainpower, are now located in the United States. A host of computer-based advanced mathematical and statistical techniques designed to assist business managers have been successfully tested in action, and more are on the way. Professional journals are packed with new ideas and new approaches. And the executive-oriented business press is liberally sprinkled with articles calculated to convince most managers that they are at least ten years behind their nearest competitor in the use of the computer.

The application possibilities are unlimited. The software is ready. A third generation of hardware is already in place. The profit potential is imposing. Yet the dollar returns expected by most companies are still found principally in promise and imagination, not in the till. Why? A growing body of evidence suggests a simple answer: too often, managers have failed to understand that the computer will contribute significantly to profits only if they themselves learn to manage in new ways with the aid of the new information it can provide.

During his first review of corporate computer activities, a new company president I know called a meeting of his top marketing and sales executives. "We are here to decide how, given perfect information, we would manage this business differently tomorrow," he told them. "Once we have made up our minds about this, we'll find out what the necessary information is going to cost."

Too few top managers perceive the opportunity so clearly. More typical is the case of another company that launched a major effort to develop an improved computer-based sales forecasting system. Managers in production and distribution as well as marketing pinned high hopes on the project. Eventually someone asked, "What would we have done differently six months ago if our forecasts had been perfect?" The answer, to everyone's surprise, turned out to be, "Very little." Since production schedules were determined by runs of economically feasible lengths rather than by month-to-month fluctuations, the items produced and the need for material would have been little affected. The same quantities of the same items would have entered the distribution system and been stored, for the most part, in the same locations. Even the regional allocation of marketing dollars to advertising, promotion, and sales efforts would not have changed significantly. In fact, the total benefit from a *perfect* sales forecast would not provide an adequate return on the contemplated investment.

Because profitable computer applications so often mean changed management methods, managing the computer effort is a uniquely difficult staff activity. Engineering, personnel administration, finance, market research, and other major corporate functions operate on the premise that basic management methods remain essentially unchanged. Computer management, in effect, brings a complex and sophisticated technology to bear on subverting this assumption. This can have serious implications at the highest management levels. To harness the computer successfully, therefore, requires a unique combination of technical sophistication and good business sense.

Most successful computer users have adopted a project approach to the planning and control of computer development activities. They evaluate systems development, operations research, and programming outlays as investments rather than expenses. This approach has two advantages. First, it casts evaluation of computer development outlays in the familiar business mold of capital investment analysis under conditions of risk and uncertainty, thereby dispelling much of the mystique that envelops computer planning in the minds of so many. Second, it provides the structure needed for a constructive dialogue between business manager and computer technician. This dialogue centers around three basic questions:

Where in the business might the computer be profitably used?

Which projects should be done first?

How can objectives be achieved?

Profitable applications

The key communications document in a formal system of planning and control of computer activities is the project description. Because of its vital importance, its development deserves intensive effort by both operating and computer management. Preferably, this description should cover, as concisely as possible: the objective of the application; expected benefits; costs; a brief description of the input and output; and a summary project evaluation.

The *objective* of a computer application is the improvement that will result from completing the project (not what will be reported). "To increase promotion effectiveness by allocating promotion dollars on the basis of item and region profitability" is a valid objective; "to report item profitability by region" is not. "To reduce turnover among promising young managers by promoting each good performer at least every two years" is a valid objective; "to report performance and promotion records of young managers" is not. Because improvements must be judged in terms of accomplishment, action, and change, the statement of objective should be developed by operating managers, not the computer staff.

It is sometimes forgotten that, in business, *benefits* means dollars. Even short-term benefits from computer applications should be quantified in terms of dollar return on the required investment. Too often a computer application is evaluated on the basis of whether it can, rather than whether it should, be done. Since there are few things that cannot be done with today's computer technology, failure to concentrate on the right question can easily lead to unproductive investments. To be sure, the danger is not equally acute in all areas of the business. Every controller has known for years that increased machine costs must be balanced by reduced clerical costs. And most production executives, with their day-to-day knowledge of actual personnel and machine performance against engineered standards, are prepared to put a dollar sign on the benefits they expect to get from a given computer application. But executives in other functional areas, such as marketing, personnel, or finance, too often tend to describe information they want from the computer as "necessary to the conduct of the business" but fail to estimate the dollar payout.

These nebulous benefits, however, can almost always be nailed down in dollar terms. Recently, for example, the marketing manager of a large consumer products company was asked to evaluate his proposed project for reporting item profitability by sales territory. This was his reply: "We conducted a sample study of item profitability in three Southeastern territories. As a result of this study we reduced our promotion costs in these territories by $5,000, with no loss of sales or profit. Extending this nationally, we expect a first-year reduction in promotion expenditures of $50,000. In addition, we are convinced we can increase this by $10,000 a year for at least five years, again with no loss of sales or profits." A five-year payoff of $350,000! Interestingly, all the data that would be required for the proposal report were already being processed by the computer for order entry and accounts payable applications. The cost of consolidating them would be less than $500! The only reason these benefits had not already been achieved was that marketing and computer management were not communicating properly. They had simply never gotten together to discuss what should be done and what information would be required to do it.

Consider another example. The marketing manager of a food products company thought the computer could help him improve advertising effectiveness and authorized a study to find out. Fourteen market areas were chosen, randomly, for testing. The suggested advertising budget from the advertising agency was adjusted, again randomly, from zero to four times the recommended level. To the surprise of everyone, including the experimenters, sales tended to go down when advertising was increased, go up when advertising was reduced as much as 50 percent, and hold steady when advertising was eliminated. As a result of this study, a concept of "advertising fatigue" was hypothesized. Half a million dollars was spent to develop a computer-based sales forecast that would relate to levels of advertising expenditures, against sales and profits generated, thus enabling the company to maximize its return from advertising dollars.

Since the real value of a computer application is determined entirely by what use management makes of it, only operating management can really estimate the dollar benefits. Where dollar benefits are difficult to determine and a major commitment of development dollars is at stake, experimentation can often supply the needed answers.

The third key element of a project description is *costs*. Large expenditures are required to develop computer applications primarily because systems, operations research, and programming personnel are so scarce and costly. But there is another factor to be considered—the opportunity cost. A programmer engaged in writing an accounts payable program, or in converting 1401 programs to a System 360/30, cannot at the same time write a program for evaluating production efficiency or promotion effectiveness. Hence the economic concept of opportunity cost—differences in return on alternative investments—is especially pertinent in systems development and programming. For example, one management considered a project that would have reduced computer costs $200,000 annually through centralization. To achieve contralization, however, would have meant tying up all systems and programming resources for six months, a lost opportunity worth slightly over $1 million. The project was turned down; the savings were just not worth the cost. Another company, in contrast, held up an evaluation of procedures used to select customers for mail promotion—a $30 million annual effort—while top operations research analyst worked for three months to establish a procedure for allocating overhead expense to its divisions.

Cost calculations, therefore, should reflect both the skills required and the time these skills would be tied up. The out-of-pocket dollar development cost of a given project can best be estimated by the data processing manager, but operating management should adjust these estimates to reflect the alternative opportunities for utilization of the required skills.

What will the computer do? Seldom will it make decisions. Rather, it will usually provide managers with information upon which decisions can be based. Consequently, the project description should describe the specific *report outputs*—and the *data inputs* needed to produce them. Without an explicit definition of output, misunderstandings between operating and computer management can spoil otherwise well-planned projects. Avoiding such misunderstandings, however, may be far from easy. In one company— an effective computer user with applications in the production area that had already repaid their cost twice over—operating executives and computer managers agreed that a production scheduling model would reduce manufacturing costs by $500,000 annually. The operating managers envisioned a day-by-day, and possibly hour-by-hour, schedule for each machine. Computer management was thinking, a bit more realistically, of a weekly production schedule for each machine, with guidelines to suggest daily production requirements. Neither group made its assumptions clear to the other, and the project nearly came a cropper when the misunderstanding came to light. Had operating management recognized its responsibility to specify the computer output required to attain the benefits, this conflict could have been prevented.

The *project summary* should give management a simple evaluation of costs, benefits, and expected return on investment. In addition, the risks—both technological and operational—should be assessed. Technological risk reflects the likelihood that the desired output from the computer cannot be achieved. For most computer applications, this risk is minimal, but it increases in the more advanced management science or operations research applications. Developing a call schedule for salesmen entails no technological risk; this has already been done many times. An effective program for routing store-door delivery salesmen whose customers will see them only from 10 to 11 a.m. on Tuesdays and Thursdays is a different matter. The complexity of the problem automatically entails a higher probability of failure.

On the other hand, operational risk—the danger that a computer application will prove not to be feasible—is high in a great many projects. An example often adduced is the program that requires a hundred salesmen, or a hundred secretaries, to do their jobs in a different and unfamiliar way. This would obviously be more difficult, and hence entail greater operational risk, than helping an eagerly cooperated manager of production planning to revise his approach to production-line scheduling.

Significantly, the likelihood of operational success often hinges upon top-management plans. In one company, marketing managers developed an elaborate plan for controlling franchise operations, quite unaware that top management was already making plans to get out of the franchise business altogether. In another company, one division undertook the development of a production control program comprising thirty-two projects. Unknown to the division personnel, top management had already set the date, six months later, when this division's production responsibilities would be transferred to other divisions, leaving it a sales organization only. In both cases, an explicit project summary would have alerted top management to what was afoot in time to prevent needless waste of time and resources. As a rule, it is the most influential element of the project descriptions as far as top management's decision on the project is concerned.

Sorting out priorities

In aggregate, the individual project descriptions provide management with a solid idea of what *could* profitably be done with the computer. They will not, in most companies, tell management what *should* be done. Available personnel resources will seldom suffice for the development of every worthwhile project. And in view of the current shortage of skilled computer personnel, enlarging the development staff is not simple matter. One company set up a committee of senior executives to locate as many profitable computer projects as possible. From more than 200 application possibilities, top management selected 27 for initiation during the next two years. Even this greatly reduced slate could be implemented only if the project computer staff, which already numbered over 100, were to be quadrupled over the two-year period.

The chief executive was entirely willing to spend the money necessary to add 300 people, since over $200 million yearly in identified dollar benefits was at stake. He did not believe, however, that the staff could be enlarged by so much so quickly. A special project was set up to investigate this question. After considering several factors that affect the growth of a technical group—turnover, experience level of available recruits, training time requirements, and so on—the study team concluded that the chief executive was right. Assuming no change in turnover patterns or recruiting policy, the staff would remain at essentially its existing size. If the turnover rate could somehow be reduced by 50 percent, a growth of about 10 perecnt a year could be expected. And if the corporate recruiting policy were revised to attract the most experienced personnel available, the best man agement could expect would be a growth rate in the neighborhood of 25 percent a year. As a result of this study, the initial project slate was reduced from 27 projects to 7—7 out of an available 200!

This story underlines the fact that selecting a project slate normally means setting priorities, often between major functional areas of the company. This is a top management responsibility. Deciding whether the vice-president of production will have to wait a year or two for his pet project while work is being done for the vice-president of marketing is no job for the data processing manager. What criteria, then, should guide top management in setting the priorities?

Return on investment This is the most important criterion, but it cannot be relied upon alone as a guide to the best project slate.

Distribution of benefits It may be desirable to include at least one project for each major operating function, both for political reasons and to broaden awareness of the computer's capabilities among operating managers, thus stimulating the identification of potentially profitable future applications.

Distribution of risk   In most cases, it is unwise for a company to tie up all its available resources in one or two major projects. With a number of projects under way simultaneously, the probability of achieving benefits is often significantly increased. To satisfy this criterion, large projects can frequently be broken into segments, each with its own identified benefits.

Balance of risk   High payback applications often entail relatively high risk. It will probably be desirable to include a few such projects in the slate, but some resources should be devoted to more conventional applications. An ideal project slate balances high risk with low risk projects.

Personnel interests and capabilities   Although personnel availability is seldom a critical constraint to be considered in defining and evaluating individual applications, the selection of the project slate as a whole should usually reflect the interests and capabilities of individuals in the data processing group.

Departmental priority   Most projects will require extensive participation by user department personnel. No matter how attractive the payout opportunity, no project should be scheduled unless the user department is prepared to commit the needed personnel resources.

Achieving benefits

The completed project slate is a plan. To a large extent, it also represents a calculated hope and a prayer. As with any plan, attainment of the stated objectives at the indicated cost is a matter of control. And, as with any plan, the appropriate control technique depends on the size and type of projects being undertaken. It may be PERT or it may be an old-fashioned Gantt chart; no single control technique is equally applicable in all situations.

Two often-ignored aspects of control are particularly relevant to computer development activities. First, the control system should relate directly to the planning system. The project system of planning provides an ideal means of control, one that is unavailable when development costs are expensed rather than capitalized. With each review of the project slate, projects already under way should also be individually reevaluated. Estimates of benefits and remaining costs, revised in the light of experience in prior development activity, should be incorporated into the project description. Management should remember that money already spent on project development is gone. Projects currently under way should be continued or abandoned on the basis of money still to be spent.

Second, control of a computer project should be continued after the programs are "on the air." Achievement of benefits will not automatically follow the printing of a report. It is contingent on successful implementation, which will mean a change in management method and may entail a realignment of organizational responsibilities or the removal of people. Since these are all hard to accomplish, post-implementation audit or reappraisal will usually be necessary—not just to determine whether the benefits have been achieved, but to indicate what action needs to be taken to make sure they are.

Thanks to the wide scope of computer applications, periodic review of all available project investment opportunities can provide the opportunity for a comprehensive appraisal of the direction of the entire business. In one food company, a review of computer opportunities identified several application possibilities in a special department that had been established to dispose of surplus fruit on the commodity market. During the presentation of the recommended project slate, the growth and profit potential of this department was brought to the president's attention for the first time. Soon afterwards the department head was made a vice-president.

As we have seen, the project approach to the planning and control of computer activities is not different in principle from management's traditional approach to the appraisal of any capital investment. Indeed, much of its value lies in its familiarity. It gives managers an opportunity to review their information needs from a business perspective. It takes the mystique out of computer planning. Most important, it puts the focus of management attention where it belongs—on the profitability of the computer as a business investment.

28. Twelve Areas to Investigate for Better MIS*

Robert W. Holmes

Computer systems directed to management planning and assistance in making decisions for most companies are still a myth. Executives failing to exploit the computer are facing a grim future, and they are well-advised to investigate in depth the reasons for their failure with the computer and to profit from the successes of others.

Impressive MIS achievements of many large companies have received wide exposure and publicity, and they should serve as models of what can be accomplished through the computer. For each instance of noteworthy achievement, however, there has been a multitude of unsatisfactory results, ranging from minor dissatisfaction to serious lack of progress and, finally, to complete failure.

Management generally has not come to associate high profit return directly with strong information capability. (By "information," I refer to all computer output after its conversion from raw data input by computer processing.) The definition of MIS put forth by the Management Information Systems Committee of the Financial Executives Institute makes clear the relationship between the two. The definition is, in part, as follows:

> "MIS is a system designed to provide selected decision-oriented information needed by management to plan, control, and evaluate the activities

*SOURCE: *Financial Executive* (July 1970), pp. 24-31. Reprinted by permission of the publisher.

of the corporation. It is designed within a framework that emphasizes profit planning, performance planning, and control at all levels. It contemplates the ultimate integration of required business information subsystems, both financial and non-financial, within the company.

"A successful management information system must consider the current and future management information needs of the administrative, financial, marketing, production, operating, and research functions. It will have the capacity to provide environmental (competitive, regulatory) information required for evaluating corporate objectives, long-range planning (strategy), and short-range planning (tactics)."

The development of MIS within a company is a continuous process, phase by phase, all blending together, with additions made as required to meet the needs of management.

By and large, senior management has been unable to come to grips with the organization and operation of its information processing function. Well-defined objectives of the function are almost nonexistent. Major applications have been hurriedly computerized, piecemeal, without overall plans, without concern for management's needs, and without updating basic systems.

Current writing reveal the strong trend toward turning over data processing activities completely to outside service organizations for facilities management. Large and small companies alike are using this escape hatch. The complexities of the computer itself, high costs with poor return on investment, shortage of qualified technicians, and problems which seem to defy solution are exhausting a disproportionate amount of top management's time and patience.

Passing off the facilities management or operational problems, however, attacks only the portion of the iceberg above water. Management is still faced with a very basic problem which extends beyond systems development and operation: the organization and managemnt of information technology for maximum competitive leverage.

The real advantages that can be gained from computers come from the operating intelligence it provides to assist management. A sensitive and quick-acting intelligence/information system can arm a company with a most formidable competitive weapon. Such a system can figure in a company's present and future strength as forcibly as the more exotic influences, like acquisitions, product research and development, new product lines, market development, and manufacturing process breakthroughs. In the present period of extraordinary high costs, management leverage through information becomes the most significant factor in insuring a maximum return on invested capital. Timely, relevant information enables management to make key decisions and to take action promptly with minimal risk. The outcome of decisions can be predicted with reasonable accuracy before they are implemented, and knowledgeable choices can be made between many alternatives.

To use outside facilities management could have the regrettable impact of allowing management to continue in its failure to exploit the computer. Management is better advised to investigate thoroughly and to deploy constructively the factors contributing to the success of a management information system. These factors, largely nontechnical, will vary with the viewpoint of the person assessing them. They are listed in the order of their importance.

12 AREAS TO INVESTIGATE FOR BETTER MIS

1 Top management's involvement with the system

2 Management's ability to organize this MIS function

3 The use of a master-plan

4 The attention given to human relations between functions involved

5 Management's ability to identify its information needs

6 Management's ability to apply judgment to information

7 The condition of basic accounting, cost, and control systems

8 The degree of confidence generated by accuracy at the input level

9 The frequeny of irrelevant or outdated data provided

10 The competence of systems technicians and their grasp of management problems

11 The justification for projects undertaken

12 Reliance on equipment vendors

Investigation of these factors will illuminate the causes of any unsatisfactory condition and, more importantly, will ascertain the proper responses leading to desired improvements.

Top mangaement's involvement with the system

Computer failures have caused disillusionment and management withdrawal at times when greater management involvement is neded. Some managers even consider the computer an encroachment on and a threat to their traditional decision-making rights. Perhaps they feel this way because the presence of decision-oriented information—specific facts and figures— can force management to take action in distaseful situations which they are otherwise able to ignore. General knowledge does not trigger action, but facts and figures cannot continually be ignored.

Management's abdication has been interpreted by technicians as a complete delegation to them of the active direction of computer systems concepts, applications, and, more important, of implementation. This unfortunate delegation of great responsibility to technicians usually does not correspond with their skills in human relations. In fact, the technicians have tended to hammer their systems creations through, sometimes against all odds. As a result, almost all implementation problems or failures are traceable to the human element.

It is interesting to note some of the impressions of top management held by persons down the line involved with systems creation, design, and implementation.

• Management has not made itself aware of the computer's capacity for developing relevant information directed toward problem solving.

• Management normally cannot define problem areas clearly, yet it quaintly regards the computer as a challenge to its decision-making prerogative.

• Management does not understand the absolute necessity of securing accurate input data to insure the success of a system, and the difficulties in accomplishing this.

• Management does not understand or appreciate the time span required to implement a system properly.

It is clear that management must come to realize much more fully the competitive significance of information systems and that, with the proper approaches, eminently successful systems can be developed. Further, management must gain a much broader knowledge of computer systems, possible applications, and implementation problems than it now possesses. With this knowledge, it can confidently demand specific information that is relevant, fresh, accurate, and obtainable.

Management should not feel incapable of understanding computers nor should it fear that computer technology challenges its decision-making rights. The computer is a valuable aid and can remove much of the guesswork and risk. The overall decision-making function, however, remains the province of management.

Finally, it is absolutely certain that any softening in interest, involvement, or support demonstrated by top management will flow freely down through all segments of the organization and present a major handicap to the success of any information system.

Members of senior management have felt that they should not try to grapple with the technical mysteries and complexities of computer systems. Computer technicians, to a large extent, have added to the confusion by failing to assist those outside technical circles in understanding the capabilities and limitations of the computer, thereby making what is a relatively simple problem unnecessarily complex.

Management's ability to organize the MIS function

Limited understanding of information systems coupled with the dynamic nature of systems have made it difficult for management to deal with policy formulation, organization, and control of this critical resource. The sum presents a continuing, nagging, and major problem for senior management.

Management is groping for answers to such questions as what skills, qualifications, and background should the head of information systems possess? Where should information systems report in the top organization? How much in the way of resources should be devoted to the function? Who should participate heavily in the planning and development of objectives? How should the function be staffed?

Another element often contributing to the problem is the incumbent head of the established information system who continually strives to convince his management that his policies, objectives, and qualifications are the best obtainable and should not be challenged. Management, in not resisting this kind of persuasion, allows the old and largely ineffectual methods to linger on.

The cornerstone of effective MIS organization and performance is the link between senior management and the personnel which form the technical staff. The individual serving as this link must have special qualifications. He must have a heavy background in upper management practices and good knowledge of computer systems and operations, and he must enjoy the confidence and cooperation of both the senior management group and the technical staff. Such qualifications are exceedingly rare, a fact which may help to explain why this position has undergone more failures in recent years than any other key management position. A common mistake has been to assign a person with only a systems background to a managerial position. In other instances, the position has been filled at a time of crisis by someone in the company not remotely qualified.

There are no hard and fast rules for guidance in setting organizational relationships. The function can report to the chief financial officer, to an "independent" executive, such as the head of administration, or directly to the president. Experience has shown that all can work successfully. The key, again, is the ability of the MIS head to gain the confidence and cooperation of senior management as a group. Likewise, the matter of centralization is dependent upon company organization, concepts of profit responsibility, and degree of commonality of the segments of the business.

The use of a master plan

Setting overall company objectives and planning to meet those objectives still leaves much to be desired in most companies. The real orphan within such imperfect planning is the information gathering system. Management's abdication of MIS leadership has required the system's technical staff to proceed with applications of its own selection. The more simple, low-risk applications have, therefore, tended to be selected on a piecemeal basis. Management information needs have been largely ignored. The result has been the failure to tap MIS' full potential.

Planning for information systems by involving management, other users of the service, technicians, and related clerical staff can save an enormous amount of backtracking, opposition, time, and expense. The full economic impact of charging ahead without planning can never be completely quantified. The costs of applications never completed, of other lost opportunities and poor decisions, however, are often painfully real. The more subtle effects of poor planning, on the other hand, usually lie hidden and manifest themselves only in general dissatisfaction and lack of steady progress.

Planning must start by setting long-term company objectives followed with a detailed profit plan. Information needs within the plan must then be determined and provided for in the creation of the data bank. All separate subsystems should be coordinated into one integrated system. Planning should cover the gathering, transmission, and dissemination of data as well as its processing. Never should individual major applications be started without a complete integrated plan. Above all, the matters of systems concepts, goals, and long-range planning must not be left to the discretion of the technical staff, but assumed entirely by top management.

Individual project planning should assign responsibilities, time schedules, and a means for project progress reviews and project monitoring.

The attention given to
human relations between functions involved

People problems in information systems cause disappointments and failures to a much greater extent than do technical problems. The lack of participation by users of the service or by related clerical staffs can result in a deficiency of interest which alone can cause the system to fail. Forcing service upon users that they neither ordered nor helped to conceive may cause the system to die. Clerical personnel, who must make the system work, will not be predisposed toward cooperation if they are brought aboard only in the final implementation stage. Sloppy input, arising out of clerical indifference, leads to erroneous information that can destroy all confidence in the system.

The success of any information system is dependent largely upon the effective use of behavioral sciences *well in advance* of the application of systems techniques. It must be realized that an effective system is composed of a prponderance of nontechnical factors—concepts, attitudes, acceptance, and enthusiasm.

How can human relations techniques be better applied to modern information systems with success? What are the approaches which should be taken to assure success? These requisites can be categorized as follows:

• All functional management as well as information systems management serve on the planning and review committee,

 • Active participation by all users of the service,

 • Clear support of technical staff by management,

 • Involvement of related clerical persons in all planning and implementation as it affects them.

The following are comments applicable to each of these requisites.

Planning and review committee

In order to achieve its maximum benefit, an information system must fulfill the needs of all company functions. In fact, to ignore certain functions is to risk aborting the effort of the entire system. A good human relations approach must be premised on a clear delineation of the technicians' role: that they should serve operating management; they are the specialists to whom management looks for technical tools. But their technical expertise must be tempered with consideration, humbleness, and patience. A group of systems managers and functional managers working together in harmony can accomplish amazing results. Comprehensive forward planning and a united implementation effort will insure a high rate of success.

The committee preferably should consist of the head of each function which reports to the chief executive or another high-level executive with decision-making authority. Information systems representation should consist of the MIS head and project managers. The committee should meet regularly, reshaping ultimate goals, assigning new major applications, and reviewing progress on existing applications. Priorities should be changed where beneficial.

Participation by users of service

After objectives and priorities for major applications are set by the planning and review committee, individual projects are set up within the context of an overall plan. It is at this juncture—establishing individual projects—that the systems technicians and the specific users of the information must be joined in the effort. Again, if projected goals are set or a new system is originated without complete user participation, failure is practically guaranteed. In many instances, the users do not make any outstanding contribution to the formulation process. If, however, their participation has been invited, they will view the system somewhat as a creation of their own and will be more likely to support it enthusiastically.

The degree of user satisfaction is probably the most useful index of measuring the success or effectiveness of an information system. A mediocre system can be eminently successful when supported by user participation, while a model technical system, without such support, can be a dismal failure. Human relations has much greater impact here than is generally realized; it at least equals technical expertise in importance.

Support of technical staff

The enthusiasm and interest with which technicians approach their assignments appears almost in direct relationship to the support openly demonstrated by higher managemnt. Management interest cannot lie on the surface; to be influential, it must be deep-rooted.

Support means involvement—active participation in both application assignments and application reviews. It means honest discussions, knowledgeable commentary, and substantial ideas. Support, above all, means commendation where appropriate.

It is virtually impossible in today's competitive market to retain the loyalty of capable computer technicians where they feel a lack of direction or interest from upper management. The choice, therefore, is to give full support or to settle for an inferior technical staff.

Involve related clerical persons

This is the area in which information system delays and ultimate failures are very prevalent. In the development of a system, extensive data must be gathered and considered. Omission of any relevant, although seemingly unimportant, particulars can create the need for extensive redesign and costly delays. Complete involvement of clerical personnel gives them the opportunity to make important contributions and encourages their support of the system, thus helping to assure its successful operation. All approaches should emphasize the objective of work simplification for them.

The time of change is time for crucial added attention to human relations. Change means resistance (usually hidden) and often creates much deeper people problems than it does technical problems. Change upsets stable routines and threatens security. The benefits of change must be shared with those affected wherever practicable. When understanding pride of accomplishment, and job satisfaction are added to the particular skills of an individual, his efforts can be astounding.

Management's ability to identify its information needs

Management chronically deplores that it "does not have enough information to go on." This criticism, more often than not, is entirely correct. Yet management often has not identified its needs, nor has it demanded that these needs be identified by subordinate staff members. Human judgment alone must decide what questions to ask.

A logical approach to defining management's information needs is to review the adequacy of the present information received. Much of this will be excellent. Management certainly will not want any major overhaul that might jeopardize what it presently finds useful.

To determine its information needs, management must review the types of decisions it is called upon to make, the frequency of these decisions, and the specific information that might assist in securing the ultimate success of the decisions. Companies well advanced in MIS can logically use their present cost of capital as a focal point for information requirements, initially comparing this to the present return on investment rate. Relative return on assets employed can be used to evaluate segments of the business. In any case, the information flow can be directed to identify problem areas and to propose solutions. Information should give deep insight into all operating areas so that necessary action is clear and timely.

Management's ability to apply judgment to information

The span of answers that modeling techniques can develop under differing situations in infinite, but human judgment must make the final selections. Present-day practices of making such selections can be dramatized by the example of the senior executive faced with a major decision who, surrounded by stacks of computer runoffs, closes his door and flips a coin.

To a great extent, seasoned management believes that decisions, even the critical ones, must be made on pure judgment and intuition alone. Many very successful businesses have been built with this type of management.

And budget-minded management members are leary of the cost to produce management-oriented information. Applications using the management sciences tend to appear exotic and are not considered to be economically sound.

Thus, the practicality of using scientific techniques, management sciences, and operations research is always a problem. Companies with basic data processing problems, including organizational problems, usually are not remotely interested in the more abstruse facilities of the computer. Management's attitudes toward the utility of simulation, risk analysis, and the relative weighting of alternatives have a strong bearing on the final successes of the scientific techniques applied. Finally, the nature of the particular business, such as the need to make frequent decisions under a multiplicity of uncertain conditions, also has a large role in determining company needs.

On the whole, company management is beginning to realize that scientific management approaches, including financial models of the company or parts of the company, are important to future success. The next few years should witness rapid growth in the use of these techniques. To exploit fully the computer and the leverage derived from information obtained by the computer, management must learn more about the computer, its power, and what it can do to serve management's information needs.

The condition of basic accounting, cost, and control systems

Computer-based information systems are not a solution to outmoded and deficient accounting, cost, and budgetary control systems. There is some tendency to concentrate attention of MIS and to neglect these basic systems. An alarmingly large number of companies today are using antiquated basic systems that have not changed to meet the needs of a dynamic business— systems that produce inaccurate and irrelevant data. Job costing on repetitive production is expensive to administer; often the cost fluctuations reported are not meaningful. To make matters worse, the causes for excess costs cannot be determined because the excesses simply flow in as unidentified cost and are neither isolated nor reported in accounts under a standard cost approach.

Overhead expense accounts are commonly not sufficiently particularized to be meaningful. Account codes are not clear, and considerable cost is reported erroneously. The principles of responsibility reporting are neglected many times. Losses in the work-in-process production flow are not currently reported and cannot be detected until inventory. For many companies, special price quotations are vital to obtaining business; yet their quotation cost data is deplorable.

Budgetary controls using historical data as the principal basis for evaluating new budgets can be most detrimental when grounded on inaccurate data.

Such deficiencies can make the most carefully developed MIS fail. Until basic foundation systems are effective, bad decisions continue to be made based on bad data fed through the computer at a faster rate. A major problem in correcting outmoded basic systems is, again, people. Changes here disrupt their ingrained working patterns and are most subtly resisted.

Continual review by qualified individuals is necessary to assure that the basic systems are meeting the changing needs of the business. Encouraging participation by the users of the systems and the systems specialists is again the most fruitful approach. Fresh and independent viewpoints by outside specialists are usually very helpful.

The degree of confidence
generated by accuracy at the input level

Well-conceived and well-designed technical systems can fail miserably with poorly directed implementation. During implementation, inaccurate careless input can produce data so erroneous that the users lose all confidence in the entire system. Moreover, the memory of failure becomes so fixed that successful operations and enthusiastic support can be set back for years. The presence of the computer has created new disciplines for obtaining accurate data. Clerical errors traditionally have prevailed in abundance. The contemporary use of formal systems for handling data on a mass basis and the recent sophistication acquired by the information user have required that much greater attention be given to input.

Important involvement of the clerical personnel and a thorough testing of the system followed by adequate training—all contribute to successful implementation. Most important, going on-stream cannot be rushed, and all inaccurate output must be traced back to its source. Data isolation and correction devices are helpful in preventing bad data from causing damage or delay.

The successful operation of major applications involves substantial time, sometimes years. The high cost of development and implementation over such long periods wears management's patience thin. They demand "something from the system." If such demands are unreasonable, companies will assure failure or set-back.

The frequency of irrelevant or stale data provided

It is unbelievable under present-day concepts of exception reporting to find stacks of machine runoffs being delivered to senior executives. Sometimes the user finds the appropriate pages to keep, but more often all is discarded. It is not uncommon to find deliveries of the data lagging three to four weeks behind the period being reported.

In these instances, it is obvious that the system technicians are completely insensitive to the process of management, and management simply goes along for the ride. Often the unfortunate consequences of this indifference is the effort by members of management, unable to deal with the situation, to set up their own informal information systems. Such independent efforts on the part of management are not isolated cases; they are appearing with alarming frequency.

For a system to be effective, MIS managers must observe the principles of exception reporting and reporting by appropriate levels. Top management cannot accept less than this.

The competence of systems technicians and their grasp of management problems

In the section covering problems of organization, the importance of the qualifications of the head of MIS was discussed. The casualty rate in MIS reaches into all levels of the technical staff. In particular, the MIS managers, including the systems project leaders and data processing supervisors, have a high turnover.

Athough the most serious failings by technical personnel have been related to human relations aspects, there have also been serious technical deficiencies in much of the systems work. Such deficiencies stem largely from the absence of a clear understanding of management's desires and objectives. Systems men do not know what they are expected to accomplish, and they usually do not have a keen sensitivity to management's needs and problems.

To a lesser extent, technical deficiencies are traceable to outright incompetency. Technical qualifications are often overlooked due to the tremendous demand for skilled senior systems designers and programmers resulting from the explosive growth of computer sciences. In spite of the shortage, however, it is usually prudent to defer systems project work until fully qualified personnel can be assigned. Continuous upgrading of the staff has been necessary in most companies to pursue a solid constructive effort. Close coordination with company management has broadened the skills of technicians and has assisted them in better understanding of management. A very successful policy has been to select highly qualified accounting supervisors and train them for systems work.

The justification for projects undertaken

A policy of economic justification for all major projects provides for the allocation of resources and for maximum payoff, and prevents time and cost from being expended beyond the reach of practical application. As an example, the basic data required might not be in the data base, or even worse, it might not be obtainable by any reasonable means. A clear disclosure of what a project will accomplish prevents subsequent controversies.

In charging ahead without a master plan, many companies undertake major projects without sufficient formalized justification. All major projects should be analyzed under the following criteria:

- Strategy for profit return maximization and investment considerations,
- Planning and decision-making information for management,
- Improved service to customers and other company units,
- Improved short- and long-term processing of data, and
- Direct cost reduction.

All assignments should be approved by the head of MIS. Major projects should be approved by an operating committee.

Projects undertaken without a sophisticated evaluation of benefits versus cost can very likely cause negative payback and abandonment soon after implementation.

Reliance on equipment vendors

Until recently, systems and programming support service was supplied on a limited basis by all equipment vendors. This service, being "free" under the equipment rental arrangements, has been used extensivly to save on in-house staffing. Equipment companies have tended to oversell their limited services and have dampened interest in developing ambitious MIS programs. As a result of the intense competition between equipment vendors, some sales representatives have put a gloss on the capabilities of their hardware. Smaller companies are frequently the victims of such a sales pitch. Many times the false confidence inspired by sales representatives has resulted in serious delays and temporary failures. Fortunately, the hardware capability problem has become less critical now that more companies have the skills necessary to review hardware proposals with a realistic approach. Reviews excluding equipment vendors' representatives are most necessary, and full reliance for equipment selection must be placed on in-house staff.

Opportunity to exploit the computer is enormous

Many of the larger, well-managed, forward-looking companies have taken advantage of modern techniques and the computer's power enabling management to plan, control, and enhance the company's future return on investment. All these companies have dealt with the factors discussed here, but they have been able to profit from past errors. Problem identification must precede problem solving.

As a business continues to grow and more blind spots appear, management tends to reach out for assistance. Positive action toward acceptance of facts, figures, and probabilities using computer systems is still a critical point and a difficult step. Realization that members of management will make the final decisions with or without MIS—but with greater chance of success with MIS—should facilitate acceptance of the new concepts.

There is enormous opportunity to profit through the exploitation of the computer's capabilities, and the degree of opportunity will intensify in the future. Although past problems and failures have generally manifested themselves as being technical in nature, very often they are not. The key to computer opportunities, optimum costs, and maximum profit leverage through information will be realized only by management involvement, solid planning, and overall company cordination.

C. Computer Applications in Systems

29. Recent Trends in Applications of Computers to Business Problems*

B. G. Grubbs

The subject of computers and the evolving applications of computers to problems both old and new is extremely important to everyone. Computers, or data processing, is not only a timely topic for our considerations, but is also a most exciting one because of the rapid advancement in the art of making computers. The increased capacity of the machines to handle larger and more sophisticated problems and the improved economies through their use make possible the consideration of applications heretofore thought not practical for a cost viewpoint. Also, the certainty that these factors will continue to improve over the next decade makes the future extremely exciting.

Every significant area of organized human activity is deeply affected by modern data processing methods. Computers — the most recent development in the data processing technology—perform with great speed and reliability a myriad of essential functions. Whether the field is medical care, education, manufacturing engineering, weather prediction, space flight or scientific research, the world would be poorer without the benefits of computer technology. In a few short years, the data processing revolution has brought about creative and varied solutions to increasingly complex problems. It is

*SOURCE: *Baylor Business Studies* (May, June, July 1968), pp. 7-27. Reprinted by permission of the publisher.

therefore appropriate to survey just what it is that these computers are doing and have been doing. Then we should isolate the important trends in the uses of computers and, by following the trends into the future, gain a perspective of what we may expect to find in the environment of the future with respect to computers and our accommodation with them.

However, before starting our discussion on computer applications, let us refresh our memories—what is a computer or a computing system? The basic elements of all data processing are data input, storage, processing and output. It follows, then, that a computer performs these basic functions. The elements of a computing system are those various devices that put information into the computer; the central processor, which stores and processes the information, and, in addition, controls the operation; and those output devices which display or produce the results of the central processor. These are the elements of the computing system. The trends we are concerned with are the typs of work these computers are doing, the continuing improvements in the capabilities of these machines, and the broad areas in which they will be used.

Applications of data processing

Computers have been programmed to perform the work of users in virtually every field. Meteorologists are using the computer to predict the weather—and may someday be using it to change the weather. The startling progress made in space exploration would not have been possible without computers.

State and municipal governments use computers for highway design and traffic flow studies. Motor vehicle departments can make an instantaneous search of registration plate listings to aid in the identification of abandoned or stolen vehicles. Farmers using computers to analyze characteristics and feed requirements of the dairy herds have increased milk production, in some cases, by as much as 50 percent.

Each person or organization adapts data processing to his own activities. For example:

1. Oceanographic research

The oceans contain vast amounts of foods and chemicals, but are less understood and explored than other areas of the earth's surface. Computers are assisting researchers in studying the motions of currents and tides, producing underwater maps, taking censuses of fish and mineral deposits, and studying desalination processes to produce potable water. In one project, a shipboard computer controls and tracks a free-running, torpedo-sized deep sea research vehicle. The vehicle's instruments measure the salinity, temperature, depth, and other proprties of the ocean and communicate information to the computer through an acoustical link.

2. Medical analysis

Computers are used to aid in analyzing digital and analog signals from instruments such as spirometers, electrocardiographs, electroencephalographs, ballistographs, and phonocardiography devices. Computers are suited to the task of analyzing and correlating many variables. This ability makes them especially useful for analyzing many kinds of patient data to assist the doctor in making an accurate diagnosis. Computers also may be used to provide on-line surveillance of patients in intensive care units and to monitor such critical patient variables as blood pressure, respiration, and pulse.

3. Computing in education

In addition to performing administrative tasks, the computer is being used increasingly as an educational tool. It is used in the classroom and is available also to students at remote terminals for solving individual problem assignments. Such uses are believed by many to be a major application area of the future.

4. Water resource management

A computer has been programmed to simulate any river system in the world, and to calculate within minutes the effect of a year's rainfall and evaporation. Such information is invaluable to the timely prediction of floods or droughts and to the calculation of needed adjustments in water flow distribution.

5. Steel mill process control

Computers monitor processes and control critical variables in steel mill operations as they take place. The computers are directly connected to sensors and other instruments in blast furnaces, basic oxygen furnaces, continuous casting operations, and finishing operations. Data gathered by computers during control of these processes is used by plant management to guide the operation of the mill.

6. Air pollution control

To help predict and control air pollution, computers will be used increasingly to study the motions of air very near the earth's surface, and to determine the impact of pollutants on living beings. In Maryland, a meteorological center is using a computer to forecast weather conditions that result in temperature inversions which prevent the escape of pollutants from the lower atmosphere. A computer in Connecticut can determine in seconds the cleanliness of the air at any of the more than 5,000 street-level locations in the state.

7. Securities transactions

Computers are used to provide up-to-the-minute price quotations and to account for the buying and selling of securities, including the calculations of total prices, commissions and taxes. Computers also handle such activities as recording the number of shares owned by each customer, preparing purchase sale confirmation forms, and printing monthly customer statements.

8. Simulation in the petroleum industry

Mathematical computer programs are employed to analyze pipeline networks, predict congestion points and study methods of controlling production flow for maximum line throughput and minimum cost. Computer simulation is also used by petroleum companies to help improve refinery efficiency and profitability by assessing factors such as available facilities, raw materials and market demand.

9. Typesetting

Computers receive text and printing control information, and prepare justified lines of text with division of words at proper places. The lines of text may be sent electronically to a photocomposer, or temporarily stored in paper tape and later read by a line casting machine which prepares metal type.

10. Electric utility operations

Computers are being used to monitor the performance of both conventional and nuclear-fired steam generator plants. In integrated power systems, which comprise many power plants and interconnecting with neighboring power systems, computers are scheduling and dispatching generating capacity to reduce fuel costs and line losses. Short circuit analyses, stability studies, and fault calculations are examples of computer applications which can help assure continuous availability of power to consumers.

11. Life insurance planning

The computer processes factors that enter into planning for individual insurance needs. Such factors as present income, number of children, marital status, age, family requirements, and home mortgage enter into the caluculations that result in a projection of family income requirements.

12. Demand deposit accounting

Banks use computers to maintain each customer's account balance by posting all debit and credit transactions. Magnetic characters are read from checks and deposit slips to provide direct input to the system. Checks are sorted by machine for return to each depositor with monthly statements.

13. Engineering design automation

To analyze complex optical, hydraulic, electronic, or mechanical networks manually is almost impossible. With recent programming systems written for the computer, engineers can quickly evaluate a new design or modify an old one. For example, the placement and routing of air conditioning and heating systems, or wiring and plumbing systems in aircraft or submarines, can be difficult problems. The computer helps the planner avoid obstructions and find the most efficient route.

However, the most common data processing application operating on computers today are mainly routine clerical and computational activities carried on in manufacturing, merchandising, and service establishments, and in financial institutions, educational institutions, and government.

While such applications are those commonly computerized today, an analysis of how these various applications are actually being done reveals some trends which point the way for the future.

Trend one

One of the major trends that becomes obvious, is that applications are becoming more complex and much more sophisticated as the size and speeds of the computers increase. Because of the speed of the machine, it has the capability of processing many more instructions per second than ever before without a corresponding increase in cost. For example, a company that has been processing its inventory control data to produce reports showing the number of items on hand for each piece of inventory at the beginning of the month, with additions and deletions to stock during the month and a new balance at the end of the month, will now be adding additional elements to this application. In addition to showing the inventory information for the previous month, the application now will show sales of the particular item for several months previously, and will forecast sales of the item for the next several months. With the new information, the application is more than a tool for the accountant. It has become a reference source for planning.

In order to have more price information regarding the status of the inventory, the company is likely to be thinking about placing remote terminals in its shopping warehouses as well as in its remote sales locations. These terminals are tied directly into the central processor so that shipments of inventory as well as sales can automatically update the inventory as these things take place. Having the inventory up-to-date at all times means that now the computer can assist in direct sales, since the sales office can make inquiries regarding how much inventory is on hand and where it is warehoused.

Some examples of the increasing complexity of computer applications are noted below:

Penney's marketing operations

At J. C. Penney, an operations-oriented system is used for day-to-day inventory at both the store level and the regional level. Every evening all of the stores from coast to coast dispatch the small tickets removed from merchandise sold during the day. At the two computer centers in New Iork and Los Angeles, the coded tickets are fed into machines so that the data can be converted to punched cards. Card data are either transferred to magnetic tape or put directly into digital computers. Every two weeks the computers check the stores' stock levels against merchandise sold, and, when merchandise is needed, the computers transmit purchase orders along with the necessary shipping instructions.

This type of marketing system is becoming more and more common in the retail industry today. One of its major advantages is that it is more than just an operations system. Since it replenishes store inventory levels on the basis of a short-term stock-planning formula, it is used for the company's planning and control functions. Thus the application is a marketing operating system with short-term inventory planning and control subsystems.

Credit bureau of Dallas

This Dallas based credit bureau organization owns about fifty bureaus and is presently converting its entire operation to computers.

The initial phase of this operation will be to place all credit information pertaining to its hundreds of thousands of people into mechanical storage units. When the various managers make inquiries to the bureau regarding credit for someone, the computing system, at the command of any one of several checks, will produce the necessary information very rapidly; thus shortening considerably the response time to the local merchant.

The system will provide for a rapid up-dating of the credit files as well as the automatic preparation of management response and billing information for the credit bureau itself.

At a later date, remote terminals will be placed in the merchants' offices allowing them to place instant inquiries into the computer's files and further shorten the wait-time for the credit information.

Trend two

Another trend that is taking place and one that is extremely important for us, is the increasing use of common carrier transmission facilities to aid in making the application more timely than it was before and also, to provide remote locations with accessibility to computers which heretofore were inaccessible. Examples of this are:

Holiday Inn of America

This company operates a chain of motor hotels. Several years ago they installed a computer network to handle reservations for the many locations. Each Holiday Inn has an especially manufactured terminal which enables the reseravtion desk to automatically make reservations at any other location. Inside the computer is stored the room status of every room within the entire chain. When a request is made at any of the motels in the system, the reservation clerk can request the type of accommodations and receive almost instantaneous confirmation. In the event no room is available to meet a specific request, the terminal linked to the computer system will report the available alternative accommodations.

This application of computers linked with communication facilities has evolved into a system which, today, provides an automatic method for fast clearance of room status to tour and travel agents throughout the world. With locations in major cities about the world, this system, called Trav-L-Dex, has control centers linking small and large hotels to international airlines, car and tour rental, and travel agents for instant access to information stored within the Trav-L-Dex system.

Trav-L-Dex centers are planned for early opening in the following cities:

Honolulu	Vienna	Berlin
San Juan	Rotterdam	Athens
St. Thomas, V.I.	Montego Bay	Amsterdam
Nassau, Bahamas	Kingston, Jamaica	Rome

Freeport, Bahamas	Mexico City	Brussels
Munich	Acapulco	Paris
Zurich	Bermuda	London
Frankfort	Copenhagen	Madrid

Designed with a job-orientation concept, the special Trav-L-Dex terminal meets the requirements of speed and accuracy in the preparation of hotel, car rental, and airline reservations. Daily more than 5,000 reservation agents use the customized Trav-L-Dex terminal.

The Holiday Inn System, which is a part of Trav-L-Dex, interconnects over 900 Inns located in more than 600 cities throughout the United States, Canada, Puerto Rico and the Bahamas. The system has become the standard for travelers.

The SABRE system at American Airlines

American Airlines' SABRE system is a large, real-time teleprocessing system designed to perform all the data collection and processing functions associated with the sale, confirmation, and control of an airline reservation. Controlled through a computing center at Briarcliff Manor, New York, 30 miles north of New York City, it provides each American reservation sales agent with direct access to every available seat of any of the airline's flights. In addition, complete information on any passenger's reservation, including name, itinerary, telephone number, and related data, is recorded on a disc at Briarcliff and is therefore available to every agent in the system.

Access to the passenger name record makes it possible for any of American's sales agents immediately to confirm, alter, or cancel all or part of a passenger's itinerary, no matter where or when the original reservation was made. Access in less than three seconds to the name record also provides authorization to the ticket agent to confirm the space and issue the passenger's ticket at an airport or city ticket office.

In addition to controlling seat inventory and maintaining passenger records, SABRE automatically:

Notifies agents when special action is required, such as calling a passenger to inform him of a change in flight status.

Maintains and quickly processes waiting lists of passengers desiring space on fully booked flights.

Sends teletype messages to other airlines requesting space, follows up if no reply is received, and answers requests for space from other airlines.

Provides arrival and departure times for all the day's flights.

Equitable's CAPS system

An interesting example of an on-line system that was developed to process sizable volumes of routine clerical data is provided by one of the largest life insurance companies in the United States. In the early 1960's, Equitable Life Assurance Society of American began conducting research to determine what type of system it should use for individual policy records. The decision was made in 1963 to put all of these records into a large computer-controlled file consisting of discs that would operate on a random-access basis.

The computer and the communications center which it controlled was to be located at headquarters with wire communications network extending from the central unit to the terminal sets located in the cashier's offices and in various headquarters departments. By means of this system, the field offices can use their sets to make inquiries, request policy disbursements, withdraw dividend credits, make changes in the policy records, and so forth. The sets can also be used to transmit data about the payment of premiums. This system was called "CAPS"—Cashiers' Automatic Processing System. CAPS is used by operating personnel responsible for the day-to-day clerical administrative functions of the organization.

Sales order entry and inventory management

Many of the larger American firms have several manufacturing plants which manufacture varied products at locations in different parts of the world. Also, these companies may have hundreds of sales offices in various cities around the world. This creates a tremendous problem in coordinating the handling of sales orders, shipments from warehouses, and preparation of manufacturing and shipping schedules to their warehouses or directly to the customer.

Computers linked by communications are enabling sales orders to be placed directly into the computing system at the time the orders are taken. The computer then automatically prepares shipping requests from inventory and prepares manufacturing schedules for the plants that would be involved. This is done using techniques of optimization which allow for maximum efficiency in handling these vital operating functions.

For these companies operating in a multi-national mode throughout the world, the rapid improvements in communication technology, including the Communications Satellite Corporation, which is rapidly being expanded, offers tremendous opportunity for the future.

Trend three

Probably the most significant trend in evidence today is the trend towards an all encompassing management information system. Most of the illustrations I have used up to now have shown computers being utilized to solve operational types of applications. These specific applications require a certain sub-set of information pertaining to the business organization as a whole. This information is used in order to provide the answers required by that specific application.

The president of one of these companies would view these individual applications as sub-sets of the total requirements of his company. Ideally, he would like to have at his fingertips the necessary information by which he could make his management decisions. If the data being used in the various sub-sets of his business could somehow be integrated so that there came to be a common data base, and if this information could be made immediately available upon demand, then many factors necessary for a decision would be at his disposal when faced with the need for making decisions. Certainly the development of a management information system will require, from some areas, inputs which are not presently available within the data processing organization. However, these necessary inputs can be planned and made available for the decision-making processes. Once the information has been made available, then advanced computing techniques can be brought to bear on the analysis of the data. Such techniques include simulation, mathematical forecasting techniques, statistics, business models, linear programming and others.

In fact, the concept of management information systems is spawning a new breed of professional management people skilled in the uses of computers and mathematical techniques. These new professionals operate as top executives in their companies and have as a primary responsibility the coordination of all aspects of data processing within the company with the end goal of providing a computing system which will not only assist the day-to-day operation of the business, but also aid top management in the decision-making processes.

Trend four

Another very significant trend in the computer industry is the trend towards outside data processing. For many years organizations have had an option as to whether they would handle their data processing requirements in-house or whether they would use a professional service to provide their needs. Because of the increasing demands for sophisticated data processing solutions, many companies have found it easier to utilize an outside professional service company than to develop the in-house capabilities.

Quite recently, the number and types of outside service bureau organizations and professional data service organizations has increased tremendously. Recently, the Texas Business Reporter in a special report said, "The computer services business is growing at a rate two and one-half times as fast as the computer industry as a whole. This rapid growth is equalled by the speed with which it is changing its complexion. A definitive analysis of the industry written almost three years ago is so completely obsolete that even its break down of services no longer holds true."

The services offered by these companies are so diversified that one should not overlook them when making decisions regarding his own data processing activities. Most of the larger companies who have their own in-house computer installations also use outside data processing services to supplement their capabilities. Formerly these larger companies used outside service only for overflow work. That is, when their processing requirements reached a peak-load situation, they were compelled to go outside for additional machine capacity. The situation has changed drastically. Companies are realizing that much of their work can be done better and cheaper by an outside organization.

Speaking at the annual convention of the Life Office Management Association, Mr. Robert L. Harmon, Vice President and General Manager of the McDonnel Automation Company, said recently—"Fast and comprehensive collection, processing and reporting of data, made possible by means of remote terminals, will cause inefficient and uneconomical methods of data handling to fade away. A growing concern by top management of many companies about the efficiency and effectiveness of their computer operations clearly shows that the "gee-whiz" attitude of a few years ago is being replaced by a dollars-per-minute cost approach. The use of an outside professional service organiaztion appeals to many companies. This type of organiaztion makes available to them all the computational power they want, but they don't have to take more than they need."

A user who has data processing equipment installed on his premises might find it necessary to supplement this capacity to:

1. Process an application which, because of the amount of processing required, or the large volume of input data, is too time-consuming to be processed on his own installation. This could occur during seasonal peak conditions or during conversion of an application.

2. Process an application requiring special equipment capabilities not available on his own installation. These capabilities might include optical character reading, mark sensing or data plotting.

3. Process an application requiring additional analytical, programming or other technical assistance, or the availability of a special programming or application package.

4. Obtain information from a special data file.

5. Preserve the confidentiality of sensitive records.

A user without an installed data processing system might wish to purchase the short-term use of equipment or services because:

1. He has continuing needs which require the periodic use of data
processing equipment, but his volume does not justify the purchase or lease
of his own equipment.

2. He may not want to assume the management of a data processing
installation.

3. He requires data processing equipment, services or information on a
one-time or occasional-use basis.

4. He may want to purchase data processing time or services to prepare
for the installation of his own equipment.

Data processing may be obtained from service bureaus throughout the
country. In addition, data processing services may be purchased from a
number of equipment manufacturers and individual users, such as banks
or aerospace companies. These organizations may provide equipment,
systems design, programming, operating and supervisory personnel, information files or any combination of services.

If a user requires equipment time, the choice of a suitable installation
depends on his individual circumstances. For instance, a user who operates
his own installation but needs additional computer time for peak loads will
tend to look for a computer as similar as possible to his own. Other factors
which may influence his choice are convenience of access, availability of
machine time, special computational capabilities, and comparative total
cost, including data conversion, transportation and communications expenses. In the final analysis, however, considerations of timeliness and
economy will usually determine the choice.

Data processing equipment may be used to provide a broad spectrum
of existing and potential "Information Services." These services use data
processing to organize particular types of information for ease in retrieval
and greater usefulness.

A number of organizations sell information in machine-sensible form,
in addition to selling the published information in printed form. Often those
who sell complete data files also offer subscriptions for periodic up-dating
of the files. Examples of entities providing complete data files for sale in
machine-sensible form include:

U.S. Bureau of the Census (and other organizations acting as its distributors): samples and summaries of the U.S. Census.

Dun & Bradstreet, Inc.: file of manufacturing industry establishments;
file of electronic manufacturer's product information.

McGraw-Hill Publishing Co.: Standard & Poor's COMPUSTAT file
containing detailed financial data of about 2,500 companies.

Sales Management Magazine: file of marketing information, showing income and consumption patterns by area.

U.S. Department of Commerce: Clearing House for Federal Scientific and Technical Information, provided by various government agencies.

Other information services currently being marketed specialize in such areas as economic data, technical and scientific information, and mailing lists and street directories.

Economic Information Services are offered by various government and private organizations. These include:

U.S. Department of Commerce: foreign trade information.

The Department of Labor and Agriculture, the Small Business Administration, the Internal Revenue Service and the Federal Housing Administration: statistical summaries and studies.

IBM Corporation: Industry Information Service, which produces customized market research reports based on two specialized data banks.

United Nations: quantity and value data on imports and exports, by country; quarter and commodity. Also, population statistics.

Time, Inc.: food consumption statistics; industrial marketing data on 18,000 industrial establishments; data on the economic structure of the U.S. economy.

A. C. Nielsen Co.: marketing services such as food and drug consumption statistics; audience ratings for television and broadcasting.

Roper Public Opinion Research Center: national or regional opinions on various topics.

Among the organizations providing technical and scientific information services are:

U.S. Department of Health, Education and Welfare: MEDLARS, and index of medical research literature.

Battelle Memorial Institute: materials properties.

American Chemical Society: chemical literature abstracts, citations, chemical compound registry.

Engineering Index: engineering literature abstracts.

Mailing lists and street directors are provided by R. L. Polk and Company, and by the Reuben H. Donnelly Corp. In addition, the telephone companies, various professional societies and other associations compile personal address information, such as telephone and membership directories and address lists.

Trend five

One of the most significant trends todays is the Computer Utility. As the capabilities of computers have increased tremendously, the price of a large-scale computing system has been steadily going up. This does not mean the cost to a user has necessarily gone up—in most cases the cost of doing an application today just as it was done a few years ago, has decreased considerably. A large-scale computing system will cost from $1½ million to $5 million today. Many companies have applications requiring one of these large scale computers, but the total use of the computer by the company is not sufficient to justify the high purchase price. Because of this need, a new industry is evolving from the service bureau concept to one which is sometimes referred to as a Computer Utility. The Computer Utility consists of a service organization providing the facilities of a large-scale computer to a large number of users, with the charge to the user being based upon the amount of service which he actually uses (very similar to the way in which a consumer pays for his electrical services).

In many instances today, the user of a computer utility will have a communication terminal installed in his place of business and the input to the computer will be made through this terminal. The information is transmitted via telephone lines directly into the computer where the computer programmer will process the data and then transmit the answers back over the telephone lines, and the results will be printed out as desired at the customer's terminal.

Remote conversational computing

Conversational time-shared computing is provided by a number of firms, enabling remote users to share the power of a large-scale data processing system. The user dials the system over a communications line. Using a terminal, he enters programming statements and data into the computer, controlling the processing and receiving answers. The system edits the programming statements introduced by the user, checks their consistency and signals errors. In this manner the entire program is introduced, line by line, in a "conversational" mode. The user can determine when he wishes to have his program executed, and can monitor preliminary results, change values, and even change programming statements. In general, he may control execution of the program to his best advantage.

Most of these facilities offer the user some file space at the central processing location for storage of programs or data. However, the lowspeed input/output tends to restrict use with volume programs.

Most of the offerings in remote conversational computing have one or a few programming languages and a simple command structure. Relatively little training is neded before the customer can derive productive use from the system.

Communications between the user and the data processing facility are usually conducted on a dial-up basis, with the user dialing a service point which connects him to the data processing system through wideband or voice-grade channels. There are a number of firms offering remote conversational computing.

Remote batch processing

Remote data processing facilities are also offered for jobs requiring large volumes of input or output. These may involve large program compilations, substantial amounts of processing or a large mass of data. The user transmits data and programs from his location to the central computer for compilation or execution. Processing may be immediate or delayed, depending on the system used. Program storage may be provided at the central computing facility.

These systems normally use medium-speed, semi-automatic terminal devices. Program and data transmission may use dial-up or leased line communications facilities, with line speeds in the 1200 to 2400 baud range. In the future, wideband facilities and higher-speed transmission may be desirable for these remote processing systems. There are at least seven or eight firms offering remote batch processing.

The benefits of computers to business operations are obvious to a majority of people who have investigated their potential.

Many individuals responsible for managing an organization or department of a major endeavor fail to make the computer a regular daily part of the management decision making process. These managers should review their thinking in light of the continuing improvements in the uses and economies of data processing services.

Certainly, computers will have an increasing effect on each of us in the foreseeable future. Our daily jobs may be sharply changed by the computer.

30. Computer Timesharing: A Primer for the Financial Executive*

Timothy P. Haidinger

The computer timesharing industry has experienced extremely rapid growth since its inception in the early 1960s. A recent report indicates that there are now over 100 timesharing firms utilizing more than 275 computer systems in their operations.[1] Services are available in 42 states and the District of Columbia, and some firms now offer nationwide hook-up to a single timeshared computer center. In less than five years, the timesharing industry has succeeded in capturing a significant share of the market for computer services, with at least six of the major hardware manufacturers selling large-scale timesharing equipment.

Despite this rapid growth, computer timesharing has had a surprisingly limited impact on business data processing. Perhaps this can be attributed to the businessman's natural concern for reliability and continuity of service, and his consequent reluctance to adopt innovations quickly. It is clear, however, that timesharing offers a great many advantages, particularly for the smaller business, burdened with a cumbersome manual system and rising clerical costs, which cannot afford an in-house computer and is hesitant to trust its data processing to a service bureau. Often the use of timesharing services will permit such a company to automate its accounting and financial reporting systems earlier than it could if in-house or service-

*SOURCE: *Financial Executive* (February 1970), pp. 26-35. Reprinted by permission of the publisher.

bureau processing were used. And automation of a company's data-processing systems may be implemented at lower cost through timesharing.

Financial executives are often required to evaluate alternative data processing methods for their companies. Timesharing is not usually a major contender in such deliberations. Few financial executives have been exposed to computer timesharing techniques, and, with few exceptions, the timesharing industry has not done a very good job of selling its wares to financial executives and accountants.

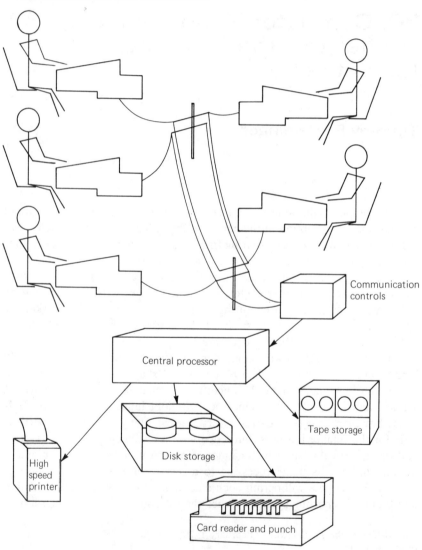

Many factors should be considered before a decision to use timeshared data processing services is made. Some of these considerations result from the unique business activities of the company; nevertheless a number of general comments can be made. The comments which follow are designed to give the reader a practical understanding of the "mechanics" of computer timesharing, guidelines for selecting a timesharing service, and system design and programming standards for business timesharing applications.

How timesharing works

The basic concept of computer timesharing is that many users, by banding together to share equipment, can have a computer capability which none of them could afford alone. Wide geographic dispersion of the users is overcome by inexpensive remote terminal devices which can serve both as input and output units for the central computer. Many of these terminals can be in operation at the same time, all sharing the same central processing unit. To avoid chaos, a switching and priority system in the central processing unit identifies each user and allocates a segment of processor time to him. Normally, the system responds so rapidly that the user feels he is working with "his" computer, and he need not concern himself with the fact that tens, or perhaps hundreds, of other users are connected to the same system.

Although the timesharing equipment currently available varies in many respects, there are more elements of similarity than difference. Most timesharing systems employ the following elements:

1. A central computer, available to many users.

2. Voice-grade telephone lines for transmitting instructions and information to and from the computer.

3. Communication couplers which convert the telephone signal to terminal-compatible impulses and vice versa.

4. Remote terminals which permit the input and output of data.

Central computer

Timesharing computers are normally third-generation, and most have fairly large central processors. Large processors are necessary because a fixed number of central processing storage units (characters of memory) is normally allocated to each user when he signs onto the system; thus the number of users on-line at any one time is limited by the size of the central processor core storage. Also, most timesharing systems use extensive software programs, which occupy a large portion of the computer's core storage.

Peripheral devices often include all those commonly found in conventional in-house configurations, such as card readers and punches, line printers, disk and tape units, and mass storage devices using magnetic cards. Disk units are used in most timesharing systems because they make available a large amount of rapidly accessible file storage at all times to multiple users. The same is true of mass storage devices which, because of their low cost, make the processing of large busines data files economically feasible. Tape units are less popular, partly because of the unavoidable delay in communicating with an operator who must mount the requested tape. To cut down on this delay, one manufacturer uses small tape reels, similar to 8-mm motion-picture film reels, which the operator mounts from the computer terminal.

Computer timesharing equipment is produced by many manufacturers, both large and small. General Electric's 420 probably holds the greatest share of the market. Other popular systems are Scientific Data Systems' 940, IBM's 360/50 and 360/67, Digital Equipment Corporation's PDP 10, Control Data Corporation's 3300/6600, and Burroughs' B5500. Several of these manufacturers are, in effect, are competing with themselves by selling timesharing hardware as well as operating their own timesharing service firms.

Voice-grade connections

Communication of data generally is accomplished over the common voice-grade telephone lines available in all business offices. Users near the computer center need make only a local telephone call to communicate with the computer. Many timesharing firms lease telephone lines which they make available to their users in distant markets free of cost or at a minimal charge.

Leased lines are economically practical, thanks to the technique of multiplexing. This is a method of coding telephone signals to permit the handling of many conversations (or data transmission) over a single line. Calls from numerous users may be multiplexed at a distant location, transmitted over a single line, and reconstructed at the computer center. This procedure is generally quite effective, although in some cases the quality of data transmission appears to be better for users who are located near the computer center than for those some distance away. Operation through office switchboards also seems to cause increased amount of transmission "noise."

All inputs are immediately checked for validity. Incorrect entries will cause error messages to be printed.

Shaded items are inputs typed by the user.

Invoice data are gathered from the customer and inventory master file and written on an invoice file. When invoices are printed, accounts receivable records will be automatically updated.

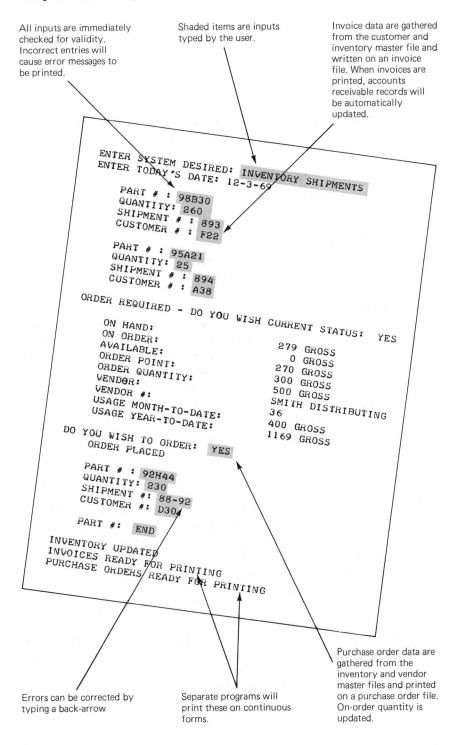

```
ENTER SYSTEM DESIRED: INVENTORY SHIPMENTS
ENTER TODAY'S DATE: 12-3-69
    PART # : 98B30
    QUANTITY: 260
    SHIPMENT # : 893
    CUSTOMER # : F22

    PART # : 95A21
    QUANTITY: 25
    SHIPMENT # : 894
    CUSTOMER # : A38

ORDER REQUIRED - DO YOU WISH CURRENT STATUS:  YES

    ON HAND:
    ON ORDER:
    AVAILABLE:
    ORDER POINT:
    ORDER QUANTITY:
    VENDOR:
    VENDOR #:
    USAGE MONTH-TO-DATE:
    USAGE YEAR-TO-DATE:

                          279 GROSS
                            0 GROSS
                          270 GROSS
                          300 GROSS
                          500 GROSS
                          SMITH DISTRIBUTING
                           36
                          400 GROSS
                         1169 GROSS

DO YOU WISH TO ORDER:  YES
    ORDER PLACED

    PART # : 92H44
    QUANTITY: 230
    SHIPMENT #: 88-92
    CUSTOMER #: D30

    PART #: END

INVENTORY UPDATED
INVOICES READY FOR PRINTING
PURCHASE ORDERS READY FOR PRINTING
```

Errors can be corrected by typing a back-arrow

Separate programs will print these on continuous forms.

Purchase order data are gathered from the inventory and vendor master files and printed on a purchase order file. On-order quantity is updated.

Communication is conducted in either the full-duplex or half-duplex mode. In the full-duplex mode, data can be transmitted from the computer to the user at the same time that other data are being transmitted from the user to the computer. With half duplex, data can be transmitted in only one direction at a time. Full duplex results in slightly faster operation because the user can input data while the terminal is typing the response to a previous processing command. The time difference, however, is not ordinarily significant.

Communication couplers

The electronic signal carried over telephone lines consists of a "carrier" signal on which the data to be transmitted are superimposed. The data and carrier signals must be joined before transmission can take place and must be unscrambled after transmission. These tasks are performed by the communication coupler.

Couplers are of three types: acoustic, magnetic, and "hard wired." Acoustic and magnetic units make use of a telephone handset to transfer sound or magnetic impulses between the terminal and the telephone lines. The "hard wired" coupler requires an actual wire connection between the terminal and the telephone line. Such couplers are probably less subject to outside noise than are acoustic and magnetic couplers, but they may require a parmanent, non-movable installation. Since all three types of couplers are permanently attached, they can usually be installed only by telephone company personnel.

Remote terminals

A wide variety of remote terminal devices is available. Probably the most popular are the Teletype Model 33 and the IBM 2741. Cathode ray tube (CRT) terminals are not suitable for most business data processing because they do not provide output of printed copy. Even though a variety of special-purpose terminals is available, none of them has yet gained the popularity of the IBM and Teletype units. But, since terminal manufacturing companies are highly innovative, many new products will undoubtedly appear in the near future.

The Teletype Model 33 is quite similar to the equipment commonly used for sending telegrams. It prints a page 72 columns wide, in uppercase characters only, at a rate of 10 characters per second. Paper tape input and output is available on the terminal. This permits paper tape to be punched and corrected in advance, so that input to the computer can be made at maximum terminal sped. Paper tape output permits large programs or files which are used infrequently to be stored on paper tape, thereby reducing on-line file storage costs (which are often quite large). Although the unit is somewhat cumbersome, it can be moved from one location to another because it requires only a telephone line, coupler, and electric outlet for operation.

The IBM 2741 terminal is based on the Selectric typewriter. It will print 130 columns in upper- and lower-case type at the rate of 15 characters per second, and the type font can be changed easily. The unit can be used as a typewriter when not being employed as a computer terminal. The terminal can be fitted with a pin-feed sprocket which permits the proper alignment of pre-printed continuous forms—a great help in preparing invoices, checks, etc. Paper tape handling equipment is not available. The installation requirements are similar to those for the Teletype 33.

Selecting a timesharing system

Business data processing makes unique demands on a timesharing system —demands which only a limited number of systems can accommodate. A thorough evaluation of the suitability of the services provided should be made before any agreement is signed with a timesharing firm.

The user ordinarily has the choice of proceeding with the evaluation and conversion of his own or hiring outside assistance. He will probably prefer unassisted conversion if the firm is experienced in the timesharing field, or if it wishes to develop its own expertise and is willing to pay the extra training cost which will be required. But one should keep in mind that the timesharing field is changing very rapidly. New firms are frequently being formed, and new or modified programming languages are announced daily. The computer hardware, computer terminals, and communication equipment in use are changing so rapidly that virtually a full-time effort is required to keep abreast of developments in the field. For this reason, a user may frequently be best advised to hire outside experts on a "for services rendered" basis to assist in evaluating alternative services and to prepare the computer programs.

Selection of a timesharing system should be based on a consideration of the following characteristics:

- Computer configuration
- Programming language
- Reliability
- Cost

The relative importance of these factors and the specific evaluation of them will be different for each application, but no decision should be made until all four have been considered.

Computer configuration

Processing characteristics of timesharing systems cover a wide range. In general, however, an extremely powerful central processor, combined with extensive peripheral devices, makes available some of the largest and fastest computer configurations now manufactured. Features of greatest interest for business applications include the numerous large on-line data files with random addressing capability, large central processor core memory, rapid computing speed, and the ability to perform "background" processing.

File size

Most business data-processing applications require the maintenance of extensive data files. For this reason, file size and method of addressing are probably the most important characteristics of the computer configuration. The file must be large enough to handle the largest of the company's master files, with an allowance for expected growth. Also, the system should permit access to more than one file by a single program at one time. File size is normally measured in terms of the number of alphabetic or numeric characters which the file can contain, and the required size is therefore fairly easy to compute.

Random addressing

The term "addressing" refers to the method by which a computer program indicates which record of a stored file is to be read into the central processor. The most flexible system of addressing permits the programmer to use a "key word" which the system will associate with a particular record on the indicated file. This key word can be any combination of alphabetic and numeric characters. For example, a part number which incorporates alphabetic and numeric characters could be used to indicate the record containing data on the price, inventory currently on hand, back order, and ordering point for the part; an employee's name or identification number could be used to indicate his compensation record.

The second common system uses a "key number" to identify each record in the master file, the key being the sequence number of the record in the file. That is, the first record has the key of one, the second record has the key of two, and so on. To recover a single record under this addressing system, the program must store a table of addresses or use some code to relate the contents of a record to its key. Although this requirement decreases operating flexibility of the system, both of these systems have the advantage of being direct-access methods in which a program needs to handle only those records for which updating is to be performed.

A third system of file addressing is "sequential addressing," in which the records of a file may be read only in strict sequence. In other words, in order to read the 30th record in the file, the preceding 29 records must first be read. Efficient processing with a sequential file addressing techniques requires that the transactions used to update the file first be stored into the same sequence in which the file is maintained. This makes it possible to update the master file in a single pass. Sorting can be a very time-consuming procedure, however, and few timesharing systems have packaged sort programs available. When transactions are prepared in the proper sequence as a matter of course, and when a large portion of the master file is to be updated, sequential addressing may not be a significant handicap. When only a small proportion of the records needs updating, the requirement that all records of the file be read may result in a considerable increase in processing time.

Processor size

The size of the central processor available to a user is important because it determines the number of instructions which can be carried out by the computer in one operation. When a large number of steps can be performed, the need to store interim calculations can be eliminated, and the speed and ease of operation of the system are improved.

One must distinguish between the total size of the computer's central processing unit and the portion of the processing unit allocated to any single user. Many systems allocate a fixed portion of the processor to each user and this is, in effect, the size of "his" central processing unit. It is of little consequence to the user that the total processor has a capacity of several hundred thousand characters of storage if only a small part of this capacity will be allocated to him. Core storage is expensive to manufacture, and the timesharing firm, with its high usage rate, can normally afford to purchase many more characters of storage than are economical for smaller in-house installations.

Speed

The central processors of timesharing computers are typically very large and very fast. Speed is of interest primarily when extensive computations with limited input and output are desired, or when the user is paying for central computer processor time, rather than terminal time. These conditions occur frequently enough to make speed an important consideration.

Background processing

Some timesharing services offer what is referred to as "background batch" processing. This type of processing uses high-speed devices, such as line printers, magnetic tapes, card readers, etc., to input and output information independent of the user's terminal. Computer time is allocated to background processing only when the allocation will not interfere with on-line timesharing users. This often entails a considerable delay, but as a result of the high-speed input and output and the ability of the computer operator to make use of otherwise idle time, background processing is freqeuntly quite inexpensive. It can best be used to process data when turnaround time is not critical and when there are large quantities of input or output.

Programming language

If the user has engaged outside consultants to perform the required system design and programming, he probably will not need to concern himself with the capabilities of the programming language used by the timesharing service. Typically, the programming contract specifies that the user will own the programs once they are completed, and that the work will be performed either for a fixed price or for an agreed hourly rate, subject to some maximum. If the user plans to do his own programming, however, the characteristics of the programming language have considerable significance. It is important that the language:

1. Be easy to learn or be a language with which the company's personnel are already familiar.

2. Have instructions available which will permit terminal input and output to be formatted to the user's specifications.

3. Permit the computer program to guide its user in inputting data and interpreting output.

The last consideration is particularly important when the operator will use the program infrequently and will need coaching on the proper procedures each time it is run.

A variety of programming languages is available to the timesharing user. Many, such as Fortran II, Fortran IV, Algol, Cobol, and, more recently, PL/1, are based on languages developed in the past for stand-alone computers. Languages developed specifically for timesharing users provide extremely simple and conversational commands which can be learned rapidly. Ease of use of these languages is achieved by reducing the control the user has over the computer's operations and by employing a great deal of system software, which occupies core storage and results in higher user charges.

The most common of these conversational languages is named "Basic." This language was developed at Dartmouth University, and has since been modified into many versions, known as Extended Basic, Super Basic, etc.

A study conducted in August 1969 indicates that the vast majority of users write their programs in Fortran or Basic, with 39.6 per cent preferring Fortran and 31.0 per cent preferring Basic.[2] For business applications, Basic is probably the overwhelming choice.

Reliability

Since the user does not control the operation of the computer in a timesharing system, he has little recourse in the event of unreliable service, other than transferring his allegiance to a different timesharing firm. If the programming language is unique—and nearly all programming languages are unique to some degree—the conversion may be quite costly.

The potential user can evaluate a service's reliability through inquiries to existing users and by performing "benchmark" tests of competitive systems. Timesharing firms are generally somewhat reluctant to release the names of their customers, but they will usually release the names if a sale is contingent upon satisfactory references. The program used in benchmark reliability tests should receive input data from a terminal, perform nominal processing upon the data, and return the related output to the terminal, with perhaps 50 to 100 repetitions of this cycle for each test. Testing should be conducted at the time of day when the operational programs are expected to be run, at the time when the computer center is likely to be experiencing its heaviest load, and at selected "off" times, such as the early morning or late evening hours.

When evaluating system reliability, the following factors should be considered:

Down time

The percentage of advertised operating time in which the computer is unavailable because of preventive maintenance or malfunction. This percentage may vary, depending on the time of day.

Line noise

Line noise is a communication malfunction which causes a character to be transmitted improperly to or from the computer center. This is an extremely important type of malfunction because its presence can often go undetected.

Training courses

If in-house programming is to be performed, the timesharing firm should have adequate facilities to train user personnel in the programming language to be used.

Design and programming assistance

A programmer should be on call at all times to answer miscellaneous questions on system operation and proper programming technique. A commitment to perform system design and program coding can be a very strong selling point if it is clear that qualified personnel will be made available.

Hours of operation

The number of hours per day and days per week in which the service is available may be important, particularly in applications which require a great deal of processing or where fast turnaround is needed.

Length of time in business

A timesharing firm which has maintained good relations with its customers over a period of years is usually preferable to one which has recently begun offering its services.

Financial stability

The timesharing firm should have sufficient financial strength to ensure that its operations will be carried on in a proper manner in the foreseeable future.

Cost

In analyzing the economics of using a computer timesharing system, four types of cost must be considered. These are (1) conversion cost (including programming costs), (2) processing cost, (3) file storage cost, and (4) terminal rental cost.

Conversion cost

Timesharing requires the user to pay only for the processing he accomplishes; any minimum charge is normally insignificant. This is in sharp contrast to in-house installations, which require a fairly large fixed monthly expenditure, regardless of usage. In addition, with timesharing there is no need to hire expensive and highly transient data-processing personnel or to construct the facilities in which to house a computer. At the same time, the user can retain nearly complete control over the processing of his transactions and has no outside service bureau apologizing for "unavoidable delays." A user with low transaction volume will not be forced to adapt his accounting to someone else's large-scale programming package, nor will he be a marginal client for a local service bureau.

The two primary conversion costs are for programming and input of beginning data files. Packaged internal accounting programs are beginning to appear, but none has yet gained wide acceptance. Most programs are custom-prepared, although it is often possible to adapt some program routines and input/output formats from one system to another. System programming performed by outside programmers will rarely cost less than $2,000, with $3,000 to $5,000 being an average for design and programming of a basic accounts receivable, inventory or similar system. In-house programming costs may be somewhat lower, but the difference dwindles in significance when all associated costs are considered.

Data conversion costs for specific applications can be estimated easily by computing the operator time and computer charges for inputting beginning data files. This can be done at the terminal or in punched card, magnetic tape, or other form. Ordinarily, conversion will be carried out at year-end or another time when the volume of data to be converted is low and conversion costs will not be significant.

Processing cost

The total monthly charge a user pays for his procesing is a function of two items: the cost base and the price. The cost base is normally either terminal hours used or central processor minutes used. If central processing unit minutes are the base, the rate may vary depending on the amount of core storage being used. Typical terminal rates range from $3 to $18 per terminal hour, and rates based on central processor time range from $5 to $16 per minute. A rough rule of thumb is that one CPU minute is required for each terminal hour, but the exact amount can vary greatly, depending on whether a program is oriented toward input/output or processing.

The majority of timesharing services charge on the basis of terminal hours used. Because inputting data at a terminal is a slow process, charges based on terminal input do not truly reflect utilization of the computer. This method is not, therefore, as suitable for business data processing purposes as is a charge based on central processor time. When the timesharing service charges for terminal time, the processing should be done on a batch basis, with input data prepared off-line on a paper tape which can be read by the terminal at high speed.

File storage cost

Most systems have a monthly charge for file storage based on the maximum number of characters stored during the month. Rates vary from several cents to as high as several dollars per thousand characters stored. The lower rates are for mass storage devices, such as the IBM data cell, and make the processing of large business data files economically feasible.

Terminal rental

The cost of a computer terminal ranges from $100 to $120 per month. The communication coupler will add another $20 to $50, as will the cost of telephone lines, printed forms, and other miscellaneous costs. The terminal rate is for unlimited usage and includes all maintenance, which is performed by the supplier.

Cathode ray tube displays and remote plotters are available for lease at rates substantially higher than those indicated above for printed-copy terminals.

System design and programming standards

Once a timesharing system has been selected, the user must concern himself with proper system design and programming. Many of the standards used for in-house systems are applicable to timesharing systems. Since it is probable, however, that the user has had limited prior experience with computer systems, he must make a particular effort to design, program, and document his system properly.

System design

The new system should be designed to permit easy conversion from the old system, with minimal disruption to those procedures not being changed. This will require that the analyst be thoroughly familiar with the procedures in effect, or that he work in close conjunction with the financial executive. Where possible, data files should be converted at year-end or at another time when the data file is at its minimum size. As with any change in processing, the conversion to a timesharing system provides an excellent opportunity to improve existing systems. In-house or outside personnel may be effectively employed at this time to conduct an overall system review.

Timesharing provides such extensive on-line processing capabilities that there is occasionally a tendency to neglect a proper audit trail. Both for outside auditors and for reconstruction of lost data, it is vitally important that an adequate trail be maintained. This will probably take the form of printed copy, retained on a predetermined schedule. Supplemental data files may also be maintained by the system as a part of the documentation available to permit reconstruction.

Programming

Certain programming standards should be maintained whether the programming is done in-house, by outside programmers as a custom application, or by the adaptation of a packaged program. Some of the standards are unique to timeshared programming, and particular caution must be exercised when programming is done by those acustomed to programming for in-house operation.

Probably the most important element of a timesharing program is the set of recovery procedures to be used in case of a communication failure. Since even the most reliable communication equipment will break down occasionally, programs must be designed to permit the operator to resume processing with as little disruption as possible. Recovery procedures are also necessary to permit the reversal of transactions or data entered improperly by the operator. Such recovery techniques take many forms and are unique to each application.

There is a natural tendency to shortcut recovery in order to complete the program as quickly as possible. However, the cost of additional programming will be quickly dwarfed by the cost of reconstructing data files after the first system breakdown. Proper recovery techniques are available, but the user must insist upon them and not leave the decision to the programmer.

Programs should be properly documented and organized. The program documentation should include a program listing, flowchart (unless the program listing contains sufficient comments that it can be used as a program flowchart), sample input and output documents, layouts of all files used by the program, a directory of all variable names, and a narrative description of the processing performed by the program. If numerous programs are being developed, documentation should be maintained in a standard format and should be required before any program is considered complete. The narrative description, system flowchart, and data input and output formats should be agreed upon before any detailed program coding is begun. To facilitate future expansion or modification, the program coding should be organized in a fashion which makes it easily understood. A modular approach to program writing, in which the program is divided into subroutines, is normally the best way to assure easy expansion.

One of the great advantages of timesharing processing is that the computer program, through the terminal, can guide the user in the proper input of data. Instructions and comments printed on the terminal by the program should be comprehensive and detailed enough to keep the error rate low, but they should not be so detailed as to be cumbersome. When a particular instruction or comment will be repeated throughout the processing, it should be made brief because the operator will become familiar with its meaning. On the other hand, those comments which will be used infrequently should be made much more explicit. In some cases, it is desirable to reduce the level of instructions after an operator has become thoroughly familiar with a program. This can usually be accomplished with minor program modifications.

Conclusion

It seems certain that timesharing will play a larger and larger role in business data processing as financial executives become increasingly aware of its capabilities. The development of standard industry languages, improved reliability, new terminal devices, and an increased marketing effort will make timesharing a question of "when," not "if," for more and more financial executives.

At the present time the opportunities for reduced clerical costs and increased flexibility make timesharing an attractive proposition. However, the rapid growth of the industry has led to a wide variety in the type and quality of services offered by timesharing firms. The financial executive is well advised to adopt a systematic and thorough approach in both the evaluation and conversion stages to assure a system which will meet his criteria for performance and cost.

NOTES

1. Lynn Colburn and James P. Magnell, "Technology Profile: Time-Sharing Services," *Modern Data Processing* (July 1969), pp. 36-50.
2. Bolidan O. Szuprowicz, "The Time-Sharing Users: Who Are They?", *Datamation* (August 1969) pp. 55-59.

31. Selecting a Timesharing Service: The Common Sense Approach*

Thomas Rullo

The evaluation procedure used to select a timesharing system has a great deal in common with the evaluation procedure used to select an automobile. Although a vital ingredient in either case, common sense is more often forgotten in the timesharing system selection process than in that for automobiles.

Selecting the family car solely on the basis of a speed test is highly illogical because more information is required. Yet, some companies evaluate timesharing systems using benchmark tests as the sole selection criteria. The intelligent car buyer knows the planned use of his automobile, specific features that he requires, and his personal resources. The prospective timesharing user should have at least this much knowledge about his timesharing requirements.

Although a performance test is a most significant and necessary step in the automobile evaluation process, it is done only after preliminary analysis and elimination steps are undertaken. It is foolish, for example, to run a performance test on a station wagon if one intends to purchase a two seater. And yet, timesharing system evaluators will sometimes run a benchmark test on a BASIC language system knowing full well they need FORTRAN.

*SOURCE: *Data Processing Magazine.* Reprinted from March, 1970 issues of *Data Processing Magazine,* the Authoratative Publication of Computer and Information Technology, pp. 43-47.

Does the test apply?

The intelligent car buyer tailors the performance test to his specific needs. He does not run speed tests unless he plans to race. And yet, many timesharing system evaluators select a system on the basis of a benchmark program that counts from one to ten thousand while the planned use of the system is for information retrieval. A car buyer does not test one car in the rain and another in clear weather because the test conditions are not equivalent. And yet, evaluators have run benchmark tests in the morning on one timesharing system and in the afternoon on another and obtained non-comparable and misleading results.

Although many more parallels can be drawn between the two evaluation processes, the automobile discussion was intended for illustration purposes only.

The remainder of this article concentrates on timesharing systems.

The first step in the evaluation process for timesharing systems is the establishment of a check list whereby all services to be considered can be qualified in the areas of system availability, operational suitability and contractual acceptability. Each system must prove satisfactory in all of these areas in order to be considered for benchmarking.

System availability

System availability, although easily checked, is sometimes overlooked. To qualify, a service must be available at an acceptable telephone cost (either free local dialing service or a reasonable fixed monthly charge) and at hours that suit the user's operational needs. If the system meets the availability requirements, the evaluator can continue his testing.

Operational suitability

A check on the operational suitability of timesharing services must be preceded by a thorough analysis of the planned use of the timesharing system. This analysis enables the user to determine the programming language and application programs he requires, the acceptable level of user assistance, and the type of terminal equipment necessary for his operation.

Programming languages

To determine which programming language is best for his planned operation, the evaluator must first consider the suitability of the language for his problem area and for the prospective users, the availability of the language, its compatibility with in-house facilities, and its potential for growth. Languages that timesharing services provide in both the conversational and remote batch modes include almost all of the programming languages available to the standard data processing user. The selection of a specific language depends upon which of the preceding factors is most critical to the user.

Of primary importance is the suitability of the language for the problem area. Although most problems can be solved by several languages (e.g., a computational problem can use BASIC or FORTRAN: a business-oriented problem can use COBOL or PL/1), some problems need a specific language. A language such as LISP or SNOBOL (for list processing applications) or AED (with design and compiler writing facilities) might be the only means of solving a user's problem. In a situation where the customer requires one of these special languages, his choice of a time sharing service can be severely limited. In most cases, the user can select one of several languages. In this situation, his selection is frequently based upon the orientation of his company's data processing group. If his company uses PL/1 exclusively in its data processing department, the user should not choose COBOL for timesharing.

Another consideration is the experience and ability of the prospective user. If the personnel who will use the timesharing service are data processing novices, a significant factor is the simplicity and ease of learning the language. The reverse is true when most of the prospective users are experienced programmers. Because most timesharing services offer multiple languages, the needs of both groups can frequently be met by the same timesharing service.

Once an appropriate language has been selected, the evaluator must then choose a particular implementation of the language. Many of the available language processors were originally provided by computer manufacturers and have been modified or enhanced subsequently to accommodate customer requirements. Thus, a wide variation in the features and capabilities of different versions of the same language are available.

Application programs

The application programs offered by a timesharing service usually require special consideration. Often these programs are the single most significant factor in the decision-making process. Application programs take the form of either a major application system offered to support a particular business or engineering activity or a general-purpose library service including complete programs or subroutines that the user can incorporate into his own program. Applications systems are generally well publicized because they are becoming one of the essential elements provided by timesharing services.

Perhaps the most difficult element to assess is the range of offerings provided in the public libraries that are available to any user of the system. Commercial timesharing services frequently do not take the time to document public library programs and routines because many of them are self-documenting. When a user calls a particular library routine, he receives a detailed description of the capabilities of the routine as well as its limitations. Except for the few services that provide comprehensive documentation of their public libraries, actual use is the only sure means for complete evaluation.

Special hardware

Another significant aspect of the operational suitability of a timesharing service is its special hardware requirements. The evaluator must first determine which terminal he requires for his operation and then eliminate those services that do not support this terminal. Teletype or Selectrictype terminals are usually no problem because of their almost universal support by the timesharing services. Plotters or video display terminals, however, are not supported by all timesharing services, so a user who requires either of these devices must consider this constraint before proceeding with the evaluation process.

User assistance

The level of user assistance and support provided by the timesharing service should also be considered in the light of the requirements of prospective users. The amount of support widely among services: some are geared to the computer novice and others are directed towards data processing professionals. Before running benchmarks, the evaluator should exclude those services that do not meet his specific requirements in the areas of user training, programing support, and systems analysis support.

Generally, remote batch timesharing services assume a higher level of user sophistication than do conversational timesharing services. Users can expect more complex documentation and less, but higher level, on-site support from the remote batch services. Once again the type of support that is acceptable depends upon the planned use of the system.

Having established guidelines for determining operational suitability, the evaluator must ascertain which systems meet his requirements in each area. If his requirements are inflexible in certain areas (e.g., only certain versions of a specific language are acceptable or a special terminal must be supported), this stage eliminates many services.

Contractual suitability

Although most systems are contractually acceptable to most users, system administrative factors must be considered before continuing the evaluation process. Some services must be excluded because they require a minimum monthly usage commitment or a lengthy commitment period.

Those services that still qualify for consideration after being tested for system availability, operational suitability, and contractural acceptability form the basis for the benchmark test. Although any intelligent evaluation process would reveal most of the problems before the final decision, it is best to eliminate services prior to the benchmarking stage because this stage requires the most effort.

Benchmark test

In the actual benchmark test, the evaluator must select a program or set of programs that typify his planned operation. The two primary considerations are the user's application type (computational, interactive, program development, or mixed) and the system parameters. If the timesharing terminal will be used to solve complex computation-oriented problems, then the benchmark program should maximize the number of calculations performed while minimizing the amount of interaction or i/o. Most of the simple benchmark programs, such as counting to a set number or performing a certain number of interactions of a set of calculations, measure the computational ability of a system.

In order to achieve a realistic measurement of a system's capabilities, the user must run a program that is more complex. The complexity of the program, however, is determined by the nature of the planned operation. If intrinsic functions such as trigonometric and logarithmic functions or complex numbers are to be common occurrences in the user's programs, they must be included in his benchmark program.

Benchmarks for timesharing

As opposed to heavily computational applications where the user inputs a few numbers and the system processes for minutes, there are many highly interactive timesharing applications where the user must input data every few seconds while the system performs a minimum of calculations. The kind of benchmark program required in this situation is not an iteration of calculations but an iteration of i/o commands, data file commands, or a combination of both.

For those who want the timesharing system to develop programs for in-house use, a different kind of benchmark program is advisable. This user is interested in the debugging facilities, program modification facilities, and compilation speed on the system, and execution speed is of little interest because he will run the completed program on an in-house system.

A good measure of these facilities evaluates the ease of entry of the source program (which contains several known logic and syntax errors), the diagnostics provided after compilation, the debugging facilities, and the facilities provided to correct an error when it is detected. This benchmark test is the most difficult to perform because it requires so much system knowledge on the part of the tester; moreover, the results of the test must be measured qualitatively.

The majority of timesharing installations have a mixture of the heavily computational, highly interactive, and program development applications. Therefore, the only valid benchmark test must check all of these facilities. In most situations, this testing requires multiple benchmark programs.

In addition to knowing the general operational characteristics of his planned system, the user designing a benchmark test must consider his specific application requirements with regard to system limitations. If his application requires multiple data files or large arrays, such data handling techniques should be built into the benchmark program. Any other size or operational requirement should be investigated through the system specifications prior to benchmark testing.

Operational variations

In order for a benchmark program to provide meaningful results, it must run under the same conditions on all systems being tested. This stipulation is extremely difficult to accomplish in a timesharing environment because the number of simultaneous users affects the operating characteristics of a system. Timesharing systems hit peak usage in the mid-morning and mid-afternoon hours; thus, a system tested during one of these peak periods will have poorer results than the same system tested during a light period such as 12 noon or 6 p.m. A program tested on a system on Saturday will run faster than one tested on Monday because there are fewer people on the system on weekends. All systems should be tested, therefore, at the same time (preferably the peak period because that is probably when the system will be used in actual operation) and on the same day.

System loading

Another factor to consider regarding subscriber loading of the system is the current system load compared to the maximum load. A recently installed system has fewer contracted users than a system that has been in operation for some time. If a program is run on a system that can handle 40 simultaneous users but has only 10 customers online, the system will perform much better than the same type of system with 30 customers.

The evaluator must realize that as a company becomes more successful in its marketing effort and adds new customers, the system response time will slow down perceptibly, and the original benchmark results will require updating. Although a new system in town usually enjoys a competitive advantage in situations based solely on benchmark tests because of low loading, this temporary success frequently becomes its downfall when it becomes a fully loaded system.

When the user determines the nature of his planned operation, he decides whether the bulk of his usage will be conversational or remote batch processing and selects the operation mode of his benchmark accordingly. Bias is created if the benchmark is run in conversational mode on one system and in batch mode on another.

Because many services offer multiple versions of the same language (i.e., FORTRAN II, FORTRAN IV, etc.), the evaluation must be sure that his benchmark program is run in the version that will be used once a system is selected. Most services have a "speed" version for production work. The language version must be consistent throughout the services tested.

Pricing structure

One of the most important factors to be considered and one of the easiest to underestimate is the pricing structure and pricing technique of the timesharing service. The pricing structure is readily obtained by consulting the service's schedule of fees. Determining the pricing technique, however, requires an analysis of the service's methods for measuring the units to be billed. There are three basic pricing considerations, terminal connect charges, central processor charge, and storage charges with many variations on the calculation of each.

Of the three basic pricing units, the terminal connect charge is the most easily evaluated. In most cases, it is simply the time the user is connected to the system, measured from the system's acceptance of the user's identification code to the user's disconnection from the system.

The central processor unit is the most difficult and elusive pricing factor to measure because in many cases the representatives of the service do not know how to evaluate it. Central processor usage can include execution time, swapping time, compilation time, or any combination of these three. The evaluator must know the exact composition of the central processor unit of each system if he is to compare the price performance accurately.

Storage price

Because storage charges are usually stated as a dollar amount per block of characters, evaluation of this factor appears to be a straightforward billing procedure. The storage pricing techniques, however, create the greatest misunderstandings. Before calculating the cost of storing a program for one month, the user must know the time of day that the storage is measured and the basis for billing.

The time that storage is measured is significant because the user can perform housekeeping on his storage areas prior to the measurement time to ensure a lower reading. The basis for billing can be either a "high water mark" (the maximum amount of storage used during a month) or an averaging method. Although the averaging method is fairer to the user, and certainly less expensive, some services do use the high water mark technique.

Thus, two services quoting the same charge per character of storage can vary widely in actual storage cost if their measuring technique and billing bases differ. This analysis of the service's pricing policies should be undertaken whether or not the evaluator intends to use benchmark programs.

Benchmark results

The preceding discussion warns about the use of benchmark programs, with the operational variations of timesharing systems noted as the prime obstacle to a valid conclusion. As long as all precautions are taken, however, meaningful results can be obtained from a benchmark test. One interesting phenomenon must be noted: an evaluator that dedicates tremendous amounts of energy to the evaluation process generally overlooks the re-evluation process entirely. After a service is chosen, the same operational variations that make the benchmarking process difficult begin to invalidate the original results. As noted before, the more successful a service becomes, the heavier the system load and, consequently, the worse the system performance.

The benchmark program used in the evaluation process should be run periodically after the service has been installed for two reasons. First, the rerun is an insurance that the benchmark test was not run on a "dummy system" (a technique not unknown to the timesharing community), Second, the rerun enables the user to determine if the system has degraded to the point where a new service must be considered, and the evaluation process must begin again.

Conclusion

The evaluation and selection process described above can be summarized as follows: know your application, determine your requirement and establish selection criteria, eliminate from consideration all that do not satisfy your requirements, test the remaining for performance, and select the one that best meets the selection criteria.

This procdure is based upon common sense and is applicable whether a timesharing system or an automobile is being evaluated. Unfortunately, common sense is sometimes neglected when something as complex as the evaluation of a system is concerned.

32. Myth of Real-Time Management Information*

John Dearden

The latest vogue in computer information systems is the so-called real-time management information system. The general idea is to have in each executive's office a remote computer terminal which is connected to a large-scale computer with a data bank containing all of the relevant information in the company. The data bank, updated continuously, can be "interrogated" by the manager at any time. Answers to questions are immediately flashed on a screen in his office. Allegedly, a real-time management information system enables the manager to obtain complete and up-to-the-minute information about everything that is happening within the company.

The purpose of this article—aimed at a time span of the next five to seven years—is to raise some serious questions concerning the utility of a real-time information system for top management. I will try to show that it would not be practicable to operate a real-time *management control* system and, moreover, that such a system would not help to solve any of the critical problems even if it could be implemented. I will also try to show that in other areas of top management concern a real-time system is, at best, of marginal value. It is my personal opinion that, of all the ridiculous things that have been foisted on the long-suffering executive in

*SOURCE: *Harvard Business Review* (May-June, 1966), pp. 123-132. Reprinted by permission of the publisher. Copyright © 1966 by the President and Fellows of Harvard College; all rights reserved.

the name of science and progress, the real-time management information system is the silliest.

Meaning of real-time

One of the problems in any new field of endeavor is that there is frequently no universally accepted definition for many of the terms. It therefore becomes nearly impossible to question the validity of the concepts underlying the terms because their meanings are different to different people. The term "real-time" is no exception. In fact, in a single issue of one computer magazine, back-to-back articles defined real-time differently; and one example, cited in the first article as an illustration of what real-time is *not*, appeared in the second article as an illustration of what a real-time system *is*.

Semantic confusion

One concept of real-time is demonstrated by these two quotations:

• "A real-time management information system—i.e., one that delivers information in time to do something about it."[1]

• "A real-time computer system may be defined as one that controls an environment by receiving data, processing them and returning results sufficiently quickly to affect the functioning of the environment at that time."[2]

The problem with both of these definitions is that they are too broad. *All* management control systems must be real-time systems under this concept. It would be a little silly to plan to provide management with budget performance reports, for instance, if they were received too late for management to take any action.

The following is a description of real-time that comes closer to the concept of real-time as it is used by most systems and computer people:

> "The delays involved in batch processing are often natural delays, and little advantage can be obtained by reducing them. But elimination of the *necessity* for such delays opens new and relatively unexplored possibilities for changing the entire nature of the data processing system— from a passive recorder of history (which, of course, is valuable for many decisions) to an active participant in the minute-to-minute operations of the organization. It becomes possible to process data in *real-time* —so that the output may be fed back immediately to control current operations. Thus the computer can interact with people on a dynamic basis, obtaining and providing information, recording the decisions of humans, or even making some of these decisions."[3]

System characteristics

To expand somewhat on this description, the term "real-time system" as used in this article will mean a computer system with the following characteristics.

(1) *Data will be maintained "on-line."* In other words, all data used in the system will be directly available to the computer — that is, they will be stored in the computer memory or in random access files attached to the computer. (This is in contrast to data maintained on magnetic tapes, which must be mounted and searched before information is available to the computer.)

(2) *Data will be updated as events occur.* (In contrast to the "batch" process, where changes are accumulated and periodically updated.)

(3) *The computer can be interrogated from remote terminals.* This means that the information stored in the computer can be obtained on request from a number of locations at a distance from the place where the data are processed and stored.

Perhaps the most widely known example of a real-time system currently in operation is the American Airlines SABRE system for making plane reservations.

Potential applications

With the new generation of computers, random access memories have become much less expensive than has been true until now. This fact, coupled with the advances made in data transmission equipment and techniques, will make many real-time applications economically feasible.

Real-time methods will improve those systems where the lack of up-to-the-minute information has in the past resulted in increased costs or loss of revenue. I believe that many companies will employ real-time methods to control all or part of their logistics (the flow of goods through the company) systems. For example:

> A manufacturer of major household appliances might have raw material and work-in-process inventories in his manufacturing plants, and finished goods inventories both in company and distributor warehouses and in dealer showrooms. There is a more or less continuous flow all along the route from raw material to retail customer. If all of the data on inventory levels and flows could be maintained centrally and updated and analyzed continuously, this would not only solve many of the problems now faced by such a manufacturers, but would make it possible to provide better all-around service with lower inventory levels and lower costs (particularly in transportation and obsolescence).

There are, of course, many other potential applications for real-time management information systems, and I believe that they will be used extensively in the next few years. However, these applications will take place almost exclusively in logistics, and, as I shall explain later on, techuniques that may improve a logistics system will not necessarily improve a management control system. I want to make it clear at this point that I am not opposed to real-time systems per se. I believe they have valuable applications in operating situations. I am only opposed to using real-time information systems where they do not apply. The balance of this article will consider top management's use of real-time systems.

Management functions

As used here, the term "top management" will apply to the president and executive vice president in centralized companies, plus divisional managers in decentralized companies. In other words, I am considering as top management those people responsible for the full range of a business activity —marketing, production, ressearch, and so forth. I am also assuming that the company or division is sufficiently large and complex so that the executive makes only a limited number of operating decisions, if any. I believe that this is a reasonable assumption in considering real-time management information systems. A company where the president makes most of the operating decisions could scarcely be considering a sophisticated and expensive computer installation.

Six categories

This part of the discussion considers, in general terms, the functions of top management. The purpose is to establish how a typical executive might spend his time so that we may later evaluate the extent to which his decision making can or cannot be helped by real-time computer systems. I have divided top management's functions into six general categories— management control, strategic planning, personnel planning, coordination, operating control, and personal appearances. Each is discussed below.

1. *Management Control.* One of the principal tasks of a manager is to exercise control over the people to whom he has delegated responsibility. Ideally, this control consists of coordinating, directing, and motivating subordinates by reviewing and approving an operating plan; by comparing periodically the actual performance against this plan; by evaluating the performance of subordinates; and by taking action with respect to subordinates where and when it becomes necessary.

The formal management control system will, of course, vary with the type and size of business as well as with the type and amount of responsibility delegated to the subordinate. Nevertheless, all effective formal management control systems need three things:

(a) A good plan, objective, or standard. The manager and the subordinate must agree as to what will constitute satisfactory performance.

(b) A system for evaluating actual performance periodically against the plan. This would include both a clear explanation of why variances have occurred and a forecast of future performance.

(c) An "early warning" system to notify management in the event that conditions warrant attention between reporting periods.

2. *Strategic Planning.* This consists of determining long-range objectives and making the necessary decisions to implement these objectives. Much of top management's strategic planning activity involves reviewing studies made by staff groups. Capital expenditure programs, acquisition proposals, and new product programs are examples of studies that fall into this area.

Another phase of strategic planning consists of developing ideas for subordinates to study—that is, instead of waiting for staff or line groups to recommend courses of action, the executive develops ideas of his own as to what the company should be doing.

3. *Personnel Planning.* This important function of management deals with making decisions on hiring, discharging, promoting, demoting, compensating, or changing key personnel. In the broadest sense, this consists of organizational planning. Personnel planning is, of course, related both to management control and strategic planning. Nevertheless, there are so many unique problems associated with personnel planning that I believe it is reasonable to consider it as a separate function.

4. *Coordination.* Here management's function is to harmonize the activities of subordinates, especially where it is necessary to solve a problem that cuts across organizational lines. For example, a quality control problem might affect several operating executives, and the solution to this problem might require top management's active participation. In general, this activity tends to be more important at the lower organization levels. The president of a large, decentralized company would perform less of this coordination function than his divisional managers because interdepartmental problems are more common at the divisional level.

5. *Operating Control.* Almost all top executives perform some operating functions. For example, I know a company president who buys certain major raw materials used by his company. Usually, the operating decisions made by top management are those which are so important to the welfare of the company that the executive believes the responsibility for making them cannot be properly delegated.

6. *Personal Appearances.* Many top executives spend much time in performing functions that require their making a personal appearance. This can vary from entertaining visiting digintaries to giving out 25-year watches. (I shall assume the activities involving such personal appearances will not be affected by a real-time management information system.)

Real-time practicality?

The purpose of this part of the article is to examine, in turn, each of the management functions described above (except #6) to see whether or not it can be improved by a real-time information system.

1. Management control

I do not see how a real-time system can be *used* in management control. In fact, I believe that any attempt to use real-time will considerably weaken even a good management control system. (In setting objectives or budgets, it may be useful to have a computer available at the time of the budget review to calculate the effects of various alternatives suggested by management. This, however, is not a real-time system, since a computer console need be installed only for the review sessions.)

Calculating Performance. In the area of performance evaluation, real-time management information systems are particularly ridiculous. When a division manager agrees to earn, say, $360,000 in 1966, he does not agree to earn $1,000 a day or $1,000/24 per hour. The only way actual performance can be compared with a budget is to break down the budget into the time periods against which performance is to be measured. If the smallest period is a month (as it usually is), nothing short of a month's actual performance is significant (with the exception of the events picked up by the early warning system to be described below). Why, then, have a computer system that allows the manager to interrogate a memory bank to show him the hour-to-hour or even day-to-day status of performance against plan?

Even assuming objectives could logically be calendarized by day or hour, we run into worse problems in calculating actual performance, and worse still in making the comparison of actual to standard meaningful. If the performance measures involve accounting data (and they most frequently do), the data will never be up-to-date until they are normalized (adjusted) at the end of the accounting period. I will not bore you with the details. Suffice it to say that a real-time accounting system which yields meaningful results on even a daily basis would be a horrendous and expensive undertaking.

Let us go one step further. Performance reports, to be meaningful, must include an explanation of the variances. This frequently involves considerable effort and often requires the analyst to spend time at the source of the variance in order to determine the cause. Would this be done every day or oftener? Ridiculous! There is one more thing about performance reports. The important message in many reports is the action being taken and the estimated effect of this action. In other words, the projection of future events is the important top management consideration. Will this be built into the real-time system? Since this involves the considered judgment of the subordinate and his staff, I do not see how this could possibly be done even on a daily basis.

Early Warning. How about real-time for providing an early warning? Here also, I do not see how it could be of help. Early warning has not been a problem in any top management control system with which I have been acquainted. In most instances, when situations deteriorate to the point where immediate action is required, top management knows about it. As the manager of a division ($100 million a year in sales) said to me, when I asked him how he knew when things might be out of hand in one of his plants, "That's what the telephone is for."

In any case, it is possible to prescribe the situations which management should be apprised of immediately, without even relying on a computer. Furthermore, the important thing is to bring the situation to top management's attention *before* something happens. For example, it is important to inform management of a threatened strike. Yet a real-time management information system would pick it up only *after* the strike had occurred.

In summary, then, early warning systems have been put into operation and have worked satisfactorily without a real-time system. I see nothing in a real-time management information system that would improve the means of early warning, and such a system would certainly be more expensive. (Note that there I am talking about management control systems. The early warning techniques of many logistical control systems, in contrast, could be greatly improved by real-time systems.)

My conclusion on management control is that real-time information cannot be made meaningful—even at an extremely high cost—and that any attempt to do so cannot help but result in a waste of money and management time. Improvements in most management control systems must come from sources other than real-time information systems.

2. Strategic planning

Since strategic planning largely involves predicting the long-run future, I fail to see how a real-time management information system will be of appreciable use here. It *is* true that past data are required to forecast future events, but these need hardly be continuously updated and immediately available. Furthermore, much of the preparation of detailed strategic plans is done by staff groups. While these groups may on occasion work with computer models, the models would certainly be stored away, not maintained on line between uses.

Perhaps the most persistent concept of a real-time management information system is the picture of the manager sitting down at his console and interacting with the computer. For example, as a strategic planning idea comes to him he calls in a simulation model to test it out, or a regression analysis to help him forecast some event; or, again, he asks for all of the information about a certain subject on which he is required to make a decision.

It seems to me that the typical manager would have neither the time nor the inclination to interact with the computer on a day-to-day basis about strategic planning. Problems requiring computer models are likely to be extremely complex. In most instances, the formulation of these problems can be turned over to staff specialists. Furthermore, I think it would be quite expensive to build a series of models to anticipate the manager's needs.

Under any conditions, strategic planning either by the manager alone or by staff groups does not appear to be improved by a real-time system. Models can be fed into the computer and coefficients can be updated as they are used. Between uses, it seems to me, these models would be most economically stored on magnetic tape.

3. Personnel planning

A real-time management information system does not help the top manager to solve his problems of personnel planning, although the computer can be useful in certain types of personnel data analysis. About the only advantage to the manager is that information becomes available somewhat more quickly. Instead of calling for the history of a particular individual and waiting for personnel to deliver it, the manager can request this information directly from the computer. Therefore, while a remote console device with a visual display unit *could* be used for retrieving personnel information, the question of whether it *should* be used is one of simple economics. Is the additional cost of storing and maintaining the information, plus the cost of the retrieval devices, worth the convenience?

4. Coordination

The coordination function is very similar to the management control function with respect to potential real-time applicability. A manager wants to know right away when there is an interdepartmental problem that will require his attention. As is the case with early warning systems developed for management control, a real-time system is not necessary (or even useful, in most cases) to convey this information. Further, I cannot see how a real-time management information system could be used in the solution of these coordination problems, except in unusual cases.

5. Operating control

There is no question that real-time methods are useful in certain types of operating systems, particularly in logistics systems.[4] To the extent that a top executive retains certain operating control functions, there is a possibility that he may be able to use a real-time information system. Because of the necessity of doing other things, however, most executives will be able to spend only a limited amount of time on operating functions. This means generally that they must work on the "exception" principle. Under most conditions, therefore, it would seem much more economical for a subordinate to monitor the real-time information and inform the top executives when a decision has to be made.

It is very difficult to generalize about this situation. Here, again, it appears to be one of simple economics. How much is a real-time system worth to the manager in relation to what it is costing? I cannot believe that there would be many instances where a manager would be concerned with operating problems to the extent that a real-time information system operating from his office would be justified.

Reporting by computer

In recent months, there have been experiments to replace traditional published reports by utilizing consoles and display devices to report information directly to management. Although these techniques, strictly speaking, are not real-time, they bear such a close relationship to real-time systems that it will be useful to consider them here.

Modus operandi

The general idea is that the information contained in the management reports would be stored in the computer memory so that the manager could ask for only the information he needed. This request would be made from the computer console, and the information would be flashed on a screen in his office. For example, a manager could ask for a report on how sales compared with quota. After looking at this, he could then ask for data on the sales of the particular regions that were below quota and, subsequently, for detail of the districts that were out of line.

The benefits claimed for this type of reporting are as follows:

- The manager will receive only the information he wants.

- Each manager can obtain the information in the format in which he wants it. In other words, each manager can design his own reports. One manager may use graphs almost exclusively, while another may use tabulation.

- The information can be assembled in whatever way the manager wants it—that is, one manager may want sales by areas, and another may want it by product line. Furthermore, the manager can have the data processed in any way that he wants.
- The information will be received more quickly.

Important considerations

Before installing such a system, it seems to me, a number of things should be taken into account.

First, what advantage, if any, does the system have over a well-designed reporting system? Since the storage and retrieval of data in a computer do not add anything that could not be obtained in a traditional reporting system, the benefits must be related to convenience. Is there enough additional convenience to justify the additional cost?

Second, is it possible that for many executives such a system will be more of a nuisance than a convenience? It may be much easier for them to open a notebook and read the information needed, since in a well-designed system the information is reported in levels of details so that only data of interest need be examined.

Finally, will the saving in time be of any value?

It seems to me that the two main considerations in installing such a system are the economics and the desires of the particular executive. There is one further possibility, however, that should be carefully considered. What will be the impact on the lower level executives? If these people do not know the kind of information their superiors are using to measure their performance, will this not create human relations problems?

Without going into the details, I can see many problems being created if this is not handled correctly. With a regular reporting system, the subordinate knows exactly what information his superior is receiving—and when he receives it—concerning his performance. Furthermore, the subordinate receives the information *first*. Any deviations in this relationship can cause problems, and the use of a computer to retrieve varying kinds of information from a data base is a deviation from this relationship.

Three fallacies

If management information on a real-time basis is so impractical and uneconomic, why are so many people evidently enamored with this concept? I believe that the alleged benefits of real-time management information systems are based on three major fallacies.

1. Improved control

Just about every manager feels, at some time, that he does not really have control of his company. Many managers feel this way frequently. This is natural, since complete control is just about impossible even with the best management control system. Since most companies have management control systems that are far from optimum, there is little wonder that a feeling of insecurity exists. In the face of this feeling of insecurity, the promise of "knowing everything that is happening as soon as it happens" has an overpowering appeal.

As explained previously, real-time will not improve management control and, consequently, will not help to eliminate the insecurity that exists. What is usually needed is a combination of improved management control systems and better selection and training of personnel. Even at best, however, the executive will have to accept responsibility for what other people do, without having full control over their actions.

2. "Scientific Management"

There appears to be considerable sentiment to the effect that the scientific way to manage is to use a computer. This fallacy implies that the executive with a computer console in his office is a scientific manager who uses man-machine communication to extend his ability into new, heretofore unavailable, realms of decision making.

I believe that it is nonsense to expect most managers to communicate directly with a computer. Every manager and every business is different. If a manager has the necessary training and wishes to do so, it may be helpful for him to use a computer to test out some of his ideas. To say, however, that *all* managers should do this, or that this is "scientific management," is ridiculous. A manager has to allocate his time so that he spends it on those areas where his contribution is greatest. If a computer is useful for testing out his ideas in a given situation, there is no reason why he should have to do it personally. The assignment can just as easily be turned over to a staff group. In other words, where a computer is helpful in solving some management problems, there is no reason for the manager to have any direct contact with the machine.

In most instances, the computer is of best use where there are complex problems to be solved. The formulation of a solution to these complex problems can generally be done best by a staff group. Not only are staff personnel better qualified (they are selected for these qualifications), but they have the uninterrupted time to do it. It seems to me that there is nothing wrong with a manager spending his time managing and letting others play "Liberace at the console."

3. Logistics similarity

This fallacy is the belief that management control systems are merely higher manifestations of logistics systems.

The fact is that the typical real-time system, either in operation or being planned, is a *logistics* system. In such a system, for example, a production plan is developed and the degree of allowable variances established in a centralized computer installation. The actual production is constantly compared to plan; and when a deviation exceeds the established norm, this fact is communicated to the appropriate source. On receiving this information, action is always taken. Either the schedules are changed or the deficiency is somehow made up.

Notice that speed in handling and transmitting vast amounts of information is essential. This is the critical problem that limits many manual logistics systems; and the computer, particularly with real-time applications, goes a long way toward solving the speed problem.

In contrast, speed in processing and transmitting large amounts of data is *not* a critical problem in *management control* systems. Consequently, the improvements that real-time techniques may effect in logistics systems cannot be extrapolated into management control systems.

The critical problems in management control are (a) determining the level of objectives, (b) determining when a deviation from the objective requires action, and (c) deciding what particular action should be taken. The higher in the organizational hierarchy the manager is positioned, the more critical these three problems tend to become. For example, they are usually much more difficult in planning divisional profit budgets than plant expense budgets. In some instances the computer can help the manager with these problems, but I do not see how it can solve them for him. Furthermore, the use of computers in solving these problems has nothing to do with real-time.

Short-term view

While real-time management information systems may be very useful in improving certain kinds of operating systems, particularly complex logistics systems, they will be of little use in improving management control. This is particularly true in the short-range time span of the next five to seven years.

The following is a checklist of questions that I believe the manager should have answer to before letting anyone install a remote computer terminal and a visual display screen in his office:

1. What will the total incremental cost of the equipment and programming be? (Be sure to consider the cost of continuing systems and programming work that the real-time systems will involve.)

2. Exactly how will this equipment be used? (Be sure to obtain a complete description of the proposed uses and the date when each application will become operational.)

3. Exactly how will each of these uses improve the ability to make decisions? In particular, how will the management control system be improved?

With precise answers to these three questions, it seems to me that a manager can decide whether or not a remote terminal and visual display device should be installed. Do not be surprised, however, if the answer is negative.

Long-range outlook

What are the prospects of real-time systems, say, 15 or 20 years from now? Some experts believe that, by that time, staff assistance to top management will have largely disappeared. Not only will the staff have disappeared, but so will most of the paper flows through present organizations. A manager in the year 1985 or so will sit in his paperless, peopleless office with his computer terminal and make decisions based on information and analyses displayed on a screen in his office.

Caution urged

It seems to me that, at the present time, the long-term potential of real-time management information systems is completely unknown. No one can say with any degree of certainty that the prediction cited above is incorrect. After all, 15 or 20 years is a long time away, and the concept of a manager using a computer to replace his staff is not beyond the realm of theoretical possibility. On the other hand, this concept could be a complete pipedream.

Under any circumstances, many significant changes in technology, organization, and managerial personnel will be required before this prediction could be a reality for business in general. As a result, if such changes do occur, they will come slowly, and there will be ample opportunity for business executives to adjust to them. For example, I believe there is little danger of a company president waking up some morning to find his chief competitor has installed a computer-based, decision-making system so effective that it will run him out of business.

I believe all executives should be open-minded to suggestions for any improvements in management information systems, but they should require evidence that any proposed real-time management information system will actually increase their effectiveness. Above all, no one should rush into this now because of its future potential.

The present state of real-time management information systems has been compared to that of the transportation field at the beginning of the Model-T era. At that time, only visionaries had any idea of how transportation would be revolutionized by the automobile. It would have been foolish, however, for a businessman to get rid of his horse-drawn vehicles just because some visionaries said that trucks would take over completely in 20 years.

It seems to me that this is the identical situation now. Even if the most revolutionary changes will eventually take place in management information systems 20 years hence, it would be silly for business executives to scrap present methods until they are positive the new methods are better.

NOTES

1. Gilbert Burck and the Editors of *Fortune, The Computer Age* (New York, Harper & Row, Publisher, 1965), p. 106.
2. James Martin, *Programming Real-Time Computer Systems* (Englewood Cliffs, New Jersey, Prentice-Hall, Inc., 1965), p. 378.
3. E. Wainright Martin, Jr., *Electronic Data Processing* (Homewood, Illinois, Richard D. Irwin, Inc., 1965), p. 381.
4. See Robert E. McGarrah, "Logistics for the International Manufacturer," HBR March-April 1966, p. 157.

33. The Multinational Computer*

Burt Nanus

In the last two decades, the number, size and influence of multinational firms have been increasing at a rapid rate. Such firms typically have some form of direct investment in a number of different countries. Their managements make decisions on production, research and marketing within a global perspective—that is, in terms of alternatives that are available to them anywhere in the world. The reasons for the growth in importance of multinational operations are well documented and need not be repeated, but several specific factors that have important operational implications can be identified.

The trend toward the aggregation of larger units for international business operations through direct foreign investment and mergers means that many multinational firms have gained considerable financial strength. This has assisted them to achieve economies of mass production and mass marketing, but in order to do so, they must be able to coordinate their operations effectively across national boundaries.

Sharp competition among the large multinational firms is causing all of them to adopt practices in production and marketing similar to those of the most successful competitors. As a result, there is a growing internationalization of the art of management which is facilitated by the sharing of consultants, textbooks and business school courses, all of which draw upon a common pool of management research and experience.

*SOURCES: Reprinted with permission from the November-December 1969 issue of the *Columbia Journal of World Business*, pp. 7-14. Copyright © 1969 by the Trustees of Columbia University.

A new breed of manager is emerging—one who is proficient in multinational operations and equally at home in a variety of countries.

If there is a single distinguishing characteristic of multinational operations, it is the necessity to accommodate to great variations in local conditions—variations in political, economic and social environments, as well as in the behavioral characteristics of workers, supervisors, suppliers and customers. As a result, many functions that are performed centrally in a national firm are performed locally in the multinational firm.

On the other hand, there are many who feel that extensive opportunities for cost savings and operational efficiency are being lost by overdecentralization and suboptimization. Clearly, the headquarters office has an opportunity to accumulate in its central staffs a great deal of business know-how collected from the experiences of all the local staff. It should be able to apply this know-how, as well as its financial resources and specialized functional skills, to a balancing and coordination of the firm's multinational operations in a way that improves the performance of the organization as a whole. Many multinational firms would probably like to coordinate their operations more closely and would do so if they could discover coordinating mechanisms that did not interfere with necessary local initiative in dealing with local circumstances.

Decision makers in multinational firms are plagued by inadequate information at every level. At headquarters, a lack of system-wide data may force decision makers to meet problems with ultraconservatism and costly delays. At the local level, inadequate information resulting from a lack of sophistication in management control techniques or from a poor flow of information from headquarters often reduces considerably the flexibility of local managers to respond to unforeseen shifts in the competitive environment. Hence, there is a great need for better management information systems designed to improve the amount and quality of information that is available to decision makers at every level. Similarly, there is a need to improve the skills of local managers in information collection and interpretation, problem identification and decision making.

These factors suggest that multinational corporations can benefit from the use of some of the newer management techniques involving large-scale information systems.

A multinational concept

To understand how these benefits could be achieved, imagine a large central computer in a headquarters office tied to satellite computers in the larger regional offices and plants in the major countries in which the multinational corporation operates. The regional offices, in turn, might be tied to hundreds of remote input/output devices located at branches and sales offices. Data would flow from the local offices to the regional computers to be assembled and used for various decision-making and performance-evaluation purposes related to current operations. Information needed by the branches would be fed back to them on remote consoles located there.

The summary data, together with special study data such as reports on economic and political conditions in the various countries, would be fed from the regional offices and plants to the central computer for storage, analysis or large-scale computation purposes. The central computer would have the capability of handling the large computational jobs and storing the main files of the corporation. In addition, it would store historical information about corporate performance and environmental information.

Within this general framework, the multinational corporate information system would have a number of service-oriented characteristics:

1. The system would be capable of operating in all the languages of the countries in which the corporation operates, at least with regard to a minimal set of operating codes. This implies the need for company-wide data collection and processing standards as a precondition to the implementation of the system.

2. The system would permit essentially simultaneous use by many remotely located users, each of whom could be independent of the others or could interact with the others at will. Furthermore, it would be designed to be available 24 hours per day to provide as much or as little computing service as each user wished.

3. The system would permit private priority access to data from the company's information files to authorized requesters and to deny such access to others. Additionally, it would have built-in memory protection to guard against the possibility of one user affecting the files of another.

4. The system would be able to provide to each user at remote stations a range of facilities similar to that which he would have if he were the sole operator at a private computer. This includes the ability to interrupt processing; to read out memory; to change previously stored data; to introduce, monitor and debug new routines and to draw upon libraries of routines.

5. The system would be designed to provide each level and position of management with the planning and control information that it needs in the conduct of its job. The information would have to be current, easily understood and preferably in a form that is under the control of the manager.

6. The system would be able to provide many forms of analysis when needed. This includes the use of mathematical models so that the impact

of management decisions could be studied and so that executives could analyze the logical relationships between the organizational units in which they are interested.

7. The system would lend itself to easy modification to accommodate corporate growth and change. Expansion might involve the addition of computers and modules to the system or the connection of the system with other special-purpose systems and data bases on either a multinational or a local basis.

The advantages of such a multinational corporate information system are of two kinds—improved decision making and economies of scale. The most direct and obvious way that the proposed system could contribute to improved decision making is by providing better information for decision makers at all levels—information that is more timely, more accurate, more convenient and more relevant. The system would permit the decision maker to use more quantitative information and to use it more effectively by taking advantage of the ability to correlate current data with historical data, to compare one country's operations and performance with those of another and to test hypotheses about the future effects of current decisions through the use of simulation and other techniques.

Some multinational firms, in responding to the need for local autonomy in certain decisions and transactions, seem to have gone overboard in decentralization and have created a disjointed composite of small businesses. They have thus deprived themselves of some of the advantages of their size. The real strength of a multinational firm is in its ability to consider opportunities available to it throughout the world.

Economies of scale

There are several ways to achieve economies of scale:

1. By reducing the time delays in the information system required to detect shortages, initiate purchases and place purchase orders, there would be less need for buffer inventories; overall inventory levels could be reduced, and cash could be freed for other purposes. Moreover, by being able to purchase critical materials for the entire organization rather than having each unit purchasing everything for itself, quantity discounts and purchases could be arranged in those countries that have the greatest competitive advantage for each resource.

2. With a company-wide perspective, it is possible to minimize transportation and warehousing costs by shipping over least-cost routes and by considering each delivery in terms of the particular combination of demand, transportation and warehousing conditions existing at a given time as well as applicable customs and duties.

3. The processing of orders, particularly when parts and finished goods may be arriving from several countries, often puts the multinational firm at a competitive disadvantage when compared to its domestic rivals. Speedup of delivery with the assistance of a multinational information system may turn out to be a key competitive factor in such operations.

4. Some economies may occur purely from the point of view of computing power. A large central computer with several satellite computers permits a balancing of input-output speeds and costs by permitting a hierarchy of storage subsystems with various access times and capacities. At the same time, users would experience faster service and turnaround time than they could get if they had to use a smaller computer, even one that was located next door. In addition, the system would permit a more economical allocation of computer power by permitting so-called "production" processing (payrolls, dividends, etc.) to be run when the on-line load is minimal from a system-wide point of view. Finally, such a system would permit the economical use of scarce programmers since all programs could be made equally available to all organizational units online to the computer, wherever they are located.

For these reasons—better decision making, competitive advantages and economies of scale—substantial benefits could be derived from a multinational information system. However, costs and feasibility must be explored as well as benefits.

Feasibility

In discussing feasibility, it is necessary to examine the concept from both a technical and an operational point of view. The first is relatively easy since anyone familiar with current hardware capability will agree that equipment exists, or will exist shortly, to fulfill all the requirements for such a system. The only reservation might be in the area of communications, since the system would require a great deal of data transmission across national boundaries and perhaps over great distances with accuracy and reliability. However, with laser technology and communication satellites, this problem is unlikely to be a major technical obstacle within a few years. With regard to other aspects of hardware—power, input-output, memory, speed, reliability, etc.—there is little doubt that the concept of a large multinational information system is technically feasible. With software, there do not seem to be any unusual demands that have not been met somewhere and implemented, cost considerations aside. Thus, technical feasibility does not seem to provide any insurmountable problems, given the current and foreseeable state of the art.

Operational feasibility, on the other hand, presents problems of a different sort. To explore this subject, it is necessary first to examine the degree of computer acceptance in the business worlds of foreign countries to establish whether sufficient human resources could be assembled for such an undertaking. Next, the economic feasibility of the undertaking must be examined and then, multinational organizational considerations must be taken into account. Finally, the question of political feasibility must be addressed.

The question to be answered on computer acceptance is whether managers in various industrialized countries are sufficiently familiar with the use of large data processing systems to permit such an undertaking at the present time. The fact is that the state of the art of business data processing in most foreign countries is considerably behind that of the United States. In fact, the United States may have from three to five times as much computer equipment as all the rest of the world together, largely because the U.S. government has supported and nurtured the computer industry by means of substantial contracts in the military and space fields. In the software and business applications spheres, the United States is also considerably ahead of other countries, many of which are plagued with serious shortages in programming talent.

What does this lag in computer know-how imply with regard to the operational feasibility of a multinational corporate information system? One must conclude that the environment in many countries is simply not yet ready for it. The sponsor of such a system would have considerable difficulty finding enough programmers with the proper training to construct the system. He might also have difficulty in making arrangements for adequate international high-speed data transmission facilities, and he would be faced with a need for a monstrous training program. These problems can, of course, be overcome by money, but the costs might be so prohibitive as to make this a serious roadblock to the current implementation of the system. However, one may conjecture that conditions will change—indeed they must change if other developed nations are to retain their advanced industrial status—and these problems may very well not be serious road-blocks within a few years.

Cost analysis

While it is not possible to do a detailed cost analysis of a system that is defined in only general terms, one can make some bold guesses based upon other large systems currently in existence. For example, given the costs of the largest computers now installed and making allowances for the fact that hardware power per dollar has been increasing greatly with time, it may be

assumed that the order of magnitude of hardware costs for the conceptualized system would be in the range of 10 to 20 million dollars, with the
software costing perhaps an additional 20 to 30 million. It is clear that
expenditures of this magnitude, even if spread out over several years, could
only be justified by the very largest multinational corporations and not even
by them unless a return on the investment of, say, 10 million dollars per
year could be expected.

It may be conjectured that such savings and more can be realized by
means of lower inventories, fewer warehouses, economies in purchasing
and economies in data processing. Even more important, there is an excellent chance that greater returns could be realized in terms of improved
decision-making efectiveness and greater coordination of the firm's operations. Although the concept appears to be economically feasible, because
of the magnitude of the expenditures and the risks involved one would not
expect a corporate stampede to implement large-scale multinational information systems in the near future.

Even assuming that the computer environment is favorable and an
economic analysis proves the benefits of the concept convincingly, one must
still ask whether executives are ready to make the kinds of personal
adjustments that would be needed to benefit from a system of this type.
Anyone who has traveled in other industrial countries must conclude that
a multinational information system would be considered a radical innovation to most of today's executives. It might be several years before they
could learn to be comfortable with and benefit from the great capability
which the system could provide. However, with the growing international
ization of managemnt and with many progressive managers attending
courses at the business schools of the industrialized countries, this situation
will probably be remedied in the coming decade.

One might predict strong political opposition to multinational information systems in many countries. Consider the situation from the point
of view of one of the countries in which a multinational corporation is
operating. It will be clear to the government of that country that control
of the enterprise is being exercised from the outside in a more direct manner
than has been the custom to date. The government will assume (probably
correctly) that the intent of the information system is to effect economies
of scale, some of which may conflict with the government's objectives. For
example, economies could be realized by transferring production, employment or capital from a high-cost country to a lower cost one, but this might
conflict with governmental desires in one or possibly both countries.

On the other hand, it is not clear whether a country, any more than a
firm, can ever afford to permit its productive resources to be used less
efficiently than its neighbor's without permanent loss of stature and power.

Obviously, if some countries forbid multinational information systems operating within their borders and others welcome them, the most efficient and sophisticated producers will be attracted to the latter. The long-range political picture is a difficult one to predict in this case, but it may be safe to assume that if the economic arguments are compelling enough, considerable political and legislative ingenuity will be exercised to make the approach politically palatable.

It is also possible to take the analysis one step further and examine the implications such a movement would have for the nature of multinational organizations and for the environments in which they operate. Will the introduction of a multinational computerized management information system cause greater centralization of control in multinational firms? Those who feel that decentralization of many such firms took place only because executives at the top were unable to get sufficient information about operations will feel that once the computer makes such information available to them, recentralization will be the natural tendency.

Decentralization effects

There are strong reasons, however, to believe that the use of computers across national boundaries will ultimately strengthen the decentralization that is needed to deal with different languages, cultures and tastes; to operate successfully with numerous governments, each with its own peculiar set of laws, traditions and patterns of interaction with business; and to cope with the differing work habits, labor practices and available skills in each country. Since most of these tasks have human, social and value-forming elements, they cannot be successfully dealt with by a centralized headquarters staff but must be handled by competent local managers who have the necessary information to relate their operations to the larger corporate picture and to act on their own initiative in a manner serving the best interests of the corporation as a whole.

This can be done by having a centralized computer collect data from decentralized sources, process them and transmit information back to the remote point for local decision making, enriched by analysis and comparison with other similar units throughout the corporation. With the informational and computational resources of the entire corporation at his fingertips, the local manager will be better equipped than he is now to make decisions on matters properly within his sphere. Thus, while one might expect to see some redistribution of decision-making authority toward the center in the multinational firm, a far more important effect is likely to be the strengthening and coordination of decision making at all levels throughout the organization.

What effects would such a concept have upon managerial skills? There are many experts who assert that the introduction of a computerized system in a large corporation leads to fewer jobs with more highly programmed content at lower levels in the management hierarchy. They feel that those who are now engaged in low-level planning functions, such as turning production decisions into parts orders or schedules, will be eliminated. There is some truth in these contentions—surely, the most programmable elements in management jobs will be relegated to the computer. However, in the case of the multinational firm, the conclusion that the lower level of management will disappear, lose its significance or decrease greatly in ,numbers, does not appear to be reasonable in view of the other forces at work. In addition to the critical human and social interactions, the dynamics of corporate growth in the multinational firm, with its emphasis upon ceaseless innovation to develop better competitive methods, will contribute to a greater demand for managers at every level.

Of course, these new managers will need a much greater understanding of the role of the information system in their organization and of the various analytical tools at their disposal than is presently found in multinational firms. This need will place many demands upon the educational systems of the countries in which multinational firms operate. It may take years to upgrade the current generation of multinational managers. The gap will have to be filled in the short run by internal management development courses. There are definite signs that multinational corporations are awakening to this challenge.

Implications for labor

The introduction of multinational information systems would almost certainly have profound effects upon workers. In the first place, it is likely to have the short-term effect that is commonly associated with the introduction of automation anywhere—the problem of worker displacement and adjustment. A second effect would be an alteration in the work content of of many jobs throughout the multinational corporation. Hundreds or thousands of people will have to receive training on how to interact with the new information system—preparing inputs, interpreting outputs, designing segments of the system, etc. For the rest of the employees, the introduction of such a system might greatly decrease the amount of routine, repetitive and boring work in the corporation.

A third effect on workers is related to the degree to which each employee will be able to reconcile his sense of patriotism with loyalty to the multinational firm of which he is a part. This problem exists to some degree today, but with the virtually complete autonomy of local management, the employee is not nearly as aware of the presence of the multinational coordinating influences as he will be when he is constantly called upon to interact with an information source in a distant country and to adjust local decision making to the needs of the overall organization.

As an illustration of such a potential conflict, an executive in the United Kingdom might be called upon to decide whether the product required to fill a Swiss order should come from an Italian plant to minimize overall production and transportation costs, or from a British plant to contribute to an improvement of the balance-of-payments situation in his own country. One might expect that as companies become more truly multinational in their operations, and staffs in each country become more international in their composition, conflicts such as these would be resolved in favor of the corporation, but the cost in terms of individual frustration might be very high.

The multinational information system would probably create a whole new framework of relationships with customers and suppliers, particularly with other multinational firms. These relationships might include, for example, more frequent negotiations at headquarters level for worldwide supply and distribution of a raw material or finished product. It might even extend to the point where large multinational customers and suppliers tie at least a portion of their information processing systems together for the purpose of coordinating shipments and production schedules for mutual benefit.

In the economic and political spheres, multinational information systems might have considerable long-term impacts:

1. There is likely to be more government involvement in the affairs of private industry. No multinational information system could be built without extensive communications linkages, and governments in most countries either own or tightly control these facilities. Moreover, every government will feel obligated to protect its citizens from at least some of the social costs of short- or long-term economic displacement caused by the introduction of computers. Governments will also wish to play a more active role in protecting national interests in such matters as labeling, advertising and financing as corporations make more of their decisions on the basis of international rather than national considerations.

2. As a result of increased integration and coordination within multinational firms across national boundaries, there will be a need for more comprehensive international trade agreements. As it becomes easier for multinational firms to shift resources among their plants and offices in various countries, differences in tax laws will serve to harm those countries whose rates are higher, and there will be strong pressures toward uniformity

or at least agreements between countries to minimize the damaging effects of such differences.

3. Labor unions will have to become truly multinational if they are to maintain their bargaining positions with large multinational companies and protect the interests of their members. At first, unions are likely to be interested mainly in ensuring equitable treatment for their members in basic matters such as wages and seniority. Eventually they may attempt to negotiate international contracts, using the threat of an international strike as a weapon.

4. There is likely to be more government support for electronic data processing. Most governments are already aware of the need to stimulate the use of electronic data processing in their countries if they are to retain their position in the industralized world. The implementation of multi-national information systems will support proponents of this view. It can be expected that the governments of many nations will considerably expand the support they provide in the field of EDP—both directly, by providing funds for training and research, and indirectly, by improving and expanding government-owned computer facilities.

In the long run, it is to be hoped that these effects will be beneficial and will provide a powerful incentive for closer cooperation between all nations and peoples. There is already a rapidly growing internationalization of tastes, attitudes, product preferences and behavioral patterns due to the expansion of international tourism and mass media communications. The multinational corporation concept, which is likely to be measurably strengthened by the type of information system discussed here, will certainly accelerate the forces already at work in this direction. This may be the most important effect of all, as Rensis Likert has pointed out: "As managers of industrial and comparable enterprises throughout the world acquire the same basic knowledge and skills, the capacity to communicate and to interact constructively in solving complex and difficult problems and conflicts will increase correspondingly. A new and much more effective resource will become available to help in the solution of the world's international conflicts. . . . This might well become the most important contribution that the art of management will make to human well-being."[1]

The world may not have to wait until the year 2000 to enjoy the benefits of this development.

NOTE

1. Rensis Likert, "Trends Toward a World-Wide Theory of Management," *Proceedings of CIOS, 13th International Management Conference*, New York, 1963.

34. The National Public Opinion Poll System—1980*

Thomas L. Wheelen

One of the phenomena of the past decade has been the impact and growth of public opinion polls. They have been extensively used by politicians and the news media.[1] The news papers are continuously showing polls (Harris, Newsweek, and Gallup) on every major issue facing our nation and especially those facing our national politicians.

Politicians have made extensive use of these polls to develop their platform issues for elections, to ascertain the sentiments of their constituents on major issues and bills pending before Congress, and possibly to solidify their voting position. Many of these respectable national surveys are based on statistical samples of 1200-2400 individuals.

This same era has also seen (1) the development of sophisticated electronic data processing equipment, (2) the development of data phones, and (3) direct communication between computers over leased lines. By the end of this decade, we should be able to combine all these elements into a feasible total system for a national public opinion poll. This system would allow every registered voter to record his opinion on all major legislation and/or issues pending before Congress or the nation. This system will provide our national leaders with an instantaneous pulse of the nation's feeling on any specific issue.

*SOURCE: *Computer Decisions* (October, 1970), p. 106. This article was adapted from "Can the Computer Make National Opinion Polls Really Nation-Wide?" by Thomas L. Wheelen. Reprint permission granted by the publisher.

The system will utilize a data phone where the individual will insert his individual identification card. The identification code wll be the person's social security number and the Congressional district number in which he is a registered voter. The card will be issued by the local election registration board. The individual will insert the card in his phone and dial the regional telephone number to record his vote. The voter will be able to record his opinion on all major legislation pending before Congress.

This will be accomplished by having the nation's newspapers provide a weekly listing of all major bills pending before the Senate and the House of Representatives. Each bill will be designated by its proper Senate or House bill number. The listing can also provide a code number for all major issues. The voter will record one of the following votes for all the issues: (1) No, (2) Yes, or (3) No Opinion. The vote will be recorded on a regional designated government computer. Daily the information from each regional computer will be transmitted and consolidated into one national data bank.

The votes will be stratified by Congressional district, state, and regional district, and could be further stratified by adding various codes to the identification card, such as age and sex. Each elected official and government executive could obtain an immediate reading of the nation's pulse on a specific bill.

This method also could modify a prevailing opinion that once I vote for a Congressman or a Senator, then he represents only his own interests and not those of the voters. The voter feels that he cannot communicate his opinions to his elected representatives. This system could overcome this problem. It also puts a strong emphasis on the apathtic vote issue. This is a way for the silent majority to express their opinion.

This would provide us with the ultimate in a democratic type of government, where each person can record his opinion on all major issues and/or legislation facing our nation. The silent majority could and would be heard from in this system if they so desired. The author feels such a system will surely be developed in the latter part of this decade. All that is actually required is the replacement of our present telephones with data phones; then, the remainder of the system could easily be developed. Another possibility to expedite the implementation of this system would be to have data phones installed at certain strategic points, such as the local post office, city or town hall, or any other designated government building. A further suggested refinement of this system would be to have the information in the central data bank published on a weekly or monthly stratified basis for the electorate. Are our elected officials and voting public ready for such a system?

NOTES

1. CBS's Special on Tuesday, May 19, 1970, was entitled "The National Environment Test." It consisted of 28 questions on the environment which were submitted to a national sample. They also had two sample votes in the studio audience. *Newsweek* of May 25, 1970, included 4 polls—(1) Nixon as President, (2) U.S. Troops in Cambodia, (3) Who's to Blame at Kent, and (4) Agnew's Stand.

2. For further discussion of points raised in this article see: "Computers May Assist Polls," by Ralph Fuller, *The Richmond Times-Dispatch,* (December 6, 1970), pp. D-1, D-11.

5 STATE OF THE ART IN EMERGING MANAGEMENT SYSTEMS

Since the advent of the computer fifteen or so years ago, the development of management information systems has been an "emerging" art. Today, some significant developments can be observed which truly may be regarded as mature rather than emerging. In particular, production process control systems, and conventional accounting data processing systems, have been widely used. However, the development of management decision systems involving the conjoining of computer-based information systems and management control systems whereby unstructured, strategic decisions may be dealt with effectively, remains an emerging art. Some idea of the difficulty associated with this aspect of systems development can be obtained from these selections.

A. Internal Control

35. Toward a System-Oriented Concept of Controllership*

John P. Fertakis

An important ingredient of the practice of management has been the ability to select from the organizational environment the kinds of information necessary to the decision process. As organizations grow and develop, so do the quantity and quality of information grow and develop. Today the manager stands in a virtual flood of potential communications and reports.

A computer-based technology of management now exists in which the orderly development and dissemination of information has become one of the primary ingredients of the management process. The integration of the information system with the management system has in the past been the task of the controller, operating primarily through the accounting system. The changing nature of information and the systems employed to generate and synthesize it are certain to have organizational consequences. Such organizational changes can easily be haphazard and troublesome unless accompanied by and accomplished through an integrative organizational approach. The subject of this paper is the development of an organizational approach to administrative management and control incorporating the information function and controllership.

*SOURCE: *Management Accounting* (December 1968), pp. 5-10, 23. Reprinted by permission of the publisher.

Nature on controllership

General agreement exists that the controller's function involves records and reports, though interpretations range from controllership being a quite narrow function to it being almost a pervasive organizational role. Two of the leading texts on the subject of controllership define the functions of the controller as follows:

> ... it becomes apparent that the really essential duties of controllership are all aspects of one basic function—designing and operating the records of the business and reporting and interpreting the information which they contain.[1]

and,

The controller is chiefly a staff executive whose primary function is to gather and interpret data which will be of assistance to other general and functional executives in the determination of sound policies and their successful execution.[2] The first concentrates upon the information and its origin, while the second considers the role of information in the management context. However, the essential focus of both views is upon the system of records and reports. Note that neither source limits the scope of controllership to accounting records or accounting-based reports.

The Committee on Ethics and Eligibility Standards of the Controllers Institute of America, in its suggested six "ideal"[3] functions of controllership, goes far beyond the passive connotation of the preceding quotations. For example, the controller is "... to measure and report on the validity of the objectives of the business and on the effectiveness of its policies, organization structure, and procedures in attaining those objectives."

A lack of agreement with respect to the role of the controller thus is apparent. Prior attempts have been made to circumscribe the controllership function by enumerating the things in which he should be involved in carrying out his role. These enumerations fail to clarify the controller's functions, being based upon an insufficient conceptual notion and lacking systematic analysis.

Nature of information

Information is defined for purposes of this paper as that data which is *relevant* to the intelligent making of choices by individuals. Data will refer to knowable things, individually or collectively. Semantic differences in the terms are beyond the scope of this paper, but *data relevance* is the key concept underlying information.

To clarify the role of the controller in relation to information and to the organization in an integrative manner, it is useful to utilize a "systems" approach in the analysis. A system is defined as:

> 1. an assemblage or combination of things or parts forming a complex or unitary whole. 2. any assemblage or set of correlated members ... 6. due method, or orderly manner of arrangement or procedure.[4]

In systems in which human beings play a part, unity, correlation, arrangement and orderliness imply interaction. Interaction, in turn, may reasonably be assumed to involve a transmittal of knowledge or directions among the component parts of the system. The usefulness of the systems approach in the present discussion lies in its contribution to orderly thinking about the job of managing.[5]

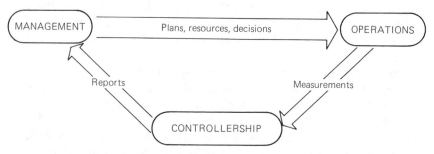

A systems concept of the organization

The basic elements of the organization, when viewed from a systems approach, might be visualized as illustrated in Exhibit I. These elements will be referred to as "sectors" or "clusters" when associated with their respective subsystems. The *management* function is the formulation or approval of plans, the allocation of resources for their implementation, and the follow-up and evaluation of results. As resources are made available, *operations* are initiated which are intended to lead toward the fulfillment of management's plans. At this stage, data is being generated and management is faced with the need to refine the data for future decisions and follow-up activity.

The increasing degree of specialization and technological sophistication found in the operations sector often makes it impractical or impossible for the manager to form valid opinions or evaluations of the operations on the basis of his own consideration of data. A further limiting factor upon good managerial evaluation is the probability that the manager himself, at higher levels, increasingly tends to be a "generalist" and is perhaps not operationally familiar with the more technical systems and flows which his allocation of resources has assembled and set in motion. Thus, a preliminary refinement of data is usually required to make it suitable for management purposes.

The function of *controllership* lies neither in operations nor in management. Its function is to provide a catalyst between the two sectors, thus promoting a favorable interaction between them.

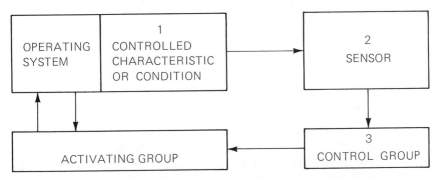

Johnson, Kast and Rosenzweig have provided a format which, with some modification, can be used to extend the concept expressed in Exhibit I into a total system design.[6] Exhibit II shows the elements of a control system as presented by these authors.

A rearrangement of the elements in Exhibits I and II allows an integration of the two concepts as shown in Exhibit III. The area shown as "Controller" may be likened to the "feedback loop" in cybernetic systems.

Feedback is essentially information to a controller about a controlled condition. A feedback loop is information about deviations from a position of equilibrium within a system which has equilibrium as a goal.[7] The concept is generally applied within the area of self-regulating or closed mechanical systems, although the concept appears to have equal validity for dynamic systems. Its use in a dynamic system concept implies the possibility of attaining a new equilibrium level which differs from the level of equilibrium before the disturbing influence, *i.e.*, an accommodation reaction within the system.

The arrangement illustrated in Exhibit III presents the three basic organizational elements or functions and comprises a simplified model of the organization from both a control viewpoint and a functional viewpoint. The duties and responsibilities of each sector stem from its position in the model and from the basic indentification and classification of functions which follows below.

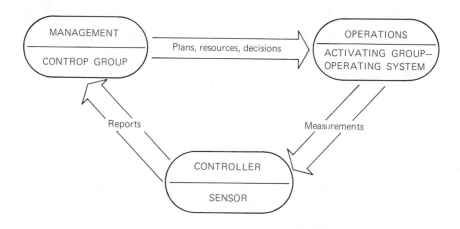

Within the organizational system outlined above are various subsystems in operation. These subsystems are related to the three basic sectors described and in turn may be visualized as clusters around each element in the diagram illustrated in Exhibit III. The position of organizational subsystems is determined by the purpose they serve—not by prestige, by position on the organization chart or by influence. The lack of organizational "levels" in such a concept should promote visualization of the organization as a functioning entity rather than as parochial areas of interest drawn together but competing for position or for limited resourses.

The management sector

A closer look at the management sector would disclose a cluster of functions having as their purpose the aiding of the planning and decision processes and of resource procurement and allocation by management. The management cluster might consist of four elements as shown in Exhibit IV.

The established activities usually identified as Staff Departments (1), which function as ongoing advisory groups or resource procurement groups, serve management in the traditional manner, but are here functionally removed from the area of operations. In a sense they serve as specialized intermediaries between management and the environment of possible firm inputs. The membership of staff departments would tend to be relatively stable and the function is in continual operation.

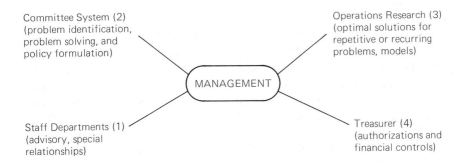

Committee System (2)
(problem identification,
problem solving, and
policy formulation)

Operations Research (3)
(optimal solutions for
repetitive or recurring
problems, models)

MANAGEMENT

Staff Departments (1)
(advisory, special
relationships)

Treasurer (4)
(authorizations and
financial controls)

A second element in the management cluster is the Committee System (2). This subsystem makes use of any person or group in the organization who can aid in problem identification and/or the search for solutions to problems of a non-routine kind. In this context, committee membership should be fluid. Problem identification and problem solving committees should be task oriented, and members should be drawn freely from any group involved or potentially affected by decisions of the committee. Policy committees may be more structured with a regular membership supplemented on occasion by others with potential contributions to the work of the committee. Committees would, by the nature of their functions, have memberships primarily drawn from the operations sector.

Another element illustrated in Exhibit IV is the Operations Research group (3) which should function to identify and suggest optimal solutions for problems of a recurring nature. This group would also contribute to any area in which mathematical techniques are applicable to aid in the management process. Problems such as inventory levels, product mix, finance mix, scheduling, and the formulation, testing and operation of models would appear ideal for consideration by this group.

The fourth element of the management group is the Treasurer (4). His special function is in the procurement, authorization and distribution of financial resources required for management plan fulfillment. He would also be visualized in this model as responsible for asset stewardship and control through the maintenance of property records and administration of the firm's cash and investments.

The management process within the organization can be aided toward rational decisions with the employment of the groups outlined. Each subsystem has clear areas of responsibility and functional duties within the administrative framework. Such an arrangement should promote an overall managerial view of the organization among those to whom decision functions have been delegated.

The operations sector

The operations element in the system illustrated in Exhibit III is charged with making operational the plans and decisions of management through detailed utilization of the resources placed at its disposal. A cluster of functions comprising this sector of the organization system is presented in Exhibit V. The carrying out of organizational acitivities takes place primarily in the areas of technology and markets. Traditional concepts of organization typically have introduced polemics into the functioning of the two areas, production and marketing, which are essentially similar in their roles within business organizations. The similarity of production and marketing in an organizational context lies in the fact that they both are involved in the movement of goods from the raw material stage to the consumption stage.

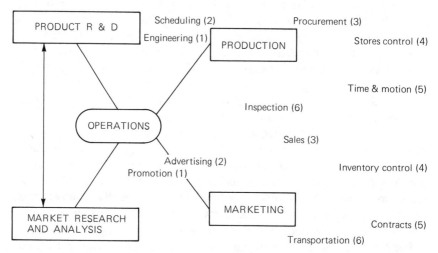

Exhibit V shows production and marketing as interrelated and functioning toward the end of interacting with the economic environment of the firm in a profitable manner. Production and marketing may each be visualized with a research arm and, of necessity, there must be clear and continuous interaction of the functions for maximum long-term benefit to the firm.

The nature of both product and market research is inquiry, while production and marketing are activity oriented. Therefore the model would lead to positions of administrative independence for the two research functions but with a strong mandate for cooperative effort with the two subsystems in immediate proximity in Exhibit V.

The controllership sector

The third basic element of the organizational system is the function of controllership. Exhibit VI illustrates the subsystems comprising the controllership sector of the concept being developed. The subsystems of General Accounting, Financial Cost Accounting and Special Managerial Cost Analysis are concerned with the basic measurement and reporting processes for management appraisal and for decisions with respect to the organization and its goals.

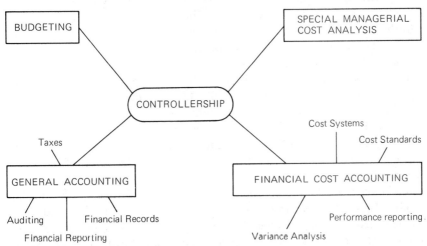

The Budgeting subsystem involves unique combinations and necessitates a degree of participation throughout the organization. The budgeting process calls for involvement in the planning and decision processes of the management sector. There must also be cooperation with the other three subsystems of the controllership sector in the development of appropriate measures, classifications and reports in order to follow up the budget procedures. The result of the budgeting procedures should be a continuing appraisal of the progress of operations with respect to management-established goals, resource allocations and limitations.

The general accounting subsystem would serve the function of meeting statutory and regulatory reporting requirements of the firm, internal control and audits, and the function of maintaining and operating the bookkeeping system and processes.

Closely allied to the general accounting subsystem, the financial cost accounting subsystem is involved primarily in the areas of production and marketing. These records serve to support the general accounting process and supply details for the cost classifications reported in the general financial statements. A close relationship to the budgeting process should be maintained for purposes of performance reporting in the operations sector. In a sense, the financial cost accounting subsystem provides feedback to the operations area in order to enhance control by every level of management and supervision concerned with the firm's operations.

The subsystem for special managerial cost analysis functions in this concept in response to management's desire for special, decision-oriented reporting with respect to any subsystem or activity. Included in these types of investigations might be financing decisions, make-or-buy decisions, pricing, data for operations research models on inventory or product mix and other special needs for information. This group would also work closely with the two research areas in the operations sector for financial and cost studies and feasibility studies, or for special breakdowns of previously measured data for studies on market segments, test areas and production costs. The special managerial cost analysis subsystem would have no regular reporting responsibilities. It should carry out a service function, responding to requests for studies—not initiating them on its own. Its results should not be distributed beyond the parties initiating the request for studies and analyses. A climate of strict neutrality and confidence will do much to dispel any reluctance on the part of managers to ask for more information, by removing the risk factors.

Again referring to the feedback concept, the controllership sector in Exhibit III is seen to stand ready to provide information to the controllers (management) about any condition over which it is desirable to maintain control. This feedback loop completes our analogy with respect to the organization as a system. The organizational system, however, is not entirely self-regulating, as is implied in the concept of cybernetics. The organization (business firm) is in constant interaction with its environment in each of the three sectors shown in Exhibit III.

Communications inputs and flows

The organization system outlined, to be fully operational, must also have a flow of reports and other communications moving in both directions between each sector. Exhibit VII presents a diagram of the flow of secondary feedback within the organization. Each sector may be seen to be in interaction with environmental forces external to the firm and to have access to specialized information of value to other sectors.

The operations sector is in constant interaction with the economic environment of markets, both as a customer and as a seller. From this

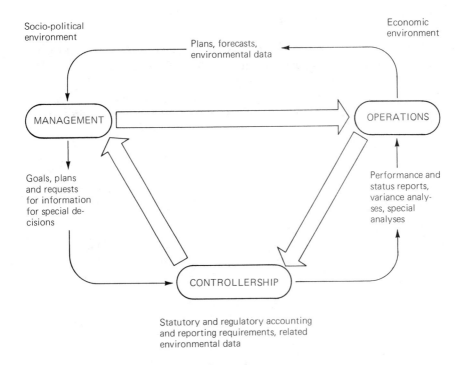

Statutory and regulatory accounting
and reporting requirements, related
environmental data

interaction a flow of information, plans, forecasts and estimates occurs, directed to management. Each area of the operations sector usually produces such flows with respect to its function. From the production subsystem, for example, will originate engineering, inspection and time and motion data in response to the needs of the operations research and other sections of the management sector. The operations research subsystem will also receive inventory data from the distribution subsystem and cost data from the special managerial cost analysis section of controllership to aid in decisions with respect to optimizing a condition.

Similarly the controllership cluster will generally provide control data to various subsystems in the form of operational and performance reports. The feedbacks in general provide for a degree of self-control activity within the operations sector. The measurement process must be keyed to the information needs of the management sector and therefore the system must provide for a dialogue between management and the groups involved in measurement. Groups in the management sector should communicate to the controllership sector their goals and plans for the controller's use in the determination of information requirements and in the development of adequate measurements.

The central processor and its role

A system-oriented concept of the role of the controller such as has been presented here is also useful in outlining the role of the data processing function in relation to other sectors of the organization. Exhibit VIII illustrates a possible conceptualization of the EDP-IDP function of the computer system within the control framework of the organization.

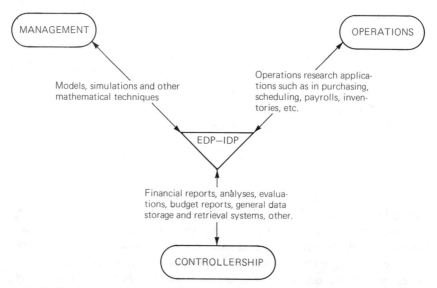

As indicated in the context illustrated in Exhibit VIII, the central data processing system should be administratively independent, yet operationally subject to the requirements of the organizational system and its subsystems. In accomplishing the information service function, programmers should be able to accept ill-structured requests and to determine output characteristics of most value to data users. In a sense, the central processor function is that of custodianship of data. Some of this data is routinely produced in report forms of various kinds and for various structured purposes. Other data is produced in non-routine forms in answer to queries from various data users. This data is structured for whatever purpose the report is to serve.

Those making queries of the data system will, of course, need to have some knowledge of the potential and the limitations of the central processor system. Processor personnel should conduct periodic get-acquainted sessions for potential data users in the three sectors of the organization system described in this paper. If the decision-making function is to be retained by the management of the firm, there must be an awareness of the nature of computer-produced reports and of the computer's potential for the production of decision-aiding summaries and analyses. Areas of programmed judgment factors and weighting used in the data manipulation must be guided by the management group and not by the model builders.

Management control will be enhanced to the extent that either of two things occurs: (1) managers are able to fully assess the value and the relevance of information produced by the computer, or (2) management can practicipate at the level of individual factors incorporated in the formula or program by which data is manipulated. If the data is correct and if it is treated in a way which gives management preferences due weight, then the final result can be more readily accepted as a basis for decisions. This implies a higher level of communication and cooperation between managers and processor personnel than is usually the case in operating systems. Some of this higher level communication and cooperation, of course, can be initiated by the controllership sector, which is by and large management oriented.

Perhaps most importantly, the computer must not become, or be regarded as, the exclusive province of any one group. Access by all should be encouraged in order to make the maximum use of the processor facilities.

Administrative control and operational control

The relationships suggested above supply a systematic view of the role of various contributors to the operation of organizations. The distinction between administrative control and operational control can now be considered within the context of the system outlined. Operational control serves to promote efficiency and coordination in the management of physical processes and resource utilization with respect to the economic environment in which the firm operates. Operational control is output oriented.

Administrative control is superimposed upon the operations area and deals with firm inputs and their sources as well as with the evaluation and approval function over the operating sector. Administrative control is goal oriented and must therefore consider the effects of current and future operations on the basis of goal satisfactions afforded to power centers both within and without the organization itself. The administrative decision processes are based on creating and preserving a desirable relationship between actual outcomes and expected outcomes in terms of goal satisfying or goal maximizing factors.

Summary

The concept developed and presented in detail in Exhibits I through VIII is summarized in Exhibit IX. The purpose of this functional model of the organization is to present a systems-oriented perspective of the basic elements of goal-oriented organizations. Hopefully, questions of role and of interaction within the organization are resolved by viewing the essential nature of the function performed. The organization, viewed in this manner, is a task-oriented system with task specialization assigned to subsystems within the structure. The interrelatedness of subgroups and their functions within the system is emphasized.

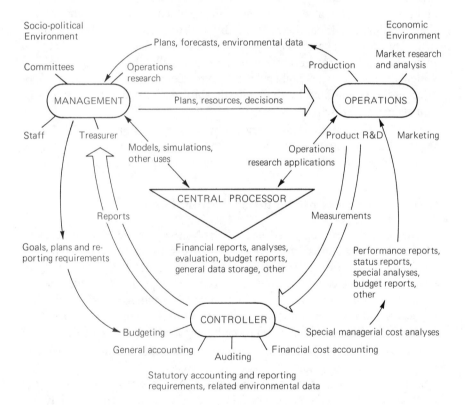

The model makes evident the fact that individuals and groups may at various times and in specific tasks be carrying out functions related to other parts of the system. Such role "crossovers" occur in real situations but are infrequently recognized as legitimate. The system concept here does not preclude such shifts and in fact is not intended to structure rigidly either formal positions or group functions. The system concept of the organization easily incorporates newer concepts of organizations such as task management and "free form" organization structures which permit mobility of executive talent.

The controller

The role and/or function of the controller is seen to be that of facilitating information flows in the areas of measurement and management reporting. His duties therefore involve the design of measurement systems and formats for reporting to management relevant information with respect to the congruence of plans and operations. He further assist management in determining the probably financial consequences of plans, as well as conducting special studies in the areas of interest to management for future planning and decision making.

The relationship of the controller to other sectors of the organization is ascertained by the systems-defined role which he fulfills. The model easily permits the adaptation and absorption of new concepts, technology, and information as they are developed and classified with respect to the management and control of organizations.

NOTES

1. David R. Anderson and Leo A. Schmidt, *Practical Controllership*, revised edition, Richard D. Irwin, Inc., Homewood, Ill., 1961, p. 12.
2. J. Brooks Heckert and James D. Willson, *Controllership*, second edition, The Ronald Press Company, New York, N.Y., 1963, p. 21.
3. Anderson and Schmidt, p. 9.
4. *American College Dictionary*, Random House, New York, N.Y., 1958, p. 1230.
5. Richard A. Johnson, Fremont E. Kast and James E. Rosenzweig. *The Theory and Management of Systems*, second edition, McGraw-Hill Series in Management, McGraw-Hill Book Co., New York, N.Y., 1967, p. 3.

36. A Control Framework for Electronic Systems*

W. Thomas Porter, Jr.

Top management, once conservative in its approach to the use of electronic data processing, has begun to realize the tremendous potential of the computer. Current EDP applications are becoming bolder in their extensions to management control functions and more sophisticated in the use of management-by-exception techniques. New systems, using EDP, have been devised to promote operational efficiency and to enhance effective decision-making.

EDP also requires management to challenge traditional methods of internal control which may no longer be efficient and effective. This article discusses the types of controls in an EDP system and their relationship to the design and implementation of a management information system. The discussion is organized in three major sections: (1) organization considerations in an EDP system, (2) administrative and operating controls in electronic installations, and (3) procedural controls. Each of these control aspects will be dealt with separately; however, they are not mutually exclusive but interrelated in such a way that serious deficiencies in any one would normally preclude the successful operation of the system as a whole.

*SOURCE: *The Journal of Accountancy*, Vol. 120, No. 4 (October, 1965), pp. 56-63. Reprinted by permission of the publisher. Copyright 1965 by the American Institute of CPAs.

Organizational considerations

Although the shape that an organizational structure takes in any particular company results from a variety of influences, one principle of organization is universally applicable: the establishment of clear lines of authority and responsibility. The division of functional responsibilities should provide for a separation between the functions of initiation and authorization of a transaction, the recording of the transaction and the custody of the resultant asset. Such a division of responsibilities, in addition to safeguarding the assets, provides for the efficiencies derived from specialization, makes possible a cross-check that promotes accuracy without duplication or wasted effort, and enhances the effectiveness of a management control system.

From a control standpoint automation has had a great effect on existing organization structures. The result has been increased centralization of data processing activities and the concentration of data processing functions.

Centralization

Before the advent of EDP systems most of the individual operating departments—shipping and receiving, production control, inventory control, marketing, budgeting, accounting—did their own clerical paperwork to a great extent. Now, to establish a "control network," we find that a separate functional and organizational entity—the data processing center—has emerged. This entity, in an attempt to tighten coordination and eliminate duplicate demands, now processes data and generates reports for the various operating departments as the basis for carrying on their individual operating activities.

EDP has also been characterized by a physical centralization of data processing activities. The major factors for this physical centralization are the high fixed cost of electronic equipment and improved data communications equipment. Such a centralization of data processing activities is characterized by the transmission of data from its source, which may be a remote point such as a warehouse or sales branch, to the processing point. The completed processing task is then returned in the desired format to the applicable locations. The systems are justified on the basis that the time and costs associated with processing data are reduced and, accordingly, management has more timely information on which to effectively control company operations.

Concentration

The centralization of data processing activities has resulted in the concentration of many processing steps into one department and the concentration of traditional accounting data along with operating data. This concentration is commonly referred to as integration, which may be defined as a concept of operation whereby the related elements in different data processing activities are combined into common and coordinated procedures and a logical work flow. The effect of integration is to prepare all desired and necessary managerial reports from only one recording of each business transaction with all transactions processed in a completely unified system.

Need for control

The centralization of data processing into one department emphasizes the importance of proper control of the data processing center itself. As noted, one of the basic principles of internal control is the separation of the people who authorize a transaction, those who have custody of the asset acquired, and those who record the accountability for the asset. This basic separation in accounting, as well as in other functions, must be maintained in order to achieve satisfactory internal control. Although there is nothing in EDP which is inconsistent with this requirement, the means for authorization and the nature of the authorization may have changed. For example, if under automated inventory management a computer prints out a purchase order because an inventory items has fallen below a certain balance, this may on the surface appear to be elimination of a separate authorization. The authorization, however, goes first from the operating people to the people who have designed the program for consideration of factors which will permit or require a purchase.

To maintain the continued integrity of the system where the authorization and recording functions are embodied in the program itself, it is necessary to separate the systems planning and programming function, the machine-operating function, and the program maintenance and tape library function. Such a separation is important because:

1. It provides an effective cross-check of the accuracy and propriety of changes which are introduced into the system.

2. It avoids the undesirable situation in which operating personnel implement revisions without prior approval and thorough checking.

3. It eliminates access to the equipment by nonoperating personnel.

In addition, such separation of duties is desirable from an operational efficiency standpoint, since the capabilities, training and skills required in carrying out these activities differ greatly.

A typical organization setup for the EDP activity in a large organization is represented by the organization chart of a manufacturing company shown in Figure 1. This chart indicates the separation of systems planning and programming functions from the EDP and EAM (electronic accounting machines or tabulating equipment) operations. Within the operations function the major control aspects include the segregation of the tape library and scheduling unit, both physically and operationally, from machine room operations; and the functioning of the data acquisition and control section.

The tape library unit is responsible for physical control of all completed computer programs and for all magnetic tape reels and the proper release of these programs and tapes for processing purposes. Personnel employed in other units and sections do not have access to the programs and tapes, except on an authorized basis.

The data acquisition and control section is responsible for all input into the EDP center and maintains control of the data being processed until the finalized output is returned to the user. The maintenance of control is achieved by comparing previously determined totals, either by the organization using it or by the data acquisition and control section itself, with the output from computer processing. This group is also responsible for meeting predetermined schedules for all input and output data and arranges the mode of reporting back to the ultimate user. Any necessary conversion of input data to machine-readable form for electronic processing also comes under the responsibility of the data acquisition and control section.

The control normally exercised by units or departments within the EDP center, similar to the data acquisition and control section, is what may be called "procedural" control. The using organization which originates the data to be processed and which receives the output from the data processing center normally exercises the "substantive" control. In large companies —where certain data procesing activities are voluminous, involve many using organizations and, in management's opinion, require extensive controls—separate control units, reporting to the controller or someone else outside the data processing department, are set up to provide much of the "substantive" control.

For example, in the company whose EDP center has been described above, a payroll control group has been established. This particular company maintains payroll records for approximately twenty thousand employees on magnetic tapes. The payroll master record consists of a "fixed" section containing permanent-type information and "variable" sections for earnings and deductions data. The fixed section includes data such as name, social security number, pay rate, budget section and year-to-date and quarter-to-date payroll totals. The variable earnings sections are used to record data for regular or normal earnings, overtime earnings, holiday pay, sick leave pay and numerous other earnings categories peculiar to the company. The variable deductions sections are used to record the twenty-five different types of payroll deductions. The payroll group:

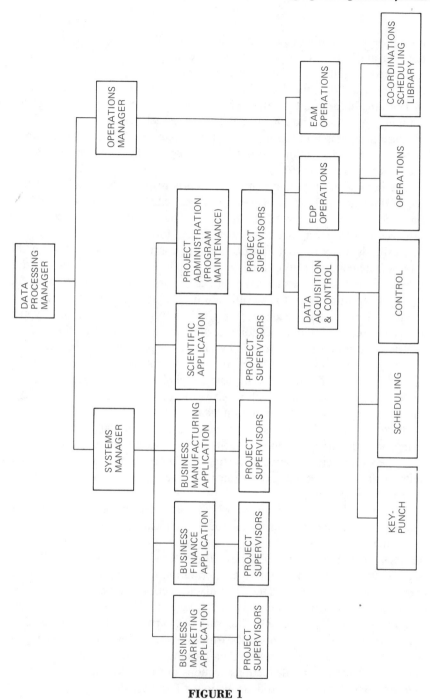

FIGURE 1

1. Reviews all changes to the payroll record, such as pay rates, new employees hired, terminations and all changes in pay deductions.

2. Compares labor hours and dollars on reports generated from the labor collection system to total hours and dollars on reports resulting from payroll processing.

3. Reviews exception reports and takes whatever action is necessary for the particular exception. The exception report lists all the transactions which are rejected because of the programed controls in the payroll program.

In smaller companies such an organization of the data processing activity described above may be impractical because of the multiplicity of functions performed by EDP people. For example, systems designers may also be programers, and computer operating personnel may maintain the tape and program library. Although segregation of duties in such an installation is more difficult to achieve, the previously stated reasons for maintaining functional segregation are still valid.

Administrative controls

Administrative controls in electronic systems can be associated with the formulation, documentation and implementation of operating procedures in: (1) systems design, (2) programming, and (3) computer operations.

Systems design

The complexity of electronic systems requires detailed systems design and programing. This detail must be adequate documented in order to evaluate and modify the system. In my opinion, one of the principal reasons for lack of control in EDP systems is a lack of documentation of a company's present and former methods of automatic data processing. Only with documentation can management accurately determine how much progress has been made and what remains to be done. When corners are cut in the quantity and depth of documentation serious delay occurs in modifying systems. Too much design work has to be done over again when the original designer has department without leaving adequate documentation. The formulation and documentation of an EDP application can be broken down into three phases: data systems survey, data systems study and programming.

The data systems survey should outline the scope and objectives of application, the plan and schedule for completion, and estimated costs and benefits. An important part of the documentation of a data systems survey, and hence an important control feature, is approval by management before proceeding to the data systems study. This approval should be made as high up in management as possible. Too often situations are encountered where management personnel do not know, much less understand, what EDP is or is not doing for the company. Conversely, systems personnel are often not aware of management policies important to the design of the system.

The data systems study should include a review of current procedures. Such a review should indicate what features and controls are necessary and beneficial in the new system and what changes can be made in improving existing procedures. After review of the current system, a new one should be designed to include adequate definition and documentation of the contents of master files, input and output requirements, methods of processing and control requirements. In addition, the documentation should include a timetable of data collection, processing and reporting; estimated execution times; required equipment; and method and timing of conversion. This documentation should be reviewed, approved and signed by all the department managers concerned to assure that the EDP applications have been thoroughly investigated, documented, and agreed upon before programming begins.

Programming

Computer programming involves the preparation of flow charts, program listings and computer operating instructions. During the planning and installation of an EDP system or application, it is desirable to document all aspects of program development as explicitly as possible. Such documentation serves both as an essential tool for understanding and controlling the programs and as a permanent history of all pertinent facts related to each program.

One extremely useful document is the *program run book*. Important run book requirements on all programs include: (1) a description of the purpose of the program, (2) a complete set of flow charts, (3) an assembly listing of the program, (4) computer operating instructions, (5) program testing documentation, and (6) a sample of all reports produced by the program.

In addition to the above document, *a console run book* should be prepared for specific use by computer operating personnel in operating each program. Normally, the console run book includes: (1) a flow chart of the portion of the system of which the program is a part, (2) identification of tape units used for input and output files, (3) console switch settings, (4) a list of all program halts and required action, and (5) a description of any exceptions to standard routines and any variable data (dates, constants, and so forth) to be entered in the program.

Efficient program development requires programming standards. *A programming manual* should be set up and maintained and should contain a written record of all policies, procedures and techniques which are to be standard throughout the organization. Its existence will facilitate communication and prevent the development of duplicate or conflicting procedures. Many areas of program development lend themselves to standardization, such as program documentation procedures, tape labeling, program-testing procedures, and tape retention policies.

The dynamic nature of most business activities causes *program changes.* Program changes require well-formulated and documented procedures to prevent the manipulation of programs for special purposes, fraudulent or otherwise. Several procedures are necessary for maintaining control over program changes:

1. The nature of the proposed procedure change should be explained in written form, and formal approval for the change should be given by a responsible individual, such as the manager of the department that will be affected.

2. Procedure changes (coding) to the program should be prepared only by the systems group, not by members of the computer operating group. The change should be supported by readable documentation in flow chart form (as opposed to direct patching of the program).

3. The change should be reviewed and approved by a person who is separate from the independent of the individual designing the change.

4. After review, this material should be given to the computer operator, who should retain control of the program changes until they are posted to the program. Then the operator should process test input data, using the original program and, next, the revised program. The output from both operations should be reviewed to ascertain that only those records which should have been affected were affected, and that only the changes contemplated were actually made. Operation of the computer during the process of making changes should be under the control of the personnel ordinarily responsible for the regular operation of this equipment and not a member of the systems (programming) group.

5. Finally, all correction sheets and print-outs should be filed in the program book, thus providing a permanent record of all changes made to the program.

Computer operations

Several forms of documentation and procedure are important to achieve control in computer operations. One of the most important controls over computer operations is the record maintained for recording and analyzing time. This *utilization record* is used to record the computer operation, the equipment used, and the time involved in processing the job. The record should be analyzed and reviewed by responsible operating personnel to determine the time spent processing each job and reasons for all lost time.

Another major control in EDP operations is the *off-premises record storage program* of the company. Since magnetic tapes are small in size, compared with other media of data storage, it is generally practicable to store a duplicate set of important tapes in an area physically separated from the computer center. Thus, at least one set of tape records will be available in the event of a fire or water leakage to the tape library. A tape library evacuation procedure should also be developed and documented. The specific tapes which should be stored off-site will depend upon the particular system. At a minimum, the program tapes and master file tapes should be stored away from the computer room.

Adequate *control procedures* are also necessary in the tape and *program library* function. Strict control over access to the library must be maintained to prevent unauthorized individuals from obtaining tapes and thereby circumventing other controls which have been established. Generally, access to the library should be limited to those personnel who require use of the program and other tapes in connection with the normal operation of the system. In very large installations, where the tape files are maintained by a tape librarian, access to the files should be limited to this person.

Apart from a tape labeling system, both internal and external, and control over access to the tapes, procedures and forms must be set up to maintain effectively the tape and program library. The reels, upon receipt, should be tested to ensure that they are not defective, and then given serial numbers. They can then be assigned to the various applications by these serial numbers, thus permitting efficient scheduling through the data processing system. To achieve efficient use of tapes and to ensure control, a rigorous record system must be maintained on the filing and status of the tapes. Such a system should provide information on: (1) the physical location of any given reel, (2) the tapes available to be written on, and (3) the usage history of each tape.

Another important control in electronic systems is *console control*. The console of a data processing system is used by the operator to control the system and monitor its operation. The console is used to start and stop the system and to restart the computer when error conditions cause it to halt. The console indicates the instruction being performed and can be used to alter the mode of operation. Using the console, the operator can determine the status of internal registers and switches and can have this data printed out. In addition, the console can be used to enter data into the system manually. In many cases the electronic equipment includes a console type-writer which can be used to create a log of console activity.

Several techniques can be employed to provide effective console control:

1. Review of the console typewriter print-out. The paper in the console typewriter should be two-part: the original for operating uses, the duplicate for supervisory review. In addition, the paper should be serially numbered for accountability. On some machines a locked recording device is available, to which the operator does not have access.

2. Rotation of duties among operators.

3. Accounting for processing time. Computer manipulation by the operator through the console takes time which would significantly increase processing time on the computer run affected. An analysis of EDP equipment utilization records by responsible personnel provides a strong console control.

4. Operation of computer in "nonstop" mode. By use of a monitor system, which quickly brings into operation the proper processing program (contained in certain magnetic tape reels mounted on specific tape units), and by use of error procedures which do not halt the computer, the EDP system precludes any manual intervention by the console operator during processing.

Procedural controls

Once management has determined its plan of organization and designed administrative controls, management must develop a system which records, processes, summarizes and reports transactions in accordance with operating responsibilities and information needs of the individuals making operating decisions. Basically, such a system includes three levels: (1) the source data level, (2) the data processing level, and (3) the reporting level.

Normally, in non-EDP systems, auditors are accustomed to three basic records: the source document, the journal, and the ledger. The processing is normally performed by people; the accuracy and propriety of the processing is insured by a segregation of duties and human review and inspection of the documents and records. EDP systems have eliminated the need for some of these records or have resulted in records not available for human inspection. Alteration of the audit trail in a system is not necessarily bad, so long as the data are recorded, processed and reported with the propriety, accuracy and timeliness required by management. The timeliness factor is achieved by the tremendous speed at which EDP equipment operates; the accuracy and propriety is achieved by source data controls, machine processing controls, and output controls. The types of procedural controls can be associated with the level of processing and the objectives of controls at each level. Each of the controls to be mentioned has been described in detail in other publications referred to at the end of this article.

Source data controls

The objectives of source data controls are:

1. To determine that all transactions have been properly recorded at the point of origin or source.

2. To determine that all transactions are transmitted from the recording point to the processing point.

In non-EDP systems these objectives are achieved largely by source document controls, such as (1) registration at the point of document entry, (2) sequential numbering with full accountability at point of document origin, and (3) grouping or "batching," with predetermined document counts or other control totals. These controls, familiar to the auditor, are largely people-oriented. In EDP systems many of these controls can be included in computer programs and can be termed computer-oriented.

In EDP systems where conventional source documents are still used, no new control problems are presented prior to processing of the data. A pre-audit of the source documents by knowledgeable personnel will detect misspellings, invalid codes, unreasonable amounts and other improper data. Key verification of punched cards or punched paper tape, the use of batch and control totals, and machine or "hard-copy" listings can be employed to determine that all source documents are correctly converted to machine-readable form for subsequent EDP processing.

In EDP systems where the source document is eliminated or is in a form that does not permit human review, there are basically two solutions to ensure proper recording. First, control can be moved to the point of origin so that access to and use of the recording and transmitting equipment is properly controlled to prevent unauthorized or improper use. A second solution is to let the computer exercise the same review of the transaction that would be made of source documents by people.

Because of the characteristics of a computer, an EDP system has unusual capabilities to examine or edit each element of information processed by it. This editing process involves the ability to inspect and accept (or reject) transactions according to the validity or reasonableness of quantities, amounts, codes and other data contained in the input record. Obviously, such an ability is also relevant to a system not using automated data collection and transmission equipment. The editing ability of the computer can be used to detect errors in input preparation that have not been detected by human review and inspection.

The editing ability of the computer is achieved by installing checks in the program of instructions for the purpose of detecting errors; hence, the term "programmed checks." Although I am now talking about programmed checks to edit the propriety and accuracy of input data, programmed checks are also used to achieve the control objectives at the data processing level. The type of programmed checks at this level will be discussed later.

Programmed checks to determine the validity of input or source data include: (1) checks to determine whether a particular transaction code is active or whether an identification number is valid (existence or valid number check); (2) checks to determine the logical relationship that exists between various data fields in a record (combination checks); (3) checks to test whether data amounts have exceeded predetermined limits (limit checks); and (4) checks to determine that the input is complete (completeness checks).

Processing controls

Processing controls established to ensure the accuracy of processing of input data have three objectives:
1. To detect loss or nonprocessing of data.
2. To determine that arithmetic functions have been performed correctly.
3. To determine that all transactions are posted to the proper record.

The accuracy of the processing is dependent upon the accuracy of programming, the checks designed and built into the equipment by the manufacturer, and the programed checks included by the user in his programs. Accurate programming depends upon the careful conception and implementation of systems design and program instructions, proper program documentation and adequate review and approval—all sound practices which were discussed earlier.

All EDP equipment manufacturers have checks built into the equipment to ensure that data is correctly read, processed, transferred within the system and recorded on output media. These checks are sometimes referred to as "hardware" controls, and include parity checks, dual read-write heads, dual circuitry and file protection rings. These hardware controls are described at length in the various publications prepared by the equipment manufacturers.

In addition to the hardware checks, data processing accuracy in an EDP system is achieved by programmed checks. Programmed checks to detect loss or nonprocessing of data include record counts, control totals and hash totals, and sequence checks. Programmed checks of arithmetic calculations include limit checks, cross-footing balance checks, proof figures, zero balancing and reverse arithmetic.

Programmed checks for proper postings may be classified as file checks and are used to achieve accuracy in file and record connections and in the changes to the files. The problem of file connections is a significant one in EDP systems because the absence of "visible" records and because of the ease with which wrong information can be written on magnetic tapes and disks. Such checks include tape labels, identification comparisons and file maintenance routines.

Output controls

The function of output controls is to determine that the processed data do not include any unauthorized alterations by the computer operations section, that data are substantially correct or reasonable, and that all errors detected in the processing of data have been corrected.

One of the biggest controls in any system is the review of reports and output data by the originating group and the taking of whatever corrective action is necessary. This review normally consists of a search for unusual or abnormal items. The use of programmed controls described above, coupled with exception reporting, actually enhances the ability of responsible personnel to take necessary action.

The most basic output control is the comparison of control totals of data processed with totals independently obtained from prior processing or original source data. Systematic sampling of individual items processed affords another output control. The testing can be performed by the originating group, the control unit or the internal audit staff.

Summary

The design of a management information system dictates that substantial amounts of time and effort be spent in the formulation of controls. Such effort is necessary to use the power of the computer most effectively and to control the cost of data processing.

REFERENCES

A. R. F. Garland, "Five Ways in Which Computer Systems Strengthen Internal Control," *N.A.A. Bulletin*, July 1962.

B. IBM, *The Auditor Encounters Electronic Data Processing*, New York, Price Waterhouse & Co. and International Business Machines Corp., 1956.

C. IBM, *Planning for an IBM Data Processing System*, New York, International Business Machines Corp., 1960.

D. IBM, *In-Line Electronic Accounting, Internal Control and Audit Trail*, New York, Price Waterhouse & Co. and International Business Machines Corp., 1960.

E. H. B. Joplin, "An Internal Control Checklist for EDP," *Management Services,* July-August 1964.

F. F. Kaufman, *Electronic Data Processing and Auditing,* New York, The Ronald Press Co., 1961.

G. F. Kaufman, "EDP Control Problems," *Lybrand Journal,* 1962.

H. A. W. Lueth, "Organizing EDP for Internal Control," *N.A.A. Bulletin,* January 1963.

I. R. E. Schlosser and D. C. Bruegman, "Effect of EDP on Internal Control," *Management Services,* March-April 1964.

J. J. R. Spellman, "Controls—The Key to Effective Data Processing," *The Arthur Anderson Chronicle,* July 1963.

37. Management Information System for Planning, Forecasting and Budgeting*

John J. Omlor

The Columbia-Hallowell Division of Standard Pressed Steel has a completely integrated management information system which provides management with timely, accurate decision making information. The system is used for business planning and profit forecasting through daily, weekly and monthly measurements. A technique has been developed whereby dollar sales forecasts plus firm orders in house are converted into a shipping forecast of specific times. The data, which includes planned increases or decreases in the inventory level, is then converted through existing computer programs to a manpower and facilities projection in terms of standard hours by product line and department. Follow-up reports indicate current accomplishments throughout the period in relation to the target.

Inputs and outputs

Basically, we can divide the system into two major categories—inputs into the computer and output reports.

*SOURCE: *Management Accounting* (March, 1970), pp. 13-16. Reprinted by permission of the publisher.

Input reports

1. Parts list: A parts list is an engineering bill of material adapted for the manufacturing stocking level. The parts list contains each item that must be manufactured, as well as the parts which are to be requisitioned in order to manufacture this part.

2. Manufacturing method sheets: These method sheets call out every operation that is to be performed to complete the part, the standard hours required and the facilities needed.

3. Fixed and variable budget rate file for each department: Our fixed budget rate is based on cost per day. Each department has its own rate file subdivided for each major category or expense per earned hour, and/or each major category of expense per day. The variable budget rates, on the other hand are based only on a rate per earned direct labor hour. An earned hour is a completed standard hour of labor.

4. Customer or manufacturing orders: These are daily routine functions.

5. Inventory transactions.

6. Labor reporting.

Output reports

1. Open order registers.
2. Scheduling documents.
3. Inventory exceptions and requirement reports.
4. Business status reports.
5. Method sheets and standards to manufacture.
6. Load hours for machine and departments.
7. Daily, weekly, and monthly variable and fixed budgets.
8. Normal accounting reports.

Business planning with MIS

The current backlog is detailed into the system by customer and by part number both in terms of sales dollars and of standard costs. The backlog data will also contain information reflecting standard hours by part, by department, and by facility to manufacture each item. All of this then becomes the basis for determining our next month's shipment forecast.

If we are going to go further out in our forecasting, either to a quarterly or to an annual plan, we will use an incoming forecast in addition to the backlog as the basis for determining the shipments for the planned period. The incoming forecast is taken from an exponentially smoothed history of incoming orders by part number, adjusted to reflect the marketing estimates of business changes. This forecast is converted into "dummy customer orders" and entered into the system exactly as though it were a customer order. These dummy orders together with the real orders we have in-house are then the basis for determining the quarterly or annual shipments forecast. For the purpose of business planning, the dummy orders and backlog are considered to be completely manufactured from beginning to end. That is, we assume no inventory changes since inventory fluctuations from month to month are not significant.

Once the forecast has been incorporated into the management information system, we can produce our shipment dollars and standard cost of goods sold, or the business status report. This report permits us to segregate our sales and standard costs by product line, and it is the basis for determining the product mix effect on the plan.

Each item forecast is exploded into the necessary manufacturing hours by department and facility. The load hours for each department are extended by the budget rate to determine the variable budget cost. This cost plus the fixed budget cost per day times the number of days equals the allowable budget dollars.

The explosion to the load hours helps us to identify machine or manpower bottlenecks. On machine bottlenecks, we can either reschedule, if possible, or use the information as a basis for our Capital Requirements Plan.

Manpower requirements are based upon the load hours by department, factored for projected performance. The performance is determined in two ways:

1. By direct labor performance.
2. By the utilization of total available labor, or the direct labor to total labor available ratio.

All manpower requirements are computed as equivalent whole people. That is, the required hours divided by eight hours per day times the number of days in the period. For example, Table 1 shows that the press shop's direct labor performance for last month was 114 percent of standard. It also shows that at the end of the month there were 81 people on the payroll although during the month only 74 equivalent whole people worked. These break down into 38 direct labor, and 36 indirect labor. The ratio of direct labor hours to total labor hours for that department was then 51.4 percent.

For November we show 8,371 standard hours required which is equivalent to 53 standard direct labor men. Factored for the 114 percent performance this is equal to 46 direct labor men. Multiplying the 46 direct labor men by the 51.4 percent direct labor to total labor ratio, we find that the department requires 83 people to produce the forecast.

TABLE 1
Manpower projection

DEPARTMENT	D. L. PERF. %	NO. OF EMP.	DL EMP. FM. WDCS 1	IND.	% DIRECT TO TOTAL LABOR	NOVEMBER— 20 DAYS				DECEMBER— 24 DAYS			
						STD. HOURS MONTH	STD. EMP.	PERF. EMP.	TOTAL MAN POWER	STD. HOURS MONTH	STD. EMP.	PERF. EMP.	TOTAL MAN POWER
Press Shop	114	81	38	36	51.4	8371	53	46	83	10336	54	48	87
Weld	92	28	15	10	60.0	3262	20	22	37	4017	21	23	38
Paint	115	19	9	9	50.0	2419	15	13	25	3058	16	14	26
Assemble	104	38	30	10	75.0	5003	31	30	40	6370	33	32	43
Pack	101	3	2	1	66.7	207	1	1	1	351	2	2	2
TOTAL	107	169	94	66	59.1	19262	120	112	186	24132	126	119	196

This report thus allows us to recognize manpower problems.

If a problem does exist, we have three alternatives:

1. Change the schedule load hours.
2. Add or delete men.
3. Change the performance forecast.

The load hours above are based on current methods of manufacture. Since performance against current methods can be distorted by changes in the standard we shoot for performance of 100 percent against this standard. Therefore, in order not to distort performance levels, we use a measurement against a fixed cost book standard. This is a trend type measurement and the standard always remains the same. Any performance change is indicated by a change in the performance percentage. These two measurements allow us to completely analyze the changes in performance.

Through the use of our Management Information System we have the ability to put together a reliable business plan, and the beauty of it is, if management rejects the results we have the ability to go back, re-do or adjust with a minimum amount of time and effort. Dummy orders, rate files, performance levels, or product mix can all be changed and in a short time we would have a completely new look at the forecast.

Performance to forecast

Let us assume that management has accepted the forecast. The next step is the measurement of performance compared to the plan. In the management information system we have the ability to measure performance to any forecast on a daily, weekly, and monthly basis.

Daily measurement

Information necessary to check the performance against plan originates with shipment and labor reporting transactions. Shipment transactions provide data on our actual shipments and standard cost of shipments through one of our existing reports—the Business Status Report. Using this computerized report helps us to prepare a shipment performance graph, Exhibit I, by product. It is a projection of the to-date shipments in comparison to the forecast shipments. The contribution effect is the volume difference multipled by the product variable margin rate.

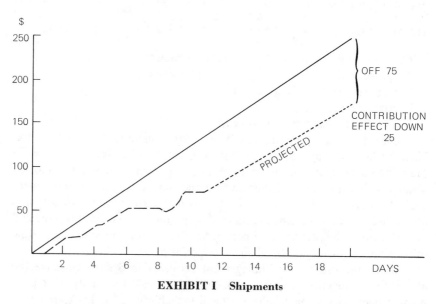

EXHIBIT I Shipments

The labor reporting transaction provides the part manufactured, the time used, the man and department where worked. This information, compared with the standard to manufacture, allows the computation of the daily performance report by department, we summarize the standard direct labor man hours earned and the direct to indirect relationship of the particular department. With this information on a daily basis, and computerized, we have the time and ability to put together reports such as Table 2 which are designed primarily to interpret data presented on the computer reports.

TABLE 2

Performance to plan manpower requirements

DEPARTMENT	*TODAY*					*BALANCE OF MONTH*		
	PLANNED STANDARD HOURS BY DEPARTMENT	STANDARD HOURS EARNED	PLAN	PERFORMANCE DAILY PERCENT	PERCENT D/L USED TO TOTAL AVAILABLE	STANDARD D/L HOURS PER DAY TO MEET PLAN	ACTUAL D/L HOURS PER DAY AT CURRENT PERFORMANCE TO MEET PLAN	EQUIVALENT WHOLE MEN REQUIRED
Press Shop	8371	529	533	108	50	360	345	86
Weld	3262	222	103	121	79	378	356	46
Paint	2419	110	121	96	68	394	306	38
Assemble	5003	220	250	78	82	775	909	114
Pack	207	26	10	98	65	0	0	0
TOTAL	19262	1107	1017	101	67	0	0	284

This is an exception type report issued to the plant manager. Detail of this performance by man in total and by job by man is issued to the foreman. In addition, each department has a graph (Exhibit II) presenting its performance to plan. The graph also portrays the amount of hours required on a monthly basis. Through a thermometer approach, we measure the department's status at a particular time.

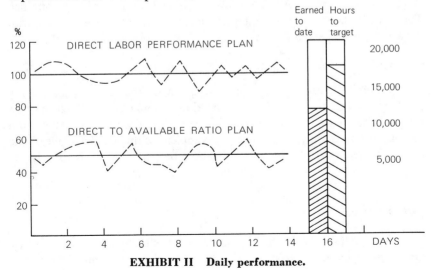

EXHIBIT II   Daily performance.

All informaton is personally delivered and interpreted by our plant accountant. At any given day, all concerned know exactly how they stand in relationship to the plan for both earned hours and shipments.

Weekly measurement

Weekly measurement techniques are very similar to those used daily. However, in measuring weekly performance, one more tool is used—the departmental budget report.

Each report shows the budget dollars or equal to the earned hours multiplied by the variable earned hour budget rate plus the fixed cost budget per day, times the number of days in the period. The variances are segregated according to direct labor and indirect labor, and the direct labor variance is identified as to wage rate and manufacturing performance variance. All this is done mechanically, allowing us time to graphically portray the information to the foremen and plant manager. Using the system to do the brute work allows time for analysis and communications.

Also on a weekly basis, the division runs what we call a "mock closing." In this procedure, we run our regular sales, cost of sales and normal accounting reports. Without going through the formal journal entries, these reports allow us to analyze total performance to plan. We do this two ways. First, we take the month-to-date and project it, assuming performance and/or shipments at the same rate as incurred in the past. Second, we contact the people responsible for the shipments and performance to determine their best estimate for the remainder of the month and prepare an outlook on this basis. Reasons for deviations are categorized as to volume, mix, manufacturing performance, and period cost. Then on each Tuesday afternoon, with this information, we have a financial review with the activity managers of the division.

Monthly measurement

The monthly performance technique is exactly the same as the weekly performance technique. However, instead of running the mock closing, we run the actual closing; and instead of running the departmental reports on the payroll basis only, the report is complete with actual supplies. The review is the same, perhaps more detailed, but the concept is exactly the same.

Conclusion

Generally, this covers the Columbia-Hallowell Division's use of their management information system for business planning. This technique is used in the annual business plan as well and is no different from that used in any quarterly forecast.

In summary, the major benefits in using this system for business planning, forecasting, and budget measurement are:

1. The ease in making changes after reviewing the forecast.

2. The timeliness of the daily, weekly, and monthly measurement technique.

3. The mechanization of the brute work, allowing accountants to be analysts and communicators of information.

38. The Computer—New Partner in Investment Management*

Arnold E. Amstutz

Many articles and forums have debated the role of the computer in investment decision making. Enthusiasts have proclaimed that "it will soon be possible for portfolio managers and financial analysts to use a high speed computer with the ease of a desk calculator." "Computer portfolio selection will eventually prove to be extremely useful to sophisticated investors." Others have vigorously objected that ". . . a computer will never tell you to buy one stock and sell another . . .[there is] no substitute . . . for flair in judgment, and a sense of timing." "Portfolio decisions must remain an art, employing at its best a fine balance of experience, judgment, and intuition all of which only a good analyst can supply."

In the absence of meaningful experience with computer based investment systems, the discussion to date has been based largely on hypothecation. The substantial cost of data acquisition and maintenance, computer time, and system development have effectively limited the generation of systems capable of providing relevant experience. Those who have devoted resources to the systematic study of security markets have offered little encouragement for the would-be practitioner of computer based investment decision making. Those who have found profitable application of the technology have preferred to enjoy a competitive advantage in the market rather than to publicize their activities.

*SOURCE: *Management Science*, Vol. 15, No. 2 (October, 1968), pp. B-91-B99. Reprinted by permission of the publisher.

Until 1963 those interested in computer-aided investment analysis faced an appalling data acquisition task. Fundamental data (sales, earnings, balance sheet, and P & L items) had to be manually culled from published reports. Technical data indicating transaction prices and volume were manually transcribed from published reports or were cumbersomely encoded from wire service lines.

In 1963, Standard Statistics, Inc., a subsidiary of Standard and Poor's, released the "Compustat" tapes containing fundamental data compiled annually from 1947 for 900 companies. Coverage has now been expanded to encompass 1800 companies with data compiled quarterly. Also in 1963, Scantlin Electronics, Ultronics, and (in 1964) Bunker-Ramo began offering price, volume, earnings, and dividend data for all listed securities. Data are now available from these sources aggregated daily, weekly, and monthly.

With "machine readable" data widely available, it has become fashionable to be "doing something" with computers. Practically every major financial institution is now quick to point out that they have a computer. Competitive considerations motivate many firms to assure their customers of active participation in the computer revolution. The resultant demand for computer output places a premium on rapid generation of computer-based numbers while largely precluding orderly conceptual development, objective formulation, testing, validation, and carefully planned implementation.

An example of successful application

This is a report on the results achieved since 1959 by a New York brokerage firm in applying computer technology to investment management. Performance to date establishes the principle that through carefully planned development the computer can become a unique and active contributor to the investment process.

Evolution

Initial research begun in 1959 was restricted to thirty securities listed on the New York Stock Exchange. Data were collected manually from published reports. Experimental IBM 650 computer programs developed to test concepts on which the present system is founded required 27 minutes to evaluate a single company.

The first experimental system was completed early in 1960, and a six-month test was undertaken to evaluate performance. Operation of this prototype was tedious and expensive. However, test results justified the allocation of additional resources to achieve increased efficiency and coverage.

In the fourth quarter of 1960, work began on an automated system designed to handle information relating to several hundred companies. Since even the experimental prototype had heavily taxed the capabilities of the IBM 650, the new system was designed for the larger, higher speed IBM 709 computer. Expanded input processing programs translated, interpreted, and filed unformated information received from news service wires. Specialized output programs presented graphic summaries of the results of analyses on printed charts.

In August 1961 following an exhaustive series of tests, the 709-based system was monitoring the activity of 300 selected securities. This second pilot operation confirmed the effectiveness of proposed analytic techniques in isolating major changes in the market for a security.

By mid-1962 operations had been expanded to monitor all common stocks traded on the New York and American Stock Exchanges. The system was particularly effective in anticipating the market decline during April and May of that year. Experience with this large scale activity revealed three areas in which major refinements were possible:

(1) Existing data sources were undependable and frequently introduced substantial errors. Constant manual review and correction were required.

(2) The system's ability to produce output far exceeded management's capacity to assimilate information.

(3) Established measures of financial performance were inadequate to distinguish between alternative models of market behavior. New concepts and measures were required to evaluate the effect of changes in criteria across the entire market over extended time periods.

In 1964 a system incorporating the proven attributes of its predecessor with significantly improved capability in the three areas of concern was implemented. This configuration employed machine-coded data, improved information-handling capabilities, and high resolution cathode ray tube graphic displays. In contrast to the 27 minutes per stock operating time cited earlier for the first prototype, this system using an IBM 7094-2 computer, analyzed a security every two seconds and handled over five billion information elements in the course of a normal week. The 1964 design included "learning" procedures through which the computer was able to contribute directly to future refinements. Heuristic rules were incorporated to permit evaluation of alternative investment approaches. Using adaptive procedures the computer developed new models and processes which contributed to the success of subsequent systems.

For almost two years the 1964 configuration was used to achieve two related but, at times, functionally incompatible objectives:

(1) In a research context, it provided flexible access to extensive data organized to facilitate systematic investigation of market process models and investment decision procedures.

(2) In an operating management context, it was the vehicle through which models and procedures validated within the research system were applied to the firm's investment activities.

In 1966 management began to separate these two functions. Detailed objectives were specified for two distinct capabilities: totally integrated research support and on-line, real-time, investment planning and decision making.

In 1966 a system meeting these research and operating objectives were completed. Their structure and application are described below.

Structure

Efficient realization of these system objectives, using hardware available in 1965, necessitated the use of five computers. The basic hardware configuration summarized in Figure 1 will be briefly outlined here to illustrate the translation of management's objectives into system structure.

Real-Time Environment Sensing. A special purpose real-time computer monitors transactions on the New York, American, Midwest, and Pacific Stock Exchanges. Transaction data in combination with earnings, dividends, and other fundamental information are transferred to on-line data files.

On-Line Processing. An on-line process computer receives and responds to transmissions from the real-time computer and two communication units.

Communication Processing. Two communication control units transfer messages between process computer and display devices.

Analysis and Control. Analytic programs operating on a large scientific computer provide central control for the system.

Report Generation. Report generation is handled by two "slave systems" controlled through magnetic tape generated by the analytic system. A small computer operating as a report generator produces printed output. A cathode ray tube display system generates graphic microfilm output which is later converted to "hard copy."

The remainder of this paper is devoted to sample outputs generated using the system configuration just described. Research and operating functions will be considered separately.

Research function

The System provides the information and structure required to evaluate process and decision models against historic or hypothetical company, market, and economic conditions. It is able to recreate conditions existing

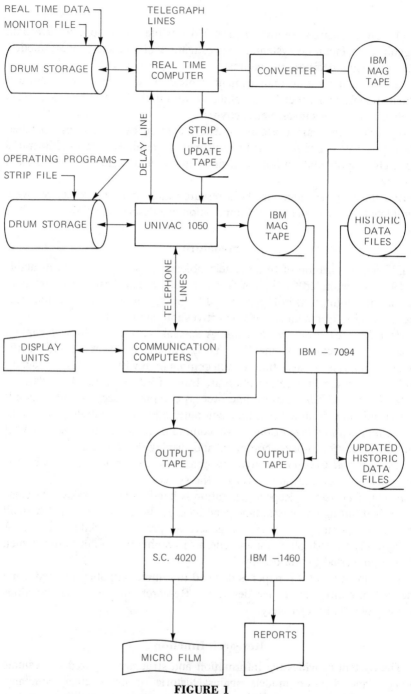

FIGURE 1
Basic hardware configuration

at any time since 1959 and to test the effect of alternative analytical approaches to determine "what would have happened if" a particular decision procedure or rule had been employed during the specified period.

Simulation Testing of Proposed Polices. Proposed policies are evaluated through investment analyses of the type illustrated in Figure 2. This report summarizes actions taken with respect to two securities under a simulated policy. The first three entries in each line indicate the date, action taken, and average action price. In the Paramount example, the stock purchased February 17, 1961, at $64.0 was sold on May 5, 1961, at an average net price of $80.3.

The Investment Report entries to the right of the reference price relate to a "Conservative Policy" governing a cash account in which only long positions are permitted, and a "Speculative Policy" controlling a margin account (50% margin during 1961) in which short as well as long positions are allowed. The computer calculates the profit per share, dollar investment, and percent return realized during the simulated period. In the Paramount example, the initial 1961 trade resulted in $16.2 per share profit on an investment of $6,405.00 in the Conservative account, and $3,302.00 in the Speculative account, yielding returns of 25.3 and 50.7 percent respectively.

After selling Paramount on May 5, 1961, the System took a short position in the margin account. This short sale, which was covered on May 17, 1963, at a price of $40.7, is noted under the Speculative Policy but does not affect the cash account. Having covered its previous short, the System established a long position in both the Conservative and Speculative accounts on May 17, 1963.

The reports presented in Figure 2 were prepared as part of a simulation test covering the time period from January, 1961 through March, 1964. The System has, therefore, closed its acounts in Paramount and U.S. Steel at the prices prevailing at the close of market on the final day of the simulated period.

Evaluation of Simulated Performance. The final performance evaluation in Figure 2 indicates the average number of weeks held and the annualized percent return on invested capital. The Conservative Policy in this simulation test produced average holding periods of 28 and 22 weeks and an annual return of 66.3 and 19.3 per cent respectively for Paramount and U.S. Steel. Under the Speculative Policy simulation holding periods averaged at 53 and 35 weeks, and annual returns were 67.9 and 40.5 percent respectively.

The simulation process permits years of hypothetical operating experience to be evaluated in a few minutes of research. Following extensive testing of alternative criteria, high performance decision procedures are implemented in the operating system.

FIGURE 2
Sample investment reports*

S.I.M.S.—II processing runs—week 277—Friday, March 20, 1964
Investment report
PXN 8250C. Paramount Pictures Corporation

DATE	ACTION	PRICE TODAY	WEEKS HELD	REFERENCE PRICE	CONSERVATIVE POLICY			SPECULATIVE POLICY		
					$ PROFIT/SHARE	INVESTMENT	RETURN	$ PROFIT/SHARE	INVESTMENT	RETURN
02/17/61	Buy	$64.0								
05/05/61	Sell	$80.3	11	$64.0	$16.2	$6405.	25.3%	$16.2	$3202.	50.7%
05/05/61	Short	$80.3								
05/17/63	Cover	$40.7	105	$80.3				$39.5	$4014.	98.5%
05/17/63	Buy	$40.7								
03/20/64	Close	$56.4	44	$40.7	$15.6	$4075.	38.3%	$15.6	$2038.	76.7%

PXN Annualized averages
   28.wks hold PRD conservative policy $4541.   66.3%
   53.wks hold PRD speculative policy $3415.   67.9%

X 110600. U.S. Steel Corporation

DATE	ACTION	PRICE TODAY	WEEKS HELD	REFERENCE PRICE	CONSERVATIVE POLICY			SPECULATIVE POLICY		
					$ PROFIT/SHARE	INVESTMENT	RETURN	$ PROFIT/SHARE	INVESTMENT	RETURN
06/30/61	Short	$81.0								
04/12/63	Cover	$51.0	93	$81.0				$30.0	$4050.	74.1%
04/12/63	Buy	$51.0								
10/25/63	Sell	$53.6	27	$51.0	$2.6	$5100.	5.1%	$2.6	$2550.	10.3%
10/25/63	Short	$53.6								
11/29/63	Cover	$52.9	5	$53.6				$0.7	$2681.	2.8%
11/29/63	Buy	$52.9								
03/20/64	Close	$58.5	16	$52.9	$5.6	$5288.	10.6%	$5.6	$2644.	21.3%

X Annualized averages
   22.wks hold PRD conservative policy $5170.   19.3%
   33.wks hold PRD speculative policy $3555.   40.5%

*The computer outputs in Figures 2, 3, 4 and 5 were set in upper and lower case for
  purposes of legibility.

Operating system functions

The majority of the operating functions defined by previously established objectives require access to a complete and extensive historical record of company and security activity. As new data are added to the System, existing file contents are updated rather than replaced. The resultant disaggregated data file is the basic reference for system evaluation of market, industry, or company conditions in light of current and historical performance measures.

Disaggregated Data Files. Disaggregated data file maintenance creates significant problems. A single status evaluation for all securities monitored may involve reference to billions of data items. However, the disaggregated file, in combination with flexible data structuring routines which aggregate to the level appropriate for analysis and/or presentation, is the foundation of the operating system. Since detailed data are maintained in chronological order, no structural biasing is imposed by aggregation along lines appropriate for analyses conducted at one point in time. If initial data files had been structured to maintain information at the level of aggregation required when the system was begun, many operations of the present System would be precluded by data limitations.

Response to Interrogation. In addition to standard reports generated on request, generalized input-output programs provide flexible communication between the computer and its human associates. The financial analyst may obtain specialized tabulations of present or historical conditions, selective reports of the existence of particular conditions, and a wide variety of visual presentations to aid in the assimilation of data. The System is able to provide output relating to a particular company, an industry, or an entire market and to aggregate present or historic information in forms specified by the analyst at time of interrogation.

The Monitor Function. Since the monitor capability is among the System's most important attributes, it may be useful to review the basic characteristics of a monitor system operating in the financial management context.

The financial analyst who is following particular situations at a time when substantive changes occur will usually note these changes and take action based on them. Unfortunately, it is impossible for an analyst to be totally "on top of" to be monitoring—all data relating to even a small portion of the relevant environment at any point in time.

The computer functions in this context to extend the coverage of the competent analyst by applying to all available data the objective reasoning which, given sufficient time and an appropriate supporting environment, the analyst would perform himself. Therefore, a small group of generalists are free to focus their attention on actionable situations confident that the market is being continuously monitored and that the System will alert them to relevant developments.

Advisory Recommendations. The System incorporates programmed procedures designed to isolate and evaluate potentially actionable market situations. Conditions meeting specified criteria are referred to management along with recommendations for action. At the time of referral a decision record identifying the recommended action is automatically updated. The Status Log containing all such decision records provides an unequivocal chronological record of the System's performance as a decision-maker. Thus, while management has the option to accept or reject system recommendations, validation of unaided system performance has been established by means of the Status Log record of actions taken under conditions existing in the monitored environment since 1958.

A sample Status Log record is illustrated in Figure 3. Entries for Abbott Laboratories traded under the symbol ABT are used as an example. The number (200) separating, the symbol from the name is a sequence control used in audit procedures. The line following the Abbott identification summarizes the status of that security at close of market on the reporting data.

The sample report indicates conditions existing on Friday, March 20, 1964. Therefore the first entry in each stock record specifies "3/20/64." The second entry defines the issue's status on that date. The Abbott Laboratories status is "CLOSED." Five status indications are possible. These are:

1. Bought—indicating that the issue was purchased on the specified data;
2. Sold—indicating that the issue was sold on the specified date;
3. Hold—indicating that the issue has previously been purchased and is now held in the system portfolio;
4. Closed—indicating that the issue has been previously sold and is not now held in the system portfolio;
5. None—indicating that, as of the reporting date, the computer has not previously purchased the specified security.

To the right of the status specification in the second and succeeding lines is the security's price at close of market on the indicated date. The last sale of Abbott Laboratories on March 20, 1964 was $114. The next entry specifies the average daily trading volume in round lots (1800 shares in the case of ABT).

The next four entries indicate the latest reported per share earning and dividend rates, the yield based on the last reported dividend, and the applicable price/earnings ratio. To the right of the company price/earnings ratio is the average price/earnings ratio for a reference industry (25.6X

FIGURE 3

S.I.M.S.—II processing run—week 277—Friday, March 20, 1964

Status log summary

DATE	STATUS	PRICE	AVERAGE VOLUME	EARNINGS PER SHARE	DIVIDENDS	YIELD	P/E RATIO CO.	P/E RATIO IND.
ABJ	100.	Abacus Fund						
— Conditions prevailing when issue was bought on 1/25/63								
— Conditions prevailing when issue was sold on 10/18/63								
— Conditions prevailing on Friday preceding data of report 3/13/64								
— Conditions prevailing on date of report generation 3/20/64								
ABT	200.	Abbott Laboratories						
03/20/64	Closed	$114.0	18.	$4.41	$2.40	2.1%	25.9X	25.6X
03/13/64	Closed	$115.1	18.	$4.41	$2.40	2.1%	26.1X	25.6X
10/18/63	Sold	$110.7	31.	$4.33			25.6X	
01/25/63	Bought	$79.2	19.					
ABC	300.	ABC Vending Corp.						
03/20/64	Hold	$14.0	27.	$1.03	$0.60	4.3%	13.6X	
03/13/64	Hold	$13.5	23.	$1.03	$0.60	4.4%	13.1X	
01/11/63	Bought	$14.5	36.					
06/09/61	Issue was split approximately 2 to 1							
ACF	400.	ACF Industries, Inc.						
03/20/64	Hold	$70.5	35.	$3.26	$1.60	2.3%	21.6X	16.7X
03/13/64	Hold	$69.5	34.	$3.26	$1.60	2.3%	21.3X	16.7X
03/06/64	Bought	$67.1	31.	$3.26	$1.60	2.4%	20.6X	
11/15/63	Bought	$55.0	29.					
ACS	500.	Acme Markets, Inc.						
03/20/64	None	$65.5	7.	$5.30	$2.00	3.1%	12.4X	14.3X
03/13/64	None	$67.0	8.	$5.30	$2.00	3.0%	12.6X	14.3X

for the Drug Industry in the case of Abbott). Data in succeeding lines summarize conditions prevailing on the preceding Friday and at the time of the most recent system actions with respect to the security.

On-Line Interaction. Much of the on-line information generated by the system is proprietary. However, portions of two representative displays are reproduced to illustrate on-line system operation. For purposes of exposition, let us imagine an analyst seated at his desk near a cathode ray tube display console.

Monitor Messages. At 10:28 on the morning of November 25, 1966, the report reproduced in Figure 4 appears on the television screen. It is a monitor message generated by the real-time computer bringing to the analyst's attention a positive (POS-2) situation in First Charter Finance. The "−2" indicates a level 2 criterion has been met.

FIGURE 4
1028 monitor display

Mon	POS-2	FCF	First	Charter	FI
1028	14.9	15.1	15.0	14.6+	15.0
15.0	9.9	12.5	14.8	14.8	14.8
73		0 103	37		
1.79	8.4/08.3		0.00	0.0/00.0	
			13+11/046		11.2

The second line of the display indicates the time of the computer's decision (10:28) and the bid, ask, high, low, and last trade (14.9, 15.1, 15.0, 14.6, and 15.0 respectively). The fourth line of the display notes that 73 round lots have been traded thus far in First Charter, and that no shares traded the preceding day. (Thanksgiving was a market holiday.) The average trading levels in that stock during two preceding reference periods were 103 and 87 round lots per day.

The first entry in the fifth line of the message indicates that the company is presently earning $1.79 per share which produces a price/earnings ratio based on the last trade of 8.4 as compared to an industry ratio of 8.3. The final item in the display notes that the system previously brought this situation to the analyst's attention as a positive (+) level 3 consideration on November 4, 1966, at which time the security was trading at 11.2.

Throughout the day the computer continues to refer actionable situations to the analyst as criteria are met.

Response to Interrogation. The analyst is able to access information in the data file at will. He might for example, request unadjusted 12-month moving cumulated earnings and dividends for a security of interest. When the display appears on his screen, he can request a printed copy from the computer to produce output of the type contained in Figure 5.

FIGURE 5
Earnings/dividends display

COPY—11/25

		Earnings-Dividends UFL		United Fin. Calif.	
Year		Quarter 1	Quarter 2	Quarter 3	Quarter 4
1964	Earnings	2.91	2.62	2.78	2.90
	Dividends	.50	.50	.50	.50
1965	Earnings	2.88	1.09	.86	.79
	Dividends	.50	.00	.00	.00
1966	Earnings	.55	.50	.42	.39
	Dividends	.00	.00	.00	.00

Summary

This paper has reported on one firm's progress in applying information technology to investment decision making.

System evolution from 1959 to 1967 has been described with emphasis placed on three characteristics of the system development process.

1. The systems have been designed to achieve specific management objectives.

2. Agreed upon measures of market and company performance are maintained in complete detail in disaggregated, chronological data files.

3. Increased system scope and sophistication have been achieved through a carefully planned process of gradual expansion and refinement.

Research and operating functions of current and earlier systems have been described. Research evaluation of market process and investment decision models was discussed with reference to simulation based analysis. Retrieval, monitor and advisory functions were illustrated by representative on-line system outputs.

The impact of the computer and systems analysis techniques has been assessed in terms of demands made on the partners of the firm. They have been called upon to establish highly specific objectives for research and investment programs. They have been asked to establish quantitative criteria which permits the computer to choose between alternatives on the basis of rational evaluation. They have been challenged to make implicit theories explicit and to discard concepts with which they have worked for many years.

It has not been easy for management to accept the computer as a partner. However, their success in incorporating computer-based systems into the investment decision process is indicative of the potential which can be realized through intelligent synthesis of advanced technology and sound management judgment.

B. Process Control

39. Process Computers Head for Wide Role in Plant Automation*

The process computer has become plant management's loyal lieutenant. It faithfully carries out orders for producing steel, chemicals, petroleum products, power, and paper at a level of efficiency beyond the reach of human operators.

At the very least, the process computer's rank in the automation hierarchy is now permanent; if present plans to broaden its command work out, it is due for a promotion.

"I don't think anyone could build a plant without a process computer," says Louis T. Rader, vice-president in charge of General Electric Co.'s Industrial Process Control Division. "Process control is here to stay," says another executive, "because a 2% improvement in plant efficiency can mean a tremendous number of dollars a day."

Such savings have been made chiefly in control of continuous processes, such as the flow of oil through a refinery. Now, manufacturers think process computers can do the same for "discrete parts"—products made one at a time.

General Motors Corp. has brought the automobile industry's first computer-managed transfer line and will use this complex of automated tools to help assemble rear axles. A Westinghouse computer will supervise the $750,000 line, made by Cross Co., when it swings into operation later this year.

*SOURCE: *Business Week* (June 29, 1968), pp. 60, 62-64. Reprinted by permission of the publisher.

Broad scope

The definition of process control duties is being broadened in other areas. International Business Machines Corp. has installed comptuers to guide the flow of city traffic; Digital Equipment Corp. sells small computers to control laboratory equipment; Mobil Oil Corp. has a process computer overseeing a 351-well oil field in Texas.

What is more, the influence of the process computer is spreading to industry's front office. "The differences between process computers and electronic data processors are shrinking," notes Bruce H. Baldridge, manager of systems application planning for Foxboro Co., a maker of industrial-control equipment.

As a result, process computers can be linked to each other and to EDP computers to form an electronic chain of command. At the bottom of this chain, powerful minicomputers handle monitoring and process details beyond the scope of the bulky, slow computers of a decade ago. Information collected at these control stations can be passed to an EDP "big brother" that can make management decisions. Such a hierarchy of control could, for example, let computers decide how much raw material must be ordered for a certain amount of finished product.

Moving in

These burgeoning prospects for process control have attracted producers of both computers and industrial control equipment. In addition to IBM and GE, a host of smaller companies, such as Foxboro, Leeds & Northrup Co., and Bailey Meter Co. have become strong in the business. They see computer control as a logical extension of their production-line sensing devices.

GE is probably the most enthusiastic advocate of computer control for parts manufacture—largely because it already makes automation controls, as well as computers. "Our entire line of numerical controls for machine tools is designed to interact with process computers," says Rader. Of course, Rader explains, "no one is going to sit down and order a plant and want it computer-directed straight off. What you do is develop 'islands of control' and then spread out from there."

Plans for putting process computers to work on discrete parts also are being spurred overseas. Britain's Molins Machine Co., Ltd., intends to build a fully automatic factory for its own use and as a prototype of others it hopes to build for customers. It expects to have the plant fully operational next year.

Hooking up

Application of the hierarchy of control concept is already under way in the U.S. Predictably, it has begun in the chemical, petroleum, and utility industries, where process control has been strongest. Monsanto Co. has been experimenting with the idea for several years. Union Carbide Corp. has already hooked up a series of process computers at its massive Taft (La.) complex.

Frederick A. Woods, associate director of engineering at Carbide, says that pooled data from this hookup could ultimately be fed into a business computer that would keep each portion of the plant's output in balance.

Before the year is out, American Oil Co. will link an IBM process computer at its Whiting (Ind.) refinery to an EDP unit 30 miles away in Chicago. American, a subsidiary of Standard Oil Co. (Indiana), says the business computer will study only payroll and inventory data; but it could also be part of a hierarchy system.

And sometime soon, Public Service Electric & Gas Co. hopes to feed process control data from its power distribution network in New Jersey to an IBM 360 at the Philadelphia headquarters of the Pennsylvania-New Jersey-Maryland interconnection. Engineers will then know how New Jersey's power needs square with those in the other two states.

Closing loops

How complete the computer takeover will be depends on a concept called direct digital control. "With DDC, computers are closing a lot of final loops," says one observer. Usually, electronic and hydraulic sensing devices are read for data on such process variables as temperature and pressure. When the sensors show changes, plant personnel act to keep the process in balance. DDC replaces men and mechanisms; the computer follows the variables, checks for discrepancies, and makes the corrections.

DDC, already a major tool in chemical production, is making headway in cement, paper, and glass making. Esso Petroleum Co., Ltd., recently installed the largest DDC system in its industry at its refinery in Fawley, England. And DDC is becoming especially attractive in the batch production of baked goods and plastics, where it takes a computer to keep track of rapid changes in recipe. Foxboro has installed one such system to handle production of up to ten varieties of polyvinyl chloride for a West German chemical company.

DDC has one major drawback, though: It can cost more than conventional controls. Some industry observers think only large plants have the money and manpower for it. "You go to DDC because it offers better control, not for savings," says Beloit Corp., which makes machinery for the paper industry.

Caution

Drawbacks notwithstanding, process control men expect the industry's sales of $100-million a year in hardware alone to more than double by 1975.

The industry is treating this potential with care, hoping to avoid mistakes made in the early years of proces control. In the early 1960s, equipment suppliers stressed computer hardware, and lots of it. But they often found that $500,000 systems could not control what they were supposed to.

"That was our trouble at Bunker-Ramo," recalls Louis B. Perillo, now a vice-president of Scientific Data Systems, Inc. Perillo thinks Bunker-Ramo concentrated too much on hardware instead of software, which ultimately became more important.

The result was that Bunker-Ramo, Philco, Daystrom, and Radio Corp. of America dropped out of the process control business. Their places have been taken by companies striving for a better balance between hardware and software and lower overall costs.

Cutting the price

Digital Equipment is among these cost-conscious companies. Its mini-computers, which can be bought for $10,000, have won converts for process control. Others are buying the low-priced IBM 1130 computer, adapted to handle process control by Digital Applications, Inc. Of course, there are still bigger, more costly control computers. But the cost of process systems is shrinking. The average price of a Westinghouse Electric system will drop from last year's $170,000 to $130,000 in 1970, predicts C. E. Hammond, industrial group vice-president.

Meanwhile, software has become so central to process control's success that it accounts for up to 50% of an installation's total cost.

Who's who

For the perplexed potential customer, confused by the profusion of suppliers and systems, there are a number of consultants who can help—both with choice and installation .Among them: Bonner & Moore Associates, Profimatics, Inc., and Digital Applications.

Now fighting to dominate the market are GE and IBM, and the battle is likely to be a long one. "GE has the lead now in systems installed and on order," says one consultant. "And GE is one of the two systems makers—Honeywell is the other—that offers a complete process package, from computers to controls. But IBM is an unbeatable marketer. It's closing the gap fast."

In the scramble, smaller makers of computers and sensing devices are helping each other penetrate such specific markets as chemicals and utilities. Leeds & Northrup buys computers from Scientific Data Systems, Inc., and then builds the finished systems. Foxboro does the same with Digital Equipment, Taylor Instrument Cos., with Systems Engineering Laboratories, Inc., and Reliance Electric Co. with Control Data Corp.

Dollar input

The need to buy computers has kept some of the controls producers from making money on process control. Foxboro, for one, loses money on it, and is considering designing its own computers. So far, though, the rapid evolution of computer technology has prevented all but Bailey Meter from taking that step.

Like the suppliers, most users of process control are still feeling their way. Says a Monsanto executive: "This isn't a field where you can make tremendous steps. It will all come, but slowly."

40. Production Planning in a Multiplant System*

Elliot Schrier

The author describes a centralized production planning system for multiplant operations, based on a research project conducted by Matson Research Corporation for a large food-processing firm. The system assigns clear responsibilities to the departments of sales, distribution, material, and production and provides organizational and functional buffers (including production inventories) to soften conflicts.

All of the procedures are within the normal reach of any manufacturing company.

There was a time in all of our memories when most products were closely identified with a single company and a single location. Kellogg made corn flakes in Battle Creek; Schlitz made beer in Milwaukee. Largely within the past two decades a new set of management problems has developed—production planning in a multiplant system. Kellogg makes corn flakes in four locations; most industries have truly national producers and distributors.

*SOURCE: Copyright 1969 by the Regents of the University of California. Reprinted from *California Management Review*, Vol. XI, No. 4 (Summer 1969), pp. 69-78, by permission of the Regents.

Multiplant systems have developed in most consumer-oriented industries through merger or acquisition, geographic expansion into new markets, or the improvement of service levels within established markets. Mergers do not always join similar product lines; even when they do, the production techniques and facilities are often dissimilar. Nor does expansion into new markets always result in comparable plants and product lines. Plants built in new areas tend to incorporate new techniques; taste perferences often require different products for different markets. Even when multiplant systems develop in response to the need for better service levels within stablished markets, the new facilties do not always resemble the old.

Diversity is not the only problem that multiplant systems have generated. Service areas have to be delineated; responsibilities have to be divided between plant managers and headquarters; and production allocation has to be added to production scheduling. Unfortunately, most multiplant systems have grown unplanned and, at least by some people, unwanted.

The unplanned system

The most prevalent characteristic of unplanned multiplant systems, particularly those composed of formerly independent regional producers, is that the plants are run as autonomous units by entrepreneurial plant managers with wide latitude in what they are allowed to make and when, so long as they meet rather general goals set by corporate management. These goals are usually expressed in qualitative terms—satisfy market requirements, operate efficiently, maintain quality. When quantitative goals are set, they are usually set in accounting terms—unit cost or total operating budget.

This entrepreneurial orientation on the part of the plant manager leads to other characteristics of the unplanned multiplant system. There is usually a close local relationship between production and marketing, with production oriented strongly to short-term market demand. With this orientation, even expert production managers are faced with either short production runs (frequent changeovers) or high inventories. This orientation to short-term market demand, in conjunction with restricted plant service areas, also leads to high unit distribution costs; the product is often shipped from the plant in small lots as orders are filled—generally less than a carload and often less than a truckload. Finally, since there is no way to use one plant to alleviate peak demand on another plant or to produce stock in anticipation of a system-wide peak, plant capacity is lost.

Restructuring operations

Trends in planning in multiplant companies. Many companies are spending a great deal of effort to restructure their operations. Three trends are emerging from these efforts:

1. Organization of a centralized production planning activity which allocates production quantities to plants and sometimes even sets production schedules.

2. Establishment of distribution centers which stock a company's entire line and serve a large market area, independently of the natural service area of any single plant.

3. Rigorous analyses of interfunctional trade-offs which look to the return to the corporation, rather than to the activity of a single function or a single plant.

A specific example

A recent example. In 1965 Matson Research Corporation was asked to study one unplanned multiplant system which had developed through acquisition of a sales-dominated organization as one of four divisions of a consumer-oriented company. Each division had its own peculiarities, with different products, seasonal variations, raw material sources, and plant locations.

All but one of the plants of the division were capable of making a full product line. The product line consisted of 102 line items in three major categories: industrial, institutional, and consumer goods. With the exception of a few bulk industrial formulations, all of the products competed for both processing and packaging facilities. The division's annual production exceeded a billion pounds, ranging from less than 100 million to over 250 million pounds per plant. Only one of the plants could be considered up to date, and several of the plants were operating at their capacity limits. Vacant land in the vicinity of all but one plant was scarce, and the nature of the manufacturing operation precluded easy expansion of capacity by the installation of larger processing units.

With a weak central organization and a dominant position in its markets, the predecessor company had allowed its plants to operate as autonomous units. According to the Vice President of Operations,

> Each plant pretty well planned its own production. We had a headquarters planning and control unit which attempted to coordinate and direct the whole. Lacking a systematic and timely body of information on which to take action, they were mostly confined to fire fighting.

Communication with Marketing, Distribution, and the plants was sketchy, informal, and often too late. Out-of-stock incidents were commonplace and emergency reallocations of finished goods, production assignments, and orders were the natural results.

To define the scope of this study we met with management to decide *whether to concentrate on interactions between products or between functions*—that is, concentrate on the distribution problem, which would involve the product lines of all four divisions or on the production planning problem in Division A, which would involve all of its functions (Figure 1). The approach concentrating on distribution would require only minimal attention to the operating problems of sales, production, materiel, or finance; it would seek ways in which all of the company's products could most efficiently be shipped, stored, and delivered as component parts of a total distribution system. The approach concentrating on production would consider alternative ways of centralizing production planning of the division for the most efficient use of its production capabilities. This approach would consider the related requirements of sales, distribution, materiel, and finance, but would neglect the product lines of the other divisions, which ultimately must influence any corporate-wide planning system.

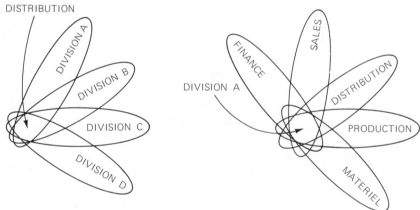

Product Line Interactions for One Function   Functional Interactions for One Product Line

FIGURE 1
Function and product interactions

Either approach would lead to more efficient operations. At that time, however, Division A production faced more pressing problems than corporate distribution. Moreover, the production planning approach showed promise of more immediate peripheral benefits across all functional lines. Management, therefore, decided to develop a centralized production planning system for Division A. The emphasis was placed on planning (forecasting and allocating demand) rather than on scheduling (fixing the order in which the various products would be made in a given plant during a given period).

Four vital elements

A production planning system must be based on *four essential elements*:
- The objectives of the organization.
- A measure of the state of the organization and its environment.
- A well-defined flow of reliable information.
- A clear assignment of functional responsibilities.

Apart from the corporate objectives, *each function within the organization has its own goals*. Some of these subgoals are defined in terms of the market (for example, customer service level), some in terms of production (plant utilization). Sometimes they are conflicting: reaching one increases the cost of reaching the other or precludes it entirely. Management must then *resolve the conflict on the basis of corporate objectives*.

The *state of the organization* can be measured by inventories, production capabilities, and other internal factors. The environment can be measured precisely only in a historical sense; for planning purposes, estimates of the future are required to supplement the historical data. In production planning such estimates generally take the form of forecasts of the shipments the plants are expected to make. The measures of the state of the organization and its environment provide the basic information for a production planning system.

Clear assignment of functional responsibilities is the last essential element of effective planning. Most contemporary industrial organizations operate with divided (and sometimes necessarily conflicting) functional responsibilities. Each function must accept its responsibilities for input, conversion, and transfer of information, and for integrated action within the planning system. *The responsibilities differentiate the functions; the information flow integrates them into a planning system*.

Functional buffers

There is a need to provide *buffers between the functions* to soften the inevitable conflicts. Given the uncertainties of the marketplace and the competition of the different marketing groups for production capacity, production has to be shielded from short-term or local changes in demand. Similarly, sales has to be shielded from short-term variations in production capabilities.

There are two types of functional buffers: *the organizational buffer* (e.g., a production planning department) and *the physical buffer* (e.g., a production inventory). The organizational buffer concentrates the planning and operational decisions within the responsible function. The physical buffer allows each function to operate at high efficiency and still meet the variable demands placed on it.

Two types of buffers

Organizational buffering is implicit in the information flow. Sales places demands only on distribution; it has no direct contact with the plants or even with production planning, unless the situation is an "exception." Although distribution is, generally, production's sole customer, when it desires to revise its plan it must call on production planning, not on plant managers. Similarly, sales must call on distribution, not on production planning. Organizational buffers are not intended to impede informal communication between functions. On the contrary, with a regular and reliable information flow, they actually improve it. But action should be generated only through the formal information flow.

Production inventories are not as widely used as distribution inventories to provide functional buffers, but they can promote effective planning and operation of a multiplant system. Sometimes the product can be shipped to a customer or a distribution warehouse directly from the end of the packaging line. Usually, however, production inventories more than repay the investment required to carry them. In a sense, production inventories are a substitute for the capacity that would otherwise be required to meet large or unexpected demands at the same customer service level. A production inventory can be thought of as an instant plant with zero start-up time, that can be put onstream and taken off-stream at a low cost.

Inventory planning

Production inventory. Any production inventory consists of three distinct parts: *cycle stock, working stock, and anticipation stock.* The cycle stock is the inventory that s available because production proceeds in batches, no product is in production for the entire planning period, and withdrawals to meet demand during the period do not match the accumulation from previous productions.

The amount of cycle stock is, of course, closely tied to the length of the production cycle. In most plants, several products compete for processing and packaging facilities. Short of building a plant with so much capacity that the utilization rate would be uneconomically low, there is no way to eliminate such conflicts. Production planning can prevent many conflicts and resolve those that do occur at the lowest possible cost.

During the cycle period all major items will be produced in sufficient quantities to meet demands until the next batches are produced in the next cycle (assuming working stock is available to cover deviations in demand). This concept is discussed in detail in the literature.[1]

In the simplest case we assume that:

- Demand for product i is continuous at rate r_i *per week*.
- When producing product i, production is at a constant rate p_i per week.
- Unfilled demand is backlogged.

And then compute that:

- Holding cost H_i—the cost of holding one unit of product for one time period.
- Back order cost B_i—the cost of having one unit of product i on back order for one time period.
- Startup and changeover costs S—the sum of all costs of startup and changeover for a complete cycle.

The following equations show how the duration of the cycle T, the average inventory I_i, and the maximum inventory level Z_i, are calculated under these assumptions.

$$T = \left[2S \middle/ \sum_{i=1}^{n} \frac{H_i r_i (1 - r_i/p_i)}{1 - H_i/B_i} \right]^{\frac{1}{2}}. \tag{1}$$

$$\bar{I}_i = \left[\frac{Tr_i}{2} \frac{(1 - r_i/p_i)}{(1 - H_i/B_i)} \right]. \tag{2}$$

$$Z = 2\bar{I}_i. \tag{3}$$

I_i and Z_i are relatively insensitive to H_i/B_i; in this case, we estimated the ratio to be in the range of 0.1 to less than 0.05, and thus the term could be ignored.

Working stock is the inventory required to permit production to meet demands which exceed the forecasts. If none is available, the plants must meet such demands by adjusting production schedules in an uneconomical manner. Working stock is also required to cover a reasonable portion of production losses due to machine breakdown or other random failures in the production system. The working stock should be large enough to meet the "maximum reasonable demand" during the period between the beginning of one production run (when the size of run is decided) and the next. Since the time between the start of successive runs is at least one period of the production cycle, the working stock should be large enough, on the average, to meet a specified service level. Since the demand distribution was close to a normal distribution, the working stock was initially set at two standard deviations (equivalent in this case to a 97.5 per cent service level). The interpretation of working stock is given in Figure 2.

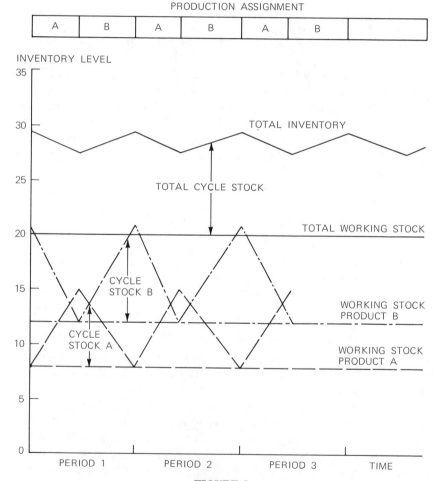

FIGURE 2
Inventory and production patterns for two products

Anticipation stocks are produced in advance of needs because of a pending promotion (for which estimated sales during the period exceed production capacity), a scheduled plant shutdown, or a future commitment. Production must know when anticipation stocks are required, particularly if promotions are frequent and large (as they were in the division under study). By anticipating demand, production can meet the demands of large bulk industrial sales more efficiently and can achieve higher levels of plant utilization over the system.

With a high level of certainty that the plants will meet demands (from either current production or plant inventory), field inventories can be kept quite low. The only lead time required to meet unexpected sales would be that required to transport the goods from the plant to the distribution warehouse or directly to the customer.

A centralized system

Production inventories are not inviolable. They are to be drawn down to zero whenever required to meet demand. It is then up to production to rebuild its inventories while it meets current demand as forecast by sales and placed by distribution.

Figure 3 is a diagram of the *centralized production planning system* that was developed for Division A. As shown by the heavy horizontal arrow in the figure, the major report from production planning details the plant production requirements by product, brand, component, and processing unit. This computer-prepared report also provides the plants with detailed listings of their output requirements for raw materials, packaging, supplies, and other necessities.

The principal information needs for the production requirements report are:

• Shipment demand forecasts for industrial, institutional, and consumer products.

• Inventory status of finished products, components, and raw materials at the plants and plant warehouses.

• Each plant's current production schedule and physical condition.

The sales forecasts generated by consumer and institutional sales are converted by distribution into shipment demands on the plants. Because of its specific contractual and formulation obligations, industrial sales sends it demand forecast directly to production planning.

Using the production requirements report and the information flowing from the plants as shown in Figure 3, production planning produces:

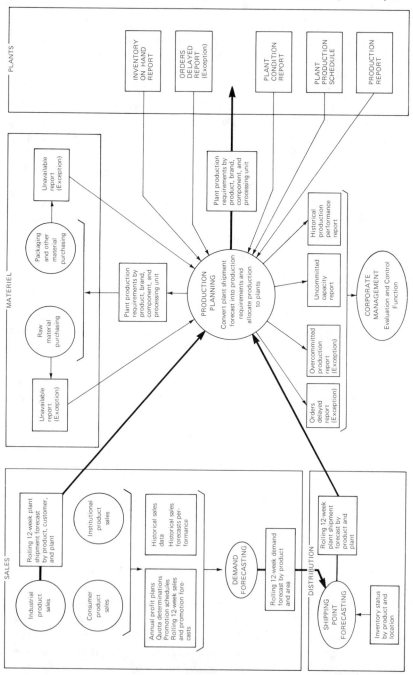

FIGURE 3

Functions and information flow for a centralized production planning system.

- An orders-delayed report and an overcommitted-production report on an "exception" basis.
- Regular reports of uncommitted production capacity.
- Actual versus planned production (historical production performance report).

A key report

Figure 4 shows the timing sequence for the *key production requirements report*. Every four weeks a major report is produced covering the next twelve weeks. Any requirements for the first two weeks are considered firm, for the second two weeks flexible, and for the last eight weeks tentative. Two weeks after the "major" production requirements report, production planning issues a "minor" report firming up the flexible two-week period. In the weeks between each major and minor report, production planning may issue a "revision" report changing the second week of the firm period as required.

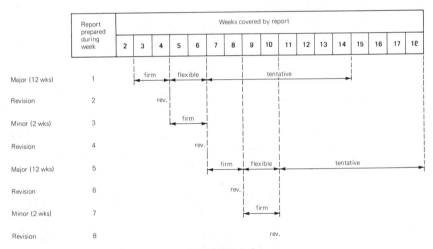

FIGURE 4
Production requirement report: time-horizon sequence

For example, production planning prepares a "major" report during week 5 detailing the production requirement for weeks 7 through 18 in terms of six two-week planning periods. The requirements for the first period—weeks 7 and 8 are considered firm by the plant managers and scheduled for production upon receipt of the report. The requirements for the next four periods—weeks 11 through 18—are used primarily to estimate material requirements and uncommitted capacity. During week 6, on the basis of a changed shipment demand forecast, a plant breakdown, an announcement of a forthcoming promotion, or some other event, production planning issues a "revision" report amending the schedules for week 8 as necessary. During week 7 production planning prepares a "minor" report firming up the requirements for weeks 9 and 10. If necessary, it amends week 10 on the basis of information received during week 8. The reporting cycle starts again during week 9 with the preparation of another "major" report.

The information flow and input data requirements for the five major reports prepared by production planning are shown in Table 1.

To prepare its shipment forecast (a necessary input to the production requirements report), distribution requires a forecast from sales. The entire system starts with that forecast. Sales is closest to the customer, and neither distribution nor production should have better information on which to base demand forecasts. Therefore, sales should be given within the company's capabilities. Similarly, distribution is in the best position to set inventory levels, choose resupply routes, and decide how to meet customer orders. Production knows best how, when, and where to make the products required to meet sales, fill the distribution pipeline, or build production inventory; and material knows best when and where to place orders with its vendors.

Allocation procedure

The system makes use of a *computer program to allocate distribution's demands to plants and to "explode" products into material and process requirements.* The allocation procedure which considers inventory status and the costs of inventory, transportation, and production is not an optimizing algorithm, but a heuristic procedure which has proved effective. It requires an input of "desired" end-of-period inventory for major end products and intermediate products. The program could, perhaps, be extended to produce individual plant schedules, but in the division under study the advantages that might be obtained from such schedules are too small to be worth the effort. Centrally produced, computer-derived schedules could not accommodate breakdowns, short-time material delays, or other problems of day-to-day production. The production requirements report, therefore, is not a schedule, but rather a list of product quantities to be produced at each plant in the period.

TABLE 1
Reports and input data time requirements

	FRE-QUENCY	PREPARED BY	PRINCIPAL DISTRIBUTION	TIMING
Production requirements	Weekly	Prod. Planning	Plants, Material	5 P.M. Friday
Consumer and inst. shipment forecast	Weekly	Distribution	Production Planning	8 A.M. Thurs. (Fri. for rev.)
Industrial shipment forecast	Weekly	Ind. Sales	Production Planning	8 A.M. Thurs. (Fri. for rev.)
W/E physical inventory	Weekly	Plants	Production Planning	8 A.M. Wednesday
Plant production schedule	Weekly	Plants	Production Planning	5 P.M. Monday
Plant condition report	Exception	Plants	Production Planning	On occurrence
Caacpity available	Weekly	Prod. Planning	Distribution, Sales, and E&C	5 P.M. Monday
Production requirement report	Weekly	Prod. Planning	Distribution, Sales, and E&C	5 P.M. Friday
Overcommitted production	Exception	Prod. Planning	Distribution, Sales, and E&C	On occurrence
Uncommitted capacity	Weekly	Prod. Planning	Distribution, Sales, and E&C	5 P.M. Monday
Daily industrial sales report	Daily	Ind. Sales	Production Planning	Noon for previous day
Exception production request	Exception	Distribution	Production Planning	On occurrence
Orders delayed	Exception	Prod. Planning	Distribution, Sales, and E&C	On occurrence
Orders delayed	Exception	Plants	Production Planning	On occurrence
Production performance	Biweekly	Prod. Planning	Distribution and E&C	5 P.M. Thursday
W/E physical inventory	Weekly	Plants	Production Planning	8 A.M. Wednesday
Plant production	Weekly	Plants	Production Planning	8 A.M. Wednesday

Production planning is normal business. Sophisticated methods of management science are not really required to develop a centralized production planning system. Most of the data that are required and most of the analyses that have to be made should be part of any manufacturing corporation's normal capabilities. Most or all of the efforts associated with the centralized production planning system should be performed even if management does not adopt a formal system.

The important goals

The major problems, briefly, are:
- The assignment of clear-cut functional responsibilties.
- The elmination of "second guessing" by members of each department of their associates in other departments.
- The establishment of generally accepted definitions for such things as orders delayed and production capacity.
- The formulation of a self-improving forecasting effort.
- Perhaps most important, the development of evaluation and control activities at both functional and divisional levels.

The problem of evaluation and control is a topic in itself. Figure 3 showed corporate management receiving four reports: orders delayed, overcommitted production, uncommitted capacity, and historical production performance. Acting for corporate management, the evluation and control function should find the causes of system malfunctions and propose operational changes to eliminate them. It should also suggest action at the corporate planning level to take advantage of opportunities uncovered by improved information. At the same time, each function in the division should establish its own evaluation and control activity to improve its performance in making forecasts, planning is operation, and supplying information for other functions within the system.

Conclusion

The centralized production planning system offers management an excellent device for controlling its operations. It accommodates change, recognizes both independent and interacting responsibilities, lends itself to computer systems, and alows opportunistic decisions to be made while easily accommodating exceptions to relatively simply routines.

NOTE

1. J. Buchan and E. Koenigsberg, *Scientific Inventory Management* (Englewood Cliffs, N.J.: Prentice-Hall, Inc., 1960); L. H. Krone, Jr., "A Note on Economic Lot Sizes for Multi-Purpose Equipment," *Management Science*, X (1964), pp. 461-464.

C. Marketing

41. Systems Approach to Marketing*

Lee Adler

More and more businessmen today recognize that corporate success is, in most cases, synonymous with marketing success and with the coming of age of a new breed of professional managers. They find it increasingly important not only to pay lip service to the marketing concept but to do something about it in terms of (a) customer orientation, rather than navel-gazing in the factory, (b) organizational revisions to implement the marketing concept, and (c) a more orderly approach to problem solving.

In an increasing number of companies we see more conscious and formal efforts to apply rational, fact-based methods for solving marketing problems, and greater recognition of the benefits these methods offer. While these benefits may be newly realized, there is nothing new about the underlying philosophy; in the parlance of military men and engineers, it is the systems approach. For, whether we like it or not, marketing is, by definition, a system, if we accept Webster's definition of system as "an assemblage of objects united by some form of regular interaction or interdependence." Certainly, the interaction of such "objects" as product, pricing, promotion, sales calls, distribution, and so on fits the definition.

There is an expanding list of sophisticated applications of systems theory —and not in one but in many sectors of the marketing front. The construction of mathematical and/or logical models to describe, quantify, and

*SOURCES: *Harvard Business Review* (May-June, 1967), pp. 105-118. Reprinted by permission of the publisher. Copyright © 1967 by the President and Fellows of Harvard College; all rights reserved.

evaluate alternate marketing strategies and mixes is an obvious case in point. So, too, is the formulation of management information systems[1] and of marketing plans with built-in performance measurements of predetermined goals. But no less vital is the role of the systems approach in the design and sale of products and services. When J. P. Stevens Company color-harmonizes linens and bedspreads, and towels and bath mats, it is creating a product system. And when Avco Corporation sells systems management to the space exploration field, involving the marriage of many scientific disciplines as well as adherence to budgetary constraints, on-time performance, and quality control, it is creating a *service* system.

In this article I shall discuss the utilization of the systems concept in marketing in both quantitative and qualitative ways with case histories drawn from various industries. In doing so, my focus will be more managerial and philosophical than technical, and I will seek to dissipate some of the hocus-pocus, glamor, mystery, and fear which pervade the field. The systems concept is not esoteric or "science fiction" in nature (although it sometimes *sounds* that way in promotional descriptions). Its advantages are not subtle or indirect; as we shall see, they are as real and immediate as decision making itself. The limitations are also real, and these, too, will be discussed.

Promising applications

Now let us look at some examples of corporate application of the systems approach. Here we will deal with specific parts or "subsystems" of the total marketing system. Exhibit I is a schematic portrayal of these relationships.

Products and services

The objective of the systems approach in product management is to provide a complete "offering" to the market rather than merely a product. If the purpose of business is to create a customer at a profit, then the needs of the customer must be carefully attended to; we must, in short, study what the customer is buying or wants to buy, rather than what we are trying to sell.

In the consumer products field we have forged ahead in understanding that the customer buys nutrition (not bread), beauty (not cosmetics), warmth (not fuel oil). But in industrial products this concept has been slower in gaining a foothold. Where it has gained a foothold, it expresses itself in two ways: the creation of a complete product system sold (1) as a unit, or (2) as a component or components which are part of a larger consumption system.

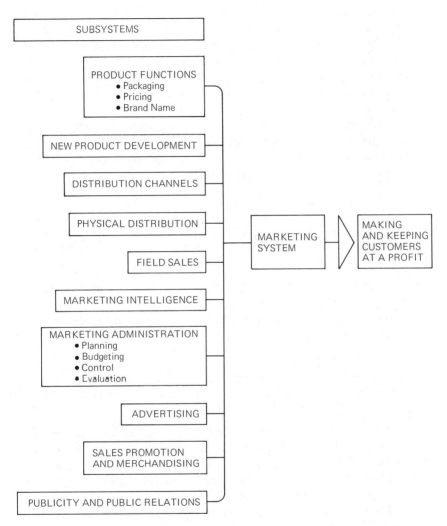

EXHIBIT I
Marketing subsystems and the total system

Perhaps the most eloquent testimony to the workability and value of the systems approach comes from companies that have actually used it. For a good example let us turn to the case of The Carborundum Company. This experience is especially noteworthy because it comes from industrial marketing, where, as just indicated, progress with the systems concept has generally been slow.

Birth of the Concept. Founded in 1894, the company was content for many years to sell abrasives. It offered an extremely broad line of grinding wheels, coated abrasives, and abrasive grain, with a reputed capacity for 200,000 different products of varying type, grade, and formulation. But the focus was on the product.

In the mid-1950's, Carborundum perceived that the market for abrasives could be broadened considerably if—looking at abrasives through customer's eyes—it would see the product as fitting into *metal polishing, cleaning,* or *removal systems.* Now Carborundum is concerned with all aspects of abrading—the machine, the contact wheel, the workpiece, the labor cost, the overhead rate, the abrasive, and, above all, the customer's objective. In the words of Carborundum's president, W. H. Wendel:

> "That objective is never the abrasive per se, but rather the creation of a certain dimension, a type of finish, or a required shape, always related to a minimum cost. Since there are many variables to consider, just one can be misleading. To render maximum service, Carborundum (must offer) a complete system."[2]

Organizational Overhaul. To offer such a system, management had to overhaul important parts of the organization:

(1) The company needed to enhance its knowledge of the total system. As Wendel explains:

> "We felt we had excellent knowledge of coated abrasive products, but that we didn't have the application and machine know-how in depth. To be really successful in the business, we had to know as much about the machine tools as we did the abrasives."[3]

To fill this need, Carborundum made three acquisitions—The Tysaman Machine Company, which builds heavy-duty snagging, billet grinding, and abrasive cut-off machines; Curtis Machine Company, a maker of belt sanders; and Pangborn Corporation, which supplied systems capability in abrasive blast cleaning and finishing.

(2) The company's abrasive divisions were reorganized, and the management of them was realigned to accommodate the new philosophy and its application. The company found that *centering responsibility for the full system in one profit center* proved to be the most effective method of coordinating approaches in application engineering, choice of distribution channels, brand identification, field sales operations, and so forth. This method was particularly valuable for integrating the acquisitions into the new program.

(3) An Abrasives Systems Center was established to handle development work and to solve customer problems.

(4) Technical conferences and seminars were held to educate customers on the new developments.

(5) Salesmen were trained in machine and application knowledge.

Planning. A key tool in the systems approach is planning—in particular, the use of what I like to call "total business plans." (This term emphasizes the contrast with company plans that cover only limited functions.) At Carborundum, total business plans are developed with extreme care by the operating companies and divisions. Very specific objectives are established, and then detailed action programs are outlined to achieve these objectives. The action programs extend throughout the organization, including the manufacturing and development branches of the operating unit. Management sets specific dates for the completion of action steps and defines who is responsible for them. Also, it carefully measures results against established objectives. This is done both in the financial reporting system and in various marketing committees.

Quantitative Methods. Carborundum has utilized various operations research techniques, like decision tree analysis and PERT, to aid in molding plans and strategies. For example, one analysis, which concerned itself with determining the necessity for plant expansion, was based on different possible levels of success for the marketing plan. In addition, the computer has been used for inventory management, evaluation of alternate pricing strategies for systems selling, and the measurement of marketing achievements against goals.

It should be noted, though, that these quantitative techniques are management tools only and that much of the application of systems thinking to the redeployment of Carborundum's business is qualitative in nature.

Gains Achieved. As a consequence of these developments, the company has opened up vast new markets. To quote Carborundum's president again:

> "Customers don't want a grinding wheel, they want metal removed. . . .
> The U.S. and Canadian market for abrasives amounts to $700 million a
> year. But what companies spend on stock removal—to bore, grind, cut,
> shape, and finish metal—amounts of $30 billion a year."[4]

Illustrating this market expansion in the steel industry is Carborundum's commercial success with three new developments—hot grinding, an arborless wheel to speed metal removal and cut grinding costs, and high-speed conditioning of carbon steel billets. All represent conversions from nonabrasive methods. Carborundum now also finds that the close relationship with customers gives it a competitive edge, opens top customer management doors, gains entree for salesmen with prospects they had never been able

EXHIBIT II. WORK FLOW AND SYSTEMS CHART FOR MANAGEMENT OF NEW PRODUCTS.

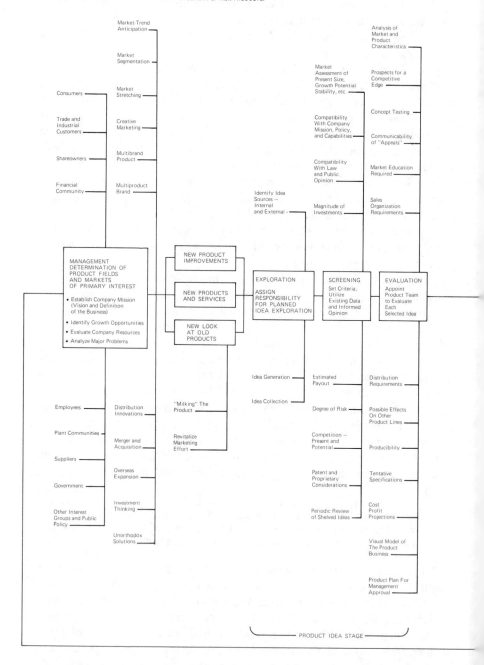

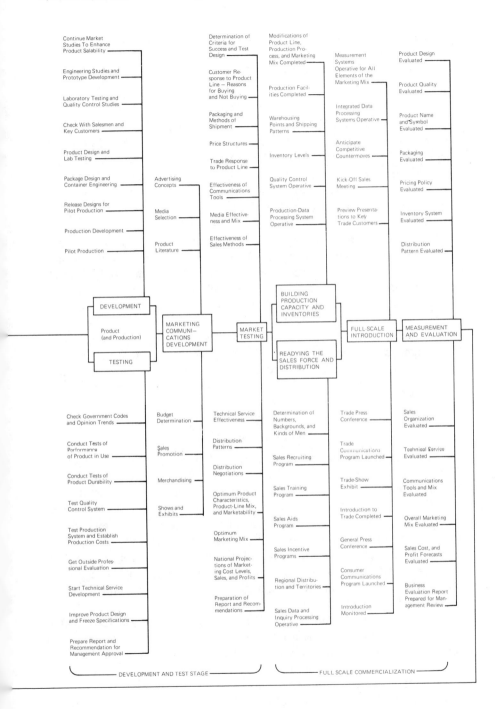

to "crack" before. Perhaps the ultimate accolade is the company's report that customers even come to the organization itself, regarding it as a consultant as well as a supplier.

Profitable innovation

The intense pressure to originate successful new products cannot be met without methodologies calculated to enhance the probabilities of profitable innovation. The systems approach has a bearing here, too. Exhibit II shows a model for "tracking" products through the many stages of ideation, development, and testing to ultimate full-scale commercialization. This diagram is in effect a larger version of the "New Product Development" box in Exhibit I.

Observe that this is a logical (specifically, sequential), rather than numerical, model. While some elements of the total system (e.g., alternate distribution channels and various media mixes) can be analyzed by means of operations research techniques, the model has not been cast in mathematical terms. Rather, the flow diagram as a whole is used as a checklist to make sure "all bases are covered" and to help organize the chronological sequence of steps in new product development. It also serves as a conceptual foundation for formal PERT application, should management desire such a step, and for the gradual development of a series of equations linking together elements in the diagrams, should it seem useful to experiment with mathematical models.

Marketing intelligence

The traditional notion of marketing research is fast becoming antiquated. For it leads to dreary chronicles of the past rather than focusing on the present and shedding light on the future. It is particularistic, tending to concentrate on the study of tiny fractions of a marketing problem rather than on the problem as a whole. It lends itself to assuaging the curiosity of the moment, to fire-fighting, to resolving internecine disputes. It is a slave to technique. I shall not, therefore, relate the term *marketing research* to the systems approach—although I recognize, of course, that some leading businessmen and writers are breathing new life and scope into the ideas referred to by that term.

The role of the systems approach is to help evolve a *marketing intelligence* system tailored to the needs of each marketer. Such a system would serve as the ever-alert nerve center of the marketing operation. It would have these major characteristics:

- Continuous surveillance of the market.
- A team of research techniques used in tandem.
- A network of data sources.

- Integrated analysis of data from the various sources.
- Effective utilization of automatic data-processing equipment to distill mountains of raw information speedily.
- Strong concentration not just on reporting findings but also on practical, non-oriented recommendations.

Concept in Use. A practical instance of the use of such an intelligence system is supplied by Mead Johnson Nutritionals (division of Mead Johnson & Company), manufacturers of Metrecal, Pablum, Bib, Nutrament, and other nutritional specialties. As Exhibit III shows, the company's Marketing Intelligence Department has provided information from these sources:

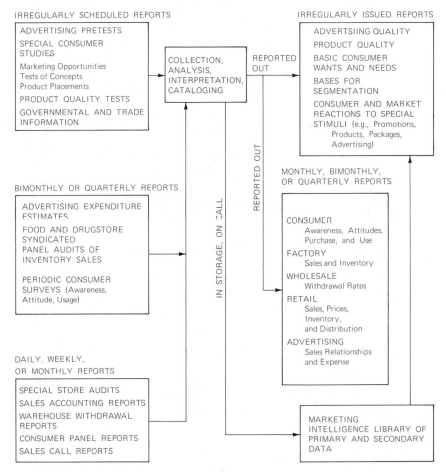

IRREGULARLY SCHEDULED REPORTS

ADVERTISING PRETESTS
SPECIAL CONSUMER STUDIES
Marketing Opportunities
Tests of Concepts
Product Placements
PRODUCT QUALITY TESTS
GOVERNMENTAL AND TRADE INFORMATION

COLLECTION, ANALYSIS, INTERPRETATION, CATALOGING

REPORTED OUT

IRREGULARLY ISSUED REPORTS

ADVERTSIING QUALITY
PRODUCT QUALITY
BASIC CONSUMER WANTS AND NEEDS
BASES FOR SEGMENTATION
CONSUMER AND MARKET REACTIONS TO SPECIAL STIMULI (e.g., Promotions, Products, Packages, Advertising)

BIMONTHLY OR QUARTERLY REPORTS

ADVERTISING EXPENDITURE ESTIMATES
FOOD AND DRUGSTORE SYNDICATED PANEL AUDITS OF INVENTORY SALES
PERIODIC CONSUMER SURVEYS (Awareness, Attitude, Usage)

REPORTED OUT

IN STORAGE, ON CALL

MONTHLY, BIMONTHLY, OR QUARTERLY REPORTS

CONSUMER
Awareness, Attitudes, Purchase, and Use
FACTORY
Sales and Inventory
WHOLESALE
Withdrawal Rates
RETAIL
Sales, Prices, Inventory, and Distribution
ADVERTISING
Sales Relationships and Expense

DAILY, WEEKLY, OR MONTHLY REPORTS

SPECIAL STORE AUDITS
SALES ACCOUNTING REPORTS
WAREHOUSE WITHDRAWAL REPORTS
CONSUMER PANEL REPORTS
SALES CALL REPORTS

MARKETING INTELLIGENCE LIBRARY OF PRIMARY AND SECONDARY DATA

EXHIBIT III
Mead Johnson's marketing intelligence system

WHAT IS TH

There seems to be agreement that the systems approach sprang to life as a semantically idenifiable term sometime during World War II. It was associated with the problem of how to bomb targets deep in Germany more effectively from British bases, with the Manhattan Project, and with studies of optimum search patterns for destroyers to use in locating U-boats during the Battle of the North Atlantic.* Subsequently, it was utilized in the defeat of the Berlin blockade. It has reached its present culmination in the success of great military systems such as Polaris and Minuteman.

Not surprisingly, the parallels between military and marketing strategies being what they are, the definition of the systems approach propounded by The RAND Corporation for the U.S. Air Force is perfectly apt for marketers:

"An inquiry to aid a decision-maker choose a course of action by systematically investigating his proper objectives, comparing quantitatively where possible the costs, effectiveness, and risks associated with the alternatives policies or strategies for achieving them, and *formulating additional alternatives if those examined are found wanting.*"†

The systems approach is thus an orderly, "architectural" discipline for dealing with complex problems of choice under uncertainty.

Typically, in such problems, multiple and possible conflicting objectives exist. The task of the systems analyst is to specify a closed operating network in which the components will work together so as to yield the optimum balance of economy, efficiency, and risk minimization. Put more broadly, the systems approach attempts to apply the "scientific method" to complex marketing problems studied *as a whole*; it seeks to discipline marketing.

But disciplining marketing is no easy matter. Marketing must be perceived as a *process* rather than as a series of isolated, discrete actions; competitors must be viewed as components of each marketer's own system. The process must also be comprehended as involving a flow and counter-flow of information and behavior between marketers and customers. Some years ago, Marion Harper, Jr., now chairman of The Interpublic Group of Companies, Inc., referred to the flow of information in marketing communications as the cycle of "listen (i.e., marketing research), publish (messages, media), listen (more

---

- A continuing large-scale consumer market study covering attitudinal and behavioral data dealing with weight control.
- Nielsen store audit data, on a bimonthly basis.
- A monthly sales audit conducted among a panel of 100 high-volume food stores in 20 markets to provide advance indications of brand share shifts.
- Supermarket warehouse withdrawal figures from Time, Inc.'s new service, Selling Areas-Marketing, Inc.
- Salesmen's weekly reports (which, in addition to serving the purposes of sales management control, call for reconnaissance on competitive promotions, new products launches, price changes, and so forth).
- Advertising expenditure data, by media class, from the company's accounting department.
- Figures on sales and related topics from company factories.
- Competitive advertising expenditure and exposure data, supplied by

'STEMS APPROACH?

marketing research), revise, publish, listen. . . ." More recently, Raymond A. Bauer referred to the "transactional" nature of communications as a factor in the motivations, frames of reference, needs, and so forth of recipients of messages. The desires of the communicator alone are but part of the picture.‡

Pushing this new awareness of the intricacies of markting communications still further, Theodore Levitt identified the interactions between five different forces—source effect (i.e., the reputation or credibility of the sponsor of the message), sleeper effect (the declining influence of source credibility with the passage of time), message effect (the character and quality of the message), communicator effect (the impact of the transmitter—e.g., a salesman), and audience effect (the competence and responsibility of the audience).§ Casting a still broader net are efforts to model the entire purchasing process, and perhaps the ultimate application of the systems concept is attempts to make mathematical models of the entire marketing process.

Mounting recognition of the almost countless elements involved in marketing and of the mind-boggling complexity of their interactions is a wholesome (though painful) experience. Nevertheless, I believe we must not ignore other ramifications of the systems approach which are qualitative in nature. For the world of marketing offers a vast panorama of non- or part-mathematical systems and opportunities to apply systems thinking. We must not become so bedazzled by the brouhaha of the operations research experts as to lose sight of the larger picture.

---

*See Glen McDaniel, "The Meaning of The Systems Movement to the Acceleration and Direction of the American Economy," in *Proceedings of the 1964 Systems Engineering Conference* (New York, Clapp & Poliak, Inc., 1964), p. I; see also E. S. Quade, editor, *Analysis for Military Decisions* (Santa Monica, California, The RAND Corporation, 1964), p. 6.
†Quade, op. cit., p. 4.
‡"Communications as a Transaction," *Public Opinion Quarterly*, Spring 1963, p. 83.
§See Theodore Levitt, *Industrial Purchasing Behavior* (Boston, Division of Research, Harvard Business School, 1965), p. 25ff.

---

the division's advertising agencies at periodic intervals.

• A panel of weight-conscious women.

To exemplify the type of outputs possible from this system, Mead Johnson will be able, with the help of analyses of factory sales data, warehouse withdrawal information, and consumer purchases from Nielsen, to monitor transactions at each stage of the flow of goods through the distribution channel and to detect accumulations or developing shortages. Management will also be able to spot sources of potential problems in time to deal with them effectively. For example, if factory sales exceed consumer purchases, more promotional pressure is required. By contrast, if factory sales lag behind consumer purchases, sales effort must be further stimulated.

Similarly, the company has been able to devise a practical measurement of advertising's effectiveness in stimulating sales—a measurement that is particularly appropriate to fast-moving packaged goods. By relating advertising outlays and exposure data to the number of prospects trying out a product during a campaign (the number is obtained from the continuing consumer survey), it is possible to calculate the advertising cost recruiting such a prospect. By persisting in such analyses during several campaigns, the relative value of alternative advertising approaches can be weighed. Since measurement of the sales, as opposed to the communications, effects of promotion is a horrendously difficult, costly, and chancy process, the full significance of this achievement is difficult to exaggerate.

Benefits Realized. Mead Johnson's marketing intelligence system has been helpful to management in a number of ways. In addition to giving executives early warning of new trends and problems, and valuable insights into future conditions, it is leading to a systematic *body* of knowledge about company markets rather than to isolated scraps of information. This knowledge in turn should lead ultimately to a theory of marketing in each field that will explain the mysteries that baffle marketers today. What is more, the company expects that the system will help to free its marketing intelligence people from fire-fighting projects so that they can concentrate on long-term factors and eventually be more consistently creative.

Despite these gains, it is important to note that Mead Johnson feels it has a long road still to travel. More work is needed in linking individual data banks. Conceptual schemes must be proved out in practice; ways must still be found to reduce an awesome volume of data, swelled periodically by new information from improved sources, so as to make intelligence more immediately acessible to decision makers. And perhaps the biggest problem of the moment, one underlying some of the others, is the difficulty in finding qualified marketing-oriented programmers.

Physical distribution

A veritable revolution is now taking place in physical distribution. Total systems are being evolved out of the former hodgepodge of separate responsibilities, which were typically scattered among different departments of the same company. These systems include traffic and transportation, warehousing, materials handling, protective packaging, order processing, production planning, inventory control, customer service, market forecasting, and plant and warehouse site selection. Motivating this revolution are the computer, company drives to reduce distribution costs, and innovations in transportation, such as jet air freight, container ships, the interstate highway network, and larger and more versatile freight cars.

Distribution is one area of marketing where the "bread-and-butter" uses of the computer are relatively easily deployed for such functions as order processing, real-time inventory level reports, and tracking the movements of goods. Further into the future lie mathematical models which will include every factor bearing on distribution. Not only will packaging, materials handling, transportation and warehouse, order processing, and related costs be considered in such models; also included will be sales forecasts by product, production rates by factory, warehouse locations and capacities, speeds of different carriers, etc. In short, a complete picture will be developed for management.

Program in Action. The experiences of the Norge Division of Borg-Warner Corporation point up the values of the systems approach in physical distribution. The firm was confronted externally with complaints from its dealers and distributors, who were trying to cope with swollen inventories and the pressures of "loading deals." Internally, because coordination of effort between the six departments involved in distribution was at a minimum, distribution costs and accounts receivable were mounting persistently.

To grapple with this situation, Norge undertook a comprehensive analysis of its distrbution system. Out of this grew a new philosophy. A company executive has described the philosophy to me as follows:

> "An effective system of physical distribution cannot begin at the end of the production line. It must also apply at the very beginning of the production process—at the planning, scheduling, and forecasting stages. Logistics, in short, is part of a larger marketing system, not just an evaluation of freight rates. We must worry not only about finished refrigerators, but also about the motors coming from another manufacturer, and even about where the copper that goes into those motors will come from. We must be concerned with *total flow.*"

To implement this philosophy, the appliance manufacturer took the following steps:

(1) It reorganized the forecasting, production scheduling, warehousing, order processing, and shipping functions into *one* department headed by a director of physical distribution.

(2) The management information system was improved with the help of EDP equipment tied into the communications network. This step made it possible to process and report data more speedily on orders received, inventory levels, and the actual movement of goods.

(3) Management used a combination of computer and manual techniques to weigh trade-offs among increased costs of multiple warehousing, reduced long-haul freight and local drayage costs, reduced inventory pipeline, and the sales value of an improved "total" product offering. Also assessed were trade-offs between shorter production runs and higher inventory levels, thereby challenging the traditional "wisdom" of production-oriented managers that the longer the run, the better.

(4) The company is setting up new regional warehouses.

As a result of these moves, Norge has been able to lower inventories throughout its sales channels and to reduce accounts receivable. These gains have led, in turn, to a reduction of the company's overall investment and a concomitant increase in profitability.

It is essential to note that even though Norge has used operations research as part of its systems approach, many aspects of the program are qualitative. Thus far, the company has found that the development of an all-encompassing model is not warranted because of (a) the time and cost involved, (b) the probability that the situation will change before the model is completed, (c) a concern that such a model would be so complex as to be unworkable, and (d) the difficulty of testing many of the assumptions used. In addition, management has not tried to quantify the impact of its actions on distributor and retailer attitudes and behavior, possible competitive countermoves, and numerous other factors contributing to results.

Toward total integration

The integration of systems developed for product management, product innovation, marketing intelligence, physical distribution, and the other functions or "subsystems" embraced by the terms *marketing* creates a total marketing system. Thus, marketing plans composed according to a step-by-step outline, ranging from enunciation of objectives and implementational steps to audit and adjustment to environmental changes, constitute a complete application of systems theory. Further, as the various subsystems of the overall system are linked quantitatively, so that the effect of modifications in one element can be detected in other elements, and as the influences of competitive moves on each element are analyzed numerically, then the total scheme becomes truly sophisticated.

Pluses and minuses

Two elements underlie the use and benefits of systems theory—order and knowledge. The first is a homely virtue, the second a lofty goal. Marketing is obviously not alone among all human pursuits in needing them; but, compared with its business neighbors, production and finance, marketing's need is acute indeed. The application of the systems concept can bring considerable advantages. It offers:

- A methodical problem-solving orientation—with a broader frame of reference so that all aspects of a problem are examined.
- Coordinated deployment of all appropriate tools of marketing.
- Greater efficiency and economy of marketing operations.

- Quicker recognition of impending problems, made possible by better understanding of the complex interplay of many trends and forces.
- A stimulus to innovation.
- A means of quantitatively verifying results.

These functional benefits in turn yield rich rewards in the marketplace. The most important gains are:

A deeper penetration of existing markets—As an illustration, the Advanced Data Division of Litton Industries has become a leader in the automatic revenue control business by designing systems meshing together "hardware" and "software."

A broadening of markets—For example, the tourist industry has attracted millions of additional travelers by creating packaged tours that are really product-service systems. These systems are far more convenient and economical than anything the consumer could assemble himself.

An extension of product lines—Systems management makes it more feasible to seek out compatibilities among independently developed systems. Evidence of this idea is the work of automatic control system specialists since the early 1950's.[5] Now similar signs are apparent in marketing. For example, Acme Visible Records is currently dovetailing the design and sale of its record-keeping systems with data-processing machines and forms.

A lessening of competition or a strengthened capacity to cope with competition—The systems approach tends to make a company's product line more unique and attractive. Carborundum's innovation in metal-removal systems is a perfect illustration of this.

Problems in practice

Having just enumerated in glowing terms the benefits of the systems approach, realism demands that I give "equal time" to the awesome difficulties its utilization presents. There is no better evidence of this than the gulf between the elegant and sophisticated models with which recent marketing literature abounds and the actual number of situations in which those models really work. For the truth of the matter is that we are still in the foothills of this development, despite the advances of a few leaders. Let us consider some of the obstacles.

Time and Manpower Costs. First of all, the systems approach requires considerable time to implement; it took one company over a year to portray its physical distribution system in a mathematical model before it could even begin to solve its problems. RCA's Electronic Data Processing Division reports models taking three to five years to build, after which holes in the data network have to be filled and the model tested against history. Add to this the need for manpower of exceptional intellectual ability, conceptual skills, and specialized education—manpower that is in exceedingly short supply. Because the problems are complex and involve all elements of the business, one man alone cannot solve them. He lacks the knowledge, tools, and controls. And so many people must be involved. If follows that the activation of systems theory can be very costly.

Absence of "Canned" Solutions. Unlike other business functions where standardized approaches to problem solving are available, systems must be tailored to the individual situation of each firm. Even the same problem in different companies in the same industry will frequently lead to different solutions because of the impact of other inputs, unique perceptions of the environment, and varying corporate missions. These factors, too, compound time and expense demands.

"Net Uncertainties." Even after exhaustive analysis, full optimization of a total problem cannot be obtained. Some uncertainty will always remain and must be dealt with on the basis of judgment and experience.

Lack of Hard Data. In the world of engineering, the systems evolved to date have consisted all or mostly of machines. Systems engineers have been wise enough to avoid the irrationalities of man until they master control of machines. Marketing model-builders, however, have not been able to choose, for the distributor, salesman, customer, and competitor are central to marketing. We must, therefore, incorporate not only quantitative measures of the dimensions of things and processes (e.g., market potential, media outlays, and shipping rates), but also psychological measures of comprehension, attitudes, motivations, intentions, needs—yes, even psychological measures of physical behavior. What is needed is a marriage of the physical and behavioral sciences—and we are about as advanced in this blending of disciplines as astronomy was in the Middle Ages.

Consider the advertising media fields as an instance of the problem:

> A number of advertising agencies have evolved linear programming or simulation techniques to assess alternate media schedules. One of the key sets of data used covers the probabilities of exposure to all or part of the audience of a TV program, magazine, or radio station. But what is exposure, and how do you measure it? What is optimum frequency of exposure, and how do you measure it? How does advertising prevail on the predispositions and perceptions of a potential customer? Is it better to judge advertising effects on the basis of exposure opportunity, "impact" (whatever that is), messages retained, message comprehension, or attitude shifts or uptrends in purchase intentions? We do not have these answers yet.

Even assuming precise knowledge of market dimensions, product performance, competitive standings, weights of marketing pressure exerted by direct selling, advertising and promotion, and so on, most marketers do not yet know, except in isolated cases, how one force will affect another. For instance, how does a company "image" affect the setting in which its salesmen work? How does a company's reputation for service affect customer buying behavior?

Nature of Marketing Men. Man is an actor on this stage in another role. A good many marketing executives, in the deepest recesses of their psyches, are artists, not analysts. For them, marketing is an art form, and, in my opinion, they really do not want it to be any other way. Their temperament is antipathetic to system, order, knowledge. They enjoy flying by the seat of their pants—though you will never get them to admit it. They revel in chaos, abhor facts, and fear research. They hate to be trammeled by written plans. And they love to spend, but are loathe to assess the results of their spending.

Obviously, such men cannot be sold readily on the value and practicality of the systems approach! It takes time, experience, and many facts to influence their thinking.

Surmounting the barriers

All is not gloom, however. The barriers described are being overcome in various ways. While operations research techniques have not yet made much headway in evolving total marketing systems and in areas where man is emotionally engaged, their accomplishments in solving inventory control problems, in sales analysis, in site selection, and in other areas have made many businessmen more sympathetic and open-minded to them.

Also, mathematical models—even the ones that do not work well yet—serve to bolster comprehension of the need for system as well as to clarify the intricacies among subsystems. Many models are in this sense learning models; they teach us how to ask more insightful questions. Moreover, they pinpoint data gaps and invite a more systematized method for reaching judgments where complete information does not exist. Because the computer abhors vague generalities, it forces managers to analyze their roles, objectives, and criteria more concretely. Paradoxically, it demands more, not less, of its human masters.

Of course, resistance to mathematical models by no means makes resistance to the systems approach necessary. There are many cases where no need may ever arise to use mathematics or computers. For the essence of the systems approach is not its technique, but the enumeration of options and their implications. A simple checklist may be the only tool needed. I would even argue that some hard thinking in a quiet room may be enough. This being the case, the whole trend to more analysis and logic in management thinking, as reflected in business periodicals, business schools, and in practices of many companies, will work in favor of the development of the systems approach.

It is important to note at this juncture that not all marketers need the systems approach in its formal, elaborate sense. The success of some companies is rooted in other than marketing talents; their expertise may lie in finance, technology, administration, or even in personnel—as in the case of holding companies having an almost uncanny ability to hire brilliant operating managers and the self-control to leave them alone. In addition, a very simple marketing operation—for example, a company marketing one product through one distribution channel—may have no use for the systems concept.

Applying the approach

Not illogically, there is a system for applying the systems approach. It may be outlined as a sequence of steps:

1. *Define the problem and clarify objectives.* Care must be exercised not to accept the view of the propounder of the problem lest the analyst be defeated at the outset.

2. *Test the definition of the problem.* Expand its parameters to the limit. For example, to solve physical distribution problems it is necessary to study the marketplace (customer preferences, usage rates, market size, and so forth), as well as the production process (which plants produce which items most efficiently, what the interplant movements of raw materials are, and so forth). Delineate the extremes of these factors, their changeability, and the limitations on management's ability to work with them.

3. *Build a model.* Portray all factors graphically, indicating logical and chronological sequences—the dynamic flow of information, decisions, and events. "Closed circuits" should be used where there is information feedback or go, no-go and recycle signals (see Exhibit II).

4. *Set concrete objectives.* For example, if a firm wants to make daily deliveries to every customer, prohibitive as the cost may be, manipulation of the model will yield one set of answers. But if the desire is to optimize service at lowest cost, then another set of answers will be needed. The more crisply and precisely targets are stated, the more specific the results will be.

5. *Develop alternative solutions.* It is crucial to be as open-minded as possible at this stage. The analyst must seek to expend the list of options rather than merely assess those given to him, then reduce the list to a smaller number of practical or relevant ones.

6. *Set up criteria or tests of relative value.*

7. *Quantify some or all of the factors or "variables."* The extent to which this is done depends, of course, on management's inclinations and the "state of the art."

8. *Manipulate the model.* That is, weigh the costs, effectiveness, profitability, and risks of each alternative.

9. *Interpret the results, and choose one or more courses of action.*

10. *Verify the results.* Do they make sense when viewed against the world as executives know it? Can their validity be tested by experiments and investigations?

Forethought and perspective

Successful systems do not blossom overnight. From primitive beginnings, they evolve over a period of time as managers and systems specialists learn to understand each other better, and learn how to structure problems and how to push out the frontiers of the "universe" with which they are dealing. Companies must be prepared to invest time, money, and energy in making systems management feasible. This entails a solid foundation of historical data even before the conceptual framework for the system can be constructed. Accordingly, considerable time should be invested at the outset in *thinking* about the problem, its appropriate scope, options, and criteria of choice before plunging into analysis.

Not only technicians, but most of us have a way of falling in love with techniques. We hail each one that comes along—*deus ex machina*. Historically, commercial research has wallowed in several such passions (e.g., probability sampling, motivation research, and semantic scaling), and now operations research appears to be doing the same thing. Significantly, each technique has come, in the fullness of time, to take its place as one, but only one, instrument in the research tool chest. We must therefore have a broad and dispassionate perspective on the systems approach at this juncture. We must recognize that the computer does not possess greater magical properties than the abacus. It, too, is a tool, albeit a brilliant one.

Put another way, executives must continue to exercise their judgment and experience. Systems analysis is no substitute for common sense. The computer must adapt itself to their styles, personalities, and modes of problem solving. It is an aid to management, not a surrogate. Businessmen may be slow, but the good ones are bright; the electronic monster, by contrast, is a speedy idiot. It demands great acuity of wit from its human managers lest they be deluged in an avalanche of useless paper. (The story is told of a sales manager who had just found out about the impressive capabilities of his company's computer and called for a detailed sales analysis of all products. The report was duly prepared and wheeled into his office on a dolly.)

Systems users must be prepared to revise continually. There are two reasons for this. First, the boundaries of systems keep changing; constraints are modified; competition makes fresh incursions; variables, being what they are, vary, and new ones crop up. Second, the analytical process is iterative. Usually, one "pass" at problem formulation and searches for solutions will not suffice, and it will be necessary to "recycle" as early hypotheses are challenged and new, more fruitful insights are stimulated by the inquiry. Moreover, it is impossible to select objectives without knowledge of their effects and costs. That knowledge can come only from anlysis, and it freqeuntly requires review and revision.

Despite all the efforts at quantification, system analysis is still largely an art. It relies frequently on inputs based on human judgment; even when the inputs are numerical, they are determined, at least in part, by judgment. Similarly, the outputs must pass through the sieve of human interpretation. Hence, there is a positive correlation between the pay-off from a system and the managerial level involved in its design. The higher the level, the more rewarding the results.

Finally, let me observe that marketing people merit their own access to computers as well as programmers who understand marketing. Left in the hands of accountants, the timing, content, and format of output are often out of phase with marketing needs.

Conclusion

Nearly 800 years ago a monk wrote the following about St. Godric, a merchant later turned hermit:

> "He laboured not only as a merchant but also as a shipman . . . to Denmark, Flanders, and Scotland; in which lands he found certain rare, and therefore more precious, wares, which he carried to other parts wherein he knew them to be least familiar, and coveted by the inhabitants beyond the price of gold itself, wherefore he exchanged these wares for others coveted by men of other lands. . . ."[6]

How St. Godric "knew" his markets we are not told, marketing having been in a primitive state in 1170. How some of us marketers today "know" is, in my opinion, sometimes no less mysterious than it was eight centuries ago. But we are trying to change that, and I will hazard the not very venturesome forecast that the era of "by guess and by gosh" marketing is drawing to a close. One evidence of this trend is marketers' intensified search for knowledge that will improve their command over their destinies. This search is being spurred on by a number of powerful developments. To describe them briefly:

- The growing complexity of technology and the accelerating pace of technological innovation.
- The advent of the computer, inspiring and making possible analysis of the relationships between systems components.
- The intensification of competition, lent impetus by the extraordinary velocity of new product development and the tendency of diversification to thrust everybody into everybody else's business.
- The preference of buyers for purchasing from as few sources as possible, thereby avoiding the problems of assembling bits and pieces themselves and achieving greater reliability, economy, and administrative convenience. (Mrs. Jones would rather buy a complete vacuum cleaner from one source than the housing from one manufacturer, the hose from another, and the attachments from still another. And industrial buyers are not much different from Mrs. Jones. They would rather buy an automated machine tool from one manufacturer than design and assemble the components themselves. Not to be overlooked, in this connection, is the tremendous influence of the U.S. government in buying systems for its military and aerospace programs.)

The further development and application of the systems approach to marketing represents, in my judgment, the leading edge in both marketing theory and practice. At the moment, we are still much closer to St. Godric than to the millenium, and the road will be rocky and tortuous. But if we are ever to convert marketing into a more scientific pursuit, this is the road we must travel. The systems concept can teach us how our businesses really behave in the marketing arena, thereby extending managerial leverage and control. It can help us to confront more intelligently the awesome complexity of marketing, to deal with the hazards and opportunities of technological change, and to cope with the intensification of competition. And in the process, the concept will help us to feed the hungry maws of our expensive computers with more satisfying fare.

NOTES

1. See, for example, Donald F. Cox and Robert E. Good, "How to Build a Marketing Information System," *Harvard Business Review* (May-June, 1967) p. 145.
2. Abrasive Maker's Systems Approach Opens New Markets," *Steel*, December 27, 1965, p. 38.
3. *Ibid.*
4. "Carborundum Grinds at Faster Clip," *Business Week*, July 23, 1966, pp. 58, 60.
5. See *Automatic and Manual Control: Papers Contributed to the Conference at Cranford, 1951*, edited by A. Tustin (London, Butterworth's Scientific Publications, 1952).
6. *Life of St. Godric*, by Reginald, a monk of Durham, c. 1170.

42. Marketing Decision-Information Systems: an Emerging View*

David B. Montgomery and Glen L. Urban

Marketing decision-information systems are composed of four key elements: a data bank, a model bank, a measurement-statistics bank, and a communications capability. If full advantage is to be taken of the new information technology, a coordinated, balanced growth of the system components must be achieved. The authors extend their initial information systems proposal to include further design concepts and practical examples.

Recent years have witnessed an increasing interest in marketing information systems. It is currently fashionable for companies to have such systems under development and the professional and popular management literature abound with articles describing system developments. In the main, these systems have tended to emphasize data collection, storage, retrieval, and display functions of a marketing information system. Yet, if the full potential of the new information technology is to be harnessed for management use, it seems imperative to take a broader view of information

*SOURCE: Journal of Marketing Research, Vol. VII (May 1970), pp. 226-234. Reprinted by permission of the American Marketing Association.

systems. Information systems can be designed to assist managers directly in planning and decision making by combining management science, statistics, computer science, and market data into an integrated decision-information system.

The principal purposes of this article are: (1) to present a conceptual model for the evolutionary development of integrated marketing information systems, (2) to illustrate the need for a planned, coordinated growth of all components in the system, (3) to present design concepts relevant to the development of the components of the system, and (4) to identify new developments which will spur the evolution of marketing information systems and broaden the base of companies which may have access to the new technology. This article extends the analysis first presented in [N].

A conceptual model of a marketing information system

A marketing information system is composed of four major internal components: (1) a data bank, (2) a measurement-statistics bank, (3) a model bank, and (4) a communications capability. These internal components interact with two external elements: (1) the manager or user, and (2) the environment. (See the figure.)

The data bank provides the capacity to store and selectively retrieve data which result from monitoring the external environment and from internal corporate records. The manager will probably not be interested in the raw data per se. For decision purposes he will generally require the data to be processed. In the simplest case, he may require sales summaries or market share information. Thus the data bank must also provide the capacity to manipulate and transform data.

The data from the data bank may be displayed directly to the manager, but in many cases it will be analyzed by statistical methods. The measurement-statistics bank provides the capacity for more complex analysis of data such as multiple regression, cluster analysis, factor analysis, and multidimensional scaling. The measurement-statistics bank should also contain procedures for obtaining and evaluating subjective marketing judgment. For example, these judgmental measurements may be in the form of sales forecasts, forecasts of competitive promotion, or subjective utility assessments. Judgmental measurements have been and are likely to continue to be important inputs to marketing models. The judgmental data may be stored in the data bank for later use.

The model bank provides a variety of marketing models at different levels of complexity appropriate to the understanding and solution of

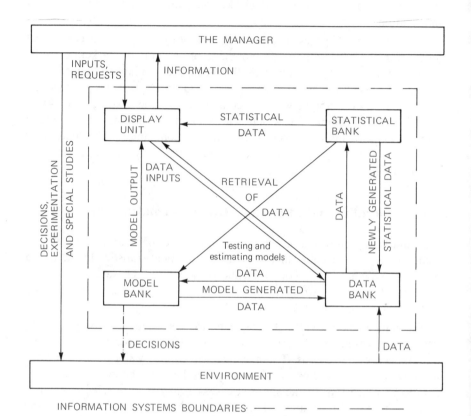

Decision-information system structure

marketing problems. Examples are budgeting models, new product planning models, and media selection models, which make use of the data from the data and measurement-statistics banks as well as direct user input and subjective measurements. The model bank interacts with the statistical components, since the adequacy of a model may be assessed by methods available in the measurement-statistics bank. In special cases models may interact with the environment, as when models are delegated authority to make routine decisions directly (e.g., as in certain inventory recorder systems and Amstutz' stock market model [C]).

The final system component is the communications capability. It gives a two-way link between the user and the system, a critical element since meaningful communication is necessary if the system is to be used.

The data bank-model bank interaction

These brief sketches indicate some of the interdependencies between system components. Perhaps the most crucial one is that between the models in the model bank and the data retained in the data bank. Marketing models generally require data for use in model formulation, choosing among alternative market response relationships, and model testing. Market data relevant to the dynamics of the market place are generated over time, often with considerable lapses between observations. Thus at any point, the development of a marketing model is constrained by the data (perhaps judgmental) available. If important information is missing, development will have to rely heavily on judgment until the appropriate data develop. While this is not meant to demean the role of judgment and sensitivity analysis of judgmental inputs to models, management's faith in models and its willingness to use them does seem positively related to the model's exposure to actual market data. Consequently, decisions made today on what data to obtain and retain in the data bank have implications for future model development.

Two recent examples from the experience of one of the authors will illustrate the point. The first example relates to a firm in the process of forming a multi-firm marketing information system in the pharmaceutical industry. One of the key elements in this new system is the development of models to assess the impact of competitive market communications. In this industry, these take three forms: journal advertising, direct mail to doctors, and details (sales calls) on doctors. Commercial data sources have existed for some time on each of these activities. Past use of the data has, however, tended to be for short-run assessment of the market. With old data discarded, data are available only back to 1967, which seriously limits the data base on which to formulate and test the dynamic measurement models. Now that models are being developed which require this data, more complete data retention in the future seems assured. The second example relates to a research study on a non U.S. market being done in conjunction with the international division of a large drug firm. In this international market, as well, much potentially valuable data (such as competitive detailing) has been discarded by its commercial supplier. Thus again, valuable raw material for model development has been lost because it was viewed as "current information" by the supplier, who gave no thought to the possibility of future model development.

These are not at all isolated examples. It is painful to contemplate the volume of potentially useful data discarded by both companies and commercial suppliers. The remedy seems clear. If a firm expects to become active in marketing models at any time in the next five years, it is imperative that it now assess something of the likely form of these models and their data requirements. This should then have an impact on decisions to obtain and retain data.

Further examples can be given of the interdependency between models and data. Models provide a framework for identifying what data should be collected and how it should be processed once obtained. In a recent paper Madansky [K] states ". . . that modeling has produced and will produce both the impetus within companies for an organized, unified, coherent data collection program and the spark for novel types of data to be collected." He cites an example in which a client, a multiproduct, multisales-area company, wanted a computer-based system to organize the vast volume of data it collected and purchased. The goal was to obtain useful information for advertising and sales promotion decisions. The first step was to structure a decision model based on variables for which data was already available or readily obtainable. The model identified additional data needs. It also prescribed the form of the data required for analysis. Thus it specified the manipulations and transformations required to provide the data in model-compatible form. In this case the transformation suggested a revision in the data collection procedure to make the data directly compatible with the model. In Madansky's words, ". . . we have gone from a decision model to a data bank organization scheme for the client." The Little-Lodish media selection model, MEDIAC, provides another example [I]. It utilizes only single media exposures and paired duplications of exposures in developing a media schedule. Hence, the model again specifies the data collection scheme—no triplication data, no quadruplication data, etc., are needed.

Integrated system implications for organization of system development

These interdependencies between systems components, particularly the intimate relation between models and data, have significant implications in composing teams assigned to develop a marketing information system. The corporate groups generally responsible for the various activities subsumed in the information system are: (1) market research, traditionally concerned with the types of data collected and programs and methods for its analysis (the measurement-statistics bank), (2) computer system group, generally responsible for maintaining computer-based data files and generating management reports (one aspect of the communications function), (3) operations research, usually responsible for models.

When the marketing information system is viewed as a data storage and retrieval system with some associated report generation and statistical analysis, the system development team will most likely be composed of representatives from marketing research and computer systems. This is not likely to lead to data and system design decisions which will serve future model development needs of the firm. What is needed is a system development team of representatives from all three functions to assure balanced system development. Perhaps the ideal would be a staff group (called something like marketing information services) with responsibility for the total system including marketing-operations research. It would have its own computer programming capability as well as access to computer hardware both internal and external to the firm. This latter point seems important in view of the frequent complaints from marketing personnel that they cannot get service from the corporate computer staff. Since most corporate computer staffs grew out of accounting type applications, large scale, routine data processing of billings, payrolls, and orders generally takes precedence over other applications. Consequently marketing will often have to access outside time sharing computer utilities and computers with remote batch processing capabilities.

The data bank

The data bank involves two primary aspects: (1) the data, and (2) computer-based and manual systems for data storage, retrieval, manipulation, and transformation. In the discussion of these two aspects, several emerging design concepts will be outlined.

The data

An extensive discussion of appropriate data for the data bank is outside the scope of this paper, but careful consideration must be given to the specification of what data will be maintained within the system. See [N] for some examples.

Data specification must give forethought to future activities in marketing models for the reasons cited before. For example, the collection and maintenance of competitive market activity data will be increasingly important (as better models are developed to assess the impact of these activities) to support the development of better models. Many of the data categories will subsequently be related to achieve a better understanding of market response. For example, data on copy and format in company advertisements may be related to advertising performance measures in order to learn systematically how the market is responding to these characteristics of ads. Cox and Good [D] report that one large consumer goods company is doing precisely that, while Diamond [E] has developed an on-line model called ADFORS which utilizes the results of such analysis.

A key concept in the design of a data bank is to maintain data in its most elemental, disaggregated form. For salesmen's call reports, disaggregated data might be details such as a person visited, time, place, sales aids used, etc. An aggregated form for such data might be simply the number of sales calls made by a salesman to accounts of a given type over some time period. Maintaining disaggregated data enhances the flexibility of its future use, to allow for organizing it differently for future, unknown purposes. Amstutz [C] discusses the benefits of future flexibility in his computerized portfolio selection system: "If initial data files had been structured to maintain information at the level of aggregation required when the system was begun, many operations of the present system would be precluded by data limitations."

Because of the high cost of physically storing disaggregated data, the data may not be maintained initially in computer disk storage, but on tapes, cards or even original work sheets. It is important, however, that it be preserved, to be accessed by model builders and managers when required.

The data bank should maintain information on who used which data and for what purposes. This should aid decisions on which data should be kept in high speed computer storage. Thus the data bank should gather information appropriate to adapting itself to better meet the needs of its users and developing specifications for the storage of disaggregated data.

Systems for processing the data

Two key issues in the development of the processing systems within the data bank are modularity and flexibility. Since the design of the data bank will be an evolving one rather than a one-shot, forever optimal system, the system must be readily adapted to change. Perfect foresight is not required if the system is flexible. Modularity in the processing systems (i.e., compartmentalization of the processing functions) will tend to minimize problems involved in adapting the processing systems to future requirements, since then existing moduals can be linked to meet the new demands.

Developing a variety of general commands to retrieve and manipulate data gives flexibility in data processing. These general commands may then operate on the data, whatever the data file may be. Although not specific to a particular data file, they greatly reduce the problems when a file is altered by additions, deletions, or reorganization. An example of an operational data handling system using such general commands is the DATA-NAL system devloped by Miller [M].

Security systems

The data bank must have security systems at both the processing systems and data levels. At the systems level the system itself must be protected from the user, to prevent inadvertent altering of the system programs. Such accidents can be costly and frustrating. A more interesting aspect is the need for data security systems. The problem here is who may have access to what. It is clear that individuals below a certain level in the organization should not have access to certain types of information. But there may be data which should not be conveniently accessible to, say, the marketing vice president. A case in point is given by Amstutz [B] in which a sales vice president was able to access very detailed information on sales results in individual territories which distracted him from his real assignment, providing overall market planning and strategy.

In addition to vertical security, there is a need for horizontal security systems. As Ackoff [A] notes, organizational harmony and efficiency are not necessarily enhanced by letting, say, marketing and production have complete access to one another's data files. Horizontal security between firms becomes important with the emergence of the multi-firm marketing information system.

Communication of data

A data bank must be accessible to the manager. An interactive man/system operation is an important system design aspect, to be discussed later. However, the capability a remote terminal provides a manager does allow the data bank to carry out one more function, "data browsing," where the manager can look at various aspects of operations data to find problems before they are severe enough to get management's attention through standard means such as exception reporting.

Although the ability to access data in a relevant form is important, it is not enough. Information systems must digest, analyze, and interpret data so the managers can improve decisions. If the data bank is more emphasized than analysis and models, the manager may suffer a data overload and receive little help in decision making. The model bank and the measurement-statistics bank are designed to help the manager analyze and make sense out of data.

The model bank

The model bank provides the marketing information system with a capability to assist directly in decision making. It should contain many models appropriate for purposes such as understanding market behavior, diagnosis, control, prediction, and strategy formulation, all likely to be frequently used. Models for analysis of one-time market situations will remain, but they will often be "back-of-the-envelope" models like Hess' price timing model [G]. Unless they have potential for recurrent use they will not be made permanent in the computrized model bank, although they may temporarily reside there.

Some model bank design aspects

The model bank should contain models of varying levels of detail within each class of models and for each marketing problem area, to reflect alternate model cost/benefit tradeoffs. More model detail is generally useful, but as more variables are included in the model, more phenomena are considered, and more disaggregation takes place, the time and financial costs of model development, input generation, operation, maintenance, and testing rapidly increase. The best level of detail in a particular application will depend on time and resource constraints on model development and operation as compared to improvement in decision because of the higher level of detail.

The model bank concept presents a partial solution to this problem by making models of varying levels of detail for a particular problem available to the decision maker. For example, SPRINTER, a model for the analysis of frequently purchased consumer goods, exists in three levels. Mod I is a very simple description of the diffusion process. Mod II adds the controllable variables of advertising and price. Mod III uses a very detailed market response model based on the behavioral buying process and adds sampling, coupons, margins, and sales calls [R]. Mod I is simple but runs at 10% of the cost of Mod III, and 50% of the cost of Mod II. With these alternatives the manager can select the model which has the best cost/benefit tradeoff for his particular problem.

The model bank might even contain a number of models at a given level of detail for a given problem with each model particularly meaningful to specific managers and their decision styles. Thus, the model bank may ultimately have several levels of model detail and multiple models at each level to service the decision needs of various marketing managers. Development of the model bank must be an evolutionary, adaptive process which adjusts to the varied and changing needs of the managers.

The models should be compatible with models at other levels of detail. Simpler models could be used to evaluate a large number of alternatives and the more detailed ones to evaluate the specific outcomes of one or a few of the alternatives generated by the less detailed model. For example, an aggregate advertising budget model might be used to specify an annual budget. Then a media allocation model could be used to indicate the best media schedule and finally this schedule could be submitted to a micro-analytic simulation to obtain detailed attitude change and micro-purchase response results by market segment. The results might indicate the need for adjustment of the preceding analysis of budget level and media schedule and provide a benchmark for control purposes once a policy has been implemented. This compatible use of models allows low cost examination of many alternatives and a high level of model detail. It should strengthen the value of the model bank and improve its ability to serve decision makers.

Trends in marketing models

The model bank concept is supported by a number of new developments in modeling.[1] The first is the emergence of a problem-centered orientation. Much of the early work in marketing models could be characterized as techniques looking for problems, which often sacrificed marketing relevance to satisfy a given solution technique. The rush to formulate the media selection problem as a linear program is a case in point. There are now hopeful signs that marketing problems will begin to dominate techniques in the formulation of marketing models. This trend has been spurred by maturing experience in structuring marketing models, the realization that successful implementation and use depend on this approach, and steady progress in management science and operations research in approaching more realistic and complex problems. Although optimization techniques are improving, the trend in marketing is to non-algorithmic techniques such as heuristic programming and simulation. These are more capable of rich representation of the interdependent and dynamic nature of marketing problems.

Another development is the growing availability of data for estimating and testing models, which should bring more realistic, detailed, and valid model structures. The trend toward realistic market response representation is aided by inclusion of more behavioral phenomena, more variables, non-linear response functions, and stochastic elements in marketing models. Dynamic aspects of markets are also increasingly being incorporated. A significant model trend emerging from development of time shared computers is that toward interactive models. An interactive model operating on a time shared computer system enables a decision maker to quickly and efficiently explore implications of his judgments on given problems. The MEDIAC [I] and ADFORS [E] models provide marketing examples here.

A major development trend is towards inclusion of dynamic effects; Little [H] has proposed a model for adjusting an advertising budget in the face of a changing environment via a series of continuing market experiments, the results of which are used to update the budget decision.

Another model trend is emerging towards building models considering competitive effects. These will have a significant interaction with the data bank. The development of competitive models must be supported by data bank capabilities in systematic monitoring and storing of competitive market data for developing, validating, and using these competitive models. It would seem important for firms to consider initiating a program of competitive data generation to match their future model intentions.

In addition to competitive and dynamic phenomena, there has been a trend towards including more behavioral content in mathematical models. For example, NOMAD has modeled the new product acceptance process basically as an updating of a brand preference vector on receipt of new advertising awareness, word-of-mouth communication, and product use experience [F]. This behavioral process approach has been utilized in SPRINTER: Mod III at a more aggregated level [R]. A general development of methods for use in behaviorally-based simulation models will play an important role in future models. While better solution methods will be evolved, principal developments will also occur in validity and sensitivity testing of complex behaviorally-based models.

The trend toward model banks with models which include competitive, dynamic, and behavioral phenomena will increase models' importance in the total information system.

The measurement-statistics bank

The measurement-statistics bank will provide a basis for measurement and estimation and methods for testing response functions and models. It should incorporate methods for both data-based and judgment-based estimation, such as procedures for estimating demand elasticities of marketing variables based on data in the data bank. It should also provide methods for judgmental assessments, such as the reference life cycle for a potential new product in an application of a new product model. In testing response functions and models it should provide techniques for assessing the adequacy of a postulated model or function in the light of available data.

Data-based measurement

The recent marketing literature makes the case for data-based measurement methods in marketing clear. The measurement-statistics bank should incorporate a wide variety of multivariate procedures, non-parametric methods, scaling techniques, and numerical estimation procedures [N].

Judgment-based methods

Marketing models, particularly normative models for planning marketing strategy, often require a certain amount of judgmental input. While much remains to be learned about effectively obtaining judgmental information, these methods should be incorporated into the system as they evolve.

One obvious example of a judgment-based method applicable in marketing is statistical decision theory. A barrier to its use, however, is the computational burden involved in problems large enough to be meaningful. A program which will perform the numerical analysis, preferably in real time from a remote console, should increase the use of this procedure. If a convenient mode is made available to marketing managers, there should be an increasingly widespread use of decision theory in marketing. Some simple steps have been made in this direction [Q].

The importance and utility of judgmental inputs and systems for their evaluation can be illustrated by examples. The first of these, which must remain anonymous for competitive reasons, relates to an application in a company whose problem was to determine which items to feature at what prices in weekly ads to increase store traffic, sales, and profits, as well as how much ad space to allocate to each featured item. Store managers and a consultant developed a simple model describing how the market would respond to this form of promotion. It was made operative on a time shared computer and made available to managers for planning their weekly promotional strategy. It required judgmental inputs from managers, and has produced excellent results in use. The consultant attributes this success to the managers' ability to provide meaningful judgmental inputs to this simple marketing model. This case reinforces the notion that useful judgmental inputs to formal analysis can be obtained from marketing managers.

Another example of the use of judgmental inputs is represented by an application of the SPRINTER: Mod O model to a new chemical product. In this case managers gave good subjective estimates of market response components, but without a model they could not combine them effectively to make the GO, ON, or NO decision and specify a best pricing strategy. Their overall subjective decision was GO for the product, but by combining their component inputs in the model and using their criteria and structure, a NO decision was indicated. Their overall subjective decision was not consistent with the logical combination of their market response judgments. A model can help produce more consistent decision procedures. In this particular case the subjective market response input and the model were also used to identify a pricing strategy predicted to generate 50% more profit.

In view of subjective inputs' importance, the system should include procedures for monitoring their performance from individuals in the firm to help identify individuals who are particularly knowledgeable and help adjust for bias in individual estimates.[2] For example, one company in a rapidly growing area combined judgmental inputs and market data in selecting sites for new outlets. In this case, monitoring of the performance of individuals supplying judgmental inputs indicated that the operations vice president tended to supply better judgmental inputs than any of the personnel on the real estate staff. When he subsequently resigned, the company not only lost a competent executive but also a valuable source of judgmental marketing information. The system should also correct any systematic bias in the estimates given by each individual. Claycamp has developed such a procedure for a manufacturer of electronic components, who asks salesmen to report an a product-by-product and customer-by-customer basis their subjective probability of realizing a sale in 30, 60, and 90 days. Each salesman's subjective probabilities are then adjusted on the basis of his past prediction performance. When aggregated across salesmen, subjective probability estimates are the basis of a short run sales forecast used by the production department.

Judgmental inputs are being used in systematic analysis of marketing problems. Interesting work has been done by Winkler on the use of experts and group judgments [S, T]. He has also proposed some incentives for managers to supply their best judgments, but more research is needed to develop procedures generating good subjective estimates.

Some design aspects of the measurement-statistics bank

Computerized statistical analysis has greatly lowered the computational burden in performing such analyses. The proliferation of readily available programs for statistical analysis makes it important that a proposed measurement-statistics bank be designed to minimize danger of misuse [J].

As an example, consider regression analysis. The measurement-statistics bank should incorporate complete econometric capability in all the available tests of assumptions which underlie the model. The measurement-statistics bank itself should warn the user of potential pitfalls and recommend appropriate tests and courses of action. Such system warnings and recommendations should help prevent naive use of this method. Sometimes the system can automatically get the user out of trouble. For example, the on-line statistical package DATANAL automatically performs a Fisher exact test when the user has specified a chi-square contingency analysis with insufficient data [M].

The design of the measurement-statistical bank is especially important since model outputs are only as good as their input. A good measurement capability is necessary for effective operation of a decision-information operation.

The user-system interface

The last major component is the subsystem which provides the user-system interface, or system input/output capability. As the only direct contact between the user and the system, it is crucial that this interface be designed to provide for convenient, efficient user-system interaction if the marketing information system is to have impact on management.

While the more traditional batch processing operations will continue to play a useful and important role in marketing information systems of the future, our attention will focus on the newer capacity for a closely coupled relationship between manager or user and the system, made feasible by the advent of time shared computers. Time shared systems allow many users to access and use a computer simultaneously. At present the most common form of interactive communication is the remote typewriter. While this form of input/output has been enormously useful and will continue to be so, computer graphics will come to play a much larger role in the future, because graphical display is often a more convenient medium in which to communicate with management.

Morton has described the use of such a graphical "management terminal system" in coordinating marketing and production planning in the consumer appliance division of Westinghouse [O]. This process originally absorbed three weeks of calendar time and six days of executive time. The new graphical system used the same data, models, and analytic approaches, adding nothing more than the capacity for interactive graphical display of such items as forecasted and observed sales, production, and inventory over several time periods by product. The graphical system changed the decision making style drastically: the three top managers coordinating marketing and production would now do so by having a session at the interactive video console. Calendar time required was reduced from three weeks to one half day, executive time from six man-days to one. Thus valuable executive time was released and the organization became more responsive to planning errors since the correction time was dramatically reduced. In addition to these objective results, it was also felt that decision making had improved as a result of the use of this system.

Consider also the problem of sales territory definition for a large sales force. A map of the area to be partitioned could be projected on a graphical display device connected to a computer containing relevant information about the area and the salesman (e.g., distribution of present and potential customers in the area). With a light pen, the sales manages could partition the graphic display area into sales territories. Once at a territory definition which he would like to consider, the computer could take the graphic input and evaluate sales and marketing implications of the proposed territorial defintions with a sales model or models using area information stored in the data bank. If the manager approved of his current territorial definition, he might decide to adopt it. Probably he would like to explore several alternatives to achieve a satisfactory (even if not globally optimal) definition. This method of user-machine interaction should enable the manager to effectively use his business judgment in creating alternatives. The computer, as an enthusiastic clerk, would then assist him in evaluating each alternative. Prototypes of this type of graphical territory definition have been developed at MIT's Project MAC for the political redistricting of Massachusetts.

Interactive systems offer several significant advantages in marketing information systems. While they have not yet been fully demonstrated in formal, scientific studies, experience with such systems to date would tend to reinforce these notions. Interactive systems offer the advantages of better data retrieval and interpretation, more timely answers to questions, and, hopefully, better solutions to problems.

Interactive systems allow effective data retrieval since data requests can be answered almost immediately and a conversational mode can lead to a succession of questions and answers meaningful to managers. For example, DATANAL allows a user to access a data base, abstract portions of it, manipulate this working data base to answer questions, and carry out statistical analyses [M]. A brand manager could access test market data to find out how many people are aware of his product, then table awareness against preference, and finally use a chi-square for significance testing. The ability to browse in the data base, ask questions, and receive answers, greatly enhances the manager's ability to interpret data and find problems. A specific marketing example is MARKINF, a language designed to retrieve, manipulate and statistically analyze sales area data [L].

Interactive systems provide more or less instant access to data, models, and measurement capabilities and thereby provide an important calendar time advantage over batch processing systems. This has two major payoffs: (1) it may make analysis feasible or enable it to be more thorough, and (2) considerable executive time may be saved. An interactive system may make analysis feasible in certain situations subject to severe time constraints and may permit more thorough analysis. Consider the corporate acquisition process. Standard practice is for the potential acquiring company to have its acquisition officer study the candidate and develop a set of alternative analyses indicating the likely future of the parent company, the candidate, and the combined companies. Inevitably, during the negotiating sessions, an officer of one of the companies involved will object to some assumption and will want to substitute an alternative. This can easily result in costly delays as well as future meetings before an agreement can be reached. Such a system, as developed by Seaman, should reduce these problems. His is in the process of further development and implementation at Raytheon [P].

In addition to a real time advantage, interactive systems, particularly interactive models, have some differential advantage in solving problems. When a manager can access a model in an interactive mode and try varying input or environmental conditions on the model to see how it reacts, he quickly gains some feeling for how the model responds and whether or not he feels that its behavior is reasonable. Once he has assured himself that it behaves reasonably, the path to management utilization of the model is much smoother. A case in point here would be Little and Lodish's MEDIAC media selection system [I]. This model operates in an interactive mode via a remote teletype. When a media planner is first exposed to this model, he generally tries a variety of alternatives to see if the recommended media schedule makes sense. If it does, his willingness to utilize the model is considerably increased.

It can be concluded that the manager-system interface is critical in the decision-information system since its effectiveness in large measure will determine the usage level of the system. While computer software will improve, a human buffer in the form of a trained specialist probably will still be needed. He would assure that the manager is accessing appropriate models and answer the input and model questions the manager will generate.

Conclusion

The interdependency between information system components should be re-emphasized. These have a significant bearing upon the evolutionary development of a marketing information system and upon the personnel required to achieve a balanced development in system components. Most existing information systems have been used for the storage, retrieval, and display of data. This emphasis is not surprising since the team which generally develops such systems is largely composed of computer systems personnel and rarely includes a member of the staff responsible for model-based market analysis. As a consequence, most marketing information systems have not achieved a balanced growth or tapped their full potential.

A balanced growth of the system components is necessary if full advantage is to be taken of the new information technology and advances in marketing models and measurements. For example, the data bank design decisions related to the level of data detail and the length of time historical data will be retained place constraints upon the type of marketing models which may be developed at any point in time.

There is also a need for a planned, balanced growth between the model bank and the data support system. For example, one of the features of future marketing model development will be richer representation of competitive interdependencies. Requisite to the development and implementation of such models will be the collection and storage of competitive data, which may involve many months or years for sufficient data to develop. The initial breakthrough will probably be made in data rich industries such as the pharmaceutical industry. It is no accident that the richest market simulation has been developed in the ethical drug market.

In planning the growth and development of a decision-information system, the manager is a key element. He sets the system goals, defines problems, and is the raison d'etre of the information system. Often, however, his lack of knowledge about models and their potential has led to an over reliance on the existing data needs and decision structures. This results in systems that function only to retrieve and display data (the data bank functions). In order to assure that the contribution of models, measurement, and statistics are fully realized, management scientists must take an active role in system development. They must make their potential contribution known and become deeply involved in the human problems of system development.

If models are to be widely used in the future, they will have to be integrated within the information system context. If the management scientist is involved in the system, his models will probably improve since he will be in a position to help assure that the system will maintain information which will be important in future formulation, estimation, and testing of marketing models. Without the participation of the management scientists, such information might not be maintained in appropriate form within the system.

Three other trends should aid in the design and utilization of decision-information systems. The first is an increasing concern with the human dimensions of system implementation. The second is towards time shared computer utilities. A computer utility offers access to powerful computers and software packages on a usage basis. Thus, what was once an enormous investment in men, machines, and systems has been reduced to much smaller and more convenient units. This lowering of the entry barriers means that most powerful computers are available to even modest sized firms.

This third and concomitant development has just begun. It is what might be called the "models utility." A model utility is one which makes a model or models available on a syndicated basis via a time shared computer utility. Such a model utility could (and does) offer models for media planning, advertising budgeting, brand management planning, and new product analysis on a time shared basis. Again, this development has lowered the barriers to smaller organizations. Modest sized firms and agencies may now feasibly have access to the new model technology. It seems safe to predict further developments on this front in the next few years. For example, model utilities and computer utilities may be combined in a multi-firm marketing information system. In such a system, an independent entity is established for the purchase of computers or computer time, collection of data, and deevelopment of data, models, and measurement banks which will be used by all the sponsors. Support of such independent efforts serves to reduce the risks and financial burdens in system development. Such a system is currently being developed in the ethical drug market.

NOTES

1. This section is designed to emphasize the directions of expansion of the state of the art, rather than the basic methodology of existing models. A detailed discussion of models is in [N].
2. This is similar in concept to the monitoring and adjustment of judgment in application of PERT.

REFERENCES

A. Russell L. Ackoff, "Management Misinformation Systems," *Management Science*, 14 (December 1967), 147-156.

B. Arnold E. Amstutz, "A Basic Market Oriented Information System," Working Paper No. 307-368, Sloan School of Management, M.I.T., 1968.

C. ————, "The Computer—New Partner in Investment Management," in Harry Stern, ed., "Information Systems in Management Science," *Management Science*, 15 (October 1968), 91-99.

D. Donald F. Cox and Robert Good, "How to Build a Marketing Information System," *Harvard Business Review*, 45 (May-June 1967), 145-154.

E. Daniel S. Diamond, "Quantitative Approach to Magazine Advertisement Format," *Journal of Marketing Research*, 5 (November 1968), 376-387.

F. Jerome D. Herniter and Victor Cook, "Nommad: Normative Models of Market Acceptance Determination," Working Paper No. P-43-5, Marketing Science Institute, Philadelphia, 1967.

G. Sidney W. Hess, "The Use of Models in Marketing Timing Decisions," *Operations Research*, 15 (July-August 1967), 720-737.

H. John D. C. Little, "A Model of Adaptive Control of Promotional Spending," *Operations Research*, 14 (November-December 1966), 175-197.

I. ———— and Leonard M. Lodish, "A Media Planning Calculus," *Operations Research*, 17 (January-February 1969), 1-35.

J. J. Leslie Livingstone and David B. Montgomery. "The Use of Regression Equations to Predict Manpower Requirements: Critical Comments," *Management Science*, 12 (March 1966), A616-A618.

K. Albert Madansky, "Models, Games and Data Banks: Implications for Data Collection," *Proceedings*, Annual Meeting, American Marketing Association, June 1968, 236-238.

L. Charles S. Mayer, Christopher E. Nugent, and Thomas E. Vollmann, "On-line Data Retrieval and Analysis," *Proceedings*, Annual Meeting, American Marketing Association, June 1969.

M. James R. Miller, "DATANAL: An Interpretive Language for On-line Analysis of Empirical Data," Working Paper No. 275-267, Sloan School of Management, M.I.T., 1967.

N. David B. Montgomery and Glen L. Urban, *Management Science in Marketing*, Englewood Cliffs, N.J.: Prentice-Hall, Inc., 1969.

O. Michael S. S. Morton, "Interactive Visual Display Systems and Management Problem Solving," *Industrial Management Review* (Fall 1967), 69-81.

P. Robert L. Seaman, "A Simulation Approach to the Analytical Aspects of Business Acquisition Evaluations," unpublished M.S. thesis, Sloan School of Management, M.I.T., 1967.

Q. Mark Allen Torozzi, "A Computer Based Teaching and Operational Aid for Applications of Statistical Decision Theory," unpublished M.S. thesis, Sloan School of Management, M.I.T., 1967.

R. Glen Urban, "SPRINTER Mod III: A Model for the Analysis of New Frequently Purchased Consumer Products," *Operations Research* (forthcoming).

S. Robert L. Winkler, "The Consensus of Subjective Probability Distributions," *Management Science* 15 (October 1968), 61-75.

T. ————, "The Quantification of Judgment: Some Methodological Suggestions," *Journal of the American Statistical Association*, 62 (1967), 1105-1120.

6 SELECTED BIBLIOGRAPHY

I. Systems Theory and Concepts

Ackoff, R. L., "Systems, Organizations and Interdisciplinary Research," *General Systems*, Vol. 5 (1960).

Andrew, G., "An Analytic System Model for Organization Theory," *Academy of Management Journal*, Vol. 8, No. 3, September, 1965.

"A Total Management System," *Data Processing for Management*, April, 1963.

Beckett, J. A., "Wanted—A Concept for Employing Systems Effectively," *Systems and Procedures Journal*, November-December, 1964.

Blank, V. F., "Management Concept in Electronic Systems," *The Journal of Accountancy*, January, 1961.

Boulding, K. E., and W. A. Spivery, "Towards a General Theory of Growth," *General Systems*. Vol. 1 (1956).

Bower, J. B. and W. R. Welke, *Financial Information Systems*. Boston: Houghton Mifflin Company, 1968.

Brewer, S. H. and J. Rosenzweig, "Rhocrematics and Organizational Adjustments," *California Management Review*, Spring 1961.

Carasso, M., "Total Systems," *Systems and Procedures Journal*, November, 1959.

Cisler, W. L., "Management's View of the Systems Function," *Systems and Procedures Journal*, July-August, 1965.

Cleland, D. I., "Why Project Management?" *Business Horizons*, Winter, 1964.

Cleland, D. I. and W. R. King, *Systems, Organization, Analysis, Management: A Book of Readings*. New York: McGraw-Hill Book Company, 1969.

Clough, D. J., *Concepts in Management Science*. New York: Prentice-Hall, Inc., 1963.

Dickey, E. R., N. L. Senensieb and H. C. Robertson, "An Integrated Approach to Administrative Systems and Data Processing," *Systems and Procedures Journal*, March-April, 1962.

Dommasch, D. O. and C. W. Laudeman, *Principles Underlying Systems Engineering*. New York: Pitman Publishing Corp., 1962.

Eckman, D. P., "Systems Research and Design," *Proceedings, First Systems Symposium, Case Institute of Technology*. New York: John Wiley & Sons, Inc., 1961.

Ellis, D. O. and F. J. Ludwig, *Systems Philosophy*, Englewood Cliffs, N.J.: Prentice-Hall, Inc., 1962.

Ewell, J. M., "How to Organize for a Total System," *Systems and Procedures Journal*, November, 1961.

————. "The Total Systems Concept and How to Organize for It," *Computers and Automation*, September, 1961.

Feigenbaum, D. S., "Good Systems Are Made Not Born," Supervisory Management, August, 1964.

————. "The Engineering and Management of Effective System," *Management Science*, August, 1968.

Fleringer, B. J., "System Reliability as a Function of System Age," *Operations Research*, January, 1960.

Gilman, G., "The Manager and The Systems Concept," *Business Horizons*, August, 1969.

Gordon, R. M., *The Total Information System and The Levels of Data Processing Today—A Progress Report*. New York: American Management Association, 1960.

Gregory, R. H. and R. L. Van Horn, *Automatic Data-Processing Systems*. Belmont, Calif.: Wadsworth Publishing Co., Inc., 1964.

Hare, Van Court, *Systems Analysis:* A Diagnostic Approach. New York: Harcourt, Brace & World, Inc., 196.

Harvey, A., "Systems Can Too Be Practical," *Business Horizons*, Summer, 1964.

Hickey, A. E., *"The Systems Approach—Can Engineers Use the Scientific Method,"* IRE Transactions on Engineering Management, June, 1960.

Hitch, C. J., "An Appreciation of Systems Analysis," *Operations Research*, November, 1955.

Hoag, M., "What Is a System?" *Operations Research*, June, 1957.

"How to Organize for a Total System," *Systems and Procedures Magazine*, November, 1961.

Jacobson, H. B. and J. S. Houcek, eds., *Automation and Society*. New York: Philosophical Library, Inc., 1959.

Johnson, R. A., "Rhocrematics—A System for Production and Marketing," *Advanced Management*, February, 1961.

Johnson, R. A., F. E. Kast, and J. E. Rosenzweig, *The Theory and Management of Systems*. New York: McGraw-Hill Book Company, 1967.

Lach, E. L., "Total Systems Concept," *Systems and Procedures Journal*, November, 1960.

Lazzaro, V., *Systems and Procedures—A Handbook for Business and Industry*. Englewood Cliffs, N.J.: Prentice-Hall, Inc., 1959.

Limberg, H., "What Management Requires from the Systems Specialists and from the System Itself, *Systems and Procedures Journal*, January-February, 1962.

McDonough, A. M., *Information Economics and Management Systems*. New York: McGraw-Hill Book Company, 1963.

McDonough, A. M. and L. J. Garrett, *Management Systems*. Homewood, Ill.: Richard D. Irwin, Inc., 1965.

McGrath, J. D., P. G. Nordlie and W. S. Vaughn, "A Systematic Framework for Comparison of System Research Methods," *Human Science Research*, November, 1959.

Machol, R. E., ed., *System Engineering Handbook*. New York: McGraw-Hill Book Company, 1965.

McKean, R. N., *Efficiency in Government Through Systems Analysis*. New York: John Wiley & Sons, Inc., 1958.

McMillan, C. and R. F. Gonzalez, *Systems Analysis—A Computer Approach to Decision Models*. Homewood, Ill.: Richard D. Irwin, Inc., 1965.

Macmillan, R. H., *Automation*. London: Cambridge University Press, 1956.

Mahler, W. R., "Systems Approach to Managing by Objectives," *Systems and Procedures Journal*, September, 1965.

Marx, M. H., *Systems and Theories in Psychology*. New York: McGraw-Hill Book Company, 1963.

Mishkin, E., ed., *Adaptive Control Systems*. New York: McGraw-Hill Book Company, 1961.

Neuschel, R. F., *Management by System*. New York: McGraw-Hill Book Company, 1960.

Neuendorf, C. W., "The Total Management Information System," *Total Systems Letter*, March, 1965.

Neuschel, R. F., "Systems Man—Architect or Journeyman," *Systems and Procedures Journal*, January-February, 1963.

Parsons, H. M., *System Trouble-Shooting*. System Development Corporation Report, SP-793, July, 1962.

Pollock, N., "Determining the Authority and Scope of Systems Personnel," *Office*, May, 1959.

Radamaker, T., *Business Systems*. Cleveland, Ohio: Systems and Procedures Association, 1963.

Rosen, N. A., "Open System Theory in an Organization Sub-System: A Field Experiment," *Organizational Behavior and Human Performance*, May, 1970.

Schoderbek, P. P., *Management Systems*, New York: John Wiley & Sons, Inc., 1967.

Seifert, W. W. and C. W. Steeg, *Control Systems Engineering*. New York: McGraw-Hill Book Company, 1960.

Sethi, N. K., "Management by System," *Personnel Journal*, April, 1963.

Self-Organizing Systems. Interdisciplinary Conference on Self-Organizing Systems, New York: Pergamon Press, Inc., 1960.

Simon, H. A., *The Shape of Automation for Men and Management*. New York: Harper & Row, Publishers, 1965.

Simon, L. and R. Sisson, "Evolution of a Total System," *Total Systems Letter*, January, 1966.

Smith, S. V., R. H. Baien, and J. E. Stafford, *Readings in Marketing Information Systems: A New Era in Marketing Research*. Boston: Houghton Mifflin Company, 1968.

Spaulding, A. T., "Is the Total System Concept Practical?" *Systems and Procedures Journal*, January, 1964.

Systems Contracting. New York: American Management Association, Purchasing Division, Management Bulletin No. 63, 1965.

"Systems for Total Management," *Data Processing for Management*, August, 1963.

Svenson, A. L., "Congruency—Driving Force in Management Systems," *Systems and Procedures Journal*, May-June, 1966.

———, "Management Systems and the Exception Principle," *Systems and Procedures Journal*, July-August, 1964.

Thurston, P. H., *Systems and Procedures Responsibility*. Boston, Mass.: Houghton Miffin Company, 1959.

————, "The Concept of a Production System," *Harvard Business Review*, November, 1963.

Tilles, S., "The Manager's Job—A Systems Approach," *Harvard Business Review*, January-February, 1963.

Tomeski, E., "Needed—Management Systems Research," *Systems and Procedures Journal*, March-April, 1964.

Tomvic, R., *Sensitivity Analysis of Dynamic Systems*. New York: McGraw-Hill Book Company, 1963.

VonBertalanffy, L., "An Outline of General Systems Theory," *British Journal of Philosophical Sciences*, 1950.

————, "General Systems Theory—A Critical Review," *Yearbook of the Society for General Systems Research*, Vol. 7, 1962.

————, "General System Theory," *General Systems*, Vol. 1, 1956.

————, "General System Theory—A New Approach to Unity of Science," *Human Biology*, December, 1951.

Young, S., *Management: A Systems Analysis*. Glenview, Ill.: Scott Foresman and Company, 1966.

II. Information Technology

Adamson, Robert E., *Implementing and Evaluating Information Processing Systems*. System Development Corporation Report, SP-1294, November, 1963.

————, *Advances in EDP and Information Systems*. New York: American Management Association, 1961.

Advances in Management Information Systems Techniques. New York: American Management Association, 1962.

Anderson, M. W., "The What and Whereto—Management Information Systems," *Total Systems Letter*, September, 1965.

Anshen, M. and G. L. Bach, eds., *Management and Corporations 1985*. New York: McGraw-Hill Book Company, 1960.

Ansoff, H. I., *Corporate Strategy*. New York: McGraw-Hill Book Company, 1965.

————, "The Firm of the Future," Harvard Business Review, September-October, 1965.

Baumann, A. L., "Single Information Flow Philosophy," *Data Processing Yearbook 1963-64*. Detroit, Mich.: American Data Processing, Inc., 1963.

Becker, J. and R. M. Hayes, *Information Storage Retrieval*. New York: John Wiley & Sons, Inc., 1963.

Bell, D. A., *Information Theory and Its Engineering Applications*. New York: Pitman Publishing Corp., 1962.

Blumberg, D. F., "Information Systems and the Planning Process, *Data Processing*, May, 1965.

Bonney, J. B., "Perceptive Feedback," *Data Processing Magazine*, August, 1964.

Bourne, C. P., *Methods of Information Handling*. New York: John Wiley & Sons, Inc., 1963.

Brillouin, L., *Science and Information Theory*. New York: Academic Press, Inc., 1962.

Burlinganie, J. F., "Information Technology and Decentralization," *Harvard Business Review*, November-December, 1961.

Cooper, H. G., "The Corporate Information and Data Automation in Perspective," *Systems and Procedures Journal*, May-June, 1966.

Dearden, J., "Can Management Information Be Automated?" *Harvard Business Review*, March-April, 1964.

————, "How to Organize Information Systems," *Harvard Business Review*, April, 1965.

Dickey, E. R., N. L. Senensieb and H. C. Robertson, "The Application of Information Technology," *Annals of the American Academy of Political and Social Science*, March, 1962.

————, "What's Ahead in Information Technology?" *Harvard Business Review*, September-October, 1965.

Elliott, C. and R. S. Wasley, *Business Information Processing Systems*. Homewood, Ill.: Richard D. Irwin, Inc., 1965.

Fairthorne, R. A., *Towards Information Retrieval*. London: Butterworths, 1961.

Feinstein, A., *Foundations of Information Theory*. New York: McGraw-Hill Book Company, 1958.

Fett, G. H., *Feedback Control Systems*. Englewood Cliffs, N.J.: Prentice-Hall, Inc., 1954.

Foy, N. S., "Computer Management—1969," *Datamation*, February, 1970.

Gallagher, J. D., *Management Information Systems and the Computer*. New York: American Management Association, 1961.

Gentle, E. C., *Data Communications in Business*. New York: American Telephone and Telegraph Company, 1965.

Gille, J. C., *Feedback Control Systems*. New York: McGraw-Hill Book Company, 1959.

Goldman, S., *Information Theory*. Englewood Cliffs, N.J.: Prentice-Hall, Inc., 1953.

Goodman, L. L., *Man and Automation*. London: Penguin Books, 1957.

Gray, P. and R. E. Machol, *Recent Developments in Information and Decision Processes*. New York: The Macmillan Company, 1962.

Green, J. C., "Information Explosion, Real or Imaginary," *Science*, May, 1964.

Greenwood, W. T., *Decision Theory and Information Systems*. Cincinnati, Ohio: South-Western Publishing Company, 1969.

————, *Management and Organizational Behavior Theories—An Interdisciplinary Approach*. Cincinnati, Ohio: South-Western Publishing Company, 1965.

Haller, G. L., "Information Revolution," *Science Digest*, May, 1964.

Hardie, A. M., *The Elements of Feedback and Control*. London: Oxford Publications, 1964.

Hartmann, H. C., "Management Control in Real-Time Is the Objective," *Systems*, September, 1965.

Hattery, L. H. and E. M. McCormick, *Information Retrieval Management*. Detroit, Mich.: American Data Processing, Inc., 1962.

Head, R. V., *Real-Time Business Systems*. New York: Holt, Rinehart & Winston, Inc., 1964.

Hockman, J., "Specifications for an Integrated Management Information System," *Systems and Procedures Journal*, January-February, 1963.

Hopkins, R. C., "Possible Applications of Information Theory to Management Control," *IRE Transactions on Engineering Management*, March, 1961.

Jackson, J. T., "Information Systems for Management Planning," *Data Processing*, March, 1962.

Jasinski, F. J., "Adapting Organization to New Technology," *Harvard Business Review*, January-February, 1959.

Johnson, R. L. and I. H. Derman, "How Intelligent Is Your MIS?" *Business Horizons*, February, 1970.

Joplin, H. B., "The Accountant's Role in Management Information Systems," *Journal of Accountancy*, March, 1966.

Klasson, C. R. and K. W. Olm, "Managerial Implications of Integrated Business Operations," *California Management Review*, Fall, 1965.

Konvalinka, J. W. and H. G. Trentin, "Management Information Systems," *Management Services*, September-October, 1965.

Martins, G. R., "Some Comments on Information Retrieval," *Datamation*, December, 1964.

Martin, J., *Design of Real-Time Computer Systems*. Englewood Cliffs, N.J.: Prentice-Hall, Inc., 1967.

————, *Programming Real-Time Computer Systems*. Englewood Cliffs, N.J.: Prentice-Hall, Inc., 1965.

Merriam, C. W., *Optimization Theory and Design of Feedback Control Systems*. New York: McGraw-Hill Book Company, 1964.

Mohan, C., R. C. Garg, and P. P. Signal, "Dependability of a Complex System," *Operations Research*, Vol. 10 (1962).

Moravec, A. F., "Basic Concepts for Designing a Fundamental Information System," *Management Services*, July-August, 1965.

————, "Basic Concepts for Planning Advanced Electronic Data Processing Systems," *Management Services*, May-June, 1965.

————, "Using Simulation to Design a Management Information System," *Management Services*, May-June, 1966.

Myers, C. A., "Management Decisions for the Next Decade," *Industrial Management Review*, Fall, 1968.

————, The Impact of Computers on Management. Cambridge: M.I.T. Press, 1967.

Nicolaus, J. J., "The Automated Approach to Technical Retrieval", *Naval Engineer Journal*, December, 1964.

Raach, F. R., "Management Information Systems," *Duns Review and Modern Industry*, January, 1966.

Reitzfeld, M., "Effective Reports: The Poor Man's Management Information System," *Records Management Journal*, Winter, 1964.

Retterer, R. W., "Computers and Communications Provide New Conception in Scientific Management," *Advanced Management Journal*, October, 1964.

Reza, F. M., *An Introduction to Information Theory*. New York: McGraw-Hill Book Company, 1961.

Savant, C. J.; *Basic Feedback Control System Design*. New York: McGraw-Hill Book Company, 1958.

Simonton, W. C., ed., *Information Retrieval Today*. Minneapolis, Minn.: University of Minnesota, Center for Continuation Study, 1963.

Sinaika, H. W., *Selected Papers on Human Factors in the Design and Use of Control Systems*. New York: Dover Publications, Inc., 1961.

Smith, O. J., *Feedback Control Systems*. New York: McGraw-Hill Book Company, 1958.

"Systems Analysts Move Into Managing," *Iron Age*, August 26, 1965.

Thurston, P. H., "Who Should Control Information Systems?" *Harvard Business Review*. November-December, 1962.

Tuthill, O. W., "The Thrust of Information Technology on Management," *Financial Executive*, January, 1966.

Vickery, B. C., On Retrieval System Theory. London: Butterworths, 1965.

Wilson, I. G. and M. E. Wilson, *Information, Computers and System Design*. New York: John Wiley & Sons, Inc., 1965.

III. The Design of a System

"Applied Psychology for the Systems Man," *Systems and Procedures Journal*, March, 1961.

Boyd, A. W., "Human Relations in Systems Change," *N.A.A. Bulletin*, July, 1959.

Brabb, G. J., "Education for Systems Analysis," *Systems and Procedures Journal*, March-April, 1966.

Bruner, W. G., "Systems Design—A Broader Role of Industrial Engineering," *Journal of Industrial Engineering*, March-April, 1962.

Chamberlain, C. J., "Coming Era in Engineering Management," *Harvard Business Review*, September-October, 1961.

Christoph, T. G., "Organization of Systems Work—Review and Preview," *Management Services*, May-June, 1966.

Concepts Associated with System Effectiveness. Bureau of Naval Weapons, *Navwaps Report 8461*, June, 1963.

Cyert, R. M., E. A. Feigenbaum and J. G. March, "Models in Behavioral Theory of the Firm," *Behavioral Science*, April, 1959.

Cyert, R. M. and J. G. March, *A Behavioral Theory of the Firm*. Englewood Cliffs, N.J.: Prentice-Hall, Inc., 1963.

DeLuca, R., "Introduction to Systems and Procedures," *Systems and Procedures*, January-February, 1961.

Doherty, P. A. and J. G. F. Wollaston, "Effective Management of a Systems Project," *Management Services*, March-April, 1965.

Ely, J. H., *Data Collection for Design and Evaluation of Man-Machine Systems*. New York: ASME-58-A-241, December, 1958.

Fulmer, R. M. and J. M. Hood, "Computerized Human Relations, *Personnel Journal*, June, 1970.

Goode, H. H. and R. E. Machol, *System Engineering—An Introduction to the Design of Large-Scale Systems*. New York: McGraw-Hill Book Company, 1957.

Grillo, E. V., "Why Not Practice Human Relations?" *Systems and Procedures Journal*, November, 1964.

Kaufman, F., "Data Systems That Cross Company Boundaries," *Harvard Business Review*, January-February, 1966.

Laden, H. N. and T. R. Gildersleeve, *System Design for Computer Applications*, New York: John Wiley & Sons, Inc., 1963.

Lipstreu, O., "Organizational Implications of Automation," *Journal of the Academy of Management*, August, 1960.

Lumsdaine, A. A., *Human Factors Methods for System Design*, Pittsburgh, Pa.: The American Institute of Research, 1960.

McGregor, D., *The Human Side of Enterprise*, New York: McGraw-Hill Book Company, 1960.

Mann, F. C. and R. L. Hoffman, *Automation and the Worker*. New York: Holt, Rinehart & Winston, Inc., 1960.

Mayo, H. R., "Putting the System in Writing," *Systems and Procedures Journal*, May, 1965.

Meistor, D. and G. F. Rabideau, *Human Factors Evaluation in Systems Development*, New York: John Wiley & Sons, Inc., 1965.

Miller, J. J., "Automation, Job Creation, and Unemployment, *Academy of Management Journal*, December, 1964.

de Neufville, R., "Systems Analysis—A Decision Process, *Industrial Management Review*, Spring, 1970.

Optner, S. L., *Systems Analysis for Business Mangement*. Englewood Cliffs, N.J.: Prentice-Hall, Inc., 1960.

————, *Systems Analysis for Business and Industrial Problem Solving*. Englewood Cliffs, N.J.: Prentice-Hall, Inc., 1965.

Postley, J. A., *Computers and People*. New York: McGraw-Hill Book Company, 1963.

Reid, P. C., "How to Survive a Systems Change," *Supervisory Management*, April, 1964.

Savant, C. J., *Control System Design*. New York: McGraw-Hill Book Company, 1964.

Schlosser, R. E., "Psychology for the Systems Analyst," *Management Services*, November-December, 1964.

Seely, S., *Dynamic Systems Analysis*. New York: Reinhold Publishing Corp., 1964.

Stoller and Van Horn, "Design of a Management Information System," *Management Technology*, January, 1960.

Wheatley, P. E., "Human Element in a Systems Survey," *Systems and Procedures Journal*, May, 1960.

Williams, L. K., "The Human Side of Change," *Systems and Procedures Journal*, July-August, 1964.

Wilson, W. E., *Concepts of Engineering System Design*. New York: McGraw-Hill Book Company, 1965.

Ziessow, B. W., "Management by Exception," *Data Processing Magazine*, October, 1965.

IV. The Role of the Computer

Anshen, M., "The Manager and the Black Box," *Harvard Business Review*, November-December, 1960.

Bates, W. J., "Business Systems in Transition," *Data Processing Magazine*, March, 1963.

Beehler, P. J., "EDP: Stimulating Systematic Corporate Planning," *Journal of Systems Management*, November, 1969.

Berkeley, E. C., *The Computer Revolution*. Garden City, N.J.: Doubleday & Company, Inc., 1962.

Blumberg, D. F., "New Directions for Computer Technology and Applications —A Long Range Prediction," *Computers and Automation*, January, 1964.

Blumenthal, S.C., "Management in Real Time," *Data Processing Magazine*, August, 1965.

Bouchardt, R., "The Catalyst in Total Systems," *Systems and Procedures Journal*, May-June, 1963.

Bower, R. S. and H. C. Simpson, "Realizing the Promise of Computer Time—Sharing in Banks," *The Bankers Magazine*, Winter, 1970.

Brabb, G. J. and E. B. Hutchins, "Electronic Computers and Management Organization," *California Management Review*, Fall, 1963.

Brady, R. H., "Computers In Top-Level Decisions Making," *Harvard Business Review*, July-August, 1967.

Bright, J. R., *Automation and Management*. Cambridge, Mass.: Harvard University Graduate School of Business Administration, 1958.

Burck, G., *The Computer and Its Potential for Management*. New York: Harper & Row, Publishers, 1965.

Business Systems. Systems and Procedures Association, 1965.

Canning, R. G., *Electronic Data Processing for Business and Industry*. New York: John Wiley & Sons, Inc., 1956.

Caples, W. G., "Automation in Theory and Practice," *Business Topics*, Autumn, 1960.

Chapin, N., *An Introduction to Automatic Computers*, Princeton, N.J.: D. Van Nostrand Co., Inc., 1957.

Chorafas, D. N., "Computer Technology in Western and Eastern Europe," *Columbia Journal of World Business*, May-June, 1966.

"Computer-Assisted Corporate Planning," *EDP Analyzer*, September, 1966.

Coyl, R. J. and J. K. Stewart, "Design of a Real-Time Programming System," *Computers and Automation*, September, 1963.

Culbertson, J. T., "Automation—Its Evolution and Future Direction," *Computers and Automation*, November and December, 1960.

"Data Transmission and the Real-Time System," *Dun's Review and Modern Industry*, September, 1965.

Dean, N. J., "The Computer Comes of Age," *Harvard Business Review*, January-February, 1968.

Desmonde, W. H., *Computers and Their Uses*. Englewood Cliffs, N.J.: Prentice-Hall, Inc., 1964.

Dickey, E. R., N. L. Senensieb and H. C. Robertson, "Automation—The New Technology," *Harvard Business Review*, September-October, 1964.

————, *Automation—The Advent of the Automatic Factory*. New York: D. Van Nostrand Co., Inc., 1952.

————, "Automation—The New Technology," *Harvard Business Review*, November-December, 1953.

————, *Beyond Automation*. New York: McGraw-Hill Book Company, 1964.

Diebold, J., "Bad Decisions on Computer Use," *Harvard Business Review*, January-February, 1969.

Dunlop, J. T., *Automation and Technological Change*. Englewood Cliffs, N.J.: Prentice-Hall, Inc., 1962.

Evans, M. K. and L. R. Hague, "Master Plan for Information Systems," *Harvard Business Review*, January-February, 1962.

Feigenbaum, E. A. and J. Feldman, *Computers and Thought*. New York: McGraw-Hill Book Company, 1963.

Fiock, Jr., L. R., "Seven Deadly Dangers in EDP," *Harvard Business Review*, May-June, 1962.

Grabbe, E. M., ed., *Automation in Business and Industry*. New York: John Wiley & Sons, Inc., 1957.

Meliz, P. W., "Impact of Electronic Data Processing on Managers," *Advanced Management*, April, 1961.

Muschamp, G. M., "Tomorrow's Integrated Office and Plants," *Automation*, May, 1961.

Porter, J. P., "What Management Should Know About Real Time System," *Price Waterhouse Review*, Autumn, 1964.

Schwab, B., "The Economics of Sharing Computers," *Harvard Business Review*, September-October, 1968.

Schwitter, J. P., "Computer Effect Upon Management Jobs," *Journal of the Academy of Management*, September, 1965.

Shultz, G. P. and T. L. Whisler, *Management Organizations and the Computer*. Chicago: University of Chicago Press, 1960.

Simon, H. A., "How Computers Will Reshape the Management Team," *Steel*, January 11, 1965.

Spett, M. C., "Standards for Evaluating Data Processing Management," *Datamation*, February, 1970.

Sprague, R. E., *Electronic Business Systems*. New York: The Ronald Press, Inc., 1962.

————, "Electronic Business Systems—Nineteen Eighty-Four," *Business Automation*, February, 1966.

————, "On Line-Real Time Systems as a Long-Range Planning Goal," *Total Systems Letter*, April, 1966.

V. State of the Art in Emerging Management Systems

Allen, B. "Dangers Ahead: Safeguard Your Computer," *Harvard Business Review,* November-December, 1968.

————, "Time Sharing Takes Off", *Harvard Business Review*, March-April, 1969.

Allison, H., "Framework for Marketing Strategy," *California Management Review*, Fall, 1961.

"AMP—System Solution to Manufacturing Planning," *Manufacturing Engineer*, December, 1965.

"A New Look in Management Reporting," *EDP Analyzer*, June 16, 1965.

Anthony, R. N., *Planning and Control Systems*, Cambridge, Mass.: Harvard University Graduate School of Business Administration, Division of Research, 1965.

Bellman, R. E., *Adaptive Control Processes*. Princeton, N.J.: Princeton University Press, 1962.

————, "Control Theory," *Scientific American*, September, 1964.

Clee, G. H. and F. A. Lindsay, "New Patterns for Overseas Operations— Systems Management Concept," *Harvard Business Review*, January, 1961.

Cox, D. F. and R. E. Good, "How to Build a Marketing Information System," *Harvard Business Review*, May-June, 1967.

Finck, N. E., "Line of Balance Gives the Answer," *Systems and Procedures Journal*, July-August, 1965.

Freed, R. N., "Computer Fraud—A Management Trap," *Business Horizons*, June, 1969.

————, "Get the Computer System You Want," *Business Horizons*, November-December, 1969.

Gibson, J. E. et al., *Control System Component*. New York: McGraw-Hill Book Company, 1969.

Guise, Jr., R. F., "File Security," *Data Systems News*, November, 1969.

Hein, L. W., *Contemporary Accounting and the Computer*. Belmont, Calif.: Dickenson Publishing Company, Inc., 1969.

Hoos, I. R., "When the Computer Takes Over the Office," *Harvard Business Review*, July, August, 1960.

Johnson, C. B., "Protection Primer for EDP Records," *Banking*, December, 1969.

Lawson, C. L., *The Total Systems Concept—Its Application to Manufacturing Operations*. New York: American Management Association, Report No. 60, 1961.

"Log Jams Block Computerized Production," *Steel*, December 15, 1969.

Malcolm, D. G. and A. J. Rowe, "Computer-Based Control Systems," *California Management Review*, Spring, 1961.

Malcolm, D. G., A. J. Rowe, and L. F. McConnell, eds., *Management Control Systems*. New York: John Wiley & Sons, Inc., 1960.

Malloy, J. P., "Computerized Cost System in Small Plant," *Harvard Business Review*, May-June, 1968.

Marill, T., "Computers in Personnel Management," *Personnel Journal*, May, 1970.

Matherne, R. J., "Introduction to Process Computer Systems," *Datamation*, December, 1969.

Morse, G. E., 'Pendulum of Management Control," *Harvard Business Review*, May, 1965.

O'Malley, R. L., S. E. Elmaghraby and J. W. Jeske, "An Operational System for Batch-Type Production," *Management Science*, June, 1966.

Parker, R. W., "The SABRE System," *Datamation*, September, 1965.

Pratt, R. N., "Computer Utilization in the Collective Bargaining Process," *Industrial Management Review*, Spring, 1970.

"Progress of Process Computers," *Iron Age*, January 29, 1970.

Wasserman, J. J., "Bridging the Computer—Auditor Gap," *Banking*, December, 1969.

Weinwurm, G. F., "Computer Management Control Systems Through the Looking Glass," *Management Science*, July, 1961.

Willoughby, T., W. Patterson, and G. Drummond, "Computer-Aided Architectural Planning," *Operational Research Quarterly*, March, 1970.

Author Index

498